DATE DUE

NO 29'00			
NO 13'01			
DE 21 02			

DEMCO 38-296

Gender and American Law

The Impact of the Law on the Lives of Women

Series Editor
Karen J. Maschke

GARLAND PUBLISHING, INC.
New York & London
1997

Contents of the Series

Feminist Legal Theories

Edited with introductions by
Karen J. Maschke

GARLAND PUBLISHING, INC.
New York & London
1997

Library of Congress Cataloging-in-Publication Data

Feminist legal theories / edited with introductions by Karen J.
  Maschke.
       p.   cm. — (Gender and American law ; 7)
    Includes bibliographical references.
    ISBN 0-8153-2521-5 (alk. paper)
       1. Women—Legal status, laws, etc.—United States. 2. Feminist
  jurisprudence—United States. I. Maschke, Karen J. II. Series.
  KF478.A5F477 1997
  346.7301'34—dc21   96-51825
                                                        CIP

Printed on acid-free, 250-year-life paper
Manufactured in the United States of America

Contents

Series Introduction

From colonial times to the present, the law has been used to both expand and contract the rights of women. Over the last two decades, a body of literature has emerged that examines the ways in which the law has had an impact on the lives of women in the United States. The topics covered in this series include the historical development of women's legal rights, matters surrounding reproduction, sexuality and the family, equal employment opportunity, educational equity, violence against women, pornography, sex work, hate speech, and developments in feminist legal thought. The articles represent multidisciplinary approaches in examining women's experiences with the law and provide theoretical insights about the nature of gender equality.

A unifying theme in these articles is that women have been constructed historically as "different," and that this characterization "has had implications in regard to the way in which women are understood as objects and subjects of law" (Fineman 1992, p. 1). Biological differences between women and men and assumptions about the different "nature" of women and men have provided the basis for legal restrictions on women's ownership of property, guardianship of their children, ability to control their reproduction, and access to the workplace and educational institutions.

Even though women have more legal rights now than at any other time in history, many of the articles show that the law can both eradicate and reinforce women's subordination. Nineteenth-century child custody law is a telling example. While "judges granted women new legal power in family affairs," they also placed "severe limits on married women's overall legal rights" (Grossberg 1983, p. 235). On the one hand, by claiming the authority to determine which parent should be granted custody, judges dismantled the practice of fathers possessing unquestioned domain over matters of child custody and guardianship. Yet judges also "ensured that women's domestic powers did not translate into extensive external political and economic authority" (Grossberg 1983, p. 237).

The limitations of legal reform are also revealed by contemporary attempts to achieve gender equality. For example, in the 1970s many local governments adopted comparable worth wage policies. Such policies were "designed to correct historically discriminatory wages of female- and minority-dominated jobs" (Evans and Nelson 1989, p. 172). However, when some local communities were forced to raise women's wages to correct discriminatory practices, they eliminated or modified various jobs and social programs. Many of these programs, such as after school latchkey programs, were developed in response to the needs of two-paycheck and female-headed families. "In other words," note Evans and Nelson, "local governments are reacting to comparable worth with threats to renege on the emerging social commitment to policies addressing what have been traditionally defined as *women's* problems" (Evans and Nelson 1989, p. 183).

Other articles provide additional evidence of how legal reforms may actually disadvantage women in ways that are unanticipated. Furthermore, they reveal the problems in employing the model of equality as a basis for achieving gender justice. The emerging "difference theories" in feminist legal thought focus on the ways in which women and men live "gendered lives," and the ways in which legal and social institutions are shaped and operate according to gendered constructs (Fineman 1992).

The articles in this series also show how the law affects women in different ways. Women of color, poor women, and single mothers may experience the power of the law in ways that are different from the experiences of white, middle-class women. Poverty reform discourses are laden with images of single mothers as "bad" and often lump these women together "with drug addicts, criminals, and other socially-defined 'degenerates' in the newly-coined category of 'underclass'" (Fineman 1992, p. 283). Consequently, current welfare policies are not designed so much to help single mothers as they are to punish them for their bad behavior.

Several authors show how in the legal matters concerning male violence against women, "the experiences of women of color are frequently the product of intersecting patterns of racism and sexism" (Crenshaw 1991, p. 1243). These authors contend that theories of gender oppression must acknowledge the intersection of race and sex, the ways in which women have contributed to the social construction of race, and the oppression of black women. They also point out that the analyses of the law's role in women's oppression must take account of the intersectional identities of women and of how the law responds to, reinforces, and stigmatizes those identities.

The articles in this series bring together an outstanding selection from a growing body of work that examines how the law treats women and gender difference. They represent some of the most intriguing theoretical writing on the subject and reflect the strong multidisciplinary character of contemporary research on women and the legal order.

Notes

Cited works are contained in volumes five, three, seven, and two, respectively.

Crenshaw, Kimberle. 1991. Mapping the Margins: Intersectionality, Identity Politics, and Violence Against Women of Color. *Stanford Law Review* 43:1241–99.
Evans, Sara M. and Barbara J. Nelson. 1989. Comparable Worth: The Paradox of Technocratic Reform. *Feminist Studies* 15:171–90.
Fineman, Martha. 1992. Feminist Theory in Law: The Difference it Makes. *Columbia Journal of Gender and Law* 2:1–23.
Grossberg, Michael. 1983. Who Gets the Child? Custody, Guardianship, and the Rise of a Judicial Patriarchy in Nineteenth-Century America. *Feminist Studies* 9:235–60.

Volume Introduction

For nearly two decades feminist legal theorists have produced a body of work about how the law treats women and gender difference. Initially, feminist legal theorists adopted an equality-based approach in their writings and in their activities as advocates for social change. Gradually, however, many legal feminists began to point out that traditional equality analysis was unable to take into account real sex differences between women and men, to recognize that gender is a social construct, to acknowledge differences among women, particularly with regard to race, and to take into account the gendered dimensions of legal and social institutions.

Traditional equality doctrine is based on the premise that there are "no legally relevant differences between men and women" (Fineman 1992, p. 1). Thus, early attempts to transform the law employed rights-based claims to equal treatment for women. The proposed Equal Rights Amendment is a good example. In 1972 the U.S. Congress proposed to the states an amendment to the Constitution which read: "Equality of rights under the law shall not be denied or abridged by the United States or by any State on account of sex." The amendment would have prohibited governmental bodies from treating men and women differently on the basis of sex-based classifications.

Legislative reforms in the 1960s and 1970s in family law, employment law, and other doctrinal areas were also based on the equal treatment approach. "Feminist reformers," notes Martha Fineman, "attacked existing classifications and categories based on gender and favored a gender-neutral paradigm of equality that linguistically assumed and asserted sameness between men and women" (Fineman 1992, p. 9). Title VII of the Civil Rights Act of 1964, which prohibits employers from discriminating against workers on the basis of race, color, religion, sex, or national origin, illustrates the equal treatment approach and its goal of assimilation. Men and women are viewed as "equals" who cannot be treated differently by employers.

The limitations of the equal treatment approach became apparent when disputes arose over employers' pregnancy-related policies. Many employers routinely refused to hire married women with children and to fire women once they became pregnant. When women challenged these discriminatory policies in the courts, they found that judges were unwilling to rule against the employers. The U.S. Supreme Court ruled in *Geduldig* v. *Aiello* that the equal protection clause of the 14th Amendment did not prohibit employers from using pregnancy-based classifications even though they were sex-based classifications. In *General Electric Co.* v. *Gilbert* the Court ruled that pregnancy discrimination was not a form of discrimination "because of sex" under Title VII. The Court reasoned in these cases that there was no discrimination because only women had the unique capacity to become pregnant.

Congress rejected the Court's approach to pregnancy-related classifications by passing the Pregnancy Discrimination Act in 1978 (PDA). The PDA makes clear that pregnancy-based classifications fall within the scope of the sex discrimination provision of Title VII. The PDA also rejects the uniqueness approach to pregnancy by declaring that pregnancy-related conditions must be treated like other medical conditions that may affect an employee's ability to work (Lindgren and Taub 1993).

Family law is another doctrinal area that illustrates the limitations of the traditional equality approach. In the 1970s, many states reformed their divorce laws by passing no-fault divorce statutes. Additional divorce law reforms also affected the legal rules and processes governing property distribution and child custody (Fineman 1991). These equality-based reforms were based on a gender-neutral paradigm and were intended to benefit women. Yet there is substantial evidence that many women have actually been disadvantaged by these reforms. As Martha Fineman states, "even though divorce is now easier to obtain, its occasion provides the justification for ongoing, extensive state supervision of the custody determination and the typical postdivorce family unit, comprised of mothers and their children" (Fineman 1991, p. 79).

Many feminist legal theorists now agree that it is necessary to move beyond equality and to establish affirmative theories of difference (Fineman 1992; Daly 1990). In doing so, the question that must be addressed is what "legally relevant differences between men and women" are "worthy of some legal accommodation" (Fineman 1992, pp. 13–14). If some differences do matter, then the question to be asked is how the law can respond to and accommodate difference without reinforcing the "unequal and inequitable position of women" (Fineman 1992, p. 15). Fineman's feminist legal theory answers this question by offering the concept of a "gendered life." She argues that because women live gendered lives, "feminist legal theory *cannot* be gender-neutral, nor can it have as its goal equality in the traditional, formal legal sense of the word" (Fineman 1992, p. 15).

Other legal feminists point out that women's lives are also shaped by racial identities. Angela Harris contends that some feminist legal theorists rely on "gender essentialism—the notion that a unitary, 'essential' women's experience can be isolated and described independently of race, class, sexual orientation, and other realities of experience" (Harris 1990, p. 585). As Martha Mahoney points out, both race and gender are social constructions. She argues that feminist theorists such as Catherine MacKinnon who emphasize the construction of gender through male power and who focus on women's sexual exploitation, "tend to obscure the importance to white women of the social construction of race" (Mahoney 1993, p. 251.). As a result, racism, and white women's complicity with racism, is often displaced by theories of the "'essential' oppression of women" (Mahoney 1993, p. 217).

Kimberle Crenshaw proposes the concept of "intersectionality" as a way to avoid erasing race from antidiscrimination doctrine and feminist theory. Rather than including black women "in an already established analytical structure," feminist theory should take into consideration "the interaction of race and gender" (Crenshaw 1989, p. 140). Such an approach would be based on the recognition that "the intersectional experience is greater than the sum of racism and sexism" and that "'women's experience' or 'the Black experience' are not adequate frames of reference for the experiences and concerns of black women" (Crenshaw 1989, p. 140).

A common thread among the various feminist legal theories that has emerged over the past two decades is the recognition that despite incremental legal reforms, patriarchal distributions of power continue to result in unequal and oppressive conditions for many women. Consequently, one task feminists face is how to determine whether there has been any progress in dismantling the structures of women's subordination. Thus, as Katherine Bartlett asks, how should feminists go about defining progress and producing change? Rather than defining progress "in opposition to tradition and the past" Bartlett proposes that feminists attempt to seek a "reconciliation between the familiar and an evolving sense of what is just and good, rather than a radical break from the past" (Bartlett 1995, p. 305). She contends that changing gender role attitudes and the oppressive conditions that shape women's experiences, depends "upon the integration of insight and past understandings." Her vision of the possibilities for feminist-based change is based on an "integrated approach to tradition and change" that will "produce a deeper kind of progress—one that both endures and serves as a foundation for future progress" (Bartlett, 1995, p. 306). Whether or not feminist visions of the future can be achieved by a movement that reflects a "never-ending narrative of change" remains to be seen (Bartlett, 1995, p. 306).

Notes

Articles marked with an asterisk (*) are included in this volume.

*Bartlett, Katharine T. 1995. Tradition, Change, and the Idea of Progress in Feminist Legal Thought. *Wisconsin Law Review* 1995:303–43.
*Crenshaw, Kimberle. 1989. Demarginalizing the Intersection of Race and Sex: A Black Feminist Critique of Antidiscrimination Doctrine, Feminist Theory and Antiracist Politics. *University of Chicago Legal Forum* 1989:139–67.
  Daly, Kathleen. 1990. Reflections on Feminist Legal Thought. *Social Justice* 17:7–24.
  Fineman, Martha Albertson. 1991. *The Illusion of Equality.* Chicago: University of Chicago Press.
* Fineman, Martha Albertson. 1992. Feminist Theory in Law: The Difference It Makes. *Columbia Journal of Gender and Law* 2:1–23.
*Harris, Angela P. 1990. Race and Essentialism in Feminist Legal Theory. *Stanford Law Review* 42:581–616.
*Mahoney, Martha R. 1993. Whiteness and Women, in Practice and Theory: A Reply to Catherine MacKinnnon. *Yale Journal of Law and Feminism* 5:217–51.
  Lindgren J. Ralph and Nadine Taub. 1993. *The Law of Sex Discrimination,* 2d ed. Minneapolis: West Publishing Co.

Feminist Legal Theories

Difference and Dominance:
On Sex Discrimination
(1984)

What is a gender question a question of? What is an inequality question a question of? These two questions underlie applications of the equality principle to issues of gender, but they are seldom explicitly asked. I think it speaks to the way gender has structured thought and perception that mainstream legal and moral theory tacitly gives the same answer to them both: these are questions of sameness and difference. The mainstream doctrine of the law of sex discrimination that results is, in my view, largely responsible for the fact that sex equality law has been so utterly ineffective at getting women what we need and are socially prevented from having on the basis of a condition of birth: a chance at productive lives of reasonable physical security, self-expression, individuation, and minimal respect and dignity. Here I expose the sameness/ difference theory of sex equality, briefly show how it dominates sex discrimination law and policy and underlies its discontents, and propose an alternative that might do something.

      •   •   •

According to the approach to sex equality that has dominated politics, law, and social perception, equality is an equivalence, not a distinction, and sex is a distinction. The legal mandate of equal treatment—which is both a systemic norm and a specific legal doctrine— becomes a matter of treating likes alike and unlikes unlike; and the sexes are defined as such by their mutual unlikeness. Put another way, gender is socially constructed as difference epistemologically;

The most memorable occasions on which I delivered a version of this speech were: Harvard Law School, Cambridge, Massachusetts, Oct. 24, 1984; Conference on the Moral Foundations of Civil Rights Policy, Center for Philosophy and Public Policy, University of Maryland, College Park, Maryland, Oct. 19, 1984; and the James McCormick Mitchell Lecture, State University of Buffalo Law School, Buffalo, New York, Oct. 19, 1984. I thank the students of Harvard Law School for their response to so many of my initial thoughts.

32

sex discrimination law bounds gender equality by difference doctrinally. A built-in tension exists between this concept of equality, which presupposes sameness, and this concept of sex, which presupposes difference. Sex equality thus becomes a contradiction in terms, something of an oxymoron, which may suggest why we are having such a difficult time getting it.

Upon further scrutiny, two alternate paths to equality for women emerge within this dominant approach, paths that roughly follow the lines of this tension. The leading one is: be the same as men. This path is termed gender neutrality doctrinally and the single standard philosophically. It is testimony to how substance gets itself up as form in law that this rule is considered formal equality. Because this approach mirrors the ideology of the social world, it is considered abstract, meaning transparent of substance; also for this reason it is considered not only to be *the* standard, but *a* standard at all. It is so far the leading rule that the words "equal to" are code for, equivalent to, the words "the same as"—referent for both unspecified.

To women who want equality yet find that you are different, the doctrine provides an alternate route: be different from men. This equal recognition of difference is termed the special benefit rule or special protection rule legally, the double standard philosophically. It is in rather bad odor. Like pregnancy, which always calls it up, it is something of a doctrinal embarrassment. Considered an exception to true equality and not really a rule of law at all, this is the one place where the law of sex discrimination admits it is recognizing something substantive. Together with the Bona Fide Occupational Qualification (BFOQ), the unique physical characteristic exception under ERA policy, compensatory legislation, and sex-conscious relief in particular litigation, affirmative action is thought to live here.[1]

The philosophy underlying the difference approach is that sex *is* a difference, a division, a distinction, beneath which lies a stratum of human commonality, sameness. The moral thrust of the sameness branch of the doctrine is to make normative rules conform to this empirical reality by granting women access to what men have access to: to the extent that women are no different from men, we deserve what they have. The differences branch, which is generally seen as patronizing but necessary to avoid absurdity, exists to value or compensate women for what we are or have become distinctively as women (by which is meant, unlike men) under existing conditions.

My concern is not with which of these paths to sex equality is preferable in the long run or more appropriate to any particular issue,

33

3

although most discourse on sex discrimination revolves about these questions as if that were all there is. My point is logically prior: to treat issues of sex equality as issues of sameness and difference *is to take a particular approach.* I call this the difference approach because it is obsessed with the sex difference. The main theme in the fugue is "we're the same, we're the same, we're the same." The counterpoint theme (in a higher register) is "but we're different, but we're different, but we're different." Its underlying story is: on the first day, difference was; on the second day, a division was created upon it; on the third day, irrational instances of dominance arose. Division may be rational or irrational. Dominance either seems or is justified. Difference *is.*

There is a politics to this. Concealed is the substantive way in which man has become the measure of all things. Under the sameness standard, women are measured according to our correspondence with man, our equality judged by our proximity to his measure. Under the difference standard, we are measured according to our lack of correspondence with him, our womanhood judged by our distance from his measure. Gender neutrality is thus simply the male standard, and the special protection rule is simply the female standard, but do not be deceived: masculinity, or maleness, is the referent for both. Think about it like those anatomy models in medical school. A male body is the human body; all those extra things women have are studied in ob/gyn. It truly is a situation in which more is less. Approaching sex discrimination in this way—as if sex questions are difference questions and equality questions are sameness questions—provides two ways for the law to hold women to a male standard and call that sex equality.

·   ·   ·

Having been very hard on the difference answer to sex equality questions, I should say that it takes up a very important problem: how to get women access to everything we have been excluded from, while also valuing everything that women are or have been allowed to become or have developed as a consequence of our struggle either not to be excluded from most of life's pursuits or to be taken seriously under the terms that have been permitted to be our terms. It negotiates what we have managed in relation to men. Legally articulated as the need to conform normative standards to existing reality, the strongest doctrinal expression of its sameness idea would prohibit taking gender into account in any way.

34

Its guiding impulse is: we're as good as you. Anything you can do, we can do. Just get out of the way. I have to confess a sincere affection for this approach. It has gotten women some access to employment[2] and education,[3] the public pursuits, including academic,[4] professional,[5] and blue-collar work;[6] the military;[7] and more than nominal access to athletics.[8] It has moved to change the dead ends that were all we were seen as good for and has altered what passed for women's lack of physical training, which was really serious training in passivity and enforced weakness. It makes you want to cry sometimes to know that it has had to be a mission for many women just to be permitted to do the work of this society, to have the dignity of doing jobs a lot of other people don't even want to do.

The issue of including women in the military draft[9] has presented the sameness answer to the sex equality question in all its simple dignity and complex equivocality. As a citizen, I should have to risk being killed just like you. The consequences of my resistance to this risk should count like yours. The undercurrent is: what's the matter, don't you want me to learn to kill . . . just like you? Sometimes I see this as a dialogue between women in the afterlife. The feminist says to the soldier, "we fought for your equality." The soldier says to the feminist, "oh, no, *we* fought for *your* equality."

Feminists have this nasty habit of counting bodies and refusing not to notice their gender. As applied, the sameness standard has mostly gotten men the benefit of those few things women have historically had—for all the good they did us. Almost every sex discrimination case that has been won at the Supreme Court level has been brought by a man.[10] Under the rule of gender neutrality, the law of custody and divorce has been transformed, giving men an equal chance at custody of children and at alimony.[11] Men often look like better "parents" under gender-neutral rules like level of income and presence of nuclear family, because men make more money and (as they say) initiate the building of family units.[12] In effect, they get preferred because society advantages them before they get into court, and law is prohibited from taking that preference into account because that would mean taking gender into account. The group realities that make women more in need of alimony are not permitted to matter, because only individual factors, gender-neutrally considered, may matter. So the fact that women will live their lives, as individuals, as members of the group women, with women's chances in a sex-discriminatory society, may not count, or else it is sex discrimination. The equality principle in this guise mobilizes the idea that the way to

35

5

get things for women is to get them for men. Men have gotten them. Have women? We still have not got equal pay,[13] or equal work,[14] far less equal pay for equal work,[15] and we are close to losing separate enclaves like women's schools through this approach.[16]

Here is why. In reality, which this approach is not long on because it is liberal idealism talking to itself, virtually every quality that distinguishes men from women is already affirmatively compensated in this society. Men's physiology defines most sports,[17] their needs define auto and health insurance coverage, their socially designed biographies define workplace expectations and successful career patterns, their perspectives and concerns define quality in scholarship, their experiences and obsessions define merit, their objectification of life defines art, their military service defines citizenship, their presence defines family, their inability to get along with each other—their wars and rulerships—defines history, their image defines god, and their genitals define sex. For each of their differences from women, what amounts to an affirmative action plan is in effect, otherwise known as the structure and values of American society. But whenever women are, by this standard, "different" from men and insist on not having it held against us, whenever a difference is used to keep us second class and we refuse to smile about it, equality law has a paradigm trauma and it's crisis time for the doctrine.

What this doctrine has apparently meant by sex inequality is not what happens to us. The law of sex discrimination that has resulted seems to be looking only for those ways women are kept down that have *not* wrapped themselves up as a difference—whether original, imposed, or imagined. Start with original: what to do about the fact that women actually have an ability men still lack, gestating children in utero. Pregnancy therefore is a difference. Difference doctrine says it is sex discrimination to give women what we need, because only women need it. It is not sex discrimination not to give women what we need because then only women will not get what we need.[18] Move into imposed: what to do about the fact that most women are segregated into low-paying jobs where there are no men. Suspecting that the structure of the marketplace will be entirely subverted if comparable worth is put into effect, difference doctrine says that because there is no man to set a standard from which women's treatment is a deviation, there is no sex discrimination here, only sex difference. Never mind that there is no man to compare with because no man would do that job if he had a choice, and of course he has because he is a man, so he won't.[19]

36

Now move into the so-called subtle reaches of the imposed category, the de facto area. Most jobs in fact require that the person, gender neutral, who is qualified for them will be someone who is not the primary caretaker of a preschool child.[20] Pointing out that this raises a concern of sex in a society in which women are expected to care for the children is taken as day one of taking gender into account in the structuring of jobs. To do that would violate the rule against not noticing situated differences based on gender, so it never emerges that day one of taking gender into account was the day the job was structured with the expectation that its occupant would have no child care responsibilities. Imaginary sex differences—such as between male and female applicants to administer estates or between males aging and dying and females aging and dying[21]—I will concede, the doctrine can handle.

I will also concede that there are many differences between women and men. I mean, can you imagine elevating one half of a population and denigrating the other half and producing a population in which everyone is the same? What the sameness standard fails to notice is that men's differences from women are equal to women's differences from men. There is an *equality* there. Yet the sexes are not socially equal. The difference approach misses the fact that hierarchy of power produces real as well as fantasied differences, differences that are also inequalities. What is missing in the difference approach is what Aristotle missed in his empiricist notion that equality means treating likes alike and unlikes unlike, and nobody has questioned it since. Why should you have to be the same as a man to get what a man gets simply because he is one? Why does maleness provide an original entitlement, not questioned on the basis of *its* gender, so that it is women—women who want to make a case of unequal treatment in a world men have made in their image (this is really the part Aristotle missed)—who have to show in effect that they are men in every relevant respect, unfortunately mistaken for women on the basis of an accident of birth?

The women that gender neutrality benefits, and there are some, show the suppositions of this approach in highest relief. They are mostly women who have been able to construct a biography that somewhat approximates the male norm, at least on paper. They are the qualified, the least of sex discrimination's victims. When they are denied a man's chance, it looks the most like sex bias. The more unequal society gets, the fewer such women are permitted to exist. Therefore, the more unequal society gets, the *less* likely the difference

37

doctrine is to be able to do anything about it, because unequal power creates both the appearance and the reality of sex differences along the same lines as it creates its sex inequalities.

The special benefits side of the difference approach has not compensated for the differential of being second class. The special benefits rule is the only place in mainstream equality doctrine where you get to identify as a woman and not have that mean giving up all claim to equal treatment—but it comes close. Under its double standard, women who stand to inherit something when their husbands die have gotten the exclusion of a small percentage of the inheritance tax, to the tune of Justice Douglas waxing eloquent about the difficulties of all women's economic situation.[22] If we're going to be stigmatized as different, it would be nice if the compensation would fit the disparity. Women have also gotten three more years than men get before we have to be advanced or kicked out of the military hierarchy, as compensation for being precluded from combat, the usual way to advance.[23] Women have also gotten excluded from contact jobs in male-only prisons because we might get raped, the Court taking the viewpoint of the reasonable rapist on women's employment opportunities.[24] We also get protected out of jobs because of our fertility. The reason is that the job has health hazards, and somebody who might be a real person some day and therefore could sue—that is, a fetus—might be hurt if women, who apparently are not real persons and therefore can't sue either for the hazard to our health or for the lost employment opportunity, are given jobs that subject our bodies to possible harm.[25] Excluding women is always an option if equality feels in tension with the pursuit itself. They never seem to think of excluding men. Take combat.[26] Somehow it takes the glory out of the foxhole, the buddiness out of the trenches, to imagine us out there. You get the feeling they might rather end the draft, they might even rather not fight wars at all than have to do it with us.

The double standard of these rules doesn't give women the dignity of the single standard; it also does not (as the differences standard does) suppress the gender of its referent, which is, of course, the female gender. I must also confess some affection for this standard. The work of Carol Gilligan on gender differences in moral reasoning[27] gives it a lot of dignity, more than it has ever had, more, frankly, than I thought it ever could have. But she achieves for moral reasoning what the special protection rule achieves in law: the affirmative rather than the negative valuation of that which has accurately distinguished women from men, by making it seem as though those attributes, with their consequences, really are somehow ours, rather than what male supremacy has attributed to us for its own use. For women to affirm difference, when difference means dominance, as it does with gender, means to affirm the qualities and characteristics of powerlessness.

Women have done good things, and it is a good thing to affirm them. I think quilts are art. I think women have a history. I think we create culture. I also know that we have not only been excluded from making what has been considered art; our artifacts have been excluded from setting the standards by which art is art. Women have a history all right, but it is a history both of what was and of what was not allowed to be. So I am critical of affirming what we have been, which necessarily is what we have been permitted, as if it is women's, ours, possessive. As if equality, in spite of everything, already ineluctably exists.

I am getting hard on this and am about to get harder on it. I do not think that the way women reason morally is morality "in a different voice."[28] I think it is morality in a higher register, in the feminine voice. Women value care because men have valued us according to the care we give them, and we could probably use some. Women think in relational terms because our existence is defined in relation to men. Further, when you are powerless, you don't just speak differently. A lot, you don't speak. Your speech is not just differently articulated, it is silenced. Eliminated, gone. You aren't just deprived of a language with which to articulate your distinctiveness, although you are; you are deprived of a life out of which articulation might come. Not being heard is not just a function of lack of recognition, not just that no one knows how to listen to you, although it is that; it is also silence of the deep kind, the silence of being prevented from having anything to say. Sometimes it is permanent. All I am saying is that the damage of sexism is real, and reifying that into differences is an insult to our possibilities.

So long as these issues are framed this way, demands for equality will always appear to be asking to have it both ways: the same when we are the same, different when we are different. But this is the way men have it: equal and different too. They have it the same as women when they are the same and want it, and different from women when they are different and want to be, which usually they do. Equal and different too would only be parity.[29] But under male supremacy, while

39

being told we get it both ways, both the specialness of the pedestal and an even chance at the race, the ability to be a woman and a person, too, few women get much benefit of either.

•   •   •

There is an alternative approach, one that threads its way through existing law and expresses, I think, the reason equality law exists in the first place. It provides a second answer, a dissident answer in law and philosophy, to both the equality question and the gender question. In this approach, an equality question is a question of the distribution of power. Gender is also a question of power, specifically of male supremacy and female subordination. The question of equality, from the standpoint of what it is going to take to get it, is at root a question of hierarchy, which—as power succeeds in constructing social perception and social reality—derivatively becomes a categorical distinction, a difference. Here, on the first day that matters, dominance was achieved, probably by force. By the second day, division along the same lines had to be relatively firmly in place. On the third day, if not sooner, differences were demarcated, together with social systems to exaggerate them in perception and in fact, *because* the systematically differential delivery of benefits and deprivations required making no mistake about who was who. Comparatively speaking, man has been resting ever since. Gender might not even code as difference, might not mean distinction epistemologically, were it not for its consequences for social power.

I call this the dominance approach, and it is the ground I have been standing on in criticizing mainstream law. The goal of this dissident approach is not to make legal categories trace and trap the way things are. It is not to make rules that fit reality. It is critical of reality. Its task is not to formulate abstract standards that will produce determinate outcomes in particular cases. Its project is more substantive, more jurisprudential than formulaic, which is why it is difficult for the mainstream discourse to dignify it as an approach to doctrine or to imagine it as a rule of law at all. It proposes to expose that which women have had little choice but to be confined to, in order to change it.

The dominance approach centers on the most sex-differential abuses of women as a gender, abuses that sex equality law in its difference garb could not confront. It is based on a reality about which little of a systematic nature was known before 1970, a reality that calls for a new conception of the problem of sex inequality. This new in-

40

10

formation includes not only the extent and intractability of sex segregation into poverty, which has been known before, but the range
of issues termed violence against women, which has not been. It
combines women's material desperation, through being relegated to
categories of jobs that pay nil, with the massive amount of rape and
attempted rape—44 percent of all women—about which virtually
nothing is done;[30] the sexual assault of children—38 percent of girls
and 10 percent of boys—which is apparently endemic to the patriarchal family;[31] the battery of women that is systematic in one quarter
to one third of our homes;[32] prostitution, women's fundamental economic condition, what we do when all else fails, and for many
women in this country, all else fails often;[33] and pornography, an industry that traffics in female flesh, making sex inequality into sex to
the tune of eight billion dollars a year in profits largely to organized
crime.[34]

These experiences have been silenced out of the difference definition of sex equality largely because they happen almost exclusively
to women. Understand: for this reason, they are considered *not* to
raise sex equality issues. Because this treatment is done almost
uniquely to women, it is implicitly treated as a difference, the sex
difference, when in fact it is the socially situated subjection of
women. The whole point of women's social relegation to inferiority
as a gender is that for the most part these things aren't done to men.
Men are not paid half of what women are paid for doing the same
work on the basis of their equal difference. Everything they touch
does not turn valueless because they touched it. When they are hit,
a person has been assaulted. When they are sexually violated, it is
not simply tolerated or found entertaining or defended as the necessary structure of the family, the price of civilization, or a constitutional right.

Does this differential describe the sex difference? Maybe so. It does
describe the systematic relegation of an entire group of people to a
condition of inferiority and attribute it to their nature. If this differential were biological, maybe biological intervention would have to
be considered. If it were evolutionary, perhaps men would have to
evolve differently. Because I think it is political, I think its politics
construct the deep structure of society. Men who do not rape women
have nothing wrong with their hormones. Men who are made sick
by pornography and do not eroticize their revulsion are not under-
evolved. This social status in which we can be used and abused and
trivialized and humiliated and bought and sold and passed around

41

and patted on the head and put in place and told to smile so that we look as though we're enjoying it all is not what some of us have in mind as sex equality.

This second approach—which is not abstract, which is at odds with socially imposed reality and therefore does not look like a standard according to the standard for standards—became the implicit model for racial justice applied by the courts during the sixties. It has since eroded with the erosion of judicial commitment to racial equality. It was based on the realization that the condition of Blacks in particular was not fundamentally a matter of rational or irrational differentiation on the basis of race but was fundamentally a matter of white supremacy, under which racial differences became invidious as a consequence.[35] To consider gender in this way, observe again that men are as different from women as women are from men, but socially the sexes are not equally powerful. To be on the top of a hierarchy is certainly different from being on the bottom, but that is an obfuscatingly neutralized way of putting it, as a hierarchy is a great deal more than that. If gender were merely a question of difference, sex inequality would be a problem of mere sexism, of mistaken differentiation, of inaccurate categorization of individuals. This is what the difference approach thinks it is and is therefore sensitive to. But if gender is an inequality first, constructed as a socially relevant differentiation in order to keep that inequality in place, then sex inequality questions are questions of systematic dominance, of male supremacy, which is not at all abstract and is anything but a mistake.

If differentiation into classifications, in itself, is discrimination, as it is in difference doctrine, the use of law to change group-based social inequalities becomes problematic, even contradictory. This is because the group whose situation is to be changed must necessarily be legally identified and delineated, yet to do so is considered in fundamental tension with the guarantee against legally sanctioned inequality. If differentiation is discrimination, affirmative action, and any legal change in social inequality, is discrimination—but the existing social differentiations which constitute the inequality are not? This is only to say that, in the view that equates differentiation with discrimination, changing an unequal status quo is discrimination, but allowing it to exist is not.

Looking at the difference approach and the dominance approach from each other's point of view clarifies some otherwise confusing tensions in sex equality debates. From the point of view of the dominance approach, it becomes clear that the difference approach adopts

42

12

the point of view of male supremacy on the status of the sexes. Simply by treating the status quo as "the standard," it invisibly and uncritically accepts the arrangements under male supremacy. In this sense, the difference approach is masculinist, although it can be expressed in a female voice. The dominance approach, in that it sees the inequalities of the social world from the standpoint of the subordination of women to men, is feminist.

If you look through the lens of the difference approach at the world as the dominance approach imagines it—that is, if you try to see real inequality through a lens that has difficulty seeing an inequality as an inequality if it also appears as a difference—you see demands for change in the distribution of power as demands for special protection. This is because the only tools that the difference paradigm offers to comprehend disparity equate the recognition of a gender line with an admission of lack of entitlement to equality under law. Since equality questions are primarily confronted in this approach as matters of empirical fit[36]—that is, as matters of accurately shaping legal rules (implicitly modeled on the standard men set) to the way the world is (also implicitly modeled on the standard men set)—any existing differences must be negated to merit equal treatment. For ethnicity as well as for gender, it is basic to mainstream discrimination doctrine to preclude any true diversity among equals or true equality within diversity.

To the difference approach, it further follows that any attempt to change the way the world actually is looks like a moral question requiring a separate judgment of how things ought to be. This approach imagines asking the following disinterested question that can be answered neutrally as to groups: against the weight of empirical difference, should we treat some as the equals of others, even when they may not be entitled to it because they are not up to standard? Because this construction of the problem is part of what the dominance approach unmasks, it does not arise with the dominance approach, which therefore does not see its own foundations as moral. If sex inequalities are approached as matters of imposed status, which are in need of change if a legal mandate of equality means anything at all, the question whether women should be treated unequally means simply whether women should be treated as less. When it is exposed as a naked power question, there is no separable question of what ought to be. The only real question is what is and is not a gender question. Once no amount of difference justifies treating women as subhuman, eliminating that is what equality law is for.

43

In this shift of paradigms, equality propositions become no longer propositions of good and evil, but of power and powerlessness, no more disinterested in their origins or neutral in their arrival at conclusions than are the problems they address.

There came a time in Black people's movement for equality in this country when slavery stopped being a question of how it could be justified and became a question of how it could be ended. Racial disparities surely existed, or racism would have been harmless, but at that point—a point not yet reached for issues of sex—no amount of group difference mattered anymore. This is the same point at which a group's characteristics, including empirical attributes, become constitutive of the fully human, rather than being defined as exceptions to or as distinct from the fully human. To one-sidedly measure one group's differences against a standard set by the other incarnates partial standards. The moment when one's particular qualities become part of the standard by which humanity is measured is a millenial moment.

To summarize the argument: seeing sex equality questions as matters of reasonable or unreasonable classification is part of the way male dominance is expressed in law. If you follow my shift in perspective from gender as difference to gender as dominance, gender changes from a distinction that is presumptively valid to a detriment that is presumptively suspect. The difference approach tries to map reality; the dominance approach tries to challenge and change it. In the dominance approach, sex discrimination stops being a question of morality and starts being a question of politics.

You can tell if sameness is your standard for equality if my critique of hierarchy looks like a request for special protection in disguise. It's not. It envisions a change that would make possible a simple equal chance for the first time. To define the reality of sex as difference and the warrant of equality as sameness is wrong on both counts. Sex, in nature, is not a bipolarity; it is a continuum. In society it is made into a bipolarity. Once this is done, to require that one be the same as those who set the standard—those which one is already socially defined as different from—simply means that sex equality is conceptually designed never to be achieved. Those who most need equal treatment will be the least similar, socially, to those whose situation sets the standard as against which one's entitlement to be equally treated is measured. Doctrinally speaking, the deepest problems of sex inequality will not find women "similarly situated"[37] to men. Far less will practices of sex inequality require that acts be intentionally discriminatory.[38] All that is required is that the status quo be maintained. As a strategy for maintaining social power first structure reality unequally, then require that entitlement to alter it be grounded on a lack of distinction in situation; first structure perception so that different equals inferior, then require that discrimination be activated by evil minds who *know* they are treating equals as less.

I say, give women equal power in social life. Let what we say matter, then we will discourse on questions of morality. Take your foot off our necks, then we will hear in what tongue women speak. So long as sex equality is limited by sex difference, whether you like it or don't like it, whether you value it or seek to negate it, whether you stake it out as a grounds for feminism or occupy it as the terrain of misogyny, women will be born, degraded, and die. We would settle for that equal protection of the laws under which one would be born, live, and die, in a country where protection is not a dirty word and equality is not a special privilege.

45

2. Difference and Dominance

1. The Bona Fide Occupational Qualification (BFOQ) exception to Title VII of the Civil Rights Act of 1964, 42 U.S.C. § 2000 e-(2)(e), permits sex to be a job qualification when it is a valid one. The leading interpretation of the proposed federal Equal Rights Amendment would, pursuing a similar analytic structure, permit a "unique physical characteristic" exception to its otherwise absolute embargo on taking sex into account. Barbara Brown, Thomas I. Emerson, Gail Falk, and Ann E. Freedman, "The Equal Rights Amendment: A Constitutional Basis for Equal Rights for Women," 80 *Yale Law Journal* 893 (1971).

2. Title VII of the Civil Rights Act of 1964, 42 U.S.C. § 2000 e; Phillips v. Martin-Marietta, 400 U.S. 542 (1971). Frontiero v. Richardson, 411 U.S. 484 (1974) is the high-water mark of this approach. *See also* City of Los Angeles v. Manhart, 435 U.S. 702 (1978); Newport News Shipbuilding and Dry Dock Co. v. EEOC, 462 U.S. 669 (1983).

3. Title IX of the Education Amendments of 1972, 20 U.S.C.§1681; Cannon v. University of Chicago, 441 U.S. 677 (1981); Mississippi University for Women v. Hogan, 458 U.S. 718 (1982); *see also* De La Cruz v. Tormey, 582 F.2d 45 (9th Cir. 1978).

4. My impression is that women appear to lose most academic sex discrimination cases that go to trial, although I know of no systematic or statistical study on the subject. One case that won eventually, elevating the standard of proof in the process, is Sweeney v. Board of Trustees of Keene State College, 439 U.S. 29 (1979). The ruling for the plaintiff was affirmed on remand, 604 F.2d 106 (1st Cir. 1979).

5. Hishon v. King & Spalding, 467 U.S. 69 (1984).

6. *See, e.g.*, Vanguard Justice v. Hughes, 471 F. Supp. 670 (D. Md. 1979); Meyer v. Missouri State Highway Commission, 567 F.2d 804, 891 (8th Cir. 1977); Payne v. Travenol Laboratories Inc., 416 F. Supp. 248 (N.D. Mass. 1976). *See also* Dothard v. Rawlinson, 433 U.S. 321 (1977) (height and weight requirements invalidated for prison guard contact positions because of disparate impact on sex).

7. Frontiero v. Richardson, 411 U.S. 484 (1974); Schlesinger v. Ballard, 419 U.S. 498 (1975).

8. This situation is relatively complex. *See* Gomes v. R.I. Interscholastic League, 469 F. Supp. 659 (D. R.I. 1979); Brenden v. Independent School District, 477 F.2d 1292 (8th Cir. 1973); O'Connor v. Board of Education of School District No. 23, 645 F.2d 578 (7th Cir. 1981); Cape v. Tennessee Secondary School Athletic Association, 424 F. Supp. 732 (E.D. Tenn. 1976), *rev'd*, 563 F.2d 793 (6th Cir. 1977); Yellow Springs Exempted Village School District Board of Education v. Ohio High School Athletic Association, 443 F. Supp. 753 (S.D. Ohio 1978); Aiken v. Lieuallen, 593 P.2d 1243 (Or. App. 1979).

9. Rostker v. Goldberg, 453 U.S. 57 (1981). *See also* Lori S. Kornblum, "Women Warriors in a Men's World: The Combat Exclusion," 2 *Law and Inequality: A Journal of Theory and Practice* 353 (1984).

240

10. David Cole, "Strategies of Difference: Litigating for Women's Rights in a Man's World," 2 *Law & Inequality: A Journal of Theory and Practice* 34 n.4 (1984) (collecting cases).

11. Devine v. Devine, 398 So. 2d 686 (Ala. Sup. Ct. 1981); Danielson v. Board of Higher Education, 358 F. Supp. 22 (S.D.N.Y. 1972); Weinberger v. Wiesenfeld, 420 U.S. 636 (1975); Stanley v. Illinois, 405 U.S. 645 (1971); Caban v. Mohammed, 441 U.S. 380 (1979); Orr v. Orr, 440 U.S. 268 (1979).

12. Lenore Weitzman, "The Economics of Divorce: Social and Economic Consequences of Property, Alimony and Child Support Awards," 28 *U.C.L.A. Law Review* 1118, 1251 (1982), documents a decline in women's standard of living of 73 percent and an increase in men's of 42 percent within a year after divorce.

13. Equal Pay Act, 29 U.S.C. § 206(d)(1) (1976) guarantees pay equality, as does case law, *but cf.* data on pay gaps, "Introduction," note 2.

14. Examples include Christenson v. State of Iowa, 563 F.2d 353 (8th Cir. 1977); Gerlach v. Michigan Bell Tel. Co., 501 F. Supp. 1300 (E.D. Mich. 1980); Odomes v. Nucare, Inc., 653 F.2d 246 (6th Cir. 1981) (female nurse's aide denied Title VII remedy because her job duties were not substantially similar to those of better-paid male orderly); Power v. Barry County, Michigan, 539 F. Supp. 721 (W.D. Mich. 1982); Spaulding v. University of Washington, 740 F. 2d 686 (9th Cir. 1984).

15. County of Washington v. Gunther, 452 U.S. 161 (1981) permits a comparable worth–type challenge where pay inequality can be proven to be a correlate of intentional job segregation. *See also* Lemons v. City and County of Denver, 17 FEP Cases 910 (D. Colo. 1978), *aff'd,* 620 F.2d 228 (10th Cir. 1977), *cert. denied,* 449 U.S. 888 (1980); AFSCME v. State of Washington, 770 F.2d 1401 (9th Cir. 1985). *See generally* Carol Jean Pint, "Value, Work and Women," 1 *Law & Inequality: A Journal of Theory and Practice* 159 (1983).

16. Combine the result in Bob Jones University v. United States, 461 U.S. 547 (1983) with Mississippi University for Women v. Hogan, 458 U.S. 718 (1982), and the tax-exempt status of women-only schools is clearly threatened.

17. A particularly pungent example comes from a case in which the plaintiff sought to compete in boxing matches with men, since there were no matches sponsored by the defendant among women. A major reason that preventing the woman from competing was found not to violate her equality rights was that the "safety rules and precautions [were] developed, designed, and tested in the context of all-male competition." Lafler v. Athletic Board of Control, 536 F. Supp. 104, 107 (W.D. Mich. 1982). As the court put it: "In this case, the real differences between the male and female anatomy are relevant in considering whether men and women may be treated differently with regard to their participating in boxing. The plaintiff *admits* that she wears a protective covering for her breasts while boxing. Such a protective covering . . . would violate Rule Six, Article 9 of the Amateur Boxing Federation rules currently in effect. The same rule *requires* contestants to wear a protective

241

17

cup, a rule obviously designed for the unique anatomical characteristics of men." Id. at 106 (emphasis added). The rule is based on the male anatomy, therefore not a justification for the discrimination but an example of it. This is not considered in the opinion, nor does the judge discuss whether women might benefit from genital protection, and men from chest guards, as in some other sports.

18. This is a reference to the issues raised by several recent cases which consider whether states' attempts to compensate pregnancy leaves and to secure jobs on return constitute sex discrimination. California Federal Savings and Loan Assn. v. Guerra, 758 F.2d 390 (9th Cir. 1985), *cert. granted* 54 U.S.L.W. 3460 (U.S. Jan. 13, 1986); *see also* Miller-Wohl v. Commissioner of Labor, 515 F. Supp. 1264 (D. Montana 1981), *vacated and dismissed*, 685 F.2d 1088 (9th Cir. 1982). The position argued in "Difference and Dominance" here suggests that if these benefits are prohibited under Title VII, Title VII is unconstitutional under the equal protection clause.

This argument was not made directly in either case. The American Civil Liberties Union argued that the provisions requiring pregnancy to be compensated in employment, without comparable coverage for men, violated Title VII's prohibition on pregnancy-based classifications and on sex. Montana had made it illegal for an employer to "terminate a woman's employment because of her pregnancy" or to "refuse to grant to the employee a reasonable leave of absence for such pregnancy." Montana Maternity Leave Act § 49-2-310(1) and (2). According to the ACLU, this provision "grants pregnant workers certain employment rights not enjoyed by other workers . . . Legislation designed to benefit women has . . . perpetuated destructive stereotypes about their proper roles and operated to deny them rights and benefits enjoyed by men. The [Montana provision] deters employers from hiring women who are or may become pregnant, causes resentment and hostility in the workplace, and penalizes men." Brief of American Civil Liberties Union, et al. *amicus curiae*, Montana Supreme Court No. 84-172, at 7. The National Organization for Women argued that the California provision, which requires employers to give pregnant workers unpaid disability leave with job security for up to four months, would violate Title VII should Title VII be interpreted to permit it. Brief of National Organization for Women, et al., United States Court of Appeals for the Ninth Circuit, 685 F.2d 1088 (9th Cir. 1982).

When Congress passed the Pregnancy Discrimination Act, amending Title VII, 42 U.S.C. § 2000 e(k), it defined "because of sex" or "on the basis of sex" to include "because of or on the basis of pregnancy, childbirth, or related medical conditions; and women affected by pregnancy, childbirth, or related medical conditions shall be treated the same for all employment-related purposes." In so doing, Congress arguably decided that one did not have to be the same as a man to be treated without discrimination, since it guaranteed freedom from discriminatory treatment on the basis of a condition that is not the same for men as it is for women. It even used the word "women" in the statute.

242

18

Further, Congress made this decision expressly to overrule the Supreme Court decision in General Electric v. Gilbert, 429 U.S. 125 (1976), which had held that failure to cover pregnancy as a disability was not sex discrimination because the line between pregnant and nonpregnant was not the line between women and men. In rejecting this logic, as the Court found it did expressly in Newport News Shipbuilding and Dry Dock Co. v. EEOC, 462 U.S. 669, 678 (1983), Congress rejected the implicit measuring of women's entitlement to equality by a male standard. Nor need all women be the same, that is, pregnant or potentially so, to have pregnancy-based discrimination be sex-based discrimination.

Upholding the California pregnancy leave and job security law, the Ninth Circuit opinion did not require sameness for equality to be delivered: "The PDA does not require states to ignore pregnancy. It requires that women be treated equally . . .[E]quality under the PDA must be measured in employment opportunity, not necessarily in amounts of money expended—or in amounts of days of disability leave expended. Equality . . . compares coverage to actual need, not coverage to hypothetical identical needs." California Federal v. Guerra, 758 F.2d 390 (9th Cir. 1985) (Ferguson, J.). "We are not the first court to announce the goal of Title VII is equality of employment opportunity, not necessarily sameness of treatment." Id. at 396 n.7.

19. Most women work at jobs mostly women do, and most of those jobs are paid less than jobs that mostly men do. *See, e.g.,* Pint, note 15 above, at 162–63 nn.19, 20 (collecting studies). To the point that men may not meet the male standard themselves, one court found that a union did not fairly represent its women in the following terms: "As to the yard and driver jobs, defendants suggest not only enormous intellectual requirements, but that the physical demands of those jobs are so great as to be beyond the capacity of any female. Again, it is noted that plaintiffs' capacity to perform those jobs was never tested, despite innumerable requests therefor. It is also noted that defendants have never suggested *which* of the innumerable qualifications they list for these jobs (for the first time) the plaintiffs might fail to meet. The court, however, will accept without listing here the extraordinary catalogue of feats which defendants argue must be performed in the yard, and as a driver. That well may be. However, one learns from this record that one cannot be too weak, too sick, too old and infirm, or too ignorant to perform these jobs, *so long as one is a man.* The plaintiffs appear to the layperson's eye to be far more physically fit than many of the drivers who moved into the yard, over the years, according to the testimony of defense witnesses . . . In short, they were all at least as fit as the men with serious physical deficits and disabilities who held yard jobs." Jones v. Cassens Transport, 617 F. Supp. 869, 892 (1985) (emphasis in original).

20. Phillips v. Martin-Marietta, 400 U.S. 542 (1971).

21. Reed v. Reed, 404 U.S. 71 (1971) held that a statute barring women from administering estates is sex discrimination. If few women were taught to read and write, as used to be the case, the gender difference would not be

243

imaginary in this case, yet the social situation would be even more sex discriminatory than it is now. Compare City of Los Angeles v. Manhart, 434 U.S. 815 (1978), which held that requiring women to make larger contributions to their retirement plan was sex discrimination, in spite of the allegedly proven sex difference that women on the average outlive men.

22. Kahn v. Shevin, 416 U.S. 351, 353 (1974).

23. Schlesinger v. Ballard, 419 U.S. 498 (1975).

24. Dothard v. Rawlinson, 433 U.S. 321 (1977); *see also* Michael M. v. Sonoma County Superior Court, 450 U.S. 464 (1981).

25. Doerr v. B.F. Goodrich, 484 F. Supp. 320 (N.D. Ohio 1979). Wendy Webster Williams, "Firing the Woman to Protect the Fetus: The Reconciliation of Fetal Protection with Employment Opportunity Goals Under Title VII," 69 *Georgetown Law Journal* 641 (1981). *See also* Hayes v. Shelby Memorial Hospital, 546 F. Supp. 259 (N.D. Ala. 1982); Wright v. Olin Corp., 697 F.2d 1172 (4th Cir. 1982).

26. Congress requires the Air Force (10 U.S.C. § 8549 [1983]) and the Navy (10 U.S.C. § 6015 [1983]) to exclude women from combat, with some exceptions. Owens v. Brown, 455 F. Supp. 291 (D.D.C. 1978), had previously invalidated the prior Navy combat exclusion because it prohibited women from filling jobs they could perform and inhibited Navy's discretion to assign women on combat ships. The Army excludes women from combat based upon its own policies under congressional authorization to determine assignment (10 U.S.C. § 3012 [e] [1983]).

27. Carol Gilligan, *In a Different Voice* (1982).

28. Id.

29. I argued this in Appendix A of my *Sexual Harassment of Working Women: A Case of Sex Discrimination* (1979). That book ends with "Women want to be equal and different, too." I could have added "Men are." As a standard, this would have reduced women's aspirations for equality to some corresponding version of men's actualities. But as an observation, it would have been true.

30. Diana Russell and Nancy Howell, "The Prevalence of Rape in the United States Revisited," 8 *Signs: Journal of Women in Culture and Society* 689 (1983) (44 percent of women in 930 households were victims of rape or attempted rape at some time in their lives).

31. Diana Russell, "The Incidence and Prevalence of Intrafamilial and Extrafamilial Sexual Abuse of Female Children," 7 *Child Abuse & Neglect: The International Journal* 133 (1983).

32. R. Emerson Dobash and Russell Dobash, *Violence against Wives: A Case against the Patriarchy* (1979); Bruno v. Codd, 90 Misc. 2d 1047, 396 N.Y.S. 2d 974 (Sup. Ct. 1977), *rev'd*, 64 A.D. 2d 582, 407 N.Y.S. 2d 165 (1st Dep't 1978), *aff'd* 47 N.Y. 2d 582, 393 N.E. 2d 976, 419 N.Y.S. 2d 901 (1979).

33. Kathleen Barry, *Female Sexual Slavery* (1979); Moira K. Griffin, "Wives, Hookers and the Law: The Case for Decriminalizing Prostitution," 10 *Student Lawyer* 18 (1982); Report of Jean Fernand-Laurent, Special Rapporteur on the Suppression of the Traffic in Persons and the Exploitation of the Prostitution of Others (a United Nations report), in *International Feminism: Networking*

244

20

against Female Sexual Slavery 130 (Kathleen Barry, Charlotte Bunch, and Shirley Castley eds.) (Report of the Global Feminist Workshop to Organize against Traffic in Women, Rotterdam, Netherlands, Apr. 6–15, 1983 [1984]).

34. Galloway and Thornton, "Crackdown on Pornography—A No-Win Battle," *U.S. News and World Report*, June 4, 1984, at 84. *See also* "The Place of Pornography," *Harper's*, November 1984, at 31 (citing $7 billion per year).

35. Loving v. Virginia, 388 U.S. 1 (1967), first used the term "white supremacy" in invalidating an antimiscegenation law as a violation of equal protection. The law equally forbade whites and Blacks to intermarry. Although going nowhere near as far, courts in the athletics area have sometimes seen that "same" does not necessarily mean "equal" nor does "equal" require "same." In a context of sex inequality like that which has prevailed in athletic opportunity, allowing boys to compete on girls' teams may diminish overall sex equality. "Each position occupied by a male reduces the female participation and increases the overall disparity of athletic opportunity which generally exists." Petrie v. Illinois High School Association, 394 N.E. 2d 855, 865 (Ill. 1979). "We conclude that to furnish exactly the same athletic opportunities to boys as to girls would be most difficult and would be detrimental to the compelling governmental interest of equalizing general athletic opportunities between the sexes." Id.

36. The scholars Tussman and tenBroek first used the term "fit" to characterize the necessary relation between a valid equality rule and the world to which it refers. J. Tussman and J. tenBroek, "The Equal Protection of the Laws," 37 *California Law Review* 341 (1949).

37. Royster Guano Co. v. Virginia, 253 U.S. 412, 415 (1920): "[A classification] must be reasonable, not arbitrary, and must rest upon some ground of difference having a fair and substantial relation to the object of the legislation, so that all persons similarly circumstanced shall be treated alike." Reed v. Reed, 404 U.S. 71, 76 (1971): "Regardless of their sex, persons within any one of the enumerated classes . . . are similarly situated . . . By providing dissimilar treatment for men and women who are thus similarly situated, the challenged section violates the Equal Protection Clause."

38. Washington v. Davis, 426 U.S. 229 (1976) and Personnel Administrator of Massachusetts v. Feeney, 442 U.S. 256 (1979) require that intentional discrimination be shown for discrimination to be shown.

245

Demarginalizing the Intersection of Race and Sex: A Black Feminist Critique of Antidiscrimination Doctrine, Feminist Theory and Antiracist Politics

Kimberle Crenshaw†

One of the very few Black women's studies books is entitled *All the Women Are White, All the Blacks Are Men, But Some of Us are Brave.*[1] I have chosen this title as a point of departure in my efforts to develop a Black feminist criticism[2] because it sets forth a problematic consequence of the tendency to treat race and gender as mutually exclusive categories of experience and analysis.[3] In this talk, I want to examine how this tendency is perpetuated by a single-axis framework that is dominant in antidiscrimination law and that is also reflected in feminist theory and antiracist politics.

I will center Black women in this analysis in order to contrast the multidimensionality of Black women's experience with the single-axis analysis that distorts these experiences. Not only will this juxtaposition reveal how Black women are theoretically erased, it will also illustrate how this framework imports its own theoretical limitations that undermine efforts to broaden feminist and an-

---

† Acting Professor of Law, University of California, Los Angeles Law School.

[1] Gloria T. Hull, et al, eds (The Feminist Press, 1982).

[2] For other work setting forth a Black feminist perspective on law, see Judy Scales-Trent, *Black Women and the Constitution: Finding Our Place, Asserting Our Rights (Voices of Experience: New Responses to Gender Discourse)*, 24 Harv CR-CL L Rev 9 (1989); Regina Austin, *Sapphire-Bound!*, forthcoming in Wisc Women's L J (1989); Angela Harris, *Race and Essentialism in Feminist Legal Theory* (unpublished manuscript on file with author); and Paulette M. Caldwell, *A Hair Piece* (unpublished manuscript on file with author).

[3] The most common linguistic manifestation of this analytical dilemma is represented in the conventional usage of the term "Blacks and women." Although it may be true that some people mean to include Black women in either "Blacks" or "women," the context in which the term is used actually suggests that often Black women are not considered. See, for example, Elizabeth Spelman, *The Inessential Woman* 114-15 (Beacon Press, 1988) (discussing an article on Blacks and women in the military where "the racial identity of those identified as 'women' does not become explicit until reference is made to Black women, at which point it also becomes clear that the category of women excludes Black women"). It seems that if Black women were explicitly included, the preferred term would be either "Blacks and white women" or "Black men and all women."

tiracist analyses. With Black women as the starting point, it becomes more apparent how dominant conceptions of discrimination condition us to think about subordination as disadvantage occurring along a single categorical axis. I want to suggest further that this single-axis framework erases Black women in the conceptualization, identification and remediation of race and sex discrimination by limiting inquiry to the experiences of otherwise-privileged members of the group. In other words, in race discrimination cases, discrimination tends to be viewed in terms of sex- or class-privileged Blacks; in sex discrimination cases, the focus is on race- and class-privileged women.

This focus on the most privileged group members marginalizes those who are multiply-burdened and obscures claims that cannot be understood as resulting from discrete sources of discrimination. I suggest further that this focus on otherwise-privileged group members creates a distorted analysis of racism and sexism because the operative conceptions of race and sex become grounded in experiences that actually represent only a subset of a much more complex phenomenon.

After examining the doctrinal manifestations of this single-axis framework, I will discuss how it contributes to the marginalization of Black women in feminist theory and in antiracist politics. I argue that Black women are sometimes excluded from feminist theory and antiracist policy discourse because both are predicated on a discrete set of experiences that often does not accurately reflect the interaction of race and gender. These problems of exclusion cannot be solved simply by including Black women within an already established analytical structure. Because the intersectional experience is greater than the sum of racism and sexism, any analysis that does not take intersectionality into account cannot sufficiently address the particular manner in which Black women are subordinated. Thus, for feminist theory and antiracist policy discourse to embrace the experiences and concerns of Black women, the entire framework that has been used as a basis for translating "women's experience" or "the Black experience" into concrete policy demands must be rethought and recast.

As examples of theoretical and political developments that miss the mark with respect to Black women because of their failure to consider intersectionality, I will briefly discuss the feminist critique of rape and separate spheres ideology, and the public policy debates concerning female-headed households within the Black community.

I. The Antidiscrimination Framework

A. The Experience of Intersectionality and the Doctrinal Response

One way to approach the problem of intersectionality is to examine how courts frame and interpret the stories of Black women plaintiffs. While I cannot claim to know the circumstances underlying the cases that I will discuss, I nevertheless believe that the way courts interpret claims made by Black women is itself part of Black women's experience and, consequently, a cursory review of cases involving Black female plaintiffs is quite revealing. To illustrate the difficulties inherent in judicial treatment of intersectionality, I will consider three Title VII[4] cases: *DeGraffenreid v General Motors,*[5] *Moore v Hughes Helicopter*[6] and *Payne v Travenol.*[7]

1. *DeGraffenreid v General Motors.*

In *DeGraffenreid,* five Black women brought suit against General Motors, alleging that the employer's seniority system perpetuated the effects of past discrimination against Black women. Evidence adduced at trial revealed that General Motors simply did not hire Black women prior to 1964 and that all of the Black women hired after 1970 lost their jobs in a seniority-based layoff during a subsequent recession. The district court granted summary judgment for the defendant, rejecting the plaintiffs' attempt to bring a suit not on behalf of Blacks or women, but specifically on behalf of Black women. The court stated:

[P]laintiffs have failed to cite any decisions which have stated that Black women are a special class to be protected from discrimination. The Court's own research has failed to disclose such a decision. The plaintiffs are clearly entitled to a remedy if they have been discriminated against. However, they should not be allowed to combine statutory remedies to create a new 'super-remedy' which would give them relief beyond what the drafters of the relevant statutes intended. Thus, this lawsuit must be examined to see if it states a cause of action for race discrimination, sex discrimination, or alternatively either, but not a combination of both.[8]

---

[4] Civil Rights Act of 1964, 42 USC § 2000e, et seq as amended (1982).
[5] 413 F Supp 142 (E D Mo 1976).
[6] 708 F2d 475 (9th Cir 1983).
[7] 673 F2d 798 (5th Cir 1982).
[8] *DeGraffenreid,* 413 F Supp at 143.

Although General Motors did not hire Black women prior to 1964, the court noted that "General Motors has hired . . . female employees for a number of years prior to the enactment of the Civil Rights Act of 1964."[9] Because General Motors did hire women—albeit *white women*—during the period that no Black women were hired, there was, in the court's view, no sex discrimination that the seniority system could conceivably have perpetuated.

After refusing to consider the plaintiffs' sex discrimination claim, the court dismissed the race discrimination complaint and recommended its consolidation with another case alleging race discrimination against the same employer.[10] The plaintiffs responded that such consolidation would defeat the purpose of their suit since theirs was not purely a race claim, but an action brought specifically on behalf of Black women alleging race *and* sex discrimination. The court, however, reasoned:

> The legislative history surrounding Title VII does not indicate that the goal of the statute was to create a new classification of 'black women' who would have greater standing than, for example, a black male. The prospect of the creation of new classes of protected minorities, governed only by the mathematical principles of permutation and combination, clearly raises the prospect of opening the hackneyed Pandora's box.[11]

Thus, the court apparently concluded that Congress either did not contemplate that Black women could be discriminated against as "Black women" or did not intend to protect them when such discrimination occurred.[12] The court's refusal in *DeGraffenreid* to

---

[9] Id at 144.

[10] Id at 145. In *Mosley v General Motors*, 497 F Supp 583 (E D Mo 1980), plaintiffs, alleging broad-based racial discrimination at General Motors' St. Louis facility, prevailed in a portion of their Title VII claim. The seniority system challenged in *DeGraffenreid*, however, was not considered in *Mosley*.

[11] Id at 145.

[12] Interestingly, no case has been discovered in which a court denied a white male's attempt to bring a reverse discrimination claim on similar grounds—that is, that sex and race claims cannot be combined because Congress did not intend to protect compound classes. White males in a typical reverse discrimination case are in no better position than the frustrated plaintiffs in *DeGraffenreid*: If they are required to made their claims separately, white males cannot prove race discrimination because white women are not discriminated against, and they cannot prove sex discrimination because Black males are not discriminated against. Yet it seems that courts do not acknowledge the compound nature of most reverse discrimination cases. That Black women's claims automatically raise the question of compound discrimination and white males' "reverse discrimination" cases do not suggest

acknowledge that Black women encounter combined race and sex discrimination implies that the boundaries of sex and race discrimination doctrine are defined respectively by white women's and Black men's experiences. Under this view, Black women are protected only to the extent that their experiences coincide with those of either of the two groups.[13] Where their experiences are distinct, Black women can expect little protection as long as approaches, such as that in *DeGraffenreid*, which completely obscure problems of intersectionality prevail.

    2. *Moore v Hughes Helicopter, Inc.*.

    Moore v Hughes Helicopters, Inc.[14] presents a different way in which courts fail to understand or recognize Black women's claims. *Moore* is typical of a number of cases in which courts refused to certify Black females as class representatives in race *and* sex discrimination actions.[15] In *Moore*, the plaintiff alleged that the employer, Hughes Helicopter, practiced race and sex discrimination in promotions to upper-level craft positions and to supervisory jobs. Moore introduced statistical evidence establishing a significant disparity between men and women, and somewhat less of a disparity between Black and white men in supervisory jobs.[16]

---

that the notion of compoundedness is somehow contingent upon an implicit norm that is not neutral but is white male. Thus, Black women are perceived as a compound class because they are two steps removed from a white male norm, while white males are apparently not perceived to be a compound class because they somehow represent the norm.

  [13] I do not mean to imply that all courts that have grappled with this problem have adopted the *DeGraffenreid* approach. Indeed, other courts have concluded that Black women are protected by Title VII. See, for example, *Jefferies v Harris Community Action Ass'n.*, 615 F2d 1025 (5th Cir 1980). I do mean to suggest that the very fact that the Black women's claims are seen as aberrant suggests that sex discrimination doctrine is centered in the experiences of white women. Even those courts that have held that Black women are protected seem to accept that Black women's claims raise issues that the "standard" sex discrimination claims do not. See Elaine W. Shoben, *Compound Discrimination: The Interaction of Race and Sex in Employment Discrimination*, 55 NYU L Rev 793, 803-04 (1980) (criticizing the *Jefferies* use of a sex-plus analysis to create a subclass of Black women).

  [14] 708 F2d 475.

  [15] See also *Moore v National Association of Securities Dealers*, 27 EPD (CCH) ¶ 32,238 (D DC 1981); but see *Edmondson v Simon*, 86 FRD 375 (N D Ill 1980) (where the court was unwilling to hold as a matter of law that no Black female could represent without conflict the interests of both Blacks and females).

  [16] 708 F2d at 479. Between January 1976 and June 1979, the three years in which Moore claimed that she was passed over for promotion, the percentage of white males occupying first-level supervisory positions ranged from 70.3 to 76.8%; Black males from 8.9 to 10.9%; white women from 1.8 to 3.3%; and Black females from 0 to 2.2%. The overall male/female ratio in the top five labor grades ranged from 100/0% in 1976 to 98/1.8% in 1979. The white/Black ratio was 85/3.3% in 1976 and 79.6/8% in 1979. The overall ratio of men to women in supervisory positions was 98.2 to 1.8% in 1976 to 93.4 to 6.6% in 1979; the Black to white ratio during the same time period was 78.6 to 8.9% and 73.6 to 13.1%

  For promotions to the top five labor grades, the percentages were worse. Between 1976

Affirming the district court's refusal to certify Moore as the class representative in the sex discrimination complaint on behalf of all women at Hughes, the Ninth Circuit noted approvingly:

> . . . Moore had never claimed before the EEOC that she was discriminated against as a female, *but only* as a Black female . . . . [T]his raised serious doubts as to Moore's ability to adequately represent white female employees.[17]

The curious logic in *Moore* reveals not only the narrow scope of antidiscrimination doctrine and its failure to embrace intersectionality, but also the centrality of white female experiences in the conceptualization of gender discrimination. One inference that could be drawn from the court's statement that Moore's complaint did not entail a claim of discrimination "against females" is that discrimination against Black females is something less than discrimination against females. More than likely, however, the court meant to imply that Moore did not claim that *all* females were discriminated against *but only* Black females. But even thus recast, the court's rationale is problematic for Black women. The court rejected Moore's bid to represent all females apparently because her attempt to specify her race was seen as being at odds with the standard allegation that the employer simply discriminated "against females."

The court failed to see that the absence of a racial referent does not necessarily mean that the claim being made is a more inclusive one. A white woman claiming discrimination against females may be in no better position to represent all women than a Black woman who claims discrimination as a Black female and wants to represent all females. The court's preferred articulation of "against females" is not necessarily more inclusive—it just appears to be so because the racial contours of the claim are not specified.

The court's preference for "against females" rather than "against Black females" reveals the implicit grounding of white female experiences in the doctrinal conceptualization of sex discrimination. For white women, claiming sex discrimination is simply a statement that but for gender, they would not have been disadvantaged. For them there is no need to specify discrimination as *white*

---

and 1979, the percentage of white males in these positions ranged from 85.3 to 77.9%; Black males 3.3 to 8%; white females from 0 to 1.4%, and Black females from 0 to 0%. Overall, in 1979, 98.2% of the highest level employees were male; 1.8% were female.

[17] 708 F2d at 480 (emphasis added).

females because their race does not contribute to the disadvantage for which they seek redress. The view of discrimination that is derived from this grounding takes race privilege as a given.

Discrimination against a white female is thus the standard sex discrimination claim; claims that diverge from this standard appear to present some sort of hybrid claim. More significantly, because Black females' claims are seen as hybrid, they sometimes cannot represent those who may have "pure" claims of sex discrimination. The effect of this approach is that even though a challenged policy or practice may clearly discriminate against all females, the fact that it has particularly harsh consequences for Black females places Black female plaintiffs at odds with white females.

Moore illustrates one of the limitations of antidiscrimination law's remedial scope and normative vision. The refusal to allow a multiply-disadvantaged class to represent others who may be singularly-disadvantaged defeats efforts to restructure the distribution of opportunity and limits remedial relief to minor adjustments within an established hierarchy. Consequently, "bottom-up" approaches, those which combine all discriminatees in order to challenge an entire employment system, are foreclosed by the limited view of the wrong and the narrow scope of the available remedy. If such "bottom-up" intersectional representation were routinely permitted, employees might accept the possibility that there is more to gain by collectively challenging the hierarchy rather than by each discriminatee individually seeking to protect her source of privilege within the hierarchy. But as long as antidiscrimination doctrine proceeds from the premise that employment systems need only minor adjustments, opportunities for advancement by disadvantaged employees will be limited. Relatively privileged employees probably are better off guarding their advantage while jockeying against others to gain more. As a result, Black women—the class of employees which, because of its intersectionality, is best able to challenge all forms of discrimination—are essentially isolated and often required to fend for themselves.

In *Moore*, the court's denial of the plaintiff's bid to represent all Blacks and females left Moore with the task of supporting her race and sex discrimination claims with statistical evidence of discrimination against Black females alone.[18] Because she was unable to represent white women or Black men, she could not use overall

---

[18] Id at 484-86.

statistics on sex disparity at Hughes, nor could she use statistics on race. Proving her claim using statistics on Black women alone was no small task, due to the fact that she was bringing the suit under a disparate impact theory of discrimination.[19]

The court further limited the relevant statistical pool to include only Black women who it determined were qualified to fill the openings in upper-level labor jobs and in supervisory positions.[20] According to the court, Moore had not demonstrated that there were any qualified Black women within her bargaining unit or the general labor pool for either category of jobs.[21] Finally, the court stated that even if it accepted Moore's contention that the percentage of Black females in supervisory positions should equal the percentage of Black females in the employee pool, it still would not find discriminatory impact.[22] Because the promotion of only two Black women into supervisory positions would have achieved the expected mean distribution of Black women within that job category, the court was "unwilling to agree that a prima facie case of disparate impact ha[d] been proven."[23]

The court's rulings on Moore's sex and race claim left her with such a small statistical sample that even if she had proved that there were qualified Black women, she could not have shown discrimination under a disparate impact theory. *Moore* illustrates yet another way that antidiscrimination doctrine essentially erases Black women's distinct experiences and, as a result, deems their discrimination complaints groundless.

3. *Payne v Travenol.*

Black female plaintiffs have also encountered difficulty in

---

[19] Under the disparate impact theory that prevailed at the time, the plaintiff had to introduce statistics suggesting that a policy or procedure disparately affects the members of a protected group. The employer could rebut that evidence by showing that there was a business necessity supporting the rule. The plaintiff then countered the rebuttal by showing that there was a less discriminatory alternative. See, for example, *Griggs v Duke Power*, 401 US 424 (1971); *Connecticut v Teal*, 457 US 440 (1982).

A central issue in a disparate impact case is whether the impact proved is statistically significant. A related issue is how the protected group is defined. In many cases a Black female plaintiff would prefer to use statistics which include white women and/or Black men to indicate that the policy in question does in fact disparately affect the protected class. If, as in *Moore*, the plaintiff may use only statistics involving Black women, there may not be enough Black women employees to create a statistically significant sample.

[20] Id at 484.

[21] The court buttressed its finding with respect to the upper-level labor jobs with statistics for the Los Angeles Metropolitan Area which indicated the there were only 0.2% Black women within comparable job categories. Id at 485 n 9.

[22] Id at 486.

[23] Id.

their efforts to win certification as class representatives in some race discrimination actions. This problem typically arises in cases where statistics suggest significant disparities between Black and white workers and further disparities between Black men and Black women. Courts in some cases[24] have denied certification based on logic that mirrors the rationale in *Moore*: The sex disparities between Black men and Black women created such conflicting interests that Black women could not possibly represent Black men adequately. In one such case, *Payne v Travenol*,[25] two Black female plaintiffs alleging race discrimination brought a class action suit on behalf of all Black employees at a pharmaceutical plant.[26] The court refused, however, to allow the plaintiffs to represent Black males and granted the defendant's request to narrow the class to Black women only. Ultimately, the district court found that there had been extensive racial discrimination at the plant and awarded back pay and constructive seniority to the class of Black female employees. But, despite its finding of general race discrimination, the court refused to extend the remedy to Black men for fear that their conflicting interests would not be adequately addressed;[27] the Fifth Circuit affirmed.[28]

Notably, the plaintiffs in *Travenol* fared better than the similarly-situated plaintiff in *Moore*: They were not denied use of meaningful statistics showing an overall pattern of race discrimination simply because there were no men in their class. The plaintiffs' bid to represent all Black employees, however, like Moore's attempt to represent all women employees, failed as a consequence

---

[24] See *Strong v Arkansas Blue Cross & Blue Shield, Inc.*, 87 FRD 496 (E D Ark 1980); *Hammons v Folger Coffee Co.*, 87 FRD 600 (W D Mo 1980); *Edmondson v Simon*, 86 FRD 375 (N D Ill 1980); *Vuyanich v Republic National Bank of Dallas*, 82 FRD 420 (N D Tex 1979); *Colston v Maryland Cup Corp.*, 26 Fed Rules Serv 940 (D Md 1978).

[25] 416 F Supp 248 (N D Miss 1976).

[26] The suit commenced on March 2, 1972, with the filing of a complaint by three employees seeking to represent a class of persons allegedly subjected to racial discrimination at the hands of the defendants. Subsequently, the plaintiffs amended the complaint to add an allegation of sex discrimination. Of the original named plaintiffs, one was a Black male and two were Black females. In the course of the three-year period between the filing of the complaint and the trial, the only named male plaintiff received permission of the court to withdraw for religious reasons. Id at 250.

[27] As the dissent in *Travenol* pointed out, there was no reason to exclude Black males from the scope of the remedy *after* counsel had presented sufficient evidence to support a finding of discrimination against Black men. If the rationale for excluding Black males was the potential conflict between Black males and Black females, then "[i]n this case, to paraphrase an old adage, the proof of plaintiffs' ability to represent the interests of Black males was in the representation thereof." 673 F2d at 837-38.

[28] 673 F2d 798 (5th Cir 1982).

of the court's narrow view of class interest.

Even though *Travenol* was a partial victory for Black women, the case specifically illustrates how antidiscrimination doctrine generally creates a dilemma for Black women. It forces them to choose between specifically articulating the intersectional aspects of their subordination, thereby risking their ability to represent Black men, or ignoring intersectionality in order to state a claim that would not lead to the exclusion of Black men. When one considers the political consequences of this dilemma, there is little wonder that many people within the Black community view the specific articulation of Black women's interests as dangerously divisive.

In sum, several courts have proved unable to deal with intersectionality, although for contrasting reasons. In *DeGraffenreid*, the court refused to recognize the possibility of compound discrimination against Black women and analyzed their claim using the employment of white women as the historical base. As a consequence, the employment experiences of white women obscured the distinct discrimination that Black women experienced.

Conversely, in *Moore*, the court held that a Black woman could not use statistics reflecting the overall sex disparity in supervisory and upper-level labor jobs because she had not claimed discrimination as a woman, but "only" as a Black woman. The court would not entertain the notion that discrimination experienced by Black women is indeed sex discrimination—provable through disparate impact statistics on women.

Finally, courts, such as the one in *Travenol*, have held that Black women cannot represent an entire class of Blacks due to presumed class conflicts in cases where sex additionally disadvantaged Black women. As a result, in the few cases where Black women are allowed to use overall statistics indicating racially disparate treatment Black men may not be able to share in the remedy.

Perhaps it appears to some that I have offered inconsistent criticisms of how Black women are treated in antidiscrimination law: I seem to be saying that in one case, Black women's claims were rejected and their experiences obscured because the court refused to acknowledge that the employment experience of Black women can be distinct from that of white women, while in other cases, the interests of Black women were harmed because Black women's claims were viewed as so distinct from the claims of either white women or Black men that the court denied to Black females representation of the larger class. It seems that I have to say that Black women are the same and harmed by being treated differently, or that they are different and harmed by being treated the same. But I cannot say both.

This apparent contradiction is but another manifestation of the conceptual limitations of the single-issue analyses that intersectionality challenges. The point is that Black women can experience discrimination in any number of ways and that the contradiction arises from our assumptions that their claims of exclusion must be unidirectional. Consider an analogy to traffic in an intersection, coming and going in all four directions. Discrimination, like traffic through an intersection, may flow in one direction, and it may flow in another. If an accident happens in an intersection, it can be caused by cars traveling from any number of directions and, sometimes, from all of them. Similarly, if a Black woman is harmed because she is in the intersection, her injury could result from sex discrimination or race discrimination.

Judicial decisions which premise intersectional relief on a showing that Black women are specifically recognized as a class are analogous to a doctor's decision at the scene of an accident to treat an accident victim only if the injury is recognized by medical insurance. Similarly, providing legal relief only when Black women show that their claims are based on race or on sex is analogous to calling an ambulance for the victim only after the driver responsible for the injuries is identified. But it is not always easy to reconstruct an accident: Sometimes the skid marks and the injuries simply indicate that they occurred simultaneously, frustrating efforts to determine which driver caused the harm. In these cases the tendency seems to be that no driver is held responsible, no treatment is administered, and the involved parties simply get back in their cars and zoom away.

To bring this back to a non-metaphorical level, I am suggesting that Black women can experience discrimination in ways that are both similar to and different from those experienced by white women and Black men. Black women sometimes experience discrimination in ways similar to white women's experiences; sometimes they share very similar experiences with Black men. Yet often they experience double-discrimination—the combined effects of practices which discriminate on the basis of race, and on the basis of sex. And sometimes, they experience discrimination as Black women—not the sum of race and sex discrimination, but as Black women.

Black women's experiences are much broader than the general categories that discrimination discourse provides. Yet the continued insistence that Black women's demands and needs be filtered through categorical analyses that completely obscure their experiences guarantees that their needs will seldom be addressed.

B. The Significance of Doctrinal Treatment of Intersectionality

DeGraffenreid, Moore and *Travenol* are doctrinal manifestations of a common political and theoretical approach to discrimination which operates to marginalize Black women. Unable to grasp the importance of Black women's intersectional experiences, not only courts, but feminist and civil rights thinkers as well have treated Black women in ways that deny both the unique compoundedness of their situation and the centrality of their experiences to the larger classes of women and Blacks. Black women are regarded either as too much like women or Blacks and the compounded nature of their experience is absorbed into the collective experiences of either group or as too different, in which case Black women's Blackness or femaleness sometimes has placed their needs and perspectives at the margin of the feminist and Black liberationist agendas.

While it could be argued that this failure represents an absence of political will to include Black women, I believe that it reflects an uncritical and disturbing acceptance of dominant ways of thinking about discrimination. Consider first the definition of discrimination that seems to be operative in antidiscrimination law: Discrimination which is wrongful proceeds from the identification of a specific class or category; either a discriminator intentionally identifies this category, or a process is adopted which somehow disadvantages all members of this category.[29] According to the dominant view, a discriminator treats all people within a race or sex category similarly. Any significant experiential or statistical variation within this group suggests either that the group is not being discriminated against or that conflicting interests exist which de-

---

[29] In much of antidiscrimination doctrine, the presence of intent to discriminate distinguishes unlawful from lawful discrimination. See *Washington v Davis*, 426 US 229, 239-45 (1976) (proof of discriminatory purpose required to substantiate Equal Protection violation). Under Title VII, however, the Court has held that statistical data showing a disproportionate impact can suffice to support a finding of discrimination. See *Griggs*, 401 US at 432. Whether the distinction between the two analyses will survive is an open question. See *Wards Cove Packing Co., Inc. v Atonio*, 109 S Ct 2115, 2122-23 (1989) (plaintiffs must show more than mere disparity to support a prima facie case of disparate impact). For a discussion of the competing normative visions that underlie the intent and effects analyses, see Alan David Freeman, *Legitimizing Racial Discrimination Through Antidiscrimination Law: A Critical Review of Supreme Court Doctrine*, 62 Minn L Rev 1049 (1978).

feat any attempts to bring a common claim.[30] Consequently, one
generally cannot combine these categories. Race and sex, moreover,
become significant only when they operate to explicitly *disadvantage* the victims; because the *privileging* of whiteness or maleness
is implicit, it is generally not perceived at all.

Underlying this conception of discrimination is a view that the
wrong which antidiscrimination law addresses is the use of race or
gender factors to interfere with decisions that would otherwise be
fair or neutral. This process-based definition is not grounded in a
bottom-up commitment to improve the substantive conditions for
those who are victimized by the interplay of numerous factors. Instead, the dominant message of antidiscrimination law is that it
will regulate only the limited extent to which race or sex interferes
with the process of determining outcomes. This narrow objective is
facilitated by the top-down strategy of using a singular "but for"
analysis to ascertain the effects of race or sex. Because the scope of
antidiscrimination law is so limited, sex and race discrimination
have come to be defined in terms of the experiences of those who
are privileged *but for* their racial or sexual characteristics. Put differently, the paradigm of sex discrimination tends to be based on
the experiences of white women; the model of race discrimination
tends to be based on the experiences of the most privileged Blacks.
Notions of what constitutes race and sex discrimination are, as a
result, narrowly tailored to embrace only a small set of circumstances, none of which include discrimination against Black
women.

To the extent that this general description is accurate, the following analogy can be useful in describing how Black women are
marginalized in the interface between antidiscrimination law and
race and gender hierarchies: Imagine a basement which contains all
people who are disadvantaged on the basis of race, sex, class, sexual preference, age and/or physical ability. These people are
stacked—feet standing on shoulders—with those on the bottom
being disadvantaged by the full array of factors, up to the very top,
where the heads of all those disadvantaged by a singular factor
brush up against the ceiling. Their ceiling is actually the floor
above which only those who are *not* disadvantaged in any way re-
side. In efforts to correct some aspects of domination, those above
the ceiling admit from the basement only those who can say that
"but for" the ceiling, they too would be in the upper room. A hatch

---

[30] See, for example, *Moore*, 708 F2d at 479.

is developed through which those placed immediately below can crawl. Yet this hatch is generally available only to those who—due to the singularity of their burden and their otherwise privileged position relative to those below—are in the position to crawl through. Those who are multiply-burdened are generally left below unless they can somehow pull themselves into the groups that are permitted to squeeze through the hatch.

As this analogy translates for Black women, the problem is that they can receive protection only to the extent that their experiences are recognizably similar to those whose experiences tend to be reflected in antidiscrimination doctrine. If Black women cannot conclusively say that "but for" their race or "but for" their gender they would be treated differently, they are not invited to climb through the hatch but told to wait in the unprotected margin until they can be absorbed into the broader, protected categories of race and sex.

Despite the narrow scope of this dominant conception of discrimination and its tendency to marginalize those whose experiences cannot be described within its tightly-drawn parameters, this approach has been regarded as the appropriate framework for addressing a range of problems. In much of feminist theory and, to some extent, in antiracist politics, this framework is reflected in the belief that sexism or racism can be meaningfully discussed without paying attention to the lives of those other than the race-, gender- or class-privileged. As a result, both feminist theory and antiracist politics have been organized, in part, around the equation of racism with what happens to the Black middle-class or to Black men, and the equation of sexism with what happens to white women.

Looking at historical and contemporary issues in both the feminist and the civil rights communities, one can find ample evidence of how both communities' acceptance of the dominant framework of discrimination has hindered the development of an adequate theory and praxis to address problems of intersectionality. This adoption of a single-issue framework for discrimination not only marginalizes Black women within the very movements that claim them as part of their constituency but it also makes the illusive goal of ending racism and patriarchy even more difficult to attain.

II. FEMINISM AND BLACK WOMEN: "AIN'T WE WOMEN?"

Oddly, despite the relative inability of feminist politics and theory to address Black women substantively, feminist theory and tradition borrow considerably from Black women's history. For example, "Ain't I a Woman" has come to represent a standard refrain in feminist discourse.[31] Yet the lesson of this powerful oratory is not fully appreciated because the context of the delivery is seldom examined. I would like to tell part of the story because it establishes some themes that have characterized feminist treatment of race and illustrates the importance of including Black women's experiences as a rich source for the critique of patriarchy.

In 1851, Sojourner Truth declared "Ain't I a Woman?" and challenged the sexist imagery used by male critics to justify the disenfranchisement of women.[32] The scene was a Women's Rights Conference in Akron, Ohio; white male hecklers, invoking stereotypical images of "womanhood," argued that women were too frail and delicate to take on the responsibilities of political activity. When Sojourner Truth rose to speak, many white women urged that she be silenced, fearing that she would divert attention from women's suffrage to emancipation. Truth, once permitted to speak, recounted the horrors of slavery, and its particular impact on Black women:

> Look at my arm! I have ploughed and planted and gathered into barns, and no man could head me—and ain't I a woman? I could work as much and eat as much as a man—when I could get it—and bear the lash as well! And ain't I a woman? I have born thirteen children, and seen most of 'em sold into slavery, and when I cried out with my mother's grief, none but Jesus heard me—and ain't I a woman?[33]

By using her own life to reveal the contradiction between the ideological myths of womanhood and the reality of Black women's experience, Truth's oratory provided a powerful rebuttal to the claim that women were categorically weaker than men. Yet Truth's personal challenge to the coherence of the cult of true womanhood

---

[31] See Phyliss Palmer, *The Racial Feminization of Poverty: Women of Color as Portents of the Future for All Women*, Women's Studies Quarterly 11:3-4 (Fall 1983) (posing the question of why "white women in the women's movement had not created more effective and continuous alliances with Black women" when "simultaneously . . . Black women [have] become heroines for the women's movement, a position symbolized by the consistent use of Sojourner Truth and her famous words, "Ain't I a Woman?"").

[32] See Paula Giddings, *When and Where I Enter: The Impact of Black Women on Race and Sex in America* 54 (William Morrow and Co, Inc, 1st ed 1984).

[33] Eleanor Flexner, *Century of Struggle: The Women's Rights Movement in the United States* 91 (Belknap Press of Harvard University Press, 1975). See also Bell Hooks, *Ain't I a Woman* 159-60 (South End Press, 1981).

was useful only to the extent that white women were willing to reject the racist attempts to rationalize the contradiction—that because Black women were something less than real women, their experiences had no bearing on true womanhood. Thus, this 19th-century Black feminist challenged not only patriarchy, but she also challenged white feminists wishing to embrace Black women's history to relinquish their vestedness in whiteness.

Contemporary white feminists inherit not the legacy of Truth's challenge to patriarchy but, instead, Truth's challenge to their forbearers. Even today, the difficulty that white women have traditionally experienced in sacrificing racial privilege to strengthen feminism renders them susceptible to Truth's critical question. When feminist theory and politics that claim to reflect *women's* experience and *women's* aspirations do not include or speak to Black women, Black women must ask: "Ain't *We* Women?" If this is so, how can the claims that "women are," "women believe" and "women need" be made when such claims are inapplicable or unresponsive to the needs, interests and experiences of Black women?

The value of feminist theory to Black women is diminished because it evolves from a white racial context that is seldom acknowledged. Not only are women of color in fact overlooked, but their exclusion is reinforced when *white* women speak for and as *women*. The authoritative universal voice—usually white male subjectivity masquerading as non-racial, non-gendered objectivity[34]—is merely transferred to those who, but for gender, share many of the same cultural, economic and social characteristics. When feminist theory attempts to describe women's experiences through analyzing patriarchy, sexuality, or separate spheres ideology, it often overlooks the role of race. Feminists thus ignore how their own race functions to mitigate some aspects of sexism and, moreover, how it often privileges them over and contributes to the domination of other women.[35] Consequently, feminist theory remains *white*, and its potential to broaden and deepen its analysis by addressing non-privileged women remains unrealized.

An example of how some feminist theories are narrowly con-

---

[34] "'Objectivity' is itself an example of the reification of white male thought." Hull et al, eds, *But Some of Us Are Brave* at XXV (cited in note 1).

[35] For example, many white females were able to gain entry into previously all white male enclaves not through bringing about a fundamental reordering of male versus female work, but in large part by shifting their "female" responsibilities to poor and minority women.

structed around white women's experiences is found in the separate spheres literature. The critique of how separate spheres ideology shapes and limits women's roles in the home and in public life is a central theme in feminist legal thought.[36] Feminists have attempted to expose and dismantle separate spheres ideology by identifying and criticizing the stereotypes that traditionally have justified the disparate societal roles assigned to men and women.[37] Yet this attempt to debunk ideological justifications for *women's* subordination offers little insight into the domination of *Black* women. Because the experiential base upon which many feminist insights are grounded is white, theoretical statements drawn from them are overgeneralized at best, and often wrong.[38] Statements such as "men and women are taught to see men as independent, capable, powerful; men and women are taught to see women as dependent, limited in abilities, and passive,"[39] are common within this literature. But this "observation" overlooks the anomalies created by crosscurrents of racism and sexism. Black men and women live in a society that creates sex-based norms and expectations which racism operates simultaneously to deny; Black men are not viewed as powerful, nor are Black women seen as passive. An effort to develop an ideological explanation of gender domination in the Black community should proceed from an understanding of how crosscutting forces establish gender norms and how the conditions

---

[36] Feminists often discuss how gender-based stereotypes and norms reinforce the subordination of women by justifying their exclusion from public life and glorifying their roles within the private sphere. Law has historically played a role in maintaining this subordination by enforcing the exclusion of women from public life and by limiting its reach into the private sphere. See, for example, Deborah L. Rhode, *Association and Assimilation*, 81 Nw U L Rev 106 (1986); Frances Olsen, *From False Paternalism to False Equality: Judicial Assaults on Feminist Community, Illinois 1869-95*, 84 Mich L Rev 1518 (1986); Martha Minow, *Foreword: Justice Engendered*, 101 Harv L Rev 10 (1987); Nadine Taub and Elizabeth M. Schneider, *Perspectives on Women's Subordination and the Role of Law*, in David Kairys, ed, *The Politics of Law* 117-39 (Pantheon Books, 1982).

[37] See works cited in note 36.

[38] This criticism is a discrete illustration of a more general claim that feminism has been premised on white middle-class women's experience. For example, early feminist texts such as Betty Friedan's *The Feminine Mystique* (W. W. Norton, 1963), placed white middle-class problems at the center of feminism and thus contributed to its rejection within the Black community. See Hooks, *Ain't I a Woman* at 185-96 (cited in note 33) (noting that feminism was eschewed by Black women because its white middle-class agenda ignored Black women's concerns).

[39] Richard A. Wasserstrom, *Racism, Sexism and Preferential Treatment: An Approach to the Topics*, 24 UCLA L Rev 581, 588 (1977). I chose this phrase not because it is typical of most feminist statements of separate spheres; indeed, most discussions are not as simplistic as the bold statement presented here. See, for example, Taub and Schneider, *Perspectives on Women's Subordination and the Role of Law* at 117-39 (cited in note 36).

of Black subordination wholly frustrate access to these norms. Given this understanding, perhaps we can begin to see why Black women have been dogged by the stereotype of the pathological matriarch[40] or why there have been those in the Black liberation movement who aspire to create institutions and to build traditions that are intentionally patriarchal.[41]

Because ideological and descriptive definitions of patriarchy are usually premised upon white female experiences, feminists and others informed by feminist literature may make the mistake of assuming that since the role of Black women in the family and in other Black institutions does not always resemble the familiar manifestations of patriarchy in the white community, Black women are somehow exempt from patriarchal norms. For example, Black women have traditionally worked outside the home in numbers far exceeding the labor participation rate of white women.[42] An analysis of patriarchy that highlights the history of white women's exclusion from the workplace might permit the inference that Black women have not been burdened by this particular gender-based expectation. Yet the very fact that Black women must work conflicts with norms that women should not, often creating personal, emotional and relationship problems in Black women's lives. Thus, Black women are burdened not only because they often have to take on responsibilities that are not traditionally feminine but, moreover, their assumption of these roles is sometimes interpreted within the Black community as either Black women's failure to live up to such norms or as another manifestation of racism's scourge upon the Black community.[43] This is one of the many aspects of intersectionality that cannot be understood

---

[40] For example, Black families have sometimes been cast as pathological largely because Black women's divergence from the white middle-class female norm. The most infamous rendition of this view is found in the Moynihan report which blamed many of the Black community's ills on a supposed pathological family structure. For a discussion of the report and its contemporary reincarnation, see pp 163-165.

[41] See Hooks, Ain't I a Woman at 94-99 (cited in note 33) (discussing the elevation of sexist imagery in the Black liberation movement during the 1960s).

[42] See generally Jacqueline Jones, Labor of Love, Labor of Sorrow; Black Women, Work, and the Family from Slavery to the Present (Basic Books, 1985); Angela Davis, Women, Race and Class (Random House, 1981).

[43] As Elizabeth Higginbotham noted, "women, who often fail to conform to 'appropriate' sex roles, have been pictured as, and made to feel, inadequate—even though as women, they possess traits recognized as positive when held by men in the wider society. Such women are stigmatized because their lack of adherence to expected gender roles is seen as a threat to the value system." Elizabeth Higginbotham, Two Representative Issues in Contemporary Sociological Work on Black Women, in Hull, et al, eds, But Some of Us Are Brave at 95 (cited in note 1).

through an analysis of patriarchy rooted in white experience.

Another example of how theory emanating from a white context obscures the multidimensionality of Black women's lives is found in feminist discourse on rape. A central political issue on the feminist agenda has been the pervasive problem of rape. Part of the intellectual and political effort to mobilize around this issue has involved the development of a historical critique of the role that law has played in establishing the bounds of normative sexuality and in regulating female sexual behavior.[44] Early carnal knowledge statutes and rape laws are understood within this discourse to illustrate that the objective of rape statutes traditionally has not been to protect women from coercive intimacy but to protect and maintain a property-like interest in female chastity.[45] Although feminists quite rightly criticize these objectives, to characterize rape law as reflecting male control over female sexuality is for Black women an oversimplified account and an ultimately inadequate account.

Rape statutes generally do not reflect *male* control over *female* sexuality, but *white* male regulation of *white* female sexuality.[46] Historically, there has been absolutely no institutional effort to regulate Black female chastity.[47] Courts in some states had gone so far as to instruct juries that, unlike white women, Black women were not presumed to be chaste.[48] Also, while it was true that the

---

[44] See generally Susan Brownmiller, *Against Our Will* (Simon and Schuster, 1975); Susan Estrich, *Real Rape* (Harvard University Press, 1987).

[45] See Brownmiller, *Against Our Will* at 17; see generally Estrich, *Real Rape*.

[46] One of the central theoretical dilemmas of feminism that is largely obscured by universalizing the white female experience is that experiences that are described as a manifestation of male control over females can be instead a manifestation of dominant group control over all subordinates. The significance is that other nondominant men may not share in, participate in or connect with the behavior, beliefs or actions at issue, and may be victimized themselves by "male" power. In other contexts, however, "male authority" might include nonwhite men, particularly in private sphere contexts. Efforts to think more clearly about when Black women are dominated as *women* and when they are dominated as *Black women* are directly related to the question of when power is *male* and when it is *white male*.

[47] See Note, *Rape, Racism and the Law*, 6 Harv Women's L J 103, 117-23 (1983) (discussing the historical and contemporary evidence suggesting that Black women are generally not thought to be chaste). See also Hooks, *Ain't I a Woman* at 54 (cited in note 33) (stating that stereotypical images of Black womanhood during slavery were based on the myth that "all black women were immoral and sexually loose"); Beverly Smith, *Black Women's Health: Notes for a Course*, in Hull et al, eds, *But Some of Us Are Brave* at 110 (cited in note 1) (noting that ". . . white men for centuries have justified their sexual abuse of Black women by claiming that we are licentious, always 'ready' for any sexual encounter").

[48] The following statement is probably unusual only in its candor: "What has been said by some of our courts about an unchaste female being a comparatively rare exception is no doubt true where the population is composed largely of the Caucasian race, but we would blind ourselves to actual conditions if we adopted this rule where another race that is largely

attempt to regulate the sexuality of white women placed unchaste women outside the law's protection, racism restored a fallen white woman's chastity where the alleged assailant was a Black man.[49] No such restoration was available to Black women.

The singular focus on rape as a manifestation of male power over female sexuality tends to eclipse the use of rape as a weapon of racial terror.[50] When Black women were raped by white males, they were being raped not as women generally, but as Black women specifically: Their femaleness made them sexually vulnerable to racist domination, while their Blackness effectively denied

---

immoral constitutes an appreciable part of the population." *Dallas v State*, 76 Fla 358, 79 So 690 (1918), quoted in Note, 6 Harv Women's L J at 121 (cited in note 47).

Espousing precisely this view, one commentator stated in 1902: "I sometimes hear of a virtuous Negro woman but the idea is so absolutely inconceivable to me . . . I cannot imagine such a creature as a virtuous Negro woman." Id at 82. Such images persist in popular culture. See Paul Grein, *Taking Stock of the Latest Pop Record Surprises*, LA Times § 6 at 1 (July 7, 1988) (recalling the controversy in the late 70s over a Rolling Stones recording which included the line "Black girls just wanna get fucked all night").

Opposition to such negative stereotypes has sometimes taken the form of sexual conservatism. "A desperate reaction to this slanderous myth is the attempt . . . to conform to the strictest versions of patriarchal morality." Smith, *Black Women's Health*, in Hull et al, eds, *But Some of Us Are Brave* at 111 (cited in note 1). Part of this reaction is reflected in the attitudes and policies of Black schools which have been notoriously strict in regulating the behavior of female students. See Gail Elizabeth Wyatt, *The Sexual Experience of Afro-American Women*, in Martha Kirkpatrick, ed, *Women's Sexual Experience: Exploration of the Dark Continent* 24 (Plenum, 1982) (noting "the differences between the predominantly Afro-American universities, where there was far more supervision regarding sexual behavior, and the majority of white colleges, where there were fewer curfews and restrictions placed on the resident"). Any attempt to understand and critique the emphasis on Black virtue without focusing on the racist ideology that places virtue beyond the reach of Black women would be incomplete and probably incorrect.

[49] Because of the way the legal system viewed chastity, Black women could not be victims of forcible rape. One commentator has noted that "[a]ccording to governing sterotypes [sic], chastity could not be possessed by Black women. Thus, Black women's rape charges were automatically discounted, and the issue of chastity was contested only in cases where the rape complainant was a white woman." Note, 6 Harv Women's L J at 126 (cited in note 47). Black women's claims of rape were not taken seriously regardless of the offender's race. A judge in 1912 said: "This court will never take the word of a nigger against the word of a white man [concerning rape]." Id at 120. On the other hand, lynching was considered an effective remedy for a Black man's rape of a white woman. Since rape of a white woman by a Black man was "a crime more horrible than death," the only way to assuage society's rage and to make the woman whole again was to brutally murder the Black man. Id at 125.

[50] See *The Rape of Black Women as a Weapon of Terror*, in Gerda Lerner, ed, *Black Women in White America* 172-93 (Pantheon Books, 1972). See also Brownmiller, *Against Our Will* (cited in note 44). Even where Brownmiller acknowledges the use of rape as racial terrorism, she resists making a "special case" for Black women by offering evidence that white women were raped by the Klan as well. Id at 139. Whether or not one considers the racist rape of Black women a "special case," such experiences are probably different. In any case, Brownmiller's treatment of the issue raises serious questions about the ability to sustain an analysis of patriarchy without understanding its multiple intersections with racism.

them any protection.[51] This white male power was reinforced by a judicial system in which the successful conviction of a white man for raping a Black woman was virtually unthinkable.[52]

In sum, sexist expectations of chastity and racist assumptions of sexual promiscuity combined to create a distinct set of issues confronting Black women.[53] These issues have seldom been explored in feminist literature nor are they prominent in antiracist politics. The lynching of Black males, the institutional practice that was legitimized by the regulation of white women's sexuality, has historically and contemporaneously occupied the Black agenda on sexuality and violence. Consequently, Black women are caught between a Black community that, perhaps understandably, views with suspicion attempts to litigate questions of sexual violence, and a feminist community that reinforces those suspicions by focusing on white female sexuality.[54] The suspicion is compounded

---

[51] Lerner, *Black Women in White America* at 173.

[52] See generally, Note, 6 Harv Women's L J at 103 (cited in note 47).

[53] Paula Giddings notes the combined effect of sexual and racial stereotypes: "Black women were seen having all of the inferior qualities of white women without any of their virtues." Giddings, *When and Where I Enter* at 82 (cited in note 32).

[54] Susan Brownmiller's treatment of the Emmett Till case illustrates why antirape politicization makes some African Americans uncomfortable. Despite Brownmiller's quite laudable efforts to discuss elsewhere the rape of Black women and the racism involved in much of the hysteria over the Black male threat, her analysis of the Till case places the sexuality of white women, rather than racial terrorism, at center stage. Brownmiller states: "Rarely has one single case exposed so clearly as Till's the underlying group-male antagonisms over access to women, for what began in Bryant's store should not be misconstrued as an innocent flirtation . . . . In concrete terms, the accessibility of all white women was on review." Brownmiller, *Against Our Will* at 272 (cited in note 44).

Later, Brownmiller argues:

> And what of the wolf whistle, Till's 'gesture of adolescent bravado'? We are rightly aghast that a whistle could be cause for murder but we must also accept that Emmett Till and J. W. Millam shared something in common. They both understood that the whistle was no small tweet of hubba-hubba or melodious approval for a well-turned ankle. Given the deteriorated situation . . . it was a deliberate insult just short of physical assault, a last reminder to Carolyn Bryant that this black boy, Till, had a mind to possess her.

Id at 273.

While Brownmiller seems to categorize the case as one that evidences a conflict over possession, it is regarded in African American history as a tragic dramatization of the South's pathological hatred and fear of African Americans. Till's body, mutilated beyond recognition, was viewed by thousands so that, in the words of Till's mother, "the world could see what they did to my boy." Juan Williams, *Standing for Justice*, in *Eyes on the Prize* 44 (Viking, 1987). The Till tragedy is also regarded as one of the historical events that bore directly on the emergence of the Civil Rights movement. "[W]ithout question it moved black America in a way the Supreme Court ruling on school desegregation could not match." Id. As Williams later observed, "the murder of Emmitt Till had a powerful impact on a generation of blacks. It was this generation, those who were adolescents when Till was killed, that would soon demand justice and freedom in a way unknown in America before."

by the historical fact that the protection of white female sexuality was often the pretext for terrorizing the Black community. Even today some fear that antirape agendas may undermine antiracist objectives. This is the paradigmatic political and theoretical dilemma created by the intersection of race and gender: Black women are caught between ideological and political currents that combine first to create and then to bury Black women's experiences.

III. WHEN AND WHERE I ENTER: INTEGRATING AN ANALYSIS OF SEXISM INTO BLACK LIBERATION POLITICS

Anna Julia Cooper, a 19th-century Black feminist, coined a phrase that has been useful in evaluating the need to incorporate an explicit analysis of patriarchy in any effort to address racial domination.[55] Cooper often criticized Black leaders and spokespersons for claiming to speak for the race, but failing to speak for Black women. Referring to one of Martin Delaney's public claims that where he was allowed to enter, the race entered with him, Cooper countered: "Only the Black Woman can say, when and where I enter . . . then and there the whole Negro race enters with me."[56]

Cooper's words bring to mind a personal experience involving two Black men with whom I had formed a study group during our first year of law school. One of our group members, a graduate from Harvard College, often told us stories about a prestigious and exclusive men's club that boasted memberships of several past United States presidents and other influential white males. He was one of its very few Black members. To celebrate completing our first-year exams, our friend invited us to join him at the club for drinks. Anxious to see this fabled place, we approached the large door and grasped the brass door ring to announce our arrival. But our grand entrance was cut short when our friend sheepishly slipped from behind the door and whispered that he had forgotten

---

Id at 57. Thus, while Brownmiller looks at the Till case and sees the vicious struggle over the possession of a white woman, African Americans see the case as a symbol of the insane degree to which whites were willing to suppress the Black race. While patriarchal attitudes toward women's sexuality played a supporting role, to place white women center stage in this tragedy is to manifest such confusion over racism as to make it difficult to imagine that the white antirape movement could be sensitive to more subtle racial tensions regarding Black women's participation in it.

[55] See Anna Julia Cooper, *A Voice from the South* (Negro Universities Press, 1969 reprint of the Aldine Printing House, Ohio, 1892).

[56] Id at 31.

a very important detail. My companion and I bristled, our training as Black people having taught us to expect yet another barrier to our inclusion; even an informal one-Black-person quota at the establishment was not unimaginable. The tension broke, however, when we learned that *we* would not be excluded because of our race, but that *I* would have to go around to the back door because I was a female. I entertained the idea of making a scene to dramatize the fact that my humiliation as a female was no less painful and my exclusion no more excusable than had we all been sent to the back door because we were Black. But, sensing no general assent to this proposition, and also being of the mind that due to our race a scene would in some way jeopardize all of us, I failed to stand my ground. After all, the Club was about to entertain its first Black guests—even though one would have to enter through the back door.[57]

Perhaps this story is not the best example of the Black community's failure to address problems related to Black women's intersectionality seriously. The story would be more apt if Black women, and only Black women, had to go around to the back door of the club and if the restriction came from within, and not from the outside of the Black community. Still this story does reflect a markedly decreased political and emotional vigilance toward barriers to Black women's enjoyment of privileges that have been won on the basis of race but continue to be denied on the basis of sex.[58]

The story also illustrates the ambivalence among Black women about the degree of political and social capital that ought to be expended toward challenging gender barriers, particularly when the challenges might conflict with the antiracism agenda. While there are a number of reasons—including antifeminist ones—why gender has not figured directly in analyses of the subordination of Black Americans, a central reason is that race is still seen by many as the primary oppositional force in Black lives.[59] If

---

[57] In all fairness, I must acknowledge that my companion accompanied me to the back door. I remain uncertain, however, as to whether the gesture was an expression of solidarity or an effort to quiet my anger.

[58] To this one could easily add class.

[59] An anecdote illustrates this point. A group of female law professors gathered to discuss "Isms in the Classroom." One exercise led by Pat Cain involved each participant listing the three primary factors that described herself. Almost without exception, white women in the room listed their gender either primarily or secondarily; none listed their race. All of the women of color listed their race first, and then their gender. This seems to suggest that identity descriptions seem to begin with the primary source of opposition with whatever the dominant norm is. See Pat Cain, *Feminist Jurisprudence: Grounding the Theories* 19-20 (unpublished manuscript on file with author) (explaining the exercise and noting that "no

one accepts that the social experience of race creates both a primary group identity as well as a shared sense of being under collective assault, some of the reasons that Black feminist theory and politics have not figured prominently in the Black political agenda may be better understood.[60]

The point is not that African Americans are simply involved in a more important struggle. Although some efforts to oppose Black feminism are based on this assumption, a fuller appreciation of the problems of the Black community will reveal that gender subordination does contribute significantly to the destitute conditions of so many African Americans and that it must therefore be addressed. Moreover, the foregoing critique of the single-issue framework renders problematic the claim that the struggle against racism is distinguishable from, much less prioritized over, the struggle against sexism. Yet it is also true that the politics of racial otherness that Black women experience along with Black men prevent Black feminist consciousness from patterning the development of white feminism. For white women, the creation of a consciousness that was distinct from and in opposition to that of white men figured prominently in the development of white feminist politics. Black women, like Black men, live in a community that has been defined and subordinated by color and culture.[61] Although patriarchy clearly operates within the Black community, presenting yet another source of domination to which Black women are vulnerable, the racial context in which Black women find themselves makes the creation of a political consciousness that is oppositional to Black men difficult.

Yet while it is true that the distinct experience of racial otherness militates against the development of an oppositional feminist consciousness, the assertion of racial community sometimes supports defensive priorities that marginalize Black women. Black

---

white woman ever mentions race, whereas every woman of color does" and that, similarly, "straight women do not include 'heterosexual' . . . whereas lesbians who are open always include 'lesbian' ").

[60] For a comparative discussion of Third World feminism paralleling this observation, see Kumari Jayawardena, *Feminism and Nationalism in the Third World* 1-24 (Zed Books Ltd, 1986). Jayawardena states that feminism in the Third World has been "accepted" only within the central struggle against international domination. Women's social and political status has improved most when advancement is necessary to the broader struggle against imperialism.

[61] For a discussion of how racial ideology creates a polarizing dynamic which subordinates Blacks and privileges whites, see Kimberle Crenshaw, *Race, Reform and Retrenchment: Transformation and Legitimation in Antidiscrimination Law*, 101 Harv L Rev 1331, 1371-76 (1988).

women's particular interests are thus relegated to the periphery in public policy discussions about the presumed needs of the Black community. The controversy over the movie *The Color Purple* is illustrative. The animating fear behind much of the publicized protest was that by portraying domestic abuse in a Black family, the movie confirmed the negative stereotypes of Black men.[62] The debate over the propriety of presenting such an image on the screen overshadowed the issue of sexism and patriarchy in the Black community. Even though it was sometimes acknowledged that the Black community was not immune from domestic violence and other manifestations of gender subordination, some nevertheless felt that in the absence of positive Black male images in the media, portraying such images merely reinforced racial stereotypes.[63] The struggle against racism seemed to compel the subordination of certain aspects of the Black female experience in order to ensure the security of the larger Black community.

The nature of this debate should sound familiar to anyone who recalls Daniel Moynihan's diagnosis of the ills of Black America.[64] Moynihan's report depicted a deteriorating Black family, foretold the destruction of the Black male householder and lamented the creation of the Black matriarch. His conclusions prompted a massive critique from liberal sociologists[65] and from civil rights leaders.[66] Surprisingly, while many critics characterized the report as racist for its blind use of white cultural norms as the standard for evaluating Black families, few pointed out the sexism apparent in Moynihan's labeling Black women as pathological for their "failure" to live up to a white female standard of motherhood.[67]

---

[62] Jack Matthews, *Three Color Purple Actresses Talk About Its Impact*, LA Times § 6 at 1 (Jan 31, 1986); Jack Matthews, *Some Blacks Critical of Spielberg's Purple*, LA Times § 6 at 1 (Dec 20, 1985). But see Gene Siskel, *Does Purple Hate Men?*, Chicago Tribune § 13 at 16 (Jan 5, 1986); Clarence Page, *Toward a New Black Cinema*, Chicago Tribune § 5 at 3 (Jan 12, 1986).

[63] A consistent problem with any negative portrayal of African Americans is that they are seldom balanced by positive images. On the other hand, most critics overlooked the positive transformation of the primary male character in *The Color Purple*.

[64] Daniel P. Moynihan, *The Negro Family: The Case for National Action* (Office of Policy Planning and Research, United States Department of Labor, 1965).

[65] See Lee Rainwater and William L. Yancey, *The Moynihan Report and the Politics of Controversy* 427-29 (MIT Press, 1967) (containing criticisms of the Moynihan Report by, among others, Charles E. Silberman, Christopher Jencks, William Ryan, Laura Carper, Frank Riessman and Herbert Gans).

[66] Id at 395-97 (critics included Martin Luther King, Jr., Benjamin Payton, James Farmer, Whitney Young, Jr. and Bayard Rustin).

[67] One of the notable exceptions is Jacquelyne Johnson Jackson, *Black Women in a*

The latest versions of a Moynihanesque analysis can be found in the Moyers televised special, *The Vanishing Black Family*,[68] and, to a lesser extent, in William Julius Wilson's *The Truly Disadvantaged*.[69] In *The Vanishing Black Family*, Moyers presented the problem of female-headed households as a problem of irresponsible sexuality, induced in part by government policies that encouraged family breakdown.[70] The theme of the report was that the welfare state reinforced the deterioration of the Black family by rendering the Black male's role obsolete. As the argument goes, because Black men know that someone will take care of their families, they are free to make babies and leave them. A corollary to the Moyers view is that welfare is also dysfunctional because it allows poor women to leave men upon whom they would otherwise be dependent.

Most commentators criticizing the program failed to pose challenges that might have revealed the patriarchal assumptions underlying much of the Moyers report. They instead focused on the dimension of the problem that was clearly recognizable as racist.[71] White feminists were equally culpable. There was little, if any, published response to the Moyers report from the white feminist community. Perhaps feminists were under the mistaken assumption that since the report focused on the Black community,

---

Racist Society, in *Racism and Mental Health* 185-86 (University of Pittsburgh Press, 1973).

[68] *The Vanishing Black Family* (PBS Television Broadcast, January 1986).

[69] William Julius Wilson, *The Truly Disadvantaged: The Inner City, The Underclass and Public Policy* (The University of Chicago Press, 1987).

[70] Columnist Mary McGrory, applauding the show, reported that Moyers found that sex was as common in the Black ghetto as a cup of coffee. McGrory, *Moynihan was Right 21 Years Ago*, The Washington Post B1 and B4 (Jan 26, 1986). George Will argued that oversexed Black men were more of a menace than Bull Conner, the Birmingham Police Chief who in 1968 achieved international notoriety by turning fire hoses on protesting school children. George Will, *Voting Rights Won't Fix It*, The Washington Post A23 (Jan 23, 1986).

My guess is that the program has influenced the debate about the so-called underclass by providing graphic support to pre-existing tendencies to attribute poverty to individual immorality. During a recent and memorable discussion on the public policy implications of poverty in the Black community, one student remarked that nothing can be done about Black poverty until Black men stop acting like "roving penises," Black women stop having babies "at the drop of a hat," and they all learn middle-class morality. The student cited the Moyers report as her source.

[71] Although the nearly exclusive focus on the racist aspects of the program poses both theoretical and political problems, it was entirely understandable given the racial nature of the subsequent comments that were sympathetic to the Moyers view. As is typical in discussions involving race, the dialogue regarding the Moyers program covered more than just the issue of Black families; some commentators took the opportunity to indict not only the Black underclass, but the Black civil rights leadership, the war on poverty, affirmative action and other race-based remedies. See, for example, Will, *Voting Rights Won't Fix It* at A23 (cited in note 70).

the problems highlighted were racial, not gender based. Whatever the reason, the result was that the ensuing debates over the future direction of welfare and family policy proceeded without significant feminist input. The absence of a strong feminist critique of the Moynihan/Moyers model not only impeded the interests of Black women, but it also compromised the interests of growing numbers of white women heads of household who find it difficult to make ends meet.[72]

William Julius Wilson's *The Truly Disadvantaged* modified much of the moralistic tone of this debate by reframing the issue in terms of a lack of marriageable Black men.[73] According to Wilson, the decline in Black marriages is not attributable to poor motivation, bad work habits or irresponsibility but instead is caused by structural economics which have forced Black unskilled labor out of the work force. Wilson's approach represents a significant move away from that of Moynihan/Moyers in that he rejects their attempt to center the analysis on the morals of the Black community. Yet, he too considers the proliferation of female-headed households as dysfunctional *per se* and fails to explain fully why such households are so much in peril. Because he incorporates no analysis of the way the structure of the economy and the workforce subordinates the interests of women, especially childbearing Black women, Wilson's suggested reform begins with finding ways to put Black men back in the family.[74] In Wilson's view, we must change the economic structure with an eye toward providing more Black jobs for Black men. Because he offers no critique of sexism, Wilson fails to consider economic or social reorganization that directly empowers and supports these single Black mothers.[75]

---

[72] Their difficulties can also be linked to the prevalence of an economic system and family policy that treat the nuclear family as the norm and other family units as aberrant and unworthy of societal accommodation.

[73] Wilson, *The Truly Disadvantaged* at 96 (cited in note 69).

[74] Id at 154 (suggestions include macroeconomic policies which promote balanced economic growth, a nationally-oriented labor market strategy, a child support assurance program, a child care strategy, and a family allowances program which would be both means tested and race specific).

[75] Nor does Wilson include an analysis of the impact of gender on changes in family patterns. Consequently, little attention is paid to the conflict that may result when gender-based expectations are frustrated by economic and demographic factors. This focus on demographic and structural explanations represent an effort to regain the high ground from the Moyers/Moynihan approach which is more psycho-social. Perhaps because psycho-social explanations have come dangerously close to victim-blaming, their prevalence is thought to threaten efforts to win policy directives that might effectively address deteriorating conditions within the working class and poor Black communities. See Kimberle Crenshaw, *A Comment on Gender, Difference, and Victim Ideology in the Study of the Black Family*, in

My criticism is not that providing Black men with jobs is undesirable; indeed, this is necessary not only for the Black men themselves, but for an entire community, depressed and subject to a host of sociological and economic ills that accompany massive rates of unemployment. But as long as we assume that the massive social reorganization Wilson calls for is possible, why not think about it in ways that maximize the choices of Black women?[76] A more complete theoretical and political agenda for the Black underclass must take into account the specific and particular concerns of Black women; their families occupy the bottom rung of the economic ladder, and it is only through placing them at the center of the analysis that their needs and the needs of their families will be directly addressed.[77]

IV. EXPANDING FEMINIST THEORY AND ANTIRACIST POLITICS BY EMBRACING THE INTERSECTION

If any real efforts are to be made to free Black people of the constraints and conditions that characterize racial subordination, then theories and strategies purporting to reflect the Black community's needs must include an analysis of sexism and patriarchy. Similarly, feminism must include an analysis of race if it hopes to express the aspirations of non-white women. Neither Black liberationist politics nor feminist theory can ignore the intersectional experiences of those whom the movements claim as their respective constituents. In order to include Black women, both movements must distance themselves from earlier approaches in which experiences are relevant only when they are related to certain clearly identifiable causes (for example, the oppression of Blacks is significant when based on race, of women when based on gender). The praxis of both should be centered on the life chances and life situations of people who should be cared about without regard to the source of their difficulties.

I have stated earlier that the failure to embrace the complexities of compoundedness is not simply a matter of political will, but

---

The Decline of Marriage Among African Americans: Causes, Consequences and Policy Implications (forthcoming 1989).

[76] For instance, Wilson only mentions in passing the need for day care and job training for single mothers. Wilson at 153 (cited in note 69). No mention at all is made of other practices and policies that are racist and sexist, and that contribute to the poor conditions under which nearly half of all Black women must live.

[77] Pauli Murray observes that the operation of sexism is at least the partial cause of social problems affecting Black women. See Murray, The Liberation of Black Women, in Jo Freeman, ed, Women: A Feminist Perspective 351-62 (Mayfield Publishing Co, 1975).

is also due to the influence of a way of thinking about discrimination which structures politics so that struggles are categorized as singular issues. Moreover, this structure imports a descriptive and normative view of society that reinforces the status quo.

It is somewhat ironic that those concerned with alleviating the ills of racism and sexism should adopt such a top-down approach to discrimination. If their efforts instead began with addressing the needs and problems of those who are most disadvantaged and with restructuring and remaking the world where necessary, then others who are singularly disadvantaged would also benefit. In addition, it seems that placing those who currently are marginalized in the center is the most effective way to resist efforts to compartmentalize experiences and undermine potential collective action.

It is not necessary to believe that a political consensus to focus on the lives of the most disadvantaged will happen tomorrow in order to recenter discrimination discourse at the intersection. It is enough, for now, that such an effort would encourage us to look beneath the prevailing conceptions of discrimination and to challenge the complacency that accompanies belief in the effectiveness of this framework. By so doing, we may develop language which is critical of the dominant view and which provides some basis for unifying activity. The goal of this activity should be to facilitate the inclusion of marginalized groups for whom it can be said: "When they enter, we all enter."

CHALLENGING LAW, ESTABLISHING DIFFERENCES: THE FUTURE OF FEMINIST LEGAL SCHOLARSHIP

Martha L. Fineman*

I. INTRODUCTION

This essay concerns the complex, difficult, and perhaps impossible goal of introducing feminist theory into legal discourse. In it I analyze existing and emerging themes that dominate contemporary feminist legal discourse and that concern me because of their limited usefulness in developing a theory of women's experience within law and legal institutions.

On the broadest level feminist legal thought seems unanchored. It drifts between the extremes of "grand theory," which is totalizing in its scope and ambitions,[1] and personal narratives, which begin and end with the presentation of one individual's unique experience.[2] Neither of these extremes does much to further the discussion of feminist issues because they obscure more than they illuminate. Be-

---

*Professor of Law, University of Wisconsin Law School. B.A. 1971, Temple University; J.D. 1975, University of Chicago. My thanks to Amy Scarr and Michael Toner for assistance on this essay.

1. Grand theory, for example, while valued in academic institutions, relies on abstractions not grounded in women's gendered life experiences. Its application to women's lives, therefore, is usually irrelevant and occasionally detrimental.

2. The personal narratives are more difficult to critique and involve an intersection of two other themes in contemporary feminist legal discourse — the fetish about difference that impedes the development of viable theoretical underpinnings for strategies and what I term the "ideal of representation." See infra part IV.

tween these extremes, in that space between something so exclusively personal as to be beyond generalization or political content, and something so general and abstract as to be removed from the everyday realities of women's lives, lies fertile ground for feminist methodology.

In my efforts to assess the future of feminist legal scholarship, I am not concerned with discussions that focus merely on including women in the legal profession, nor with those directed at ensuring that, once included, women in law share power and positions equally with men. Women's presence in the legal profession has not caused feminist theory to follow. In fact, all too often in order to be successful, women have adopted assimilation as their intellectual strategy and equal treatment as their substantive principle.

My version of feminist theory is decidedly antiassimilationist. It does not adopt existing legal norms and merely require equal entitlement for women to the benefits and burdens distributed throughout our system of legal regulations. Rather, my version of feminist theory questions both the asserted universal "ideal" of equality espoused in dominant legal thought and the existing distributions of power and economic benefits held in place by the structure and nature of law. It goes beyond considerations of gender and addresses questions of value (what we deem worthwhile) and knowledge (how we construct truth).

I begin with my version of the ideally antagonistic interaction of feminist theory with the law.[3] I locate my discussion between the extremes of grand theory and unique experience. I consider the central, pressing task of feminist theory to be challenging existing law and legal doctrines through the articulation and establishment of a theory of difference. In this essay I divide my discussion of the theory of difference into two sections. The first section concerns the theoretical and political necessity of establishing the differences between men and women. Articulation of the extent of this manifestation of difference illustrates that the law primarily represents and reflects male experiences and norms. Critiquing the law from a feminist perspective requires understanding how women's perceptions and experiences differ from men's and how such differences are relevant to the development and implementation of legal doctrines and theories.

The second theoretical consideration involved in developing a theory of difference is the realization that important differences exist among women.[4] Feminists must overcome these differences in both

---

3. See *infra* text accompanying notes 6-28.
4. See *infra* text accompanying notes 46-47.

practice and theory because the existence of these differences is misused to divide women. The task of feminist theory in this regard is to encourage women to work together, across differences, so that the similar, shared gendered aspects of our lives do not continue to be invisible and unspoken in law.

Finally, I will address questions about the notion of "representation."[5] I focus on the concept of representation as a legitimating selection criterion that affects our acceptance of an individual possessing an identified characteristic as "typical" of a class or group. Representation implies that an individual can typify a group or class merely by possessing a shared characteristic that serves the functions of both distinguishing him or her from the whole and unifying him or her with an identifiable subgroup. In this regard, representation is a totalizing concept even though its premise initially lies in the recognition of difference. Representation depends upon identifying and privileging one characteristic from among the many that an individual may possess. The characteristic thus serves to identify the individual as well as the group that the individual represents. The characteristic, so designated, publicly becomes the most politically, and perhaps socially, salient feature that the individual possesses. The theme of representation is integrally related to and is an outgrowth of my earlier considerations of differences.

II. FEMINIST THEORY AND LAW

Recently, the interest in feminist scholarship has increased. Law has been an area relatively untouched by the postmodern currents that have washed through other disciplines, but it now appears to be caught within tides of critical methodologies and conclusions that threaten its very roots. An examination of the concept of feminist legal theory reveals both a subject and a methodology that are still in the process of being born. There are no "right" paths, clearly defined. The scholarship, however, can be described as sharing the objective of raising questions about women's relationships to law and legal institutions.

A. *Theory and Practice*

Given the newness of the inquiry, many "practitioners" of feminist legal theory may prefer to describe their work as examples of feminist "methodology" rather than as expositions of "theory." In fact, in regard

---

5. *See infra* part IV.

to feminist scholarship, it is appropriate to conclude that method *is* theory in its most relevant form.

My approach has been to reject the resort to abstractions and to concentrate on understanding why little relation exists between women's lives and material circumstances and the specific doctrinal representations of those lives and circumstances.[6] My choice has been to "do" feminist theory as an exercise in the concrete, both by focusing on a specific area of law and by using empirical information and stories of specific lives. This emphasis on specifics relates to my understanding of the insights feminist methodology has produced for scholars. The real distinction between feminist theory (legal and otherwise) and more traditional legal theory is this belief in the desirability of the concrete. Such an emphasis also has had rather honorable nonfeminist adherents. For example, Robert Merton coined the term "theory of the middle range" to describe work that mediated between "stories" and "grand theory."[7] He described such scholarship as being superior to mere storytelling or mindless empiricism, as well as superior to vague references to the relationships between ill-defined abstractions.[8] Clifford Geertz[9] and James Boyd White,[10] among others, have noted that language or rhetoric itself is specific and tied to given material concerns. White has stated,

> Like law, rhetoric invents; and, like law, it invents out of something rather than out of nothing. It always starts in a particular culture and among particular people. There is always one speaker addressing others in a particular situation,

---

6. *See, e.g.*, M. FINEMAN, THE ILLUSION OF EQUALITY: RHETORIC AND REALITY IN DIVORCE REFORM (forthcoming 1991); Fineman, *Implementing Equality, Ideology Contradiction and Social Change: A Study of Rhetoric and Results in the Regulation of the Consequences of Divorce*, 1983 WIS. L. REV. 789.

7. R. MERTON, *On Sociological Theories of the Middle Range*, in ON THEORETICAL SOCIOLOGY: FIVE ESSAYS, OLD AND NEW 39, 68 (1967).

8. *Id.* at 68.

9. Geertz stated in regard to grand anthropological concepts:

   If anthropological interpretation is constructing a reading of what happens, then to divorce it from what happens — from what, in this time or that place, specific people say, what they do, what is done to them, from the whole vast business of the world — is to divorce it from its applications and render it vacant. A good interpretation of anything — a poem, a person, a history, a ritual, an institution, a society — takes us into the heart of that of which it is the interpretation.

C. GEERTZ, *Thick Description: Toward an Interpretive Theory of Culture*, in THE INTERPRETATION OF CULTURES 18 (1973).

10. White, *Law as Rhetoric, Rhetoric as Law: The Arts of Cultural and Communal Life*, 52 U. CHI. L. REV. 684 (1985).

about concerns that are real and important to somebody, and speaking a particular language. Rhetoric always takes place with given materials. One cannot idealize rhetoric and say, "Here is how it should go on in general". . . . [R]hetoric is always specific to its material.[11]

At least in nonlaw areas, feminist scholarship has tended to focus on specifics.[12] Feminist legal scholarship, however, seems to be drifting toward abstract grand-theory presentations. Carol Smart recently warned that feminist legal theorists are in danger of creating the impression that one specific form of feminist jurisprudence represents the "superior" (or true) version as opposed to various other feminist legal theories. Smart labeled this totalizing tendency, evident in the work of many of the most well-known North American legal feminists, the construction of a "scientific feminism" and was explicitly critical of such grand theorizing.[13]

While I agree with Smart's assertion, I am aware that the tenure, hiring, and promotion committees, in addition to the law reviews of elite American law schools, often prefer grand theory over middle-level theory:[14] the grander the feminist theory, the more it resembles mainstream scholarly format and content. Grand theorizing represents the creation of a new form of positivism in a search for universal truth discoverable within the methodology of critical legal analysis. In contrast, middle-range theory mediates between the material circumstances of women's lives and the grand realizations that law is gendered, that law is a manifestation of power, and that law works to the detriment of women. These realizations previously have been hidden or ignored in considerations of the laws that regulate women's

---

11. *Id.* at 695.

12. Grand theory represents a belief that an existing "truth" waits to be discovered and rejects the idea that theory is constantly in process. *See* C. WEEDON, FEMINIST PRACTICE AND POSTSTRUCTURALIST THEORY 11 (1987) (defining her feminist project as "hold[ing] on to feminism as a politics" and "mobiliz[ing] theory in order to develop strategies for change on behalf of feminist interests," rather than coming up with a "definitive feminist theory — a totalizing theory of patriarchy").

13. C. SMART, FEMINISM AND THE POWER OF LAW 70-71 (1989); *see also* West, *Jurisprudence and Gender*, 55 U. CHI. L. REV. 1 (1988) (the need for a more experience-based jurisprudence). *But cf.* Olsen, *Feminist Theory in Grand Style*, 89 COLUM. L. REV. 1147, 1166-77 (1989) (a defense of grand theorizing in the context of reviewing the work of Catharine MacKinnon).

14. Academia has created a set of relatively well-defined scholarly norms which, to a certain extent, feminist theory seeks to expose and ultimately erode. *See, e.g.,* Flax, *Postmodernism and Gender Relations in Feminist Theory*, 12 SIGNS: J. WOMEN IN CULTURE & SOC'Y 621 (1987).

lives.[15] They are best exposed by referencing and emphasizing those lives.

Increasingly, I have become aware of the difficulty of trying to use middle-range feminist methodology within the confines of legal theory. Not only does the pull toward grand theory categorize less grand scholarship as nontheoretical, but I fear that feminist sensibilities become lost or absorbed into the morass of legal concepts and words. I have lost faith. Feminism, it seems, has not transformed, and perhaps cannot transform the law. Rather, the law, when it becomes the battleground, threatens to transform feminism. This result stems from the obvious power of the law as a "dominant discourse" — one which is self-contained (though incomplete and imperfect), self-congratulatory (though not introspective or self-reflective), and self-fulfilling (though not inevitable nor infallible).

The transformative potential of feminist thought is blunted because in order to be incorporated into and considered compatible with legal theory, feminist thought must adapt, even if it does not totally conform, to the words and concepts of legal discourse. Feminism may enter as the challenger, but the tools inevitably employed are those of the androphile master. And the character of the tools largely determines the shape and design of the resulting construction. Therefore, the task of feminists concerned with the law and legal institutions must be to create and explicate feminist methods and theories that explicitly challenge and compete with the totalizing nature of grand legal theory. Such a feminist strategy would set its middle-range theory in opposition to law — outside of formal legal categories.

B. *Feminist Methodologies*

In my opinion, there are several characteristics that, in various permutations and combinations, provide the ingredients for feminist legal analyses that effectively can challenge existing legal theory and paradigms. First, feminist methodology should be critical. This critical

---

15. For example, family law regulates intimacy, employment law regulates market activity, and constitutional law regulates sexuality and reproduction.

16. I have written extensively on the problems associated with the gender neutrality paradigm within the context of family law. *See, e.g.*, M. FINEMAN, *supra* note 6; Fineman, *Dominant Discourse, Professional Language, and Legal Change in Child Custody Decisionmaking*, 101 HARV. L. REV. 727 (1988) [hereinafter Fineman, *Dominant Discourse*]; Fineman, *Illusive Equality: On Weitzman's Divorce Revolution*, 1986 AM. B. FOUND. RES. J. 781 [hereinafter Fineman, *Illusive Equality*]; Fineman, *supra* note 6; Fineman & Opie, *The Uses of Social Science Data in Legal Policymaking: Custody Determinations at Divorce*, 1987 WIS. L. REV. 107.

stance is developed by adopting an explicitly woman-focused perspective, a perspective informed by women's experiences. Feminist theory cannot be "gender neutral" and often will be explicitly critical of that paradigm as historically having excluded the woman's perspective from legal thought.[16] "Gender-sensitive" feminism, however, cannot be viewed as lacking legitimacy because of an inappropriate bias. Rather, it is premised on the need to expose and correct an *existing* bias. "Gender-sensitive" feminism seeks to correct the imbalance and unfairness in the legal system that result from implementing perspectives that exclude attention to the circumstances of women's gendered lives, even on issues that intimately affect those lives.[17]

Feminist analysis, if recognized at all, often is seen as marginal to legal thought.[18] Traditional legal scholarship tends to view the status quo as unbiased or neutral.[19] This belief in the possibility of a neutral stance is the logical place for feminist analysis to begin: as an explicit challenge to the use of the concept of bias, as contrasted with the concepts of perspective and position, when introducing previously excluded voices into legal discourse and analysis. Feminist theory can demonstrate that the status quo is *not* neutral; that it is as "biased" as, and certainly no more "correct" than, that which challenges it. And there can be no refuge in the status quo. Law has developed in

---

17. For a development of the term "gendered lives," see *infra* text accompanying notes 41-45. Recent changes in the family law illustrate measures denying the existence of women's gendered lives. In property reform, for example, measures promoted in the 1970s sought to impose a 50-50 distribution scheme. This distribution was consistent with the partnership metaphor that liberal feminists had chosen to characterize marriage. Liberal feminists adopted this metaphor because of their uncritical acceptance of the need to establish "equality" through sameness of treatment. However, in light of the social and economic inequalities women experience, one half of the accumulated assets seldom suffice to provide adequately for divorced women and their children. *See* L. WEITZMAN, THE DIVORCE REVOLUTION: THE UNEXPECTED SOCIAL AND ECONOMIC CONSEQUENCES FOR WOMEN AND CHILDREN IN AMERICA 70-109 (1985). I have criticized these "rule equality" reforms elsewhere. *See* Fineman, *supra* note 6, at 833-42; *see also* Fineman, *Illusive Equality, supra* note 16, at 781. Similarly, in child custody disputes, courts have retreated from the historic preference accorded women under the "tender years" doctrine (an evidentiary presumption under which women, unless "unfit," received custody of their young children) in favor of equality based custody norms like joint custody. *See* Fineman & Opie, *supra* note 16, at 107, 112; *see also* Fineman, *Dominant Discourse, supra* note 16, at 727.

18. Few law schools offer courses in feminist legal theory, and it seldom is included in courses on jurisprudence. Other forms of themed analysis, such as law and economics and critical legal studies, also are excluded.

19. One aspect of feminist scholarship has been uncovering and exposing male-infused, male-dominated thinking masquerading as neutral, objective theory. *See, e.g.*, N. NODDINGS, CARING: A FEMININE APPROACH TO ETHICS & MORAL EDUCATION (1984); E. REED, SEXISM AND SCIENCE (1978); Fineman & Opie, *supra* note 16.

the context of theories and institutions which are controlled by men and reflect their concerns. Historically, law has been a "public" arena, and its focus has been on public concerns. Traditionally, women have belonged to the "private" recesses of society: in families, in relationships controlled and defined by men, and in silence.

In addition to exposing the inevitability of bias, feminist analysis critically evaluates not only outcomes but also fundamental concepts, values, and assumptions embedded in legal thought.[20] Results or outcomes in cases decided under existing legal doctrines are relevant to this inquiry, but criticizing them is only a starting point. Too many legal scholars end their inquiry with a critique of results and recommendations for "tinkering"-type reforms without considering how the conceptual structure of legal thought condemns such reforms merely to replicating injustices.[21] When, as is often the case, the basic tenets of legal ideology clash with women's gendered lives, reforms based on those tenets will do little more than the original rules did to validate and accommodate women's experiences.

From this perspective, feminism is a political theory concerned with issues of power. It challenges the conceptual bases of the status quo by assessing the ways that power controls the production of values and standards against which specific results and rules are measured. Law represents both a discourse and a process of power. Norms created by and enshrined in law are manifestations of power relationships. These norms are applied coercively and are justified in part by the perception that they are "neutral" and "objective." Appreciating this phenomenon, many feminist scholars have focused their attention on the legislative and political processes rather than on the judiciary.[22] The recognition that law is power also has led many feminists to concentrate on social and cultural perceptions and manifestations of law and legality rather than to focus narrowly on formal legal doctrinal developments.[23]

---

20. See MacKinnon, *Feminism, Marxism, Method and the State: An Agenda for Theory?*, 7 SIGNS: J. WOMEN IN CULTURE & SOC'Y 515, 534-36 (1982) (discussing the political implications of method); *see also* Fineman & Opie, *supra* note 16, at 107.

21. For a further discussion and critique of this tendency, see Fineman, *Illusive Equality*, *supra* note 16, at 781.

22. *See, e.g.*, AT THE BOUNDARIES OF LAW: FEMINISM AND LEGAL THEORY (1990) [hereinafter BOUNDARIES].

23. For two excellent illustrations of works analyzing the interplay between formal legal developments and their application in practice, see Girdner, *Child Custody Determination: Ideological Dimensions of a Social Problem*, in REDEFINING SOCIAL PROBLEMS 165 (1986); McCann, *Battered Women and the Law: The Limits of the Legislation*, in WOMEN IN LAW: EXPLORATIONS IN LAW, FAMILY & SEXUALITY 71 (1985) [hereinafter WOMEN IN LAW].

Implicit in my assertion that feminism must be a politically rather than a legally focused theory is my belief about the relative powerlessness of law, as compared to other ideological institutions within our culture, to transform society. While law can reflect, and even facilitate, social change, law can seldom, if ever, initiate it. Regardless of the formal legal articulation, legal rules will tend to track and reflect the dominant conclusions of the majority culture. Thus, while law perhaps highlights the social and political aspects it reflects, it is more a mirror than a catalyst in regard to enduring social change.[24]

An additional characteristic of feminist legal methodology is that it seeks to present alternatives to the existing order.[25] The construction of alternatives may be, of course, a natural outgrowth of other characteristics of feminist legal thought, particularly that feminist legal thought is critical and political. I place the construction of alternatives as a separate characteristic, however, because an independent goal of much of feminist work is to present oppositional values.[26] Feminist analysis often is radically nonassimilationist, and it resists the mere inclusion in dominant social institutions as the solution to the problems in women's gendered lives. In fact, the larger social value of feminist methodology may lie in its ability to make explicit oppositional stances vis-á-vis the existing culture. The task of the moment for feminism may be to transform society by challenging dominant values and defiantly refusing to assimilate into the status quo. The point of making women's experiences and perspectives central factors in developing social theory is to change "things," not merely to change women's perspectives on their positions within existing power relationships. To many feminist scholars, therefore, assimilation is failure, while opposition is essential for feminist methodology applied to law.[27]

It seems to me important to emphasize that feminist theory that effectively challenges existing paradigms will be characteristically evolutionary in nature. Feminist legal theory, therefore, will not represent doctrine carved in stone or even printed in statute books. Feminist methodology at its best generates contributions to what is recognized as a series of ongoing debates that start with the premises

---

24. No-fault divorce reform illustrates this phenomenon. Prior to these statutes, lawyers often would counsel clients on how to "create" divorce grounds. *See* L. FRIEDMAN, A HISTORY OF AMERICAN LAW 438-40 (1973). Thus, rather than representing any legal "change," no-fault reforms actually mirrored existing practice.

25. *See* West, *supra* note 13, at 72 (discussing the construction of present goals in light of a feminist utopian vision).

26. *See, e.g.,* BOUNDARIES, *supra* note 22.

27. In the context of family law, for example, many scholars refuse to accept the dictates of formal rule-equality. *See* M. FINEMAN, *supra* note 6.

that "truth" changes over time as circumstances change and that gains and losses, along with recorded wisdom, are mutable parts of an evolving story. As feminist legal theory references women's lives, it must define and undertake the "tasks of the moment." The tasks of the future cannot yet be defined, and each piece of feminist legal scholarship is only one step in the long journey feminist legal scholars have begun.

Feminist legal thought contains explicit criticism as well as implicit disagreements about the wisdom of pragmatic uses of law, the effectiveness of law as an instrument of social change and, most broadly, the importance of law as a focus for feminist study. Some feminist scholarship reveals antagonistic, even violent, disagreement with other feminist works.[28] Disagreements aside, however, feminist legal theory has lessons for all of society, not just for women or legal scholars. Ultimately, the members of our audience will judge the effectiveness and genuineness of our individual and collective voices.

Our scholarship is critical, political, and controversial; it is concerned with the processes that comprise law. The best feminist legal scholarship is about law in its broadest form, as a manifestation of power in society, and recognizes no division between law and power. Law is not found only in courts and cases, and legislatures and statutes, but in implementing institutions, such as social work and law enforcement, as well. Law is found in the discourse used in everyday life. Law is evident in the beliefs and assumptions we hold about the world in which we live and in the norms and values we cherish.

III. FEMINIST METHODOLOGY AND ISSUES OF DIFFERENCES

Not surprisingly, much of feminist legal methodology considers the issue of "differences."[29] This examination is not an easy task. In fact, much of the rather antagonistic interaction among legal feminists has arisen from disagreement about the fundamental question of whether or not there are cognizable differences between men and women.[30] The early, "founding mother" members of a broadly defined legal feminist community would disagree with the exploration of such differences and would deny their existence or significance.[31] More recently,

---

28. *See, e.g.*, Williams, *The Equality Crisis: Some Reflections on Culture, Courts, and Feminism*, 7 WOMEN'S RTS. L. REP. 175 (1982).

29. For a collection of essays organized around the differences theme, see 3 WIS. WOMEN'S L.J. (1987), a compilation of papers presented at the 1986 Feminism and Legal Theory Conference held in Madison, Wisconsin.

30. *See* Williams, *supra* note 28, at 175.

31. *See* McElroy, *The Roots of Individualist Feminism in 19th-Century America*, in FREE-DOM, FEMINISM, AND THE STATE 3-26 (W. McElroy ed. 1982).

some feminist scholarship has emphasized that there are differences *among* women,[32] and the question arises whether these differences should be considered legally, as well as theoretically, significant.

Focusing on differences is particularly difficult for women trained in the law because any recognition of differences challenges dominant legal equality theory and its accompanying paradigms, such as sameness of treatment.[33] The initial approach of early contemporary legal feminists trying to break the barriers of the profession, therefore, was to develop the existing rhetoric of equality and to seek laws that were gender neutral.[34] Equality in the market and in the home were their articulated goals, and, as a strategy, early feminist theoreticians and lawyers minimized or denied the existence of significant differences between men and women.[35]

Recently, the representation of equality embodied in the "gender-neutrality" paradigm has undergone sustained attacks. Gender neutrality as a universal concept has been recognized as an objective that accepts the terms and structures of the status quo, the dominant culture.[36] To argue that gender neutrality is or should be the goal of feminist reformist law is to further legitimate the underlying institutions constructed and maintained in the context of patriarchy and dominance as neutral, objective, and value-free.

Strong voices within the feminist legal community are joining in a chorus to celebrate the liberating realization that anything we legitimately can call *"feminist"* legal theory must begin with a conceptual statement about differences because, by its very definition, *feminist* theory must be a gendered theory. Feminist theory is woman centered and is, therefore, gendered by its very nature. It takes as its raw building materials women's experiences. Because women live gendered lives in our culture, any analysis that begins with their experiences necessarily must be a gendered analysis.[37] It cannot be a gender-neutral theory, nor can it have as its goal equality in the traditional, formal legal sense of the word.

---

32. *See infra* text accompanying note 47.

33. *See* Smart & Brophy, *Locating Law: A Discussion of the Place of Law in Feminist Politics*, in WOMEN IN LAW, *supra* note 23, at 1 (discussing the historic and contemporary conflict between strict, or "rule equality," and special treatment, or "result equality," in British feminist thought); *see also* M. FINEMAN, *supra* note 6.

34. Fineman, *supra* note 6, at 789-96, 811-34, 845, 851-52 (discussing this conflict within the context of American feminism).

35. Williams, *supra* note 28.

36. *Cf.* MacKinnon, *supra* note 20, at 535-41 (discussing human sexuality as a gendered experience).

37. *Id.* at 535 (discussing feminism as "the theory of women's point of view" and of different ways of knowing).

Because the differences between men and women have been the source of women's past oppression, to recognize these differences as the basis of feminist theory is to risk being dismissed as naïve or being accused of advocating a position that will harm women.[38] Furthermore, advocates of difference recently have faced the possibility of being labeled "essentialists" — those who advocate a belief in an "essential womanhood" that exists outside of language and society, and who are insensitive to race, class, and other differences among women. The "essentialist" label is more significant and, therefore, more difficult to address. I recognize that there are some differences among women that may, in some instances, be more significant than are the gendered life differences between men and women.[39] However, in the aggregate, I believe women's shared or collective gendered experiences, both actual *and* potential, differ significantly from men's experiences in our society. These gendered experiences require adequate reflection and consideration in our legal system. These gendered experiences may be cultural and linguistic constructions, but they define the parameters of women's lives — even if only as constraints to resist. Incorporation of women's gendered life experiences is not accomplished by rules conceived in and constrained by a system that refuses to recognize gender as a relevant perspective, imposing "neutral" conclusions on women's circumstances.[40] Furthermore, the recognition that there are differences among women should not defeat the attempt to "gender" law.

The possibility that women's perspectives differ from men's is relevant because, given their perspective and positions, women often may make different observations, ask different questions, and consider different issues from similarly situated men. A difference in *perspective* often is reflected as a difference in *perception*. Women from different

---

38. Equal treatment also has contributed to the oppression of women, particularly poor, nonprofessional women.

39. Rae identified three different types of equalities: "simple," "segmental," and "bloc." *See* D. RAE, EQUALITIES 20 (1981). "Simple equality" compares individuals, while "segmental equality" compares equality within a subclass. *Id.* at 20, 29. By contrast, "bloc equality" compares groups or blocs and thus "asks for something very different from simple or segmental equality." *Id.* at 35. Liberal feminist reform efforts tend to adopt a simple or individual model of equality. As a result, such efforts generally fail to assess seriously the implications of the total failure of women to achieve bloc equality with men in the economic sphere. Moreover, the differences among women present complicated segmental equality questions.

40. *See* West, *supra* note 13, at 70 (discussing need for a "true" description of women's experience and subjectivity in order to change masculine jurisprudence). For a critique of essentialism, see Harris, *Race and Essentialism in Feminist Legal Theory*, 42 STAN. L. REV. 581 (1990).

cultures, classes, races, and economic circumstances might argue about conclusions, tactics, and values, but they also understand a common gendered-life reference point that unites them in interest and urgency around certain shared cultural and social experiences. Therefore, legal theory that is uninformed or uninfluenced by these different perspectives and perceptions is incomplete, inequitable, and indefensible.

A.   *Differences Between Women and Men*

The assertion of a gendered existence is contested in our legal culture.[41] Even when accepted, the premise generates issues concerning how much significance should be attached to such a realization.[42] My exploration of these issues has led me to reach some tentative (and perhaps totally idiosyncratic) conclusions about the types of gender differences that might be significant in legal theory.

I believe that many women experience society in ways significantly different from the ways that men experience society. I believe certain real *or* potential experiences can be described as constituting the basis for a feminist development of the concept of "gendered life." These experiences lead many women to develop a perspective qualitatively different from what is reflected in dominant legal ideology. This is *not* to assert that all women think alike or have identical experiences. My position is based on experiential, not essential differences.[43]

Women's gendered existence is comprised of a variety of experiences — material, psychological, physical, social, and cultural. Some of these experiences may be described as biologically based, while others seem more rooted in culture and custom. The actual or potential experiences of rape, sexual harassment, pornography, and other sexual violence that women may suffer in our culture shape individual experiences. So, too, the potential for reproductive events such as pregnancy, breast feeding, and abortion has an impact on women's constructions of their gendered lives. Further, some gendered experiences, such as aging, are events shared by men. But women often live or experience such events in unique ways. Thus, while both men and women age, the implications of aging from both a social and economic perspective are different for the genders in our culture.[44]

---

41. *See* Williams, *supra* note 28.

42. *See* Kay, *Models of Equality*, 1985 U. ILL. L. REV. 39.

43. "Essentialist" also implies that the categories of gender, race, or class are inherently meaningful and, therefore, universal. Even if one is "sensitive" to race and class, one may still be essentialist by, for example, espousing a belief in an "essence of woman" that cuts across all differences.

44. *See* P. ZOPF, AMERICAN WOMEN IN POVERTY 109-11 (1989).

Human beings are the product of their experiences. As organisms, they have little or no independent "essence" distinct from their experiences. Of course, certain physical and chemical components or characteristics of human beings both provoke experiences and act as filters through which such experiences are processed. A person, therefore, is the sum of these physical attributes as acted upon, by, and through his or her social and cultural experiences. What we call knowledge, what we label virtuous, grows out of these experiences. The very questions we ask, along with the answers we fashion, express these experiences. Therefore, if women collectively have different actual and potential experiences from men, they are likely to have different perspectives — different sets of values, beliefs, and concerns as a group.

I am not arguing that *all* women react the same way to or reach identical conclusions about issues in our society, nor do I believe that all women experience any one or more of the gendered experiences. Uniformity in interpretation and experiences is not necessary to the concept of gendered life. Individual experiences may differ from the socially constructed and culturally defined nexus, but they are still affected by them. Unadorned, uninterpreted events are not in and of themselves what one "experiences." Interpretation of events is an extremely significant aspect of this process of individual experiencing. Experiences do not take place in an interpretive vacuum, however, but are part of a social, interactive process. Culture and society provide the media through which experiences are understood. Our twentieth-century society has universal, totalizing cultural representations of women and women's experiences.[45] Even those critical of such cultural constructions of essentialist images of women must recognize the force these images hold. None of us completely escapes the dominant images of the society within which we operate. Interpretation of events, the process whereby events are given meaning, is not an autonomistic, individualistic procedure. Social action and interaction, as well as dominant cultural images, significantly contribute to individual interpretations of and reactions to events.

Further, I recognize that individual responses to similar experiences may differ as individual options (economic and otherwise) vary due to external circumstances such as race, sexuality, and social class.

---

45. One example is that of motherhood. The construction of women as mothers affects all women's experiences in the culture whether they individually choose to be mothers or not. As women they are at least partially identified and defined as mothers, potential mothers, or past mothers.

Additionally, previous experiences may filter new ones, having in some instances much more significance than gender. To recognize that there may be differences *among* women does not, however, refute the observation that women's actual *and* potential shared experiences are female experiences, inescapably gendered within the larger culture and society.

B. *Differences Among Women*

A tendency to question the ability of any group of women to speak for others has begun to emerge in feminist legal theory. Initially, this perspective developed in response to minority women's criticisms that feminism was a "white middle-class, heterosexual movement."[46] Such criticism has made many feminist theorists reluctant to speak unless they have first disclaimed the notion that they are representing anything other than their individual (and, perhaps, their own class, race, and sexual preference) perspective. Many feel they must rattle off a litany of differences among women at the beginning of any discussion about feminism, society, and law — a distance placed between groups of women filled with assumptions about the nature of "representation" and about the essential and determinative character of race, class, and sexuality in defining an individual or group.

While few would dispute that characteristics such as race, class, and sexuality may be significant to one's experiences, it is a mistake to regard these markers of difference as the only relevant ones. Women may have other characteristics that give them a basis for cooperation and empathy. For example, in addition to race, class, and sexual preference, factors such as age, physical characteristics (including "handicaps" *and* "beauty" or lack thereof), religion, marital status, the level of male identification (which is independent of both marital status and sexual preference — what Gerda Lerner has referred to as "the man in our head"[47]), birth order, motherhood, grandmotherhood, intelligence, rural or urban existence, responsiveness to change or ability to accept ambivalence in one's personal life or in society, sources of income (self, spouse, or state), degree of poverty or wealth,

---

46. For recent critiques of mainstream feminist legal theory for its white middle-class, heterosexual bias, see E. SPELMAN, INESSENTIAL WOMAN: PROBLEMS OF EXCLUSION IN FEMINIST THOUGHT (1988); Harris, *supra* note 40; Kline, *Race, Racism, and Feminist Legal Theory*, 12 HARV. WOMEN'S L.J. 115 (1989).

47. From conversations between Gerda Lerner and the author. For a general discussion of male hegemony over that which is defined socially as "universal truth," see G. LERNER, THE CREATION OF PATRIARCHY 217-29 (1986).

and substance dependency, among others, shape how individual women experience the world.

Separating out a few differences as conclusively and exclusively determinative results in analyses that are impoverished reflections of the very complexity of women's gendered lives, which feminists should seek to understand and address. Such separation also results in a privileging that fosters the creation of hierarchies of oppression and claims of exclusive or genuine oppression. These, in turn, lead to a competition among oppressions that serves only the interests of the dominant social group. It is members of this group who are benefited when dominated groups fight among themselves at the margins of powerful institutions, which condescendingly have made room for only a few outsiders.

Privileging any one or two characteristics when so many have the potential to inform and create women's gendered lives is simplistic and will impede an articulation of the problems women share in society. Hierarchies limit participation and exclude voices necessary for the creation of solutions relevant to a broad spectrum of women. It would be interesting to consider how some characteristics or clusters of characteristics may cancel out, compensate for, or compete with others. For example, how do we place people with multiple sources of oppression in relation to others? If a white woman also is a welfare mother, can we consider her legitimately placed with the dominant group in society merely because she shares their skin color? I would argue clearly not, but where, then, does she fit among the oppressed? Can she really be considered *always* more privileged simply because of her race in a ranking of oppressions? A hierarchy of oppression that always places race at the top would consider her so. I believe oppression to be much more complex. Exclusion leads to conflict and competition. This disunity impedes the aggregation of power necessary for women of all groups to push back the barriers excluding most of us and our experiences.

The competition should not be with each other in the margins of society but with the powerful, dominant main structures whose visions and versions of reality are reflected in society's institutions. The task, then, for feminists of all races, classes, characteristics, and orientations, as well as for men who seek significant change in our social and cultural institutions, is to find common ground and work together. We must learn about and be sensitive to the many differences among us. Those differences, however, must not divide us to the point where we fight only among ourselves, each internal group urging its unifying source or sources of oppression as the only "true" oppression and seeking to silence others. The task should be to bring the many manifestations of women's gendered lives into consideration, not to argue that only one version of gendered existence is entitled to be heard or addressed.

IV. QUESTIONS OF REPRESENTATION

The current obsession with differences among women has a negative impact in that it provides yet another means to decide who is given a voice and who is silenced. It also reveals a problem with the idea of "representation." At least initially, it seems problematic that, by merely "having" or embodying a characteristic or set of characteristics, an individual has the authority and legitimacy to represent definitively the position of women sharing such characteristics. While characteristics may indicate experiences or potential experiences, they should not be considered in and of themselves sufficient or even necessary. It should not be the characteristics of the *speaker* which are considered most relevant but the quality and nature of that which is *spoken*. We must focus on the discourse, the ideology. No groups or persons should be immune from a critical and political assessment of what they advocate.

In contemporary critical thought there is a trend toward excessive reliance on the individual characteristics of the speaker to legitimate discourses. This focus erroneously furthers the idea that the individual is the agent of social action and change and masks the manifold ways in which oppression takes place and is fostered within the structures and dominant ideologies of our society. It operates to place some discourses beyond criticism; they are accepted as authentic, not because of the nature of the rhetoric, but because of the nature of the individual speaker. Additionally, from the most rudimentary political perspective, adhering to the notion that authority or authenticity is located exclusively in individuals as supposed representatives of groups with which they share characteristics, risks conveying the impression that the token inclusions of such individuals are "solutions" to the problems suffered by those groups.

This version of representation was evident in the earlier, token moves to incorporate women into law. By merely conceding a need for the presence of a woman or even several women in the legal profession, social institutions and legal ideology remained unchanged in accommodating feminist concerns and criticisms. This manifestation of "representation" equates one woman with another, making us fungible objectifications of the essential woman. This type of representation, in which one woman is deemed capable of acting for the whole, is totally insensitive to differences among women. It is also likely to act to eradicate the perception of differences between women and men because it is a characteristic-focused, not an experientially or ideologically focused, strategy. Not surprisingly, a woman chosen to "represent" her gender often is one whose interests and values coincide with those of the normalized male institutions that have deigned to include her. Furthermore, since ideology and structure are not relevant in the selection of a representative, the representative woman also often finds herself accommodating the behavioral norms and the professional standards of the institution, not challenging them, even if she initially had oppositional ideals.

This individualized concept of representation, initially adopted by feminists, has been refined and more finely tuned by the addition of other "authenticating" characteristics to gender, such as sexuality or race. Perhaps these additions are concessions to the notion of experiences and ideology; however, the basic tenet in this view of representation is still that an individual's possession of a characteristic or set of characteristics is both a necessary and a sufficient indication of "authenticity." The focus continues to be on the characteristics of the individual. The underlying assumption is circular: an individual having the designated characteristic can and does represent members of a community now defined by that characteristic.

This notion of representation currently is used simultaneously to legitimate and to privilege some women's voices. The process of legitimation is accomplished within unchanged institutions which use the representative woman against the radical potential and challenge of a discourse of gendered experience and ideology. The gendered experience, however, is not capable of location within any individual woman. The notion of individual representation facilitates tokenism; furthermore, it can empower an individual woman while it renders her the most effective weapon to silence the interests and voices of the women she is supposed to represent. The individualized mode of representation operates to exclude discordant voices, to prompt the drawing of boundaries and the placing of barriers, and to divide women on the basis of one or some of their potentially shared characteristics. At the same time, the individual-based representation minimizes or ignores the importance of other characteristics that might operate in a more inclusive manner.

Thus, a notion of representation that is dependent on the individual poses serious difficulties. It carries with it not only the potential for divisiveness but also the certainty of exclusion within the hypothetically available community of feminists. Moreover, individual-based representation allows tokenism to flourish and nurtures continued resistance to the radical potential for change through the ideological and structural implications of feminism within institutions.

V. Conclusion

Feminist concerns are, and must continue to be, the subject of discourses located outside of law. Law as a dominant rhetorical system has established concepts that limit and contain feminist criticisms. Feminist theory must develop free of the restraints imposed by legal concepts of equality and neutrality, or it will be defined by them. Law is too crude an instrument to be employed for the development of a theory anchored in an appreciation of differences. Law can and should be the *object* of feminist inquiry, but to position law and law reform as the *objective* of such theorizing is to risk having incompletely developed feminist innovations distorted and appropriated by the institutionalized and intractable dictates of law.

In developing feminist legal theory outside of the constraints of law, we will be free to confront the inevitable tensions that occur in undertaking any theoretical exploration, such as those that arise in any consideration of differences. Both politically and theoretically, feminists should explore the differences between women and men to expose the exclusion of women's experience in law and to reveal the underlying power imbalance this exclusion represents. At the same time, focusing on the differences among women, while of theoretical significance, can and will be used politically to continue and justify exclusion. Feminism as a political, pragmatic methodology must be able to live with this type of tension which, given the current political arena, cannot be avoided. There are different urgencies in considering differences that are dependent upon the contexts in which feminists must operate. Theory that arises from the circumstances in which women find themselves is destined to contain paradoxes.

Race and Essentialism in Feminist Legal Theory

Angela P. Harris*

bein alive & bein a woman & bein colored is a metaphysical dilemma [1]
— ntozake shange

I. INTRODUCTION

A. *Prologue: The Voices in Which We Speak*

1. *Funes the Memorious.*

In *Funes the Memorious*,[2] Borges tells of Ireneo Funes, who was a rather ordinary young man (notable only for his precise sense of time) until the age of nineteen, when he was thrown by a half-tamed horse and left paralyzed but possessed of perfect perception and a perfect memory.

After his transformation, Funes

> knew by heart the forms of the southern clouds at dawn on the 30th of April, 1882, and could compare them in his memory with the mottled streaks on a book in Spanish binding he had only seen once and with the outlines of the foam raised by an oar in the Río Negro the night before the Quebracho uprising. These memories were not simple ones; each visual image was linked to muscular sensations, thermal sensations, etc. He could reconstruct all his dreams, all his half-dreams. Two or three times he had reconstructed a whole day; he never hesitated, but each reconstruction had required a whole day.[3]

---

* Acting Professor, University of California at Berkeley (Boalt Hall). B.A., University of Michigan, Ann Arbor, 1981; M.A., University of Chicago, 1983; J.D., University of Chicago, 1986. An earlier version of this essay was presented at the first annual Conference on Critical Race Theory, sponsored by the University of Wisconsin Institute for Legal Studies, July 7-12, 1989; my indescribable gratitude to all the participants in that conference, but especially to Derrick Bell, Teri Miller, and Ginger Patterson. Thanks also to the many other people who provided insightful comments and criticism, including Herma Hill Kay, Kristin Luker, Robert Post, and Deborah Rhode.

1. NTOZAKE SHANGE, *no more love poems #4,* in FOR COLORED GIRLS WHO HAVE CONSIDERED SUICIDE/WHEN THE RAINBOW IS ENUF 45 (1977) (The poem in part reads, "bein alive & bein a woman & bein colored is a metaphysical dilemma/ i havent conquered yet/ do you see the point/ my spirit is too ancient to understand the separation of soul & gender/ my love is too delicate to have thrown back on my face").

2. JORGE LUIS BORGES, LABYRINTHS: SELECTED STORIES AND OTHER WRITINGS 59 (D. Yates & J. Irby eds. 1964).

3. *Id.* at 63-64.

73

Funes tells the narrator that after his transformation he invented his own numbering system. "In place of seven thousand thirteen, he would say (for example) *Máximo Pérez*; in place of seven thousand fourteen, *The Railroad*; other numbers were Luis Melián Lafinur, Olimar, sulphur, the reins, the whale, the gas, the caldron, Napoleon, Agustín de Vedia."[4] The narrator tries to explain to Funes "that this rhapsody of incoherent terms was precisely the opposite of a system of numbers. I told him that saying 365 meant saying three hundreds, six tens, five ones, an analysis which is not found in the 'numbers' *The Negro Timoteo* or *meat blanket*. Funes did not understand me or refused to understand me."[5]

In his conversation with Funes, the narrator realizes that Funes' life of infinite unique experiences leaves Funes no ability to categorize: "With no effort, he had learned English, French, Portuguese and Latin. I suspect, however, that he was not very capable of thought. To think is to forget differences, generalize, make abstractions. In the teeming world of Funes, there were only details, almost immediate in their presence."[6] For Funes, language is only a unique and private system of classification, elegant and solipsistic. The notion that language, made abstract, can serve to create and reinforce a community is incomprehensible to him.

2. *"We the People."*

Describing the voice that speaks the first sentence of the Declaration of Independence, James Boyd White remarks:

> It is not a person's voice, not even that of a committee, but the "unanimous" voice of "thirteen united States" and of their "people." It addresses a universal audience—nothing less than "mankind" itself, located neither in space nor in time—and the voice is universal too, for it purports to know about the "Course of human events" (all human events?) and to be able to discern what "becomes necessary" as a result of changing circumstances.[7]

The Preamble of the United States Constitution, White argues, can also be heard to speak in this unified and universal voice. This voice claims to speak

> for an entire and united nation and to do so directly and personally, not in the third person or by merely delegated authority. . . . The instrument thus appears to issue from a single imaginary author, consisting of all the people of the United States, including the reader, merged into a single identity in this act of self-constitution. "The People" are at once the author and the audience of this instrument.[8]

---

4. *Id.* at 64.
5. *Id.* at 65.
6. *Id.* at 66.
7. James Boyd White, When Words Lose Their Meaning 232 (1984).
8. *Id.* at 240.

Despite its claims, however, this voice does not speak for everyone, but for a political faction trying to constitute itself as a unit of many disparate voices; its power lasts only as long as the contradictory voices remain silenced.

In a sense, the "I" of Funes, who knows only particulars, and the "we" of "We the People," who know only generalities, are the same. Both voices are monologues; both depend on the silence of others. The difference is only that the first voice knows of no others, while the second has silenced them.

3. *Law and literature.*

The first voice, the voice of Funes, is the voice toward which literature sometimes seems driven. In an essay, Cynthia Ozick describes a comment she once overheard at a party: "For me, the Holocaust and a corncob are the same."[9] Ozick understands this comment to mean that for a writer, all experience is equal. Literature has no moral content, for it exists purely in the domain of the imagination, a place where only aesthetics matter. Thus, a poet may freely replace the Holocaust with a corncob, just as Funes replaces "7013" with *Máximo Pérez*. Poetic language is only a game of words; the poet need not and in fact should not worry about social responsibility. Literary language is purely self-referential.

Law, however, has not been much tempted by the sound of the first voice. Lawyers are all too aware that legal language is not a purely self-referential game, for "legal interpretive acts signal and occasion the imposition of violence upon others."[10] In their concern to avoid the social and moral irresponsibility of the first voice, legal thinkers have veered in the opposite direction, toward the safety of the second voice, which speaks from the position of "objectivity" rather than "subjectivity," "neutrality" rather than "bias." This voice, like the voice of "We the People," is ultimately authoritarian and coercive in its attempt to speak for everyone.[11]

In both law and literature there are theorists who struggle against their discipline's grain. Literary theorists such as Henry Louis Gates, Jr., Gayatri Spivak, and Abdul JanMohamed are attempting to "read specific verbal and visual texts against complex cultural codes of power, assertion, and domination which these texts both reflect and, indeed,

---

9. Cynthia Ozick, *Innovation and Redemption: What Literature Means*, in Art and Ardor 238, 244 (1983).

10. Robert M. Cover, *Violence and the Word*, 95 Yale L.J. 1601, 1601 (1986); *see also* Robert Weisberg, *The Law-Literature Enterprise*, 1 Yale J.L. & Humanities 1, 45 (1988) (describing how students of legal interpretation are initially drawn to literary interpretation because of its greater freedom, and then almost immediately search for a way to reintroduce constraints).

11. *See* Peter Goodrich, *Historical Aspects of Legal Interpretation*, 61 Ind. L.J. 331, 333 (1986) (arguing that legal interpretation is theological in derivation and "unjustifiably authoritarian in its practice").

reinforce."[12] Legal theorists such as Mari Matsuda, Pat Williams, and Derrick Bell juxtapose the voice that "allows theorists to discuss liberty, property, and rights in the aspirational mode of liberalism with no connection to what those concepts mean in real people's lives"[13] with the voices of people whose voices are rarely heard in law. In neither law nor literature, however, is the goal merely to replace one voice with its opposite. Rather, the aim is to understand both legal and literary discourse as the complex struggle and unending dialogue between these voices.

The metaphor of "voice" implies a speaker. I want to suggest, however, that both the voices I have described come from the same source, a source I term "multiple consciousness." It is a premise of this article that we are not born with a "self," but rather are composed of a welter of partial, sometimes contradictory, or even antithetical "selves." A unified identity, if such can ever exist, is a product of will, not a common destiny or natural birthright. Thus, consciousness is "never fixed, never attained once and for all";[14] it is not a final outcome or a biological given, but a process, a constant contradictory state of becoming, in which both social institutions and individual wills are deeply implicated. A multiple consciousness is home both to the first and the second voices, and all the voices in between.

As I use the phrase, "multiple consciousness" as reflected in legal or literary discourse is not a golden mean or static equilibrium between two extremes, but rather a process in which propositions are constantly put forth, challenged, and subverted. Cynthia Ozick argues that "a redemptive literature, a literature that interprets and decodes the world, beaten out for the sake of humanity, must wrestle with its own body, with its own flesh and blood, with its own life."[15] Similarly, Mari Matsuda, while arguing that in the legal realm "[h]olding on to a multiple consciousness will allow us to operate both within the abstractions of standard jurisprudential discourse, *and* within the details of our own special knowledge,"[16] acknowledges that "this constant shifting of consciousness produces sometimes madness, sometimes genius, sometimes both."[17]

---

12. Henry Louis Gates, Jr., *Editor's Introduction: Writing "Race" and the Difference It Makes,* in "RACE," WRITING AND DIFFERENCE 1, 16 (H.L. Gates, Jr. ed. 1986).

13. Mari J. Matsuda, *When the First Quail Calls: Multiple Consciousness as Jurisprudential Method,* 11 WOMEN'S RTS. L. REP. 7, 9 (1989).

14. Teresa de Lauretis, *Feminist Studies/Critical Studies: Issues, Terms, and Contexts,* in FEMINIST STUDIES/CRITICAL STUDIES 1, 8 (T. de Lauretis ed. 1986).

15. C. OZICK, *supra* note 9, at 247.

16. Matsuda, *supra* note 13, at 9.

17. *Id.* at 8.

B. *Race and Essentialism in Feminist Legal Theory*

1. *Methodology.*

In this article, I discuss some of the writings of feminist legal theorists Catharine MacKinnon and Robin West. I argue that their work, though powerful and brilliant in many ways, relies on what I call gender essentialism—the notion that a unitary, "essential" women's experience can be isolated and described independently of race, class, sexual orientation, and other realities of experience. The result of this tendency toward gender essentialism, I argue, is not only that some voices are silenced in order to privilege others (for this is an inevitable result of categorization, which is necessary both for human communication and political movement), but that the voices that are silenced turn out to be the same voices silenced by the mainstream legal voice of "We the People"—among them, the voices of black women.

This result troubles me for two reasons. First, the obvious one: As a black woman, in my opinion the experience of black women is too often ignored both in feminist theory and in legal theory, and gender essentialism in feminist legal theory does nothing to address this problem. A second and less obvious reason for my criticism of gender essentialism is that, in my view, contemporary legal theory needs less abstraction and not simply a different sort of abstraction. To be fully subversive, the methodology of feminist legal theory should challenge not only law's content but its tendency to privilege the abstract and unitary voice, and this gender essentialism also fails to do.

In accordance with my belief that legal theory, including feminist legal theory, is in need of less abstraction, in this article I destabilize and subvert the unity of MacKinnon's and West's "woman" by introducing the voices of black women, especially as represented in literature. Before I begin, however, I want to make three cautionary points to the reader. First, my argument should not be read to accuse either MacKinnon or West of "racism" in the sense of personal antipathy to black people. Both writers are steadfastly anti-racist, which in a sense is my point. Just as law itself, in trying to speak for all persons, ends up silencing those without power, feminist legal theory is in danger of silencing those who have traditionally been kept from speaking, or who have been ignored when they spoke, including black women. The first step toward avoiding this danger is to give up the dream of gender essentialism.

Second, in using a racial critique to attack gender essentialism in feminist legal theory, my aim is not to establish a new essentialism in its place based on the essential experience of black women. Nor should my focus on black women be taken to mean that other women are not silenced either by the mainstream culture or by feminist legal theory. Accordingly, I invite the critique and subversion of my own generalizations.

77

Third and finally, I do not mean in this article to suggest that either feminism or legal theory should adopt the voice of Funes the Memorious, for whom every experience is unique and no categories or generalizations exist at all. Even a jurisprudence based on multiple consciousness must categorize; without categorization each individual is as isolated as Funes, and there can be no moral responsibility or social change. My suggestion is only that we make our categories explicitly tentative, relational, and unstable, and that to do so is all the more important in a discipline like law, where abstraction and "frozen" categories are the norm. Avoiding gender essentialism need not mean that the Holocaust and a corncob are the same.

2. *Feminist legal theory.*

As a Black lesbian feminist comfortable with the many different ingredients of my identity, and a woman committed to racial and sexual freedom from oppression, I find I am constantly being encouraged to pluck out some one aspect of myself and present this as the meaningful whole, eclipsing or denying the other parts of self.[18]

— Audre Lorde

The need for multiple consciousness in feminist movement—a social movement encompassing law, literature, and everything in between—has long been apparent. Since the beginning of the feminist movement in the United States, black women have been arguing that their experience calls into question the notion of a unitary "women's experience."[19] In the first wave of the feminist movement, black women's[20] realization that the white leaders of the suffrage movement intended to take neither issues of racial oppression nor black women themselves seriously was instrumental in destroying or preventing

---

18. AUDRE LORDE, *Age, Race, Class, and Sex: Women Redefining Difference*, in SISTER OUTSIDER 114, 120 (1984).

19. For example, in 1851, Sojourner Truth told the audience at the woman's rights convention in Akron, Ohio:

That man over there says women need to be helped into carriages, and lifted over ditches, and to have the best place everywhere. Nobody ever helps me into carriages, or over mud-puddles, or gives me any best place! And ain't I a woman? Look at me! Look at my arm! I have ploughed, and planted, and gathered into barns, and no man could head me! And ain't I a woman? I could work as much and eat as much as a man—when I could get it—and bear the lash as well! And ain't I a woman? I have borne thirteen children, and seen them most all sold off to slavery, and when I cried out with my mother's grief, none but Jesus heard me! And ain't I a woman?

Address by Sojourner Truth (1851), *reprinted in* BLACK WOMEN IN NINETEENTH-CENTURY AMERICAN LIFE: THEIR WORDS, THEIR THOUGHTS, THEIR FEELINGS 234, 235 (B.J. Loewenberg & R. Bogin eds. 1976).

20. I use "black" rather than "African-American" because some people of color who do not have African heritage and/or are not Americans nevertheless identify themselves as black, and in this essay I am more interested in stressing issues of culture than of nationality or genetics. I use "black" rather than "Black" because it is my contention in this essay that race and gender issues are inextricably intertwined, and to capitalize "Black" and not "Woman" would imply a privileging of race with which I do not agree.

political alliances between black and white women within the movement.[21] In the second wave, black women are again speaking loudly and persistently,[22] and at many levels our voices have begun to be heard. Feminists have adopted the notion of multiple consciousness as appropriate to describe a world in which people are not oppressed only or primarily on the basis of gender, but on the bases of race, class, sexual orientation, and other categories in inextricable webs.[23] Moreover, multiple consciousness is implicit in the precepts of feminism itself. In Christine Littleton's words, "[f]eminist method starts with the very radical act of taking women seriously, believing that what we say about ourselves and our experience is important and valid, even when (or perhaps especially when) it has little or no relationship to what has been or is being said *about* us."[24] If a unitary "women's experience" or "feminism" must be distilled, feminists must ignore many women's voices.[25]

In feminist legal theory, however, the move away from univocal toward multivocal theories of women's experience and feminism has been

---

21. For a discussion of white racism in the suffrage movement, see ANGELA Y. DAVIS, WOMEN, RACE AND CLASS 110-26 (1981); PAULA GIDDINGS, WHEN AND WHERE I ENTER: THE IMPACT OF BLACK WOMEN ON RACE AND SEX IN AMERICA 159-70 (1984). *See also* P. GIDDINGS, *supra*, at 46-55 (white racism in the abolitionist movement).

22. *See, e.g.*, A. DAVIS, *supra* note 21; BELL HOOKS, AIN'T I A WOMAN? BLACK WOMEN AND FEMINISM (1981) [hereinafter B. HOOKS, AIN'T I A WOMAN?]; BELL HOOKS, FEMINIST THEORY: FROM MARGIN TO CENTER (1984) [hereinafter B. HOOKS, FEMINIST THEORY]; BELL HOOKS, TALKING BACK: THINKING FEMINIST, THINKING BLACK (1989) [hereinafter B. HOOKS, TALKING BACK]; GLORIA I. JOSEPH & JILL LEWIS, COMMON DIFFERENCES: CONFLICTS IN BLACK AND WHITE FEMINIST PERSPECTIVES (1981); THIS BRIDGE CALLED MY BACK: WRITINGS BY RADICAL WOMEN OF COLOR (C. Moraga & G. Anzaldúa 2d ed. 1983) [hereinafter THIS BRIDGE CALLED MY BACK]; Hazel V. Carby, *White Woman Listen! Black Feminism and the Boundaries of Sisterhood*, in THE EMPIRE STRIKES BACK: RACE AND RACISM IN 70s BRITAIN 212 (Centre for Contemporary Cultural Studies ed. 1982); Martía C. Lugones & Elizabeth V. Spelman, *Have We Got a Theory for You! Feminist Theory, Cultural Imperialism and the Demand for "The Woman's Voice,"* 6 WOMEN'S STUD. INT'L F. 573 (1983).

23. *See, e.g.*, de Lauretis, *supra* note 14, at 9 (characterizing the feminist identity as "multiple, shifting, and often self-contradictory").

24. Christine A. Littleton, *Feminist Jurisprudence: The Difference Method Makes* (Book Review), 41 STAN. L. REV. 751, 764 (1989). MacKinnon's definition of feminist method is the practice of "believing women's accounts of sexual use and abuse by men." CATHARINE A. MACKINNON, *Introduction: The Art of the Impossible*, in FEMINISM UNMODIFIED 1, 5 (1987). Littleton argues that MacKinnon's major contribution to feminist jurisprudence has been "more methodological than programmatic." Littleton, *supra*, at 753-54. In Littleton's view, "the essence of MacKinnon's view on 'feminisms' comes down to a single choice: feminist method or not." *Id.* at 752-53.

25. *See* Jane Flax, *Postmodernism and Gender Relations in Feminist Theory*, 12 SIGNS 621, 633 (1987):

> [W]ithin feminist theory a search for a defining theme of the whole or a feminist viewpoint may require the suppression of the important and discomforting voices of persons with experiences unlike our own. The suppression of these voices seems to be a necessary condition for the (apparent) authority, coherence, and universality of our own.

Elizabeth Spelman sees this as "the paradox at the heart of feminism: Any attempt to talk about all women in terms of something we have in common undermines attempts to talk about the differences among us, and vice versa." ELIZABETH V. SPELMAN, INESSENTIAL WOMAN: PROBLEMS OF EXCLUSION IN FEMINIST THOUGHT 3 (1988).

slower than in other areas. In feminist legal theory, the pull of the second voice, the voice of abstract categorization, is still powerfully strong: "We the People" seems in danger of being replaced by "We the Women." And in feminist legal theory, as in the dominant culture, it is mostly white, straight, and socioeconomically privileged people who claim to speak for all of us.[26] Not surprisingly, the story they tell about "women," despite its claim to universality, seems to black women to be peculiar to women who are white, straight, and socioeconomically privileged—a phenomenon Adrienne Rich terms "white solipsism."[27]

Elizabeth Spelman notes:

> [T]he real problem has been how feminist theory has confused the condition of one group of women with the condition of all.
>
> . . . A measure of the depth of white middle-class privilege is that the apparently straightforward and logical points and axioms at the heart of much of feminist theory guarantee the direction of its attention to the concerns of white middle-class women.[28]

The notion that there is a monolithic "women's experience" that can be described independent of other facets of experience like race, class, and sexual orientation is one I refer to in this essay as "gender essentialism."[29] A corollary to gender essentialism is "racial essentialism"—the belief that there is a monolithic "Black Experience," or "Chicano Experience." The source of gender and racial essentialism (and all other essentialisms, for the list of categories could be infinitely multiplied) is the second voice, the voice that claims to speak for all. The result of essentialism is to reduce the lives of people who experience multiple forms of oppression to addition problems: "racism + sexism = straight black women's experience," or "racism + sexism + homophobia = black lesbian experience."[30] Thus, in an essentialist

---

26. *See, e.g.,* CATHARINE A. MACKINNON, *On Collaboration,* in FEMINISM UNMODIFIED, *supra* note 24, at 198, 204 ("I am here to speak for those, particularly women and children, upon whose silence the law, including the law of the First Amendment, has been built.").

27. Rich defines white solipsism as the tendency to "think, imagine, and speak as if whiteness described the world." ADRIENNE RICH, *Disloyal to Civilization: Feminism, Racism, Gynephobia,* in ON LIES, SECRETS, AND SILENCE 275, 299 (1979).

28. E. SPELMAN, *supra* note 25, at 4.

29. Elizabeth Spelman lists five propositions which I consider to be associated with gender essentialism:

1. Women can be talked about "as women."
2. Women are oppressed "as women."
3. Gender can be isolated from other elements of identity that bear on one's social, economic, and political position such as race, class, ethnicity; hence sexism can be isolated from racism, classism, etc.
4. Women's situation can be contrasted to men's.
5. Relations between men and women can be compared to relations between other oppressor/oppressed groups (whites and Blacks, Christians and Jews, rich and poor, etc.), and hence it is possible to compare the situation of women to the situation of Blacks, Jews, the poor, etc.

Id. at 165.

30. *See* Deborah K. King, *Multiple Jeopardy, Multiple Consciousness: The Context of a Black Feminist Ideology,* 14 SIGNS 42, 51 (1988) ("To reduce this complex of negotiations to an addi-

world, black women's experience will always be forcibly fragmented before being subjected to analysis, as those who are "only interested in race" and those who are "only interested in gender" take their separate slices of our lives.

Moreover, feminist essentialism paves the way for unconscious racism. Spelman puts it this way:

> [T]hose who produce the "story of woman" want to make sure they appear in it. The best way to ensure that is to be the storyteller and hence to be in a position to decide which of all the many facts about women's lives ought to go into the story, which ought to be left out. Essentialism works well in behalf of these aims, aims that subvert the very process by which women might come to see where and how they wish to make common cause. For essentialism invites me to take what I understand to be true of me "as a woman" for some golden nugget of womanness all women have as women; and it makes the participation of other women inessential to the production of the story. How lovely: the many turn out to be one, and the one that they are is me.[31]

In a racist society like this one, the storytellers are usually white, and so "woman" turns out to be "white woman."

Why, in the face of challenges from "different" women and from feminist method itself, is feminist essentialism so persistent and pervasive? I think the reasons are several. Essentialism is intellectually convenient, and to a certain extent cognitively ingrained. Essentialism also carries with it important emotional and political payoffs. Finally, essentialism often appears (especially to white women) as the only alternative to chaos, mindless pluralism (the Funes trap), and the end of the feminist movement. In my view, however, as long as feminists, like theorists in the dominant culture, continue to search for gender and racial essences, black women will never be anything more than a crossroads between two kinds of domination, or at the bottom of a hierarchy of oppressions; we will always be required to choose pieces of ourselves to present as wholeness.[32]

Part II of this article examines some of Catharine MacKinnon's writings, the ways in which the voices of black women in those works are

---

tion problem (racism + sexism = black women's experience) is to define the issues, and indeed black womanhood itself, within the structural terms developed by Europeans and especially white males to privilege their race and their sex unilaterally."); *see also* E. SPELMAN, *supra* note 25, at 114-32 (chapter entitled "Gender & Race: The Ampersand Problem in Feminist Thought"); Barbara Smith, *Notes for Yet Another Paper on Black Feminism, or Will the Real Enemy Please Stand Up?*, 5 CONDITIONS 123, 123 (1979) (the effect of multiple oppression is "not merely arithmetic").

31. E. SPELMAN, *supra* note 25, at 159.

32. Audre Lorde writes:

> As a Black lesbian feminist comfortable with the many different ingredients of my identity, and a woman committed to racial and sexual freedom from oppression, I find I am constantly being encouraged to pluck out some one aspect of myself and present this as the meaningful whole, eclipsing or denying the other parts of self.

A. LORDE, *supra* note 18, at 120.

suppressed in the name of commonality, and the damage this process does to MacKinnon's analysis of male domination.[33] Part III examines the underpinnings of Robin West's more explicit essentialism and argues that here, as well, the experience of white women is used to define the experience of all women. Part IV discusses some of the reasons why feminist essentialism, despite its violation of feminist method, is so attractive. Part V offers no answers, but suggests that the experience of black women can be important in moving beyond essentialism and toward a jurisprudence of multiple consciousness, and that storytelling is the right way to begin the process.

II. MODIFIED WOMEN AND UNMODIFIED FEMINISM: BLACK WOMEN IN DOMINANCE THEORY[34]

Catharine MacKinnon describes her "dominance theory," like the Marxism with which she likes to compare it, as "total": "[T]hey are both theories of the totality, of the whole thing, theories of a fundamental and critical underpinning of the whole they envision."[35] Both her dominance theory (which she identifies as simply "feminism") and Marxism "focus on that which is most one's own, that which most makes one the being the theory addresses, as that which is most taken away by what the theory criticizes. In each theory you are made who you are by that which is taken away from you by the social relations the theory criticizes."[36] In Marxism, the "that" is work; in feminism, it is sexuality.

MacKinnon defines sexuality as "that social process which creates, organizes, expresses, and directs desire, creating the social beings we know as women and men, as their relations create society."[37] Moreover, "the organized expropriation of the sexuality of some for the use of others defines the sex, woman. Heterosexuality is its structure, gender and family its congealed forms, sex roles its qualities generalized to social persona, reproduction a consequence, and control its issue."[38] Dominance theory, the analysis of this organized expropriation, is a theory of power and its unequal distribution.

In MacKinnon's view, "[t]he idea of gender difference helps keep

---

33. In my discussion I focus on Catharine A. MacKinnon, *Feminism, Marxism, Method, and the State: An Agenda for Theory*, 7 SIGNS 515 (1982) [hereinafter MacKinnon, *Signs I*], and Catharine A. MacKinnon, *Feminism, Marxism, Method, and the State: Toward Feminist Jurisprudence*, 8 SIGNS 635 (1983) [hereinafter MacKinnon, *Signs II*], but I make reference to the essays in C. MACKINNON, FEMINISM UNMODIFIED, *supra* note 24, as well.

34. After this article was nearly finished, I came across Marlee Kline's article, *Race, Racism, and Feminist Legal Theory*, 12 HARV. WOMEN'S L.J. 115 (1989), which contains a similar (and thus, to my mind, remarkably insightful) critique of MacKinnon's work. I recommend Kline's article to all interested in the challenge women of color pose to MacKinnon's theory.

35. C. MACKINNON, *Desire and Power*, in FEMINISM UNMODIFIED, *supra* note 24, at 46, 49.

36. *Id.* at 48.

37. MacKinnon, *Signs I, supra* note 33, at 516 (footnote omitted).

38. *Id.*

the reality of male dominance in place."[39] That is, the concept of gender difference is an ideology which masks the fact that genders are socially constructed, not natural, and coercively enforced, not freely consented-to. Moreover, "the social relation between the sexes is organized so that men may dominate and women must submit and this relation is sexual—in fact, is sex."[40]

For MacKinnon, male dominance is not only "perhaps the most pervasive and tenacious system of power in history, but . . . it is metaphysically nearly perfect."[41] The masculine point of view is point-of-viewlessness; the force of male dominance "is exercised as consent, its authority as participation, its supremacy as the paradigm of order, its control as the definition of legitimacy."[42] In such a world, the very existence of feminism is something of a paradox. "Feminism claims the voice of women's silence, the sexuality of our eroticized desexualization, the fullness of 'lack,' the centrality of our marginality and exclusion, the public nature of privacy, the presence of our absence."[43] The wonder is how feminism can exist in the face of its theoretical impossibility.

In MacKinnon's view, men have their foot on women's necks,[44] regardless of race or class, or of mode of production: "Feminists do not argue that it means the same to women to be on the bottom in a feudal regime, a capitalist regime, and a socialist regime; the commonality argued is that, despite real changes, bottom is bottom."[45] As a political matter, moreover, MacKinnon is quick to insist that there is only one "true," "unmodified" feminism: that which analyzes women *as women*, not as subsets of some other group and not as gender-neutral beings.[46]

Despite its power, MacKinnon's dominance theory is flawed by its essentialism. MacKinnon assumes, as does the dominant culture, that there is an essential "woman" beneath the realities of differences between women[47]—that in describing the experiences of "women" issues

---

39. C. MacKinnon, *supra* note 24, at 3.
40. *Id.* Thus, MacKinnon disagrees both with feminists who argue that women and men are really the same and should therefore be treated the same under the law, and with feminists who argue that the law should take into account women's differences. Feminists who argue that men and women are "the same" fail to take into account the unequal power relations that underlie the very construction of the two genders. Feminists who want the law to recognize the "differences" between the genders buy into the account of women's "natural difference," and therefore (inadvertently) perpetuate dominance under the name of inherent difference. *See id.* at 32-40, 71-77.
41. MacKinnon, *Signs II, supra* note 33, at 638.
42. *Id.* at 639.
43. *Id.*
44. *See* C. MacKinnon, *Difference and Dominance: On Sex Discrimination,* in Feminism Unmodified, *supra* note 24, at 32, 45.
45. MacKinnon, *Signs I, supra* note 33, at 523.
46. *See* C. MacKinnon, *supra* note 24, at 16.
47. Although MacKinnon's explicit position is that until women are free from male domination, we simply don't know what we might be like, as Katharine Bartlett notes, in *Feminism Unmodified* MacKinnon
  speaks of "women's point of view," "woman's voice," woman's "distinctive contribu-

of race, class, and sexual orientation can therefore be safely ignored, or relegated to footnotes.[48] In her search for what is essential womanhood, however, MacKinnon rediscovers white womanhood and introduces it as universal truth. In dominance theory, black women are white women, only more so.

Essentialism in feminist theory has two characteristics that ensure that black women's voices will be ignored. First, in the pursuit of the essential feminine, Woman leached of all color and irrelevant social circumstance, issues of race are bracketed as belonging to a separate and distinct discourse—a process which leaves black women's selves fragmented beyond recognition. Second, feminist essentialists find that in removing issues of "race" they have actually only managed to remove black women—meaning that white women now stand as the epitome of Woman. Both processes can be seen at work in dominance theory.

MacKinnon begins *Signs I* promisingly enough: She says she will render "Black" in upper-case, because she does not regard

> Black as merely a color of skin pigmentation, but as a heritage, an experience, a cultural and personal identity, the meaning of which becomes specifically stigmatic and/or glorious and/or ordinary under specific social conditions. It is as much socially created as, and at least in the American context no less specifically meaningful or definitive than, any linguistic, tribal, or religious ethnicity, all of which are conventionally recognized by capitalization.[49]

By the time she has finished elaborating her theory, however, black women have completely vanished; remaining are only white women with an additional burden.

A. *Dominance Theory and the Bracketing of Race*

MacKinnon repeatedly seems to recognize the inadequacy of theories that deal with gender while ignoring race, but having recognized the problem, she repeatedly shies away from its implications. Thus, she at times justifies her essentialism by pointing to the essentialism of the dominant discourse: "My suggestion is that what we have in common is not that our conditions have no particularity in ways that matter. But we are all measured by a male standard for women, a standard that is not ours."[50] At other times she deals with the challenge of black wo-

---

tion," of standards that are "not ours," of empowering women "on our own terms," and of what we "really want." These references all suggest a reality beyond social construct that women will discover once freed from the bonds of oppression. Katharine T. Bartlett, *MacKinnon's Feminism: Power on Whose Terms?* (Book Review), 75 CALIF. L. REV. 1559, 1566 (1987) (citations omitted).

    48. *See, e.g.,* MacKinnon, *Signs II, supra* note 33, at 639 n.8 ("This feminism seeks to define and pursue women's interest as the fate of all women bound together. It seeks to extract the truth of women's commonalities out of the lie that all women are the same.").

    49. MacKinnon, *Signs I, supra* note 33, at 516 n.*.

    50. C. MACKINNON, *On Exceptionality: Women as Women in Law*, in FEMINISM UNMODIFIED, *supra* note 24, at 70, 76.

men by placing it in footnotes. For example, she places in a footnote without further comment the suggestive, if cryptic, observation that a definition of feminism "of coalesced interest and resistance" has tended both to exclude and to make invisible "the diverse ways that many women—notably Blacks and working-class women—have *moved* against their determinants."[51] In another footnote generally addressed to the problem of relating Marxism to issues of gender and race, she notes that "[a]ny relationship *between* sex and race tends to be left entirely out of account, since they are considered parallel 'strata,' "[52] but this thought simply trails off into a string cite to black feminist and social feminist writings.

Finally, MacKinnon postpones the demand of black women until the arrival of a "general theory of social inequality";[53] recognizing that "gender in this country appears partly to comprise the meaning of, as well as bisect, race and class, even as race and class specificities make up, as well as cross-cut, gender,"[54] she nevertheless is prepared to maintain her "colorblind" approach to women's experience until that general theory arrives (presumably that is someone else's work).

The results of MacKinnon's refusal to move beyond essentialism are apparent in the most tentative essay in *Whose Culture? A Case Note on Martinez v. Santa Clara Pueblo.*[55] Julia Martinez sued her Native American tribe, the Santa Clara Pueblo, in federal court, arguing that a tribal ordinance was invalid under a provision of the Indian Civil Rights Act guaranteeing equal protection of the laws. The ordinance provided that if women married outside the Pueblo, the children of that union were not full tribal members, but if men married outside the tribe, their children were full tribal members. Martinez married a Navajo man, and her children were not allowed to vote or inherit her rights in communal land. The United States Supreme Court held that this question was a matter of Indian sovereignty to be resolved by the tribe.[56]

MacKinnon starts her discussion with an admission: "I find *Martinez* a difficult case on a lot of levels, and I don't usually find cases difficult."[57] She concludes that the Pueblo ordinance was wrong, because it "did nothing to address or counteract the reasons why Native women were vulnerable to white male land imperialism through marriage—it gave in to them, by punishing the *woman*, the Native person."[58] Yet she reaches her conclusion, as she admits, without knowledge other than

---

51. MacKinnon, *Signs I, supra* note 33, at 518 & n.3.
52. *Id.* at 537 n.54.
53. C. MACKINNON, *supra* note 24, at 3.
54. *Id.* at 2.
55. C. MACKINNON, *Whose Culture? A Case Note on Martinez v. Santa Clara Pueblo,* in FEMINISM UNMODIFIED, *supra* note 24, at 63.
56. Santa Clara Pueblo v. Martinez, 436 U.S. 49, 71-72 (1978).
57. C. MACKINNON, *supra* note 55, at 66.
58. *Id.* at 68.

"word of mouth" of the history of the ordinance and its place in Santa Clara Pueblo culture.

MacKinnon has Julia Martinez ask her tribe, "Why do you make me choose between my equality as woman and my cultural identity?"[59] But she, no less than the tribe, eventually requires Martinez to choose; and the correct choice is, of course, that Martinez's female identity is more important than her tribal identity. MacKinnon states,

> [T]he aspiration of women to be no less than men—not to be punished where a man is glorified, not to be considered damaged or disloyal where a man is rewarded or left in peace, not to lead a derivative life, but to do everything and be anybody at all—is an aspiration indigenous to women across place and across time.[60]

What MacKinnon does not recognize, however, is that though the aspiration may be everywhere the same, its expression must depend on the social historical circumstances. In this case, should Julia Martinez be content with struggling for change from within,[61] or should the white government have stepped in "on her behalf"? What was the meaning of the ordinance within Pueblo discourse, as opposed to a transhistorical and transcultural feminist discourse? How did it come about and under what circumstances? What was the status of women within the tribe, both historically and at the time of the ordinance and at the present time, and was Martinez's claim heard and understood by the tribal authorities or simply ignored or derided? What were the Pueblo traditions about children of mixed parentage,[62] and how were those traditions changing? In a jurisprudence based on multiple consciousness, rather than the unitary consciousness of MacKinnon's dominance theory, these questions would have to be answered before the ordinance could be considered on its merits and even before the Court's decision to stay out could be evaluated.[63] MacKinnon does not answer these questions, but leaves the essay hanging with the idea that the male supremacist ideology of some Native American tribes may be adopted from white culture and therefore invalid.[64] MacKinnon's tentativeness may be due to not wanting to appear a white cultural imperialist, speaking for a Native American tribe, but to take up Julia Martinez's claim at all is to take that risk. Without a theory that can shift focus from gender to race and other facets of identity and back again, MacKinnon's essay is ultimately crippled. Martinez is made to choose her gender over her race, and her experience is distorted in the

---

59. *Id.* at 67.

60. *Id.* at 68.

61. As she did. *See* Martinez v. Santa Clara Pueblo, 402 F. Supp. 5, 11 (D.N.M. 1975), *rev'd*, 540 F.2d 1039 (10th Cir. 1976), *rev'd*, 436 U.S. 49 (1978).

62. The district court hints that such questions were decided on a case-by-case basis. *Id.* at 16. Why was an ordinance thought necessary?

63. In her article *Dependent Sovereigns: Indian Tribes, States, and the Federal Courts*, 56 U. CHI. L. REV. 671 (1989), Judith Resnik begins to address some of these issues.

64. C. MACKINNON, *supra* note 55, at 69.

process.[65]

B. *Dominance Theory and White Women as All Women*

The second consequence of feminist essentialism is that the racism that was acknowledged only in brackets quietly emerges in the feminist theory itself—both a cause and an effect of creating "Woman" from white woman. In MacKinnon's work, the result is that black women become white women only more so.

In a passage in *Signs I*, MacKinnon borrows a quote from Toni Cade Bambara describing a black woman with too many children and no means with which to care for them as "grown ugly and dangerous from being nobody for so long," and then explains:

> By using her phrase in altered context, I do not want to distort her meaning but to extend it. Throughout this essay, I have tried to see if women's condition is shared, even when contexts or magnitudes differ. (Thus, it is very different to be "nobody" as a Black woman than as a white lady, but neither is "somebody" by male standards.) This is the approach to race and ethnicity attempted throughout. I aspire to include all women in the term "women" in some way, without violating the particularity of any woman's experience. Whenever this fails, the statement is simply wrong and will have to be qualified or the aspiration (or the theory) abandoned.[66]

I call this the "nuance theory" approach to the problem of essentialism[67]: by being sensitive to the notion that different women have different experiences, generalizations can be offered about "all women" while qualifying statements, often in footnotes, supplement the general account with the subtle nuances of experience that "different" women add to the mix. Nuance theory thus assumes the commonality of all women—differences are a matter of "context" or "magnitude"; that is, nuance.

The problem with nuance theory is that by defining black women as "different," white women quietly become the norm, or pure, essential woman.[68] Just as MacKinnon would argue that being female is more than a "context" or a "magnitude" of human experience,[69] being black

---

65. Elsewhere, MacKinnon explicitly asserts that gender oppression is more significant than racial oppression. *See* C. MACKINNON, *Francis Biddle's Sister: Pornography, Civil Rights, and Speech,* in FEMINISM UNMODIFIED, *supra* note 24, at 163, 166-68.

66. MacKinnon, *Signs I, supra* note 33, at 520 n.7.

67. The reference is to an article in *Newsweek* called *Feminism: "The Black Nuance,"* NEWSWEEK, Dec. 17, 1973, at 89-90; *cf.* E. SPELMAN, *supra* note 25, at 114-15 (describing article in the *New York Times* in which the women are white and the blacks are men).

68. MacKinnon recognizes a similar process in Marxism, whereby gender oppression becomes merely a variant form of class oppression. *See* MacKinnon, *Signs I, supra* note 33, at 524-27. What MacKinnon misses is that her own theory reduces racial oppression to a mere intensifier of gender oppression.

69. *See, e.g.,* C. MACKINNON, *supra* note 65, at 169 ("Defining feminism in a way that connects epistemology with power as the politics of women's point of view, [the discovery of

is more than a context or magnitude of all (white) women's experience. But not in dominance theory.

For instance, MacKinnon describes how a system of male supremacy has constructed "woman":

> Contemporary industrial society's version of her is docile, soft, passive, nurturant, vulnerable, weak, narcissistic, childlike, incompetent, masochistic, and domestic, made for child care, home care, and husband care. . . . Women who resist or fail, including those who never did fit— for example, black and lower-class women who cannot survive if they are soft and weak and incompetent, assertively self-respecting women, women with ambitions of male dimensions—are considered less female, lesser women.[70]

In a peculiar symmetry with this ideology, in which black women are something less than women, in MacKinnon's work black women become something more than women. In MacKinnon's writing, the word "black," applied to women, is an intensifier: If things are bad for everybody (meaning white women), then they're even worse for black women. Silent and suffering, we are trotted onto the page (mostly in footnotes) as the ultimate example of how bad things are.[71]

Thus, in speaking of the beauty standards set for (white) women, MacKinnon remarks, "Black women are further from being able concretely to achieve the standard that no woman can ever achieve, or it would lose its point."[72] The frustration of black women at being unable to look like an "All-American" woman is in this way just a more dramatic example of all (white) women's frustration and oppression. When a black woman speaks on this subject, however, it becomes clear that a black woman's pain at not being considered fully feminine is different qualitatively, not merely quantitatively, from the pain MacKinnon describes. It is qualitatively different because the ideology of beauty concerns not only gender but race. Consider Toni Morrison's

---

feminism] can be summed up by saying that women live in another world: specifically, a world of *not* equality, a world of inequality.").

70. MacKinnon, *Signs I, supra* note 33, at 530. Yet, having acknowledged that black women have never been "women," MacKinnon continues in the article to discuss "women," making it plain that the "women" she is discussing are white.

71. Applied to men, however, the word "black" ameliorates: MacKinnon concedes that black men are not quite as bad as white men, although they are still bad, being men. For instance, in a footnote she qualifies her statement that "*[P]ower to create the world from one's point of view is power in its male form,*" *id.* at 537, with the recognition that black men have "less" power: "But to the extent that they cannot create the world from their point of view, they find themselves unmanned, castrated, literally or figuratively." *Id.* at 537 n.54. The last clause of this statement appears, puzzlingly, to be a reference to lynching; but it was not for *failing* to create the world but for the more radical sin of *making the attempt* that black men were "literally castrated."

72. *Id.* at 540 n.59. Similarly, in *Feminism Unmodified*, MacKinnon reminds us that the risk of death and mutilation in the course of a botched abortion is disproportionately borne by women of color, C. MacKinnon, *Not by Law Alone: From a Debate with Phyllis Schlafly*, in Feminism Unmodified, *supra* note 24, at 21, 25, but only in the context of asserting that "[n]one of us can afford this risk," *id.*

analysis of the influence of standards of white beauty on black people in *The Bluest Eye*.[73] Claudia MacTeer, a young black girl, muses, "Adults, older girls, shops, magazines, newspapers, window signs—all the world had agreed that a blue-eyed, yellow-haired, pink-skinned doll was what every girl child treasured."[74] Similarly, in the black community, "high yellow" folks represent the closest black people can come to beauty, and darker people are always "lesser. Nicer, brighter, but still lesser."[75] Beauty is whiteness itself; and middle-class black girls

> go to land-grant colleges, normal schools, and learn how to do the white man's work with refinement: home economics to prepare his food; teacher education to instruct black children in obedience; music to soothe the weary master and entertain his blunted soul. Here they learn the rest of the lesson begun in those soft houses with porch swings and pots of bleeding heart: how to behave. The careful development of thrift, patience, high morals, and good manners. In short, how to get rid of the funkiness. The dreadful funkiness of passion, the funkiness of nature, the funkiness of the wide range of human emotions.
>
> Wherever it erupts, this Funk, they wipe it away; where it crusts, they dissolve it; wherever it drips, flowers, or clings, they find it and fight it until it dies. They fight this battle all the way to the grave. The laugh that is a little too loud; the enunciation a little too round; the gesture a little too generous. They hold their behind in for fear of a sway too free; when they wear lipstick, they never cover the entire mouth for fear of lips too thick, and they worry, worry, worry about the edges of their hair.[76]

Thus, Pecola Breedlove, born black and ugly, spends her lonely and abused childhood praying for blue eyes.[77] Her story ends in despair and the fragmentation of her mind into two isolated speaking voices, not because she's even further away from ideal beauty than white women are, but because Beauty *itself* is white, and she is not and can never be, despite the pair of blue eyes she eventually believes she has. There is a difference between the hope that the next makeup kit or haircut or diet will bring you salvation and the knowledge that nothing can. The relation of black women to the ideal of white beauty is not a more intense form of white women's frustration: It is something other, a com-

---

73. TONI MORRISON, THE BLUEST EYE (1970).
74. *Id.* at 14.
75. *Id.* at 57.
76. *Id.* at 64.
77.
It had occurred to Pecola some time ago that if her eyes, those eyes that held the pictures, and knew the sights—if those eyes of hers were different, that is to say, beautiful, she herself would be different. Her teeth were good, and at least her nose was not big and flat like some of those who were thought so cute. If she looked different, beautiful, maybe [her father] would be different, and Mrs. Breedlove too. Maybe they'd say, "Why, look at pretty-eyed Pecola. We mustn't do bad things in front of those pretty eyes."
Id. at 34.

plex mingling of racial and gender hatred from without, self-hatred from within.

MacKinnon's essentialist, "color-blind" approach also distorts the analysis of rape that constitutes the heart of *Signs II*. By ignoring the voices of black female theoreticians of rape, she produces an ahistorical account that fails to capture the experience of black women.

MacKinnon sees sexuality as "a social sphere of male power of which forced sex is paradigmatic."[78] As with beauty standards, black women are victimized by rape just like white women, only more so: "Racism in the United States, by singling out Black men for allegations of rape of white women, has helped obscure the fact that it is men who rape women, disproportionately women of color."[79] In this peculiar fashion MacKinnon simultaneously recognizes and shelves racism, finally reaffirming that the divide between men and women is more fundamental and that women of color are simply "women plus." MacKinnon goes on to develop a powerful analysis of rape as the subordination of women to men, with only one more mention of color: "[R]ape comes to mean a strange (read Black) man knowing a woman does not want sex and going ahead anyway."[80]

This analysis, though rhetorically powerful, is an analysis of what rape means to white women masquerading as a general account; it has nothing to do with the experience of black women.[81] For black women, rape is a far more complex experience, and an experience as deeply rooted in color as in gender.

For example, the paradigm experience of rape for black women has historically involved the white employer in the kitchen or bedroom as much as the strange black man in the bushes. During slavery, the sexual abuse of black women by white men was commonplace.[82] Even af-

---

78. MacKinnon, *Signs II, supra* note 33, at 646.

79. *Id.* at 646 n.22; *see also* C. MACKINNON, *A Rally Against Rape*, in FEMINISM UNMODIFIED, *supra* note 24, at 81, 82 (black women are raped four times as often as white women); DIANA RUSSELL, SEXUAL EXPLOITATION 185 (1984) (black women, who comprise 10% of all women, accounted for 60% of rapes reported in 1967).

Describing SUSAN BROWNMILLER, AGAINST OUR WILL: MEN, WOMEN AND RAPE (1976), MacKinnon writes, "Brownmiller examines rape in riots, wars, pogroms, and revolutions; rape by police, parents, prison guards; and rape motivated by racism—seldom rape in normal circumstances, in everyday life, in ordinary relationships, by men as men." MacKinnon, *Signs II, supra* note 33, at 646.

80. MacKinnon, *Signs II, supra* note 33, at 653; *cf.* SUSAN ESTRICH, REAL RAPE 3 (1987) (remarking, while telling the story of her own rape, "His being black, I fear, probably makes my account more believable to some people, as it certainly did with the police."). Indeed, Estrich hastens to assure us, though, that "the most important thing is that he was a stranger." *Id.*

81. *See* ALICE WALKER, *Advancing Luna—and Ida B. Wells*, in YOU CAN'T KEEP A GOOD WOMAN DOWN 93 (1981) ("Who knows what the black woman thinks of rape? Who has asked her? Who *cares*?").

82. As Barbara Omolade notes:
To [the white slave holder the black woman slave] was a fragmented commodity whose feelings and choices were rarely considered: her head and her heart were separated from her back and her hands and divided from her womb and vagina. Her

ter emancipation, the majority of working black women were domestic servants for white families, a job which made them uniquely vulnerable to sexual harassment and rape.[83]

Moreover, as a legal matter, the experience of rape did not even exist for black women. During slavery, the rape of a black woman by any man, white or black, was simply not a crime.[84] Even after the Civil War, rape laws were seldom used to protect black women against either white or black men, since black women were considered promiscuous by nature.[85] In contrast to the partial or at least formal protection white women had against sexual brutalization, black women frequently had no legal protection whatsoever. "Rape," in this sense, was something that only happened to white women; what happened to black women was simply life.

Finally, for black people, male and female, "rape" signified the terrorism of black men by white men, aided and abetted, passively (by silence) or actively (by "crying rape"), by white women. Black women have recognized this aspect of rape since the nineteenth century. For example, social activist Ida B. Wells analyzed rape as an example of the

---

back and muscle were pressed into field labor where she was forced to work with men and work like men. Her hands were demanded to nurse and nurture the white man and his family as domestic servant whether she was technically enslaved or legally free. Her vagina, used for his sexual pleasure, was the gateway to the womb, which was his place of capital investment—the capital investment being the sex act and the resulting child the accumulated surplus, worth money on the slave market.
Barbara Omolade, *Hearts of Darkness*, in POWERS OF DESIRE: THE POLITICS OF SEXUALITY 354 (A. Snitow, C. Stansell & S. Thompson eds. 1983).

    83. *See* JACQUELINE JONES, LABOR OF LOVE, LABOR OF SORROW 150 (1985). In *Beloved*, Toni Morrison tells the story of Ella, whose "puberty was spent in a house where she was shared by father and son, whom she called 'the lowest yet.'" It was 'the lowest yet' who gave her a disgust for sex and against whom she measured all atrocities." TONI MORRISON, BE-LOVED 256 (1987). Ella knew "[t]hat anybody white could take your whole self for anything that came to mind. Not just work, kill, or maim you, but dirty you. Dirty you so bad you couldn't like yourself anymore. Dirty you so bad you forgot who you were and couldn't think it up." *Id.* at 251. Sethe, one of the protagonists in *Beloved*, kills her own baby daughter rather than relinquish her to such a life. *Cf.* Omolade, *supra* note 82, at 355 (" 'Testimony seems to be quite widespread to the fact that many if not most southern boys begin their sexual experiences with Negro girls.' " (quoting JOHN DOLLARD, CASTE AND CLASS IN A SOUTHERN TOWN 139 (rev. ed. 1949))).

    84. *See* Jennifer Wriggins, *Rape, Racism, and the Law*, 6 HARV. WOMEN'S L.J. 103, 118 (1983).

    85. Susan Estrich gives an example: When a black man raped a white woman, the death penalty was held to be justified by the Virginia Supreme Court; but when a black man raped a black woman, his conviction was reversed, on the grounds that the defendant's behavior, "though extremely reprehensible, and deserving of punishment, does not involve him in the crime which this statute was designed to punish." Christian v. Commonwealth, 64 Va. (23 Gratt.) 954, 959 (1873), *quoted in* S. ESTRICH, *supra* note 80, at 35-36. On the intertwining of gender and race oppression in the law of rape and its connection to lynching, see Jacquelyn Dowd Hall, *"The Mind that Burns in Each Body": Women, Rape, and Racial Violence*, in POWERS OF DESIRE: THE POLITICS OF SEXUALITY, *supra* note 82, at 328; Wriggins, *supra* note 84, at 103. On the intertwining of gender and race oppression in the miscegenation laws, see Karen A. Getman, *Sexual Control in the Slaveholding South: The Implementation and Maintenance of a Racial Caste System*, 7 HARV. WOMEN'S L.J. 115 (1984). *See generally* Paul A. Lombardo, *Miscegenation, Eugenics, and Racism: Historical Footnotes to* Loving v. Virginia, 21 U.C. DAVIS L. REV. 421 (1988).

inseparability of race and gender oppression in *Southern Horrors: Lynch Law in All Its Phases*, published in 1892. Wells saw that both the law of rape and Southern miscegenation laws were part of a patriarchal system through which white men maintained their control over the bodies of all black people: "[W]hite men used their ownership of the body of the white female as a terrain on which to lynch the black male."[86] Moreover, Wells argued, though many white women encouraged interracial sexual relationships, white women, protected by the patriarchal idealization of white womanhood, were able to remain silent, unhappily or not, as black men were murdered by mobs.[87] Similarly, Anna Julia Cooper, another nineteenth-century theorist, "saw that the manipulative power of the South was embodied in the southern patriarch, but she describes its concern with 'blood,' inheritance, and heritage in entirely female terms and as a preoccupation that was transmitted from the South to the North and perpetuated by white women."[88]

Nor has this aspect of rape become purely a historical curiosity. Susan Estrich reports that between 1930 and 1967, 89 percent of the men executed for rape in the United States were black;[89] a 1968 study of rape sentencing in Maryland showed that in all 55 cases where the death penalty was imposed the victim had been white, and that between 1960 and 1967, 47 percent of all black men convicted of criminal assaults on black women were immediately released on probation.[90] The case of Joann Little is testimony to the continuing sensitivity of black women to this aspect of rape. As Angela Davis tells the story:

> Brought to trial on murder charges, the young Black woman was accused of killing a white guard in a North Carolina jail where she was the

---

86. Hazel V. Carby, *"On the Threshold of Woman's Era": Lynching, Empire, and Sexuality in Black Feminist Theory*, in "RACE," WRITING, AND DIFFERENCE, *supra* note 12, at 301, 309.

87. Carby notes, "Those that remained silent while disapproving of lynching were condemned by Wells for being as guilty as the actual perpetrators of lynching." *Id.* at 308.

Of course, courageous white women have spoken out against lynching and even about the white women's complicity in its occurrence by choosing to remain silent. *See* A. DAVIS, *supra* note 21, at 194-96; Hall, *supra* note 85, at 337-40 (discussing the work of Jessie Daniel Ames and the Association of Southern Women for the Prevention of Lynching in the 1930s). However, as Davis also points out, such forms of intervention were sadly belated. A. DAVIS, *supra* note 21, at 195.

88. Carby, *supra* note 86, at 306 (discussing Anna Julia Cooper, *A Voice from the South* (1892)). Carby continues:

> By linking imperialism to internal colonization, Cooper thus provided black women intellectuals with the basis for an analysis of how patriarchal power establishes and sustains gendered and racialized social formations. White women were implicated in the maintenance of this wider system of oppression because they challenged only the parameters of their domestic confinement; by failing to reconstitute their class and caste interests, they reinforced the provincialism of their movement.

Id. at 306-07.

89. S. ESTRICH, *supra* note 80, at 107 n.2.

90. Wriggins, *supra* note 84, at 121 n.113. According to the study, "the average sentence received by Black men, exclusive of cases involving life imprisonment or death, was 4.2 years if the victim was Black, 16.4 years if the victim was white." *Id.* I do not know whether a white man has ever been sentenced to death for the rape of a black woman, although I could make an educated guess as to the answer.

only woman inmate. When Joann Little took the stand, she told how the guard had raped her in her cell and how she had killed him in self-defense with the ice pick he had used to threaten her. Throughout the country, her cause was passionately supported by individuals and organizations in the Black community and within the young women's movement, and her acquittal was hailed as an important victory made possible by this mass campaign. In the immediate aftermath of her acquittal, Ms. Little issued several moving appeals on behalf of a Black man named Delbert Tibbs, who awaited execution in Florida because he had been falsely convicted of raping a white woman.

Many Black women answered Joann Little's appeal to support the cause of Delbert Tibbs. But few white women—and certainly few organized groups within the anti-rape movement—followed her suggestion that they agitate for the freedom of this Black man who had been blatantly victimized by Southern racism.[91]

The rift between white and black women over the issue of rape is highlighted by the contemporary feminist analyses of rape that have explicitly relied on racist ideology to minimize white women's complicity in racial terrorism.[92]

Thus, the experience of rape for black women includes not only a vulnerability to rape and a lack of legal protection radically different from that experienced by white women, but also a unique ambivalence. Black women have simultaneously acknowledged their own victimization and the victimization of black men by a system that has consistently ignored violence against women while perpetrating it against men.[93] The complexity and depth of this experience is not captured, or even acknowledged, by MacKinnon's account.

MacKinnon's essentialist approach recreates the paradigmatic woman in the image of the white woman, in the name of "unmodified feminism." As in the dominant discourse, black women are relegated to the margins, ignored or extolled as "just like us, only more so." But "Black women are not white women with color."[94] Moreover, feminist essentialism represents not just an insult to black women, but a broken promise—the promise to listen to women's stories, the promise of feminist method.

---

91. A. DAVIS, *supra* note 21, at 174.

92. For example, Susan Brownmiller describes the black defendants in publicized Southern rape trials as "pathetic, semiliterate fellows," S. BROWNMILLER, *supra* note 79, at 237, and the white female accusers as innocent pawns of white men, *see, e.g., id.* at 233 ("confused and fearful, they fell into line"). *See also* A. DAVIS, *supra* note 21, at 196-99.

93. *See* Carby, *supra* note 86, at 307 (citing Ida B. Wells, *Southern Horrors*, (1892), *reprinted in* IDA B. WELLS, ON LYNCHINGS 5-6 (1969)) (miscegenation laws, directed at preventing sexual relations between white women and black men, "pretended to offer 'protection' to white women but left black women the victims of rape by white men and simultaneously granted to these same men the power to terrorize black men as a potential threat to the virtue of white womanhood").

94. Barbara Omolade, *Black Women and Feminism*, in THE FUTURE OF DIFFERENCE 247, 248 (H. Eisenstein & A. Jardine eds. 1980).

III. ROBIN WEST'S "ESSENTIAL WOMAN"

While MacKinnon's essentialism is pervasive but covert, Robin West expressly declares her essentialism. In the last section of *The Difference in Women's Hedonic Lives: A Phenomenological Critique of Feminist Legal Theory*,[95] West argues:

> Both the liberal and the radical legalist have accepted the Kantian assumption that *to be human* is to be in some sense autonomous—meaning, minimally, to be differentiated, or individuated, from the rest of social life.
>
> Underlying and underscoring the poor fit between the proxies for subjective well-being endorsed by liberals and radicals—choice and power—and women's subjective, hedonic lives is the simple fact that women's lives—*because of our biological, reproductive role*—are drastically at odds with this fundamental vision of human life. Women's lives are *not* autonomous, they are profoundly relational.[96]

In West's view, women are ontologically distinct from men, because "Women, and *only* women, and *most* women, transcend *physically* the differentiation or individuation of biological self from the rest of human life trumpeted as the norm by the entire Kantian tradition."[97] That is, because only women can bear children, and because women have the social responsibility for raising children, our selves are profoundly different from male selves. "To the considerable degree that our potentiality for motherhood defines ourselves, women's lives are relational, not autonomous. As mothers we nurture the weak and we depend upon the strong. More than do men, we live in an interdependent and hierarchical natural web with others of varying degrees of strength."[98]

This claim about women's essential connectedness to the world becomes the centerpiece of *Jurisprudence and Gender*.[99] West begins the article with the question, "What is a human being?" She then asserts that "perhaps the central insight of feminist theory of the last decade has been that wom[e]n are 'essentially connected,' not 'essentially separate,' from the rest of human life, both materially, through pregnancy, intercourse, and breast-feeding, and existentially, through the moral and practical life."[100] For West, this means that "all of our modern legal theory—by which I mean 'liberal legalism' and 'critical legal theory' collectively—is essentially and irretrievably masculine."[101] This is

---

95. 3 WIS. WOMEN'S L.J. 81 (1987).
96. *Id.* at 140.
97. *Id.*
98. *Id.* at 141.
99. 55 U. CHI. L. REV. 1 (1988).
100. *Id.* at 3. West further posits a "fundamental contradiction" in women's experience equivalent to the "fundamental contradiction" posited by some critical legal scholars between autonomy and connection; whereas men experience a fundamental contradiction between autonomy and connection, women experience a fundamental contradiction between invasion and intimacy. *See id.* at 53-58.
101. *Id.* at 2.

so because modern legal theory relies on the "separation thesis," the claim that human beings are distinct individuals first and form relationships later.[102]

Black women are entirely absent from West's work, in contrast to MacKinnon's; issues of race do not appear even in guilty footnotes. However, just as in MacKinnon's work, the bracketing of issues of race leads to the installation of white women on the throne of essential womanhood.

West's claims are clearly questionable on their face insofar as the experience of some women—"mothers"—is asserted to stand for the experience of all women. As with MacKinnon's theory, West's theory necessitates the stilling of some voices—namely, the voices of women who have rejected their "biological, reproductive role"—in order to privilege others. One might also question the degree to which motherhood, or our potential for it, defines us.[103] For purposes of this article, however, I am more interested in the conception of self that underlies West's account of "women's experience."

West argues that the biological and social implications of motherhood shape the selfhood of all, or at least most, women. This claim involves at least two assumptions.[104] First, West assumes (as does the liberal social theory she criticizes) that everyone has a deep, unitary "self" that is relatively stable and unchanging. Second, West assumes that this "self" differs significantly between men and women but is the same for all women and for all men despite differences of class, race, and sexual orientation: that is, that this self is deeply and primarily gendered. In a later part of the article, I will argue that black women can bring the experience of a multiple rather than a unitary self to feminist theory.[105] Here I want to argue that the notion that the gender difference is primary to an individual's selfhood is one that privileges white women's experience over the experience of black women.

---

102. *Id.*

103. The danger of such a theory is that, like some French feminist scholarship, it threatens to reembrace the old belief, used against women for so long, that anatomy is destiny:

A good deal of French feminist scholarship has been concerned with specifying the nature of the feminine . . . . This principle of femininity is sought in the female body, sometimes understood as the pre-oedipal mother and other times understood naturalistically as a pantheistic principle that requires its own kind of language for expression. In these cases, gender is not constituted, but is considered an essential aspect of bodily life, and we come very near the equation of biology and destiny, that conflation of fact and value, which Beauvoir spent her life trying to refute.

Judith Butler, *Variations on Sex and Gender: Beauvoir, Wittig and Foucault,* in FEMINISM AS CRITIQUE: ESSAYS ON THE POLITICS OF GENDER 128, 140 (S. Benhabib & D. Cornell eds. 1987).

Curiously, MacKinnon's dominance theory, which claims to be "total," says very little about motherhood at all. *See* Littleton, *supra* note 24, at 762 n.54.

104. I have taken this analysis from Nancy Fraser and Linda Nicholson's analysis of Nancy Chodorow's work. Nancy Fraser & Linda Nicholson, *Social Criticism Without Philosophy: An Encounter Between Feminism and Postmodernism,* in UNIVERSAL ABANDON? THE POLITICS OF POSTMODERNISM 83, 96 (A. Ross ed. 1988). *See generally* NANCY CHODOROW, THE REPRODUCTION OF MOTHERING: PSYCHOANALYSIS AND THE SOCIOLOGY OF GENDER (1978).

105. *See* text accompanying notes 125-135 *infra.*

The essays and poems in *This Bridge Called My Back* [106] describe experiences of women of color that differ radically from one another. Some contributors are Lesbians; some are straight; some are class-privileged, and others are not. What links all the writings, however, is the sense that the self of a woman of color is not primarily a female self or a colored self, but a both-and self. In her essay "Brownness," [107] Andrea Canaan describes both-and experience:

> The fact is I am brown and female, and my growth and development are tied to the entire community. I must nurture and develop brown self, woman, man, and child. I must address the issues of my own oppression and survival. When I separate them, isolate them, and ignore them, I separate, isolate, and ignore myself. I am a unit. A part of brownness. [108]

A personal story may also help to illustrate the point. At a 1988 meeting of the West Coast "fem-crits," Pat Cain and Trina Grillo asked all the women present to pick out two or three words to describe who they were. None of the white women mentioned their race; all of the women of color did.

In this society, it is only white people who have the luxury of "having no color"; only white people have been able to imagine that sexism and racism are separate experiences. [109] Far more for black women than for white women, the experience of self is precisely that of being unable to disentangle the web of race and gender—of being enmeshed always in multiple, often contradictory, discourses of sexuality and color. The challenge to black women has been the need to weave the fragments, our many selves, into an integral, though always changing and shifting, whole: a self that is neither "female" nor "black," but both-and. [110] West's insistence that every self is deeply and primarily gendered, then, with its corollary that gender is more important to personal identity than race, is finally another example of white solipsism. By suggesting that gender is more deeply embedded in self than race, her theory privileges the experience of white people over all others, [111]

---

106. THIS BRIDGE CALLED MY BACK, *supra* note 22.
107. *Id.* at 232.
108. *Id.* at 234.
109. *Cf.* E. SPELMAN, *supra* note 25, at 167 (describing the phrase "as a woman" as "the Trojan horse of feminist ethnocentrism, for its use typically makes it look as if one can neatly isolate one's gender from one's race or class").
110. *See, e.g.,* ZORA NEALE HURSTON, THEIR EYES WERE WATCHING GOD (1937) (protagonist, Janie, slowly creates herself out of the oppressions of gender and race); TONI MORRISON, SONG OF SOLOMON (1977) (one of the strongest characters is a woman with no navel—a woman who has literally created herself); N. SHANGE, *supra* note 1, at 31, 34 (the "lady in red" daily creates herself as a bold, wild, sexy woman, then, in the morning, sends the man she's attracted home and becomes an "ordinary/ brown braided woman/ with big legs & full lips/ reglar"); ALICE WALKER, THE COLOR PURPLE (1982) (two sisters, Celie and Nettie, construct healthy selves out of the potentially killing circumstance of being abused young black girls from a "broken home").
111. Feminist essentialism also strengthens the wall between the genders. The binary character of essentialism tends to make men into enemies, rather than beings who are also

and thus serves to reproduce relations of domination in the larger culture.[112] Like MacKinnon's essential woman, West's essential woman turns out to be white.

IV. THE ATTRACTIONS OF GENDER ESSENTIALISM

Strategies become institutions.[113]

— Cynthia Ozick

If gender essentialism is such a terrible thing, why do two smart and politically committed feminists like Catharine MacKinnon and Robin West rely on it? In this section I want to briefly sketch some of the attractions of essentialism.

First, as a matter of intellectual convenience, essentialism is easy. Particularly for white feminists—and most of the people doing academic feminist theory in this country at this time are white—essentialism means not having to do as much work, not having to try and learn about the lives of black women, with all the risks and discomfort that that effort entails.[114] Essentialism is also intellectually easy because the dominant culture is essentialist—because it is difficult to find materials on the lives of black women, because there is as yet no academic infrastructure of work by and/or about black women or black feminist theory.[115]

Second, and more important, essentialism represents emotional safety. Especially for women who have relinquished privilege or had it taken away from them in their struggle against gender oppression, the feminist movement comes to be an emotional and spiritual home, a place to feel safe, a place that must be kept harmonious and free of difference. In an essay, Minnie Bruce Pratt describes her early involvement in the women's movement after having lost her children in a cus-

---

crippled by the dominant discourse, though in different ways. Compare this to Joan C. Williams's view in *Deconstructing Gender*, 87 MICH. L. REV. 797, 841 (1989) ("To break free of traditional gender ideology, we need at the simplest level to see how men nurture people and relationships and how women are competitive and powerful.").

112. In this sense, my point about feminist essentialism is analogous to the point Joan Williams has made about the ideology of domesticity, a Victorian notion that some feminists have used to argue that women are "'more nurturing than men ('focused on relationships'), less tied to the questionable virtues of capitalism, and ultimately more moral than men." *Id.* at 807 (Note the resemblance to West's picture of the essential woman). Williams argues powerfully that this critique, though attractive because it seems less "strident" than traditional radical arguments, in the end leaves women open to the same old patterns of discrimination, only now justified by "choice." *Id.* at 801, 820-21.

113. CYNTHIA OZICK, *Literature and the Politics of Sex: A Dissent*, in ART & ARDOR 287 (1983).

114. At an international conference on women's history in 1986, a white feminist, in response to questions about why Western women's history is still white women's history, answered, "We have enough of a burden trying to get a feminist viewpoint across, why do we have to take on this extra burden?" E. SPELMAN, *supra* note 25, at 8.

115. Moreover, essentialism is built into the structure of academia. There are "black studies" and "women's studies" departments, but no departments of Gender and Ethnicity or "race and gender studies."

tody fight for being a lesbian, and her reluctance to look for or recognize struggle and difference within the movement itself:

> We were doing "outreach," that disastrous method of organizing; *we* had gone forward to a new place, women together, and now were throwing back safety lines to other women, to pull them in as if they were drowning, to save them. I understood then how important it was for me to have this new place; it was going to be my home, to replace the one I had lost. I needed desperately to have a place that was mine with other women, where I felt hopeful. But because of my need, I did not push myself to look at what might separate me from other women. I relied on the hopefulness of all women together: what I felt, deep down, was hope that they would join me in my place, which would be the way I wanted it. I didn't want to have to *limit* myself.
>
> I didn't understand what a limited, narrow space, and how short lasting, it would be, if only *my* imagination and knowledge and abilities were to go into the making and extending of it. I didn't understand how much I was still inside the restrictions of my culture, in my vision of how the world could be. I, and the other women I worked with, limited the effectiveness of our struggle for that place by our own racism and anti-Semitism.[116]

Many women, perhaps especially white women who have rejected or been rejected by their homes of origin, hope and expect that the women's movement will be a new home—and home is a place of comfort, not conflict.

Third, feminist essentialism offers women not only intellectual and emotional comfort, but the opportunity to play all-too-familiar power games both among themselves and with men. Feminist essentialism provides multiple arenas for power struggle which cross-cut one another in complex ways. The gameswomanship is palpable at any reasonably diverse gathering of feminists with a political agenda. The participants are busy constructing hierarchies of oppression, using their own suffering (and consequent innocence) to win the right to define "women's experience" or to demand particular political concessions for their interest group. White women stress women's commonality, which enables them to control the group's agenda; black women make reference to 200 years of slavery and argue that their needs should come first. Eventually, as the group seems ready to splinter into mutually suspicious and self-righteous factions, someone reminds the group that after all, women are women and we are all oppressed by men, and solidarity reappears through the threat of a common enemy.[117] These

---

116. Minnie Bruce Pratt, *Identity: Skin Blood Heart*, in ELLY BULKIN, MINNIE BRUCE PRATT & BARBARA SMITH, YOURS IN STRUGGLE: THREE FEMINIST PERSPECTIVES ON ANTI-SEMITISM AND RACISM, at 9, 30 (1984).

117. But this peace is only temporary, for the divisions between women remain real even when suppressed.

The idea of 'common oppression' was a false and corrupt platform disguising and mystifying the true nature of women's varied and complex social reality. Women are divided by sexist attitudes, racism, class privilege, and a host of other prejudices.

are the strategies of zero-sum games; and feminist essentialism, by purveying the notion that there is only one "women's experience," perpetuates these games.

Finally, as Martha Minow has pointed out, "Cognitively, we need simplifying categories, and the unifying category of 'woman' helps to organize experience, even at the cost of denying some of it."[118] Abandoning mental categories completely would leave us as autistic as Funes the Memorious, terrorized by the sheer weight and particularity of experience.[119] No categories at all, moreover, would leave nothing of a women's movement, save perhaps a tepid kind of "I've got my oppression, you've got yours" approach.[120] As Elizabeth Spelman has put the problem:

> At the heart of anything that can coherently be called a "women's movement" is the shared experience of being oppressed as women. The movement is, as it has to be, grounded in and justified by the fact of this shared experience: without it there would be neither the impulse nor the rationale for the political movement (whatever else is true of the movement). That is, unless in some important sense women speak in a single voice, the voice each has as a woman, there are no solid grounds for a "women's movement."[121]

The problem of avoiding essentialism while preserving "women" as a meaningful political and practical concept has thus often been posed as a dilemma.[122] The argument sometimes seems to be that we must choose: use the traditional categories or none at all.[123]

Sustained woman bonding can occur only when these divisions are confronted and the necessary steps are taken to eliminate them. Divisions will not be eliminated by wishful thinking or romantic reverie about common oppression despite the value of highlighting experiences all women share.
B. HOOKS, FEMINIST THEORY, *supra* note 22, at 44.

118. Martha Minow, *Feminist Reason: Getting It and Losing It*, 38 J. LEGAL EDUC. 47, 51 (1988); *see also* Martha Minow, *The Supreme Court 1986 Term—Foreword: Justice Engendered*, 101 HARV. L. REV. 10, 64-66 (1987) [hereinafter Minow, *Justice Engendered*]. Minow also suggests that gender essentialism is part of our early childhood experience and thus is built into our psyches. Her reference on this point, however, is to Chodorow's work, which, as Minow concedes, "underplays . . . the significance of early formation of racial, religious, and national identities, which are layered into the psychodynamic process of individuation with perhaps as much power as gender identities." Minow, *Feminist Reason: Getting It and Losing It, supra*, at 52 n.23.

119. *See* E. SPELMAN, *supra* note 25, at 2 (footnote omitted) (using the metaphor of the multiplicity of pebbles on a beach).

120. *See, e.g.*, Littleton, *supra* note 24, at 753 n.11 (rejecting "uncritical pluralism"); *see also* Elly Bulkin, *Hard Ground: Jewish Identity, Racism, and Anti-Semitism*, in E. BULKIN, M.B. PRATT & B. SMITH, *supra* note 116, at 89, 99 (noting the danger of " 'hunkering down in one's oppression,' refusing to look beyond one's identity as an oppressed person").

121. E. SPELMAN, *supra* note 25, at 15.

122. *See id.*; Seyla Benhabib & Drucilla Cornell, *Introduction: Beyond the Politics of Gender*, in FEMINISM AS CRITIQUE, *supra* note 103, at 1, 13; Fraser & Nicholson, *supra* note 104, at 97; Mary E. Hawkesworth, *Knowers, Knowing, Known: Feminist Theory and Claims of Truth*, 14 SIGNS 533, 537 (1989).

123. *See* J.M. Balkin, *Deconstructive Practice and Legal Theory*, 96 YALE L.J. 743, 753 (1987) ("The history of ideas, then, is not the history of individual conceptions, but of favored conceptions held in opposition to disfavored conceptions."); *see also* GEORGE LAKOFF & MARK

V. Beyond Essentialism: Black Women and Feminist Theory

[O]ur future survival is predicated upon our ability to relate within equality. As women, we must root out internalized patterns of oppression within ourselves if we are to move beyond the most superficial aspects of social change. Now we must recognize differences among women who are our equals, neither inferior nor superior, and devise ways to use each others' difference to enrich our visions and our joint struggles.[124]

— Audre Lorde

In this part of the article, I want to talk about what black women can bring to feminist theory to help us move beyond essentialism and toward multiple consciousness as feminist and jurisprudential method. In my view, there are at least three major contributions that black women have to offer post-essentialist feminist theory: the recognition of a self that is multiplicitous, not unitary; the recognition that differences are always relational rather than inherent; and the recognition that wholeness and commonality are acts of will and creativity, rather than passive discovery.

A. The Abandonment of Innocence

Black women experience not a single inner self (much less one that is essentially gendered), but many selves. This sense of a multiplicitous self is not unique to black women, but black women have expressed this sense in ways that are striking, poignant, and potentially useful to feminist theory. bell hooks describes her experience in a creative writing program at a predominantly white college, where she was encouraged to find "her voice," as frustrating to her sense of multiplicity.

> It seemed that many black students found our situations problematic precisely because our sense of self, and by definition our voice, was not unilateral, monologist, or static but rather multi-dimensional. We were as at home in dialect as we were in standard English. Individuals who speak languages other than English, who speak patois as well as standard English, find it a necessary aspect of self-affirmation not to feel compelled to choose one voice over another, not to claim one as more authentic, but rather to construct social realities that celebrate, acknowledge, and affirm differences, variety.[125]

This experience of multiplicity is also a sense of self-contradiction, of containing the oppressor within oneself. In her article *On Being the Object of Property*,[126] Patricia Williams writes about herself writing about her great-great-grandmother, "picking through the ruins for my

---

Johnson, Metaphors We Live By 14-19 (1980) (discussing the concepts underlying binary spatial metaphors such as GOOD IS UP and BAD IS DOWN); A. Lorde, *supra* note 18, at 114 ("Much of Western European history conditions us to see human differences in simplistic opposition to each other: dominant/subordinate, good/bad, up/down, superior/inferior.").

124. A. Lorde, *supra* note 18, at 122.

125. b. hooks, Talking Back, *supra* note 22, at 11-12.

126. 14 Signs 5 (1988).

roots."[127] What she finds is a paradox: She must claim for herself "a heritage the weft of whose genesis is [her] own disinheritance."[128] Williams's great-great-grandmother, Sophie, was a slave, and at the age of about eleven was impregnated by her owner, a white lawyer named Austin Miller. Their daughter Mary, Williams's great-grandmother, was taken away from Sophie and raised as a house servant.

When Williams went to law school, her mother told her, "The Millers were lawyers, so you have it in your blood."[129] Williams analyzes this statement as asking her to acknowledge contradictory selves:

> [S]he meant that no one should make me feel inferior because someone else's father was a judge. She wanted me to reclaim that part of my heritage from which I had been disinherited, and she wanted me to use it as a source of strength and self-confidence. At the same time, she was asking me to claim a part of myself that was the dispossessor of another part of myself; she was asking me to deny that disenfranchised little black girl of myself that felt powerless, vulnerable and, moreover, rightly felt so.[130]

The theory of black slavery, Williams notes, was based on the notion that black people are beings without will or personality, defined by "irrationality, lack of control, and ugliness."[131] In contrast, "wisdom, control, and aesthetic beauty signify the whole white personality in slave law."[132] In accepting her white self, her lawyer self, Williams must accept a legacy of not only a disinheritance but a negation of her black self: To the Millers, her forebears, the Williamses, her forebears, did not even have selves as such.

Williams's choice ultimately is not to deny either self, but to recognize them both, and in so doing to acknowledge guilt as well as innocence. She ends the piece by invoking "the presence of polar bears"[133]: bears that mauled a child to death at the Brooklyn Zoo and were subsequently killed themselves, bears judged in public debate as simultaneously "innocent, naturally territorial, unfairly imprisoned, and guilty."[134]

This complex resolution rejects the easy innocence of supposing oneself to be an essential black self with a legacy of oppression by the guilty white Other. With such multilayered analyses, black women can bring to feminist theory stories of how it is to have multiple and contradictory selves, selves that contain the oppressor as well as the oppressed.[135]

---

127. *Id.* at 5.
128. *Id.* at 6-7.
129. *Id.* at 6.
130. *Id.*
131. *Id.* at 11.
132. *Id.* at 10.
133. *Id.* at 24.
134. *Id.* at 22.
135. Donna Haraway, in her essay *A Manifesto for Cyborgs: Science, Technology, and Socialist*

B.　*Strategic Identities and "Difference"*

A post-essentialist feminism can benefit not only from the abandonment of the quest for a unitary self, but also from Martha Minow's realization that difference—and therefore identity—is always relational, not inherent.[136] Zora Neale Hurston's work is a good illustration of this notion.

In an essay written for a white audience, *How It Feels to Be Colored Me*,[137] Hurston argues that her color is not an inherent part of her being, but a response to her surroundings. She recalls the day she "became colored"—the day she left her home in an all-black community to go to school: "I left Eatonville, the town of the oleanders, as Zora. When I disembarked from the river-boat at Jacksonville, she was no more. It seemed that I had suffered a sea change. I was not Zora of Orange County any more, I was now a little colored girl."[138] But even as an adult, Hurston insists, her colored self is always situational: "I do not always feel colored. Even now I often achieve the unconscious Zora of Eatonville before the Hegira. I feel most colored when I am thrown against a sharp white background."[139]

As an example, Hurston describes the experience of listening to music in a jazz club with a white male friend:

> My pulse is throbbing like a war drum. I want to slaughter something—give pain, give death to what, I do not know. But the piece ends. The men of the orchestra wipe their lips and rest their fingers. I creep back slowly to the veneer we call civilization with the last tone and find the white friend sitting motionless in his seat, smoking calmly.
>
> "Good music they have here," he remarks, drumming the table with his fingertips.
>
> Music. The great blobs of purple and red emotion have not touched him. He has only heard what I felt. He is far away and I see him but dimly across the ocean and the continent that have fallen between us. He is so pale with his whiteness then and I am *so* colored.[140]

In reaction to the presence of whites—both her white companion

---

Feminism in the 1980s, 15 Socialist Rev. 65 (1985), argues that postmodernist theorists (who reject the idea of a "self" altogether, preferring to speak instead of multiple "subject positions") offer feminists the chance to abandon the dream of a common language and the power games of guilt and innocence in favor of "a powerful infidel heteroglossia." *Id.* at 101. Haraway's symbol for this alternate path is the cyborg, a being that transgresses the familiar boundaries of nature vs. culture, animate vs. inanimate, and born vs. made. She suggests that " 'women of color' might be understood as a cyborg identity, a potent subjectivity synthesized from fusions of outsider identities," *id.* at 93, and that the writings of women of color are a tool for subverting Western culture without falling under its spell, *id.* at 94.

136. Minow, *Justice Engendered, supra* note 118, at 34-38.

137. Zora Neale Hurston, *How It Feels to Be Colored Me*, in I Love Myself When I am Laughing . . . And Then Again When I am Looking Mean and Impressive 152 (A. Walker ed. 1979).

138. *Id.* at 153.

139. *Id.* at 154.

140. *Id.*

and the white readers of her essay—Hurston invokes and uses the traditional stereotype of black people as tied to the jungle, "living in the jungle way."[141] Yet in a later essay for a black audience, *What White Publishers Won't Print*,[142] she criticizes the white "folklore of 'reversion to type' ":

> This curious doctrine has such wide acceptance that it is tragic. One has only to examine the huge literature on it to be convinced. No matter how high we may *seem* to climb, put us under strain and we revert to type, that is, to the bush. Under a superficial layer of western culture, the jungle drums throb in our veins.[143]

The difference between the first essay, in which Hurston revels in the trope of black person as primitive, and the second essay, in which she deplores it, lies in the distinction between an identity that is contingent, temporary, and relational, and an identity that is fixed, inherent, and essential. Zora as jungle woman is fine as an argument, a reaction to her white friend's experience; what is abhorrent is the notion that Zora can always and only be a jungle woman.[144] One image is in flux, "inspired" by a relationship with another;[145] the other is static, unchanging, and ultimately reductive and sterile rather than creative.

Thus, "how it feels to be colored Zora" depends on the answer to these questions: " 'Compared to what? As of when? Who is asking? In what context? For what purpose? With what interests and presuppositions?'. What Hurston rigorously shows is that questions of difference and identity are always functions of a specific interlocutionary situation—and the answers, matters of strategy rather than truth."[146] Any "essential self" is always an invention; the evil is in denying its artificiality.[147]

---

141. *Id.*
142. Z. HURSTON, *What White Publishers Won't Print*, in I LOVE MYSELF WHEN I AM LAUGHING . . . AND THEN AGAIN WHEN I AM LOOKING MEAN AND IMPRESSIVE, *supra* note 137, at 169.
143. *Id.* at 172.
144. As Barbara Johnson perceptively notes,
    In the first [essay], Hurston can proclaim "I am this"; but when the image is repeated as "you are that," it changes completely. The content of the image may be the same, but its interpersonal use is different. The study of Afro-American literature as a whole poses a similar problem of address: any attempt to lift out of a text an image or essence of blackness is bound to violate the interlocutionary strategy of its formulation.
    Barbara Johnson, *Thresholds of Difference: Structures of Address in Zora Neale Hurston*, in "RACE," WRITING, AND DIFFERENCE, *supra* note 12, at 322-23.
145. *See* Barbara Smith & Beverly Smith, *Across the Kitchen Table: A Sister-to-Sister Dialogue*, in THIS BRIDGE CALLED MY BACK, *supra* note 22, at 113, 119 (two sisters discuss the black selves they miss when they are with white women: "Because the way you act with Black people is because they inspire the behavior. And I *do* mean inspire.").
146. Johnson, *supra* note 144, at 323-24.
147. bell hooks makes a related point about the self's relationality:
    Discarding the notion that the self exists in opposition to an other that must be destroyed, annihilated (for when I left the segregated world of home and moved in and among white people, and their ways of knowing, I learned this way of understanding the social construction of self). I evoked the way of knowing I had learned from unschooled southern black folks. We learned that the self existed in relation, was

To be compatible with this conception of the self, feminist theorizing about "women" must similarly be strategic and contingent, focusing on relationships, not essences. One result will be that men will cease to be a faceless Other and reappear as potential allies in political struggle.[148] Another will be that women will be able to acknowledge their differences without threatening feminism itself. In the process, as feminists begin to attack racism and classism and homophobia, feminism will change from being only about "women as women" (modified women need not apply), to being about all kinds of oppression based on seemingly inherent and unalterable characteristics.[149] We need not wait for a unified theory of oppression;[150] that theory can be feminism.

C. *Integrity as Will and Idea*

> *Because each had discovered years before that they were neither white nor male, and that all freedom and triumph was forbidden to them, they had set about creating something else to be.*[151]
>
> — Toni Morrison

Finally, black women can help feminist movement move beyond its fascination with essentialism through the recognition that wholeness of the self and commonality with others are asserted (if never completely achieved) through creative action, not realized in shared victimization. Feminist theory at present, especially feminist legal theory, tends to focus on women as passive victims. For example, for MacKinnon, women have been so objectified by men that the miracle is how they are able to exist at all. Women are the victims, the acted-upon, the helpless, until by radical enlightenment they are somehow empowered to act for themselves.[152] Similarly, for West, the "fundamental fact" of women's lives is pain—"the violence, the danger, the boredom, the ennui, the

---

dependent for its very being on the lives and experiences of everyone, the self not as signifier of one "I" but the coming together of many "I"s, the self as embodying collective reality past and present, family and community.
B. HOOKS, TALKING BACK, *supra* note 22, at 30-31.

148. Thus Joan Williams argues that feminism must move away from "the destructive battle between 'sameness' and 'difference' toward a deeper understanding of gender as a system of power relations." Williams, *supra* note 111, at 836. In her view, gender must be "deconstructed." *See id.* at 841, *quoted in* note 111 *supra*. The deconstruction approach would make clear the payoff of feminism for men as well as women. This change will also encourage women of color to identify themselves as feminists. *See* B. HOOKS, FEMINIST THEORY, *supra* note 22, at 70 ("Many black women refused participation in feminist movement because they felt an anti-male stance was not a sound basis for action.").

149. *See* B. HOOKS, FEMINIST THEORY, *supra* note 22, at 31 ("Focus on social equality with men as a definition of feminism led to an emphasis on discrimination, male attitudes, and legalistic reforms. Feminism as a movement to end sexist oppression directs our attention to systems of domination and the inter-relatedness of sex, race, and class oppression.").

Elizabeth Spelman suggests that feminism be expanded by conceiving of not just two genders, but many—a function of race and class as well as sex. E. SPELMAN, *supra* note 25, at 174-77.

150. *See* note 53 *supra* and accompanying text.

151. TONI MORRISON, SULA 52 (1974).

152. As Andrew Ross has noted, even the female "collaborators" MacKinnon attacks

non-productivity, the poverty, the fear, the numbness, the frigidity, the isolation, the low self-esteem, and the pathetic attempts to assimilate."[153]

This story of woman as victim is meant to encourage solidarity by emphasizing women's shared oppression, thus denying or minimizing difference, and to further the notion of an essential woman—she who is victimized. But as bell hooks has succinctly noted, the notion that women's commonality lies in their shared victimization by men "directly reflects male supremacist thinking. Sexist ideology teaches women that to be female is to be a victim."[154] Moreover, the story of woman as passive victim denies the ability of women to shape their own lives, whether for better or worse. It also may thwart their abilities. Like Minnie Bruce Pratt, reluctant to look farther than commonality for fear of jeopardizing the comfort of shared experience, women who rely on their victimization to define themselves may be reluctant to let it go and create their own self-definitions.

At the individual level, black women have had to learn to construct themselves in a society that denied them full selves. Again, Zora Neale Hurston's writings are suggestive. Though Hurston plays with being her "colored self" and again with being "the eternal feminine with its string of beads,"[155] she ends *How It Feels to Be Colored Me* with an image of herself as neither essentially black nor essentially female, but simply

> a brown bag of miscellany propped against a wall. Against a wall in company with other bags, white, red and yellow. Pour out the contents, and there is discovered a jumble of small things priceless and worthless. A first-water diamond, an empty spool, bits of broken glass, lengths of string, a key to a door long since crumbled away, a rusty knife-blade, old shoes saved for a road that never was and never will be, a nail bent under the weight of things too heavy for any nail, a dried flower or two still fragrant. In your hand is the brown bag. On the ground before you is the jumble it held—so much like the jumble in the bags, could they be emptied, that all might be dumped in a single heap and the bags refilled without altering the content of any greatly. A bit of colored glass more or less would not matter. Perhaps that is how the Great Stuffer of Bags filled them in the first place—who knows?[156]

Hurston thus insists on a conception of identity as a construction, not an essence—something made of fragments of experience, not discovered in one's body or unveiled after male domination is eliminated.

This insistence on the importance of will and creativity seems to threaten feminism at one level, because it gives strength back to the concept of autonomy, making possible the recognition of the element

---

with fury are seen as stupid, not as wrong or evil. Andrew Ross, *Politics Without Pleasure* (Book Review), 1 YALE J.L. & HUMANITIES 193, 200 (1989).

153. West, *supra* note 95, at 143.
154. B. HOOKS, FEMINIST THEORY, *supra* note 22, at 45.
155. Z. HURSTON, *supra* note 137, at 155.
156. *Id.*

of consent in relations of domination,[157] and attributes to women the power that makes culpable the many ways in which white women have actively used their race privilege against their sisters of color.[158] Although feminists are correct to recognize the powerful force of sheer physical coercion in ensuring compliance with patriarchal hegemony,[159] we must also "come to terms with the ways in which women's culture has served to enlist women's support in perpetuating existing power relations."[160]

However, at another level, the recognition of the role of creativity and will in shaping our lives is liberating, for it allows us to acknowledge and celebrate the creativity and joy with which many women have survived and turned existing relations of domination to their own ends. Works of black literature like *Beloved*, *The Color Purple*, and *Song of Solomon*, among others, do not linger on black women's victimization and

157. As Gramsci points out, hegemony consists of two strands: "1. the 'spontaneous' consent given by the great masses of the population [and] 2. the apparatus of state coercive power which 'legally' enforces discipline on those groups who do not 'consent' either actively or passively." ANTONIO GRAMSCI, SELECTIONS FROM THE PRISON NOTEBOOKS 12 (Q. Hoare & G. Smith trans. 1971). Consent, however, is not liberal consent, freely given, but a " 'contradictory consciousness' mixing approbation and apathy, resistance and resignation." T.J. Jackson Lears, *The Concept of Cultural Hegemony: Problems and Possibilities*, 90 AM. HIST. REV. 567, 570 (1985).

158. For example, during slavery,
[w]hite women performed acts of violence against Black slave women with whom their husbands had sexual relations. Often these racist acts were shaped by feelings of sexual jealousy rooted in and sustained by sexism: for such jealousy is a function of the sexism that makes the "proper" attention of her husband a condition of a woman's sense of self-worth.
E. SPELMAN, *supra* note 25, at 106 (footnotes omitted); *see also* B. HOOKS, FEMINIST THEORY, *supra* note 22, at 49 ("Historically, many black women experienced white women as the white supremacist group who most directly exercised power over them, often in a manner far more brutal and dehumanizing than that of racist white men.").

159. MacKinnon, for example, points out that her dominance approach is based on a reality that includes
not only the extent and intractability of sex segregation into poverty, which has been known before, but the range of issues termed violence against women, which has not been. It combines women's material desperation, through being relegated to categories of jobs that pay nil, with the massive amount of rape and attempted rape—44 percent of all women—about which virtually nothing is done; the sexual assault of children—38 percent of girls and 10 percent of boys—which is apparently endemic to the patriarchal family; the battery of women that is systematic in one quarter to one third of our homes; prostitution, women's fundamental economic condition, what we do when all else fails, and for many women in this country, all else fails often; and pornography, an industry that traffics in female flesh, making sex inequality into sex to the tune of eight billion dollars a year in profits largely to organized crime.
C. MACKINNON, *supra* note 44, at 41 (footnotes omitted).

160. Williams, *supra* note 111, at 829. Williams, for instance, analyzes how women use women's culture against themselves, "as they do every time a woman 'chooses' to subordinate her career 'for the good of the family' and congratulates herself on that choice as a mature assessment of her own 'priorities.' " *Id.* at 830.
Black women have often actively embraced patriarchal stereotypes in the name of racial solidarity. *See* P. GIDDINGS, *supra* note 21, at 322-23 (discussing women's concessions to male chauvinism in the civil rights movement of the 1960s); A. LORDE, *supra* note 18, at 119-21 (discussing refusal to confront sexism and homophobia within the black community).

misery; though they recognize our pain, they ultimately celebrate our transcendence.[161]

Finally, on a collective level this emphasis on will and creativity reminds us that bridges between women are built, not found. The discovery of shared suffering is a connection more illusory than real; what will truly bring and keep us together is the use of effort and imagination to root out and examine our differences, for only the recognition of women's differences can ultimately bring feminist movement to strength. This is hard work, and painful work;[162] but it is also radical work, real work. As Barbara Smith has said, "What *I* really feel is radical is trying to make coalitions with people who are different from you. I feel it is radical to be dealing with race and sex and class and sexual identity all at one time. I think *that* is really radical because it has never been done before."[163]

D. *Epilogue: Multiple Consciousness*

I have argued in this article that gender essentialism is dangerous to feminist legal theory because in the attempt to extract an essential female self and voice from the diversity of women's experience, the experiences of women perceived as "different" are ignored or treated as variations on the (white) norm. Now I want to return to an earlier point: that legal theory, including feminist legal theory, has been entranced for too long and to too great an extent by the voice of "We the People." In order to energize legal theory, we need to subvert it with narratives and stories, accounts of the particular, the different, and the hitherto silenced.

Whether by chance or not, many of the legal theorists telling stories these days are women of color. Mari Matsuda calls for "multiple consciousness as jurisprudential method";[164] Patricia Williams shows the way with her multilayered stories and meditations.[165] These writings

---

161. *See* T. MORRISON, *supra* note 83, at 273 ("[M]e and you, we got more yesterday than anybody. We need some kind of tomorrow.").

162. As Bernice Johnson Reagon has written:

Coalition work is not work done in your home. Coalition work has to be done in the streets. And it is some of the most dangerous work you can do. And you shouldn't look for comfort. Some people will come to a coalition and they rate the success of the coalition on whether or not they feel good when they get there. They're not looking for a coalition; they're looking for a home! They're looking for a bottle with some milk in it and a nipple, which does not happen in a coalition. You don't get a lot of food in a coalition. You don't get fed in a coalition. In a coalition you have to give, and it is different from your home. You can't stay there all the time. You go to the coalition for a few hours and then you go back and take your bottle wherever it is, and then you go back and coalesce some more.

Bernice Johnson Reagon, *Coalition Politics: Turning the Century*, in HOME GIRLS: A BLACK FEMINIST ANTHOLOGY 359 (B. Smith ed. 1983).

163. Smith & Smith, *supra* note 145 at 126.

164. Matsuda, *supra* note 13, at 9.

165. *See, e.g.*, Patricia J. Williams, *Alchemical Notes: Reconstructing Ideals from Deconstructed Rights*, 22 HARV. C.R.-C.L. L. REV. 401 (1987); Williams, *supra* note 126.

are healthy for feminist legal theory as well as legal theory more generally. In acknowledging "the complexity of messages implied in our being,"[166] they begin the task of energizing legal theory with the creative struggle between Funes and We the People: the creative struggle that reflects a multiple consciousness.

---

166. Williams, *supra* note 126, at 24.

Feminist Critical Theories

Deborah L. Rhode*

Heidi Hartmann once described the relation between Marxism and feminism as analogous to that of husband and wife under English common law: "Marxism and feminism are one, and that one is Marxism." In Hartmann's view, "either we need a healthier marriage or we need a divorce."[1] Responding to that metaphor, Gloria Joseph underscored the exclusion of black women from the wedding and redescribed the interaction between Marxist, feminist, and minority perspectives as an "incompatible menage à trois."[2]

The relations between critical legal studies (CLS) and feminism have provoked similar concerns. The origins of this article are a case in point. The piece grows out of an invitation to offer a feminist perspective for an anthology on critical legal studies.[3] Such invitations are problematic in several respects. Almost any systematic statement about these two bodies of thought risks homogenizing an extraordinarily broad range of views. Moreover, providing some single piece on the "woman question" perpetuates a tradition of tokenism that has long characterized left political movements.[4]

Whatever the risks of other generalizations, one threshold observation is difficult to dispute: Feminism takes gender as a central category

---

* B.A., J.D., Yale University; Professor, Stanford Law School; Director, Institute for Research on Women and Gender, Stanford University. The comments of Peter Chadwick, Katharine Bartlett, Thomas Grey, Regenia Gagnier, Henry Greely, Mark Kelman, Christine Littleton, Frances Olsen, Robert Post, Carol Sanger, Reva Siegel, William Simon, and John Stick are gratefully acknowledged.

1. Heidi Hartmann, *The Unhappy Marriage of Marxism and Feminism: Toward a More Progressive Union*, in WOMAN AND REVOLUTION 2, 2 (L. Sargent ed. 1981).

2. Gloria Joseph, *The Incompatible Menage á Trois: Marxism, Feminism and Racism*, in WOMAN AND REVOLUTION, *supra* note 1, at 91.

3. Deborah Rhode, *Feminist Critical Theories*, in CRITICAL LEGAL THEORY — (J. Stick ed. 1990) (forthcoming).

4. For inadequacies in the way Marxism, socialism, and critical theory have coped with "women's issues," see RICHARD J. EVANS, THE FEMINISTS 156-77 (1977); 1 PHILIP S. FONER, WOMEN AND THE AMERICAN LABOR MOVEMENT 133, 271-85 (1979); Nancy Fraser, *What's Critical About Critical Theory: The Case of Habermas and Gender*, 35 NEW GERMAN CRITIQUE 97 (1985), *reprinted in* FEMINISM AS CRITIQUE 31 (S. Benhabib & D. Cornell eds. 1987); SUSAN MOLLER OKIN, JUSTICE, GENDER AND THE FAMILY — (1989) (forthcoming); BARBARA TAYLOR, EVE AND THE NEW JERUSALEM: SOCIALISM AND FEMINISM IN THE NINETEENTH CENTURY ix-xviii, 217-60 (1983). *See generally* ALISON M. JAGGAR, FEMINIST POLITICS AND HUMAN NATURE (1983); note 5 *infra*. It is also instructive to survey the silences in intellectual histories of these movements. For example, the index to Jay's account of the Frankfurt school has no entries under women, sex, gender, or feminism. MARTIN JAY, THE DIALECTICAL IMAGINATION (1973).

of analysis, while the core texts of critical legal studies do not.[5] To be sure, many of these texts make at least some reference to problems of sex-based subordination, and to the existence (if not the significance) of feminist scholarship. Yet most critical legal theory and the traditions on which it relies have not seriously focused on gender inequality. Why then should feminists continue participating in enterprises in which their perspectives are added but not integrated, rendered separate but not equal?

Efforts to provide the "woman's point of view" also risk contributing to their own marginalization. In effect, feminists are invited to explain how their perspectives differ from others associated with critical legal studies or with more mainstream bodies of legal theory. Such invitations impose the same limitations that have been characteristic for women's issues in conventional legal ideology. Analysis has fixated on how women are the same or different from men; men have remained the unstated standard of analysis.[6]

In recent years, these concerns have increasingly emerged within the critical legal studies movement. During the last decade, issues of gender as well as race and ethnicity dominated the agendas of several national CLS conferences, and feminist theorists organized regional groups around common interests. A growing body of feminist and critical race scholarship also developed along lines that paralleled, intersected, and challenged critical legal theory.[7]

This essay charts relationships among these bodies of work. Although no brief overview can adequately capture the range of scholarship that coexists under such labels, it is at least possible to identify some crosscutting objectives, methodologies, and concerns. The point

---

5. *See* Carrie Menkel-Meadow, *Feminist Legal Theory, Critical Legal Studies, and Legal Education or "The Fem-Crits Go to Law School,"* 38 J. LEGAL EDUC. 61 (1988); Robin West, *Deconstructing the CLS-Fem Split,* 2 WIS. WOMEN'S L.J. 85 (1986). Early collections of critical legal scholarship did not explore gender issues and included no, or only a token number of, essays focusing on feminist concerns. For the relevant omissions, see, e.g., THE POLITICS OF LAW: A PROGRESSIVE CRITIQUE (D. Kairys ed. 1982); *Critical Legal Studies Symposium,* 36 STAN. L. REV. 1 (1984); 6 CARDOZO L. REV. 691 (1985) (Critical Legal Studies Symposium).

6. For a discussion of the marginalization and homogenization of feminist perspectives in legal circles, see, e.g., Deborah L. Rhode, *The "Woman's Point of View,"* 38 J. LEGAL EDUC. 39 (1988), and companion articles in that symposium, as well as in *Gender and the Law,* 40 STAN. L. REV. 1163 (1988). For problems with the sameness/difference approach toward gender issues, see CATHARINE A. MACKINNON, FEMINISM UNMODIFIED 32-45 (1987); DEBORAH L. RHODE, JUSTICE AND GENDER 117-25 (1989); Deborah L. Rhode, *Definitions of Difference,* in THEORETICAL PERSPECTIVES ON SEXUAL DIFFERENCE 197 (D. Rhode ed. 1990); Lucinda M. Finley, *Transcending Equality Theory: A Way Out of the Maternity and the Workplace Debate,* 86 COLUM. L. REV. 1118 (1986); Ann E. Freedman, *Sex Equality, Sex Differences, and the Supreme Court,* 92 YALE L.J. 913 (1983); Herma Hill Kay, *Models of Equality,* 1985 U. ILL. L. REV. 39; Sylvia A. Law, *Rethinking Sex and the Constitution,* 132 U. PA. L. REV. 955 (1984); Christine A. Littleton, *Reconstructing Sexual Equality,* 75 CALIF. L. REV. 1279 (1987); Stephanie M. Wildman, *The Legitimation of Sex Discrimination: A Critical Response to Supreme Court Jurisprudence,* 63 OR. L. REV. 265 (1984).

7. *See* Menkel-Meadow, *supra* note 5; *Minority Critiques of the Critical Legal Studies Movement,* 22 HARV. C.R.-C.L. L. REV. 297 (1987); *Voices of Experience: New Responses to Gender Discourse,* 24 HARV. C.R.-C.L. L. REV. 1 (1989).

of this approach is neither to develop some unifying Grand Theory nor simply to compare feminism with other critical frameworks. Rather it is to underscore the importance of multiple frameworks that avoid universal or essentialist claims and that yield concrete strategies for social change.

The following discussion focuses on a body of work that may be loosely identified as feminist critical theories. Although they differ widely in other respects, these theories share three central commitments. On a political level, they seek to promote equality between women and men. On a substantive level, feminist critical frameworks make gender a focus of analysis; their aim is to reconstitute legal practices that have excluded, devalued, or undermined women's concerns. On a methodological level, these frameworks aspire to describe the world in ways that correspond to women's experience and that identify the fundamental social transformations necessary for full equality between the sexes. These commitments are for the most part mutually reinforcing, but they occasionally pull in different directions. This essay explores various ways that feminists have sought to fuse a political agenda that is dependent on both group identity and legalist strategies with a methodology that is in some measure skeptical of both.

What distinguishes feminist critical theories from other analysis is both the focus on gender equality and the conviction that it cannot be obtained under existing ideological and institutional structures. This theoretical approach partly overlaps, and frequently draws upon other critical approaches, including CLS and critical race scholarship. At the most general level, these traditions share a common goal: to challenge existing distributions of power. They also often employ similar deconstructive or narrative methodologies aimed at similar targets—certain organizing premises of conventional liberal legalism. Each tradition includes both internal and external critiques. Some theorists focus on the inadequacy of conventional legal doctrine in terms of its own criteria for coherence, consistency, and legitimacy. Other commentators emphasize the role of legal ideology in legitimating unjust social conditions. Yet these traditions also differ considerably in their theories about theory, in their critiques of liberal legalism, in their strategies for change, and in their alternative social visions.

I. Theoretical Premises

Critical feminism, like other critical approaches, builds on recent currents in social theory that have made theorizing increasingly problematic. Post-modern and post-structural traditions that have influenced left legal critics presuppose the social construction of knowledge.[8] To varying degrees, critics within these traditions deny

---

8. Critics such as Francois Lyotard invoke the term post-modernism to describe the present age's collapse of faith in traditional Grand Narratives. Since the Enlightenment, these

the possibility of any universal foundations for critique. Taken as a whole, their work underscores the cultural, historical, and linguistic construction of human identity and social experience.[9]

Yet such a theoretical stance also limits its own aspirations to authority. For feminists, this post-modern paradox creates political as well as theoretical difficulties. Adherents are left in the awkward position of maintaining that gender oppression exists while challenging our capacity to document it.[10] Such awkwardness is, for example, especially pronounced in works that assert as unproblematic certain "facts" about the pervasiveness of sexual abuse while questioning the possibility of any objective measure.[11]

To take an obvious illustration, feminists have a stake both in quantifying the frequency of rape, and in questioning the conventional definitions on which rape statistics are based. Victims of sexual assault by acquaintances often respond to questions such as, "Have you ever been raped?" with something like, "Well . . . not exactly." What occurs in the pause between "well" and "not exactly" suggests the gap between the legal understanding and social experience of rape, and the ways in

---

metanarratives have sought to develop principles of objective science, universal morality, and autonomous art. For discussion of post-modernism's denial that categorical, noncontingent, abstract theories derived through reason or human nature can serve as the foundation for knowledge, see JEAN FRANCOIS LYOTARD, THE POSTMODERN CONDITION (1984); POST-ANALYTIC PHILOSOPHY (J. Rajchmand & C. West eds. 1985); Nancy Fraser & Linda Nicholsen, *Social Criticism Without Philosophy: An Encounter Between Feminism and Postmodernism*, in UNIVERSAL ABANDON?: THE POLITICS OF POSTMODERNISM 83 (A. Ross ed. 1988); Sandra Harding, *The Instability of the Analytical Categories of Feminist Theory*, 11 SIGNS 645 (1986); David Luban, *Legal Modernism*, 84 MICH. L. REV. 1656 (1986); Robin West, *Feminism, Critical Social Theory and Law*, 1989 U. CHI. LEGAL F. 59.

Post-structuralism, which arises from and contributes to this post-modern tradition, refers to theories of interpretation that view meaning as a cultural construction mediated by arrangements of language or symbolic form. What distinguishes post-structuralism from other interpretive schools is the premise that these arrangements are unstable and contradictory, and that readers create rather than simply discover meaning. For a useful overview, see CHRISTOPHER NORRIS, DECONSTRUCTION: THEORY AND PRACTICE (1982); Peter Fitzpatrick & Alan Hunt, *Critical Legal Studies: Introduction*, 14 J.L. & SOC'Y 1 (1987); David Kennedy, *Critical Theory, Structuralism and Contemporary Legal Scholarship*, 21 NEW ENG. L. REV. 209 (1986).

9. J.F. LYOTARD, *supra* note 8; Jane Flax, *PostModernism and Gender Relations in Feminist Theory*, 12 SIGNS 621 (1987). Critical legal studies scholars have responded in varying ways, ranging from Roberto Unger's and Jürgen Habermas's continued embrace of universalist claims, to Duncan Kennedy's reliance on deconstructive technique. *Compare* ROBERTO MANGABEIRA UNGER, KNOWLEDGE AND POLITICS (1975) *and* JÜRGEN HABERMAS, LEGITIMATION CRISIS (1975) *with* Peter Gabel & Duncan Kennedy, *Roll Over Beethoven*, 36 STAN. L. REV. 1 (1984).

10. As Nancy Cott notes, "in deconstructing categories of meaning, we deconstruct not only patriarchal definitions of 'womanhood' and 'truth' but also the very categories of our own analysis—'woman' and 'feminism' and 'oppression' " (*quoted in* Frances E. Macia-Lees, Patricia Sharpe & Colleen Ballerino Cohen, *The Postmodernist Turn in Anthropology: Cautions From a Feminist Perspective*, 15 SIGNS 7, 27 (1989)).

11. *Compare* C. MACKINNON, *supra* note 6, at 81-92 (discussing the social construction of rape and sexual violence) *with id.* at 23 (asserting "facts" about its prevalence). *See also* CATHARINE A. MACKINNON, TOWARD A FEMINIST THEORY OF THE STATE 100 (1989) (acknowledging without exploring the difficulty).

which data on abuse are constructed, not simply collected.[12]

Although responses to this dilemma vary widely, the most common feminist strategies bear mention. The simplest approach is to decline to address the problem—at least at the level of abstraction at which it is customarily formulated. The revolution will not be made with slogans from Lyotard's *Postmodern Condition*, and the audiences that are most in need of persuasion are seldom interested in epistemological anxieties. Critiques of existing ideology and institutions can proceed under their own standards without detailed discussions of the philosophy of knowledge. Yet, even from a purely pragmatic view, it is helpful to have some self-consciousness about the grounding for our claims about the world and the tensions between our political and methodological commitments.

Critical feminism's most common response to questions about its own authority has been reliance on experiential analysis. This approach draws primarily on techniques of consciousness-raising in contemporary feminist organizations, but also on pragmatic philosophical traditions. A standard practice is to begin with concrete experiences, integrate these experiences into theory, and rely on theory for a deeper understanding of the experiences.[13] One distinctive feature of feminist critical analysis is, as Katharine Bartlett emphasizes, a grounding in practical problems and a reliance on "practical reasoning."[14] Rather than working deductively from abstract principles and overarching conceptual schemes, such analysis builds from the ground up. Many feminist legal critics are also drawn to narrative styles that express the personal consequences of institutionalized injustice.[15] Even those commentators most wedded to broad categorical claims usually situate their works in the lived experience of pornography or sexual harassment rather than, for example, in the deep structure of Blackstone's *Commentaries* or the fundamental contradictions in Western political thought.[16]

---

12. For discussion of the "not really" phenomena, see *id.* and DIANA E. H. RUSSELL, RAPE IN MARRIAGE 44-48, 207 (1982).

13. According to Catharine MacKinnon, "Consciousness raising is the major technique of analysis, structure of organization, method of practice, and theory of social change of the women's movement." Catharine A. MacKinnon, *Feminism, Marxism, Method and the State: An Agenda for Theory*, 7 SIGNS 515, 519 (1982); *see also* Nancy Hartsock, *Fundamental Feminism: Process and Perspective*, 2 QUEST 67, 71-79 (1975); Elizabeth M. Schneider, *The Dialectic of Rights and Politics: Perspectives from the Women's Movement*, 61 N.Y.U. L. REV. 589, 602-03 (1986).

14. See, for example, the work of Amelie Rorty, discussed in Katharine T. Bartlett, *Feminist Legal Methods*, 103 HARV. L. REV. 829 (1990); Margaret Jane Radin, *The Pragmatist and the Feminist*, 63 S. CAL. L. REV — (1990) (forthcoming).

15. *See, e.g.,* Patricia Williams, *Spirit Murdering the Messenger: The Discourse of Fingerpointing as the Law's Response to Racism*, 42 U. MIAMI L. REV. 127 (1987); Mari J. Matsuda, *Public Response to Racist Speech: Considering the Victim's Story*, 87 MICH. L. REV. 2320 (1989); Robin L. West, *The Difference in Women's Hedonic Lives: A Phenomenological Critique of Feminist Legal Theory*, 3 WIS. WOMEN'S L.J. 81 (1987).

16. *See* Duncan Kennedy, *The Structure of Blackstone's Commentaries*, 28 BUFFALO L. REV. 205 (1979); R.M. UNGER, *supra* note 9.

In part, this pragmatic focus reflects the historical origins and contemporary agenda of feminist legal theory. Unlike critical legal studies, which began as a movement within the legal academy and took much of its inspiration from the Grand Theory of contemporary Marxism and the Frankfurt School, feminist legal theories emerged against the backdrop of a mass political movement. In America, that struggle has drawn much of its intellectual inspiration not from overarching conceptual schemes, but from efforts to provide guidance on particular substantive issues. As Carrie Menkel-Meadow has argued, the strength of feminism "originates" in the experience of "*being* dominated, not just in thinking about domination," and in developing concrete responses to that experience.[17] Focusing on women's actual circumstances helps reinforce the connection between feminist political and analytic agendas, but it raises its own set of difficulties. How can critics build a unified political and analytical stance from women's varying perceptions of their varying experiences? And what entitles that stance to special authority?

The first question arises from a longstanding tension in feminist methodology. What gives feminism its unique force is the claim to speak from women's experience. But that experience counsels sensitivity to its own diversity across such factors as time, culture, class, race, ethnicity, sexual orientation, and age. As Martha Minow has noted, "[c]ognitively we need simplifying categories, and the unifying category of 'woman' helps to organize experience, even at the cost of denying some of it."[18] Yet to some constituencies, particularly those who are not white, heterosexual, and economically privileged, that cost appears prohibitive since it is their experience that is most often denied.

A variation of this problem arises in discussions of "false consciousness." How can feminists wedded to experiential analysis respond to women who reject feminism's basic premises as contrary to *their* experience? In an extended footnote to an early article, Catharine MacKinnon noted:

> Feminism aspires to represent the experience of all women as women see it, yet criticizes antifeminism and misogyny, including when it appears in female form. . . . [Conventional responses treat] some women's views as unconscious conditioned reflections of their oppression, complicitous in it. . . . [T]his approach criticizes the substance of a view because it can be accounted for by its determinants. But if both feminism and antifeminism are responses to the condition of women, how is feminism exempt from devalidation by the same account? That feminism is critical, and antifeminism is not, is not enough, because the question is the basis on which we know something is one or the other

---

17. Menkel-Meadow, *supra* note 5, at 61; *see also* MacKinnon, *supra* note 13; West, *supra* note 15.

18. Martha Minow, *Feminist Reason: Getting It and Losing It*, 38 J. LEGAL EDUC. 47, 51 (1988).

when women, all of whom share the condition of women, disagree.[19]
Yet having raised the problem, MacKinnon declined to pursue it. As a
number of feminist reviewers have noted, MacKinnon has never reconciled her unqualified condemnation of opponents with her reliance on
experiential methodology.[20]

The issue deserves closer attention particularly since contemporary
survey research suggests that the vast majority of women do not experience the world in the terms that most critical feminists describe.[21] Nor
do these feminists agree among themselves about which experiential
accounts of women's interests should be controlling in disputes involving, for example, pornography, prostitution, surrogate motherhood, or
maternity leaves.[22]

A related issue is how any experiential account can claim special authority. Most responses to this issue take one of three forms. The first
approach is to invoke the experience of exclusion and subordination as
a source of special insight. According to Menkel-Meadow, the "feminist critique starts from the experiential point of view of the oppressed,
dominated, and devalued, while the critical legal studies critique begins—and, some would argue, remains—in a male-constructed, privileged place in which domination and oppression can be described and
imagined but not fully experienced."[23] Yet such "standpoint" theories,

---

19. MacKinnon, *supra* note 13, at 637 n.5. For a similar point, see C. MacKinnon, *supra*
note 11, at 115-16.

20. *See* West, *supra* note 15, at 117-18. For critiques of MacKinnon's position in works
such as *On Collaboration*, in Feminism Unmodified, *supra* note 6, at 198-205, see Katharine T.
Bartlett, *MacKinnon's Feminism: Power on Whose Terms?* (Book Review), 75 Calif. L. Rev. 1559,
1564 (1987); Christina B. Whitman, *Law and Sex* (Book Review), 86 Mich. L. Rev. 1369, 1399-
1400 (1988). *See generally* Ruth Colker, *Feminism, Sexuality, and Self: A Preliminary Inquiry Into the
Politics of Authenticity*, 68 B.U.L. Rev. 217 (1988); Angela P. Harris, *Race and Essentialism in
Feminist Legal Theory*, 42 Stan. L. Rev. 581 (1990); Christine A. Littleton, *Feminist Jurisprudence:
The Difference Method Makes* (Book Review), 41 Stan. L. Rev. 751 (1989); Frances Olsen, *Feminist Theory in Grand Style* (Book Review), 89 Colum. L. Rev. 1147 (1989).

21. *See, e.g.*, D. Rhode, Justice and Gender, *supra* note 6, at 66 (1989); Lisa Belkin, *Bars
to Equality of Sexes Seen as Eroding Slowly*, N. Y. Times, Aug. 20, 1989, at 1, 16 (61% of wives felt
husbands did less than fair share of house work; 70% of women with full time jobs felt women
had equal or better chance of promotion than men where they worked; and only 39% of Black
women and 22% of white women believed organized women's groups had made their lives
better); *Rosy Outlook Among Women Ages 18 to 44*, San Francisco Examiner, Aug. 23, 1988, at A7,
col. 3 (finding that nearly 90% of women of childbearing ages are satisfied with their lives).
For more qualitative research, see Spouse, Parent, Worker: On Gender and Multiple
Roles (F. Crosby ed. 1987).

22. For differences on pornography, compare West, *supra* note 15, at 134-39 with Mackinnon, *supra* note 6, at 127-213. For differences on maternity policies, compare Finley, *supra*
note 6, Herma Hill Kay, *Equality and Difference: The Case of Pregnancy*, 1 Berkeley Women's L.J.
1 (1985), and Reva B. Siegel, *Employment Equality Under the Pregnancy Discrimination Act of 1978*,
94 Yale L.J. 929 (1984-1985) (student author) with Nadine Taub, *From Parental Leaves to Nurturing Leaves*, 13 N.Y.U. Rev. L. & Soc. Change 381 (1985) and Wendy W. Williams, *Equality's
Riddle: Pregnancy and the Equal Treatment/Special Treatment Debate*, 13 N.Y.U. Rev. L. & Soc.
Change 325 (1984-85). For differences on prostitution, see sources cited in D. Rhode, Justice and Gender, *supra* note 6, at 257-62. For differences on surrogate motherhood, see *id.* at
223-29, and Martha A. Field, Surrogate Motherhood (1988).

23. Menkel-Meadow, *supra* note 5, at 61.

if left unqualified, present their own problems of privilege. There remains the issue of whose standpoint to credit, since not all women perceive their circumstances in terms of domination and not all who share that perception agree on its implications. Nor is gender the only source of oppression. Other forms of subordination, most obviously class, race, ethnicity, and sexual orientation, can yield comparable, and in some instances competing, claims to subjugated knowledge. To privilege any single trait risks impeding coalitions and understating other forces that constitute our identities.[24]

A second feminist strategy is to claim that women's distinctive attributes promote a distinctive form of understanding. Robin West has argued, for example, that

> [t]here is surely no way to know with any certainty whether women have a privileged access to a way of life that is more nurturant, more caring, more natural, more loving, and thereby more moral than the lives which both men and women presently pursue in the public sphere, including the legal sphere of legal practice, theory, and pedagogy. But it does seem that whether by reason of sociological role, psychological upbringing or biology, women are *closer* to such a life . . . .[25]

Such claims occur in more muted form in much of the legal scholarship that draws on relational strands of feminist theory. This line of analysis, popularized by Carol Gilligan, argues that women tend to reason in "a different voice"; they are less likely than men to privilege abstract rights over concrete relationships and are more attentive to values of care, connection, and context.[26] The strength of this framework lies in its demand that values traditionally associated with women *be valued* and that legal strategies focus on altering societal structures, not just assimilating women within them. Such an approach can yield theoretical and political cohesiveness on initiatives that serve women's distinctive needs.

Yet such efforts to claim an authentic female voice illustrate the difficulty of theorizing from experience without essentializing or homogenizing it. There is no "generic woman,"[27] or any uniform "condition of women."[28] To divide the world solely along gender lines is to ig-

---

24. For standpoint theory, see, e.g., Nancy C. Hartsock, Money, Sex & Power: Toward a Feminist Historical Materialism 117-18, 135, 231-47 (1983). For a critique of such theories, see Sandra Harding, The Science Question in Feminism 163-96 (1986); Bartlett, *supra* note 14.

25. West, *supra* note 8, at 48.

26. *See* Carol Gilligan, In a Different Voice (1982); Mary Field Belenky, Blythe McVickar Clinchy, Nancy Rule Goldberger & Jill Mattuck Tarule, Women's Ways of Knowing (1986); Colker, *supra* note 20; Carrie Menkel-Meadow, *Portia in A Different Voice: Speculations on a Woman's Lawyering Process*, 1 Berkeley Women's L.J. 39 (1985).

27. The phrase is Elizabeth V. Spelman's in Inessential Woman: Problems of Exclusion in Feminist Thought 187 (1988). *See also* Adrienne Rich, *Disloyal to Civilization: Feminism, Racism, Gynephobia*, in On Lies, Secrets and Silence 275 (1979).

28. MacKinnon, *supra* note 13, at 637 n.5, *quoted in* text accompanying note 19 *supra*.

nore ways in which biological constraints are experienced differently by different groups under different circumstances.[29] If, as critical feminists generally maintain, women's experience has been shaped through culturally contingent patterns of subordination, no particular experience can claim universal authentic status. Moreover, to emphasize only the positive attributes traditionally associated with women is to risk overclaiming and oversimplifying their distinctive contributions. Most empirical work on moral reasoning and public values discloses less substantial gender differences than relational frameworks generally suggest.[30] These frameworks also reinforce dichotomous stereotypes—such as males' association with abstract rationality and females' with empathetic nurturance—that have restricted opportunities for both sexes.

Such concerns underpin those strands of critical feminism that focus on challenging rather than celebrating sex-based difference. The virtue of their approach lies in revealing how legal ideology has misdescribed cultural constructions as biological imperatives.[31] Yet the strengths of this framework also suggest its limitations. Affirmations of similarity between the sexes may inadvertently institutionalize dominant social practices and erode efforts to build group solidarity. Denying difference can, in some contexts, reinforce values that critics seek to change.

A more promising response to the "difference dilemma," and to more general questions about feminist epistemology, is to challenge the framework in which these issues are typically debated. The crucial issue becomes not difference, but the difference difference makes.[32] In legal contexts, the legitimacy of sex-based treatment should not depend on whether the sexes are differently situated. Rather, analysis should turn on whether legal recognition of gender distinctions is likely to reduce or reinforce gender disparities in power, status, and economic security. Since such issues cannot be resolved in the abstract, this strategy requires contextual judgments, not categorical choices. It asks which perspective on difference can best serve particular theoretical or practical objectives, and recognizes that there may be tradeoffs between them. Such an approach demands that feminists shift self-con-

---

29. *See, e.g.,* Harris, *supra* note 20; Marlee Kline, *Race, Racism and Feminist Legal Theory,* 12 HARV. WOMEN'S L.J. 115 (1989); Judy Scales-Trent, *Black Women and the Constitution: Finding Our Place, Asserting Our Rights,* 24 HARV. C.R.-C.L. L. REV. 9 (1989); Kimberle Crenshaw, *Demarginalizing the Intersection of Race and Sex: A Black Feminist Critique of Antidiscrimination Doctrine, Feminist Theory and Antiracist Politics,* 1989 U. CHI. LEGAL F. 139. For analysis of how the significance of gender varies in different settings, see Kay Deaux & Brenda Major, *A Social Psychological Model of Gender,* in THEORETICAL PERSPECTIVES ON SEXUAL DIFFERENCE, *supra* note 6, at 89.

30. D. RHODE, JUSTICE AND GENDER, *supra* note 6, at 311-12.

31. *See, e.g.,* Frances Olsen, *Statutory Rape: A Feminist Critique of Rights Analysis,* 63 TEX. L. REV. 387 (1984); Wendy W. Williams, *The Equality Crisis: Some Reflections on Culture, Courts, and Feminism,* 7 WOMEN'S RTS. L. REP. 175 (1982); Williams, *supra* note 22.

32. *See* C. MACKINNON, *supra* note 6, at 32-45; Littleton, *supra* note 6; D. RHODE, JUSTICE AND GENDER, *supra* note 6, at 81-111; JOAN WALLACH SCOTT, GENDER AND THE POLITICS OF HISTORY 175-77 (1988).

sciously among needs to acknowledge both distinctiveness and commonality between the sexes and unity and diversity among their members.

On the more general question of what validates any particular feminist claim, the first step is to deconstruct the dualistic framework of truth and falsehood in which these issues are often discussed. As postmodernist theorists remind us, all perspectives are partial, but some are more incomplete than others.[33] To disclaim objective standards of truth is not to disclaim all value judgments. We need not become positivists to believe that some accounts of experience are more consistent, coherent, inclusive, self-critical, and so forth. Critical feminism can illuminate the process by which claims about the world are constituted as well as the effects of marginalizing women and other subordinate groups in that process. Such a framework can subject traditional forms of argument and criteria of relevance to sustained scrutiny. It can challenge exclusionary institutions in which knowledge is constructed. And it can press for social changes that would encourage deeper understanding of our experience and the forces that affect it.

Although critical feminists by no means speak with one voice on any of these issues, part of our strength lies in building on our differences as well as our commonalities. Precisely because we do not share a single view on this, or other more substantive concerns, we need theories but not Theory. Our objective should be multiple accounts that avoid privileging any single universalist or essentialist standpoint. We need understandings that can resonate with women's shared experience without losing touch with our diversity. The factors that divide us can also be a basis for enriching our theoretical perspectives and expanding our political alliances. Any framework adequate to challenge sex-based oppression must simultaneously condemn the other forms of injustice with which it intersects.

What allies this method with other critical accounts is its skepticism toward everything, including skepticism. Critical feminist theories retain a commitment to locate judgment within the patterns of social practice, to subject that judgment to continuing critique, and to promote gender equality as a normative ideal. Those commitments may take us in multiple directions but, as Martha Minow maintains, they are unifying commitments nonetheless.[34]

---

33. See BARBARA HERRNSTEIN SMITH, CONTINGENCIES OF VALUE 94, 166-79 (1988); Flax, *supra* note 9; Fraser & Nicholsen, *supra* note 8, at 91; Mary E. Hawkesworth, *Knower, Knowing, Known: Feminist Theory and Claims of Truth*, 14 SIGNS 533, 557 (1989) (arguing that "[i]n the absence of claims of universal validity, feminist accounts derive their justificatory force from their capacity to illuminate existing social relations [and] to demonstrate the deficiencies of alternative interpretations").

34. Martha Minow, *Beyond Universality*, 1989 U. CHI. LEGAL F. 115. See generally Susan Griffin, *The Way of All Ideology*, in FEMINIST THEORY: A CRITIQUE OF IDEOLOGY 273 (N. Keohane, M. Rosaldo & B. Gelpi eds. 1982); Deborah L. Rhode, *Introduction: Theoretical Perspectives on Sexual Difference*, in THEORETICAL PERSPECTIVES ON SEXUAL DIFFERENCE, *supra* note 6.

II.   Liberal Legalism

For CLS theorists, the most frequent unifying theme is opposition to a common target: the dominance of liberal legalism and the role law has played in maintaining it.[35] On this issue, critical feminism offers more varied and more ambivalent responses. This diversity in part reflects the diversity of perspectives within the liberal tradition. The target appearing in many critical legal studies accounts, and in some critical feminist analyses, is only one version of liberal legalism, generally the version favored by law and economics commentators. Under a more robust framework, many inequalities of greatest concern to feminists reflect limitations less in liberal premises than in efforts to realize liberalism's full potential.[36]

From both a philosophical and pragmatic standpoint, feminist legal critics have less stake in the assault on liberalism than CLS. Their primary target is gender inequality, whatever its pedigree, and their allies in many concrete political struggles have come as often from liberal as from radical camps. Thus, when critical feminist theorists join the challenge to liberal legalism, they often do so on somewhat modified grounds. Their opposition tends to focus on the particular form of liberalism embodied in existing legal and political structures and on the gender biases it reflects.

Although they differ widely in other respects, liberal theorists generally begin from the premise that the state's central objective lies in maximizing individuals' freedom to pursue their own objectives to an extent consistent with the same freedom for others. Implicit in this vision are several assumptions about the nature of individuals and the subjectivity of values. As conventionally presented, the liberal state is composed of autonomous, rational individuals. Their expressed choices reflect a stable and coherent understanding of their independent interests. Yet, while capable of full knowledge of their own preferences, these liberal selves lack similar knowledge about others. Accordingly, the good society remains as neutral as possible about the meaning of the good life: It seeks simply to provide the conditions necessary for individuals to maximize their own preferences through voluntary transactions. Although liberal theorists differ widely about what

---

35.   Robert W. Gordon, *New Developments in Legal Theory*, in The Politics of Law: A Progressive Critique, *supra* note 5, at 281; A. Hutchinson, *Introduction* to Critical Legal Studies (A. Hutchinson ed. 1989).

36.   For example, although Susan Okin criticizes John Rawls's work for its assumptions about egoism and his insensitivity to gender inequalties, she believes that his framework can be consistent with feminist principles. *See* Susan Moller Okin, *Reason and Feeling in Thinking About Justice*, 99 Ethics 229, 230, 248 (1989). For a contrary view, see Mari Matsuda, *Liberal Jurisprudence and Abstracted Visions of Human Nature: A Feminist Critique of Rawls' Theory of Justice* 16 N.M.L. Rev. 613 (1986). *See generally* Charles Larmore, Patterns of Moral Complexity 107-29 (1987) (arguing that liberalism understood as a political rather than metaphysical doctrine need not appeal to individualism as a general value); Robin L. West, *Liberalism Rediscovered: A Pragmatic Definition of the Liberal Vision*, 46 U. Pitt. L. Rev. 673 (1985).

those background conditions entail, they share a commitment to preserving private zones for autonomous choices, free from public intervention.[37] Critical feminist theorists have challenged this account along several dimensions. According to theorists such as West, these liberal legalist selves are peculiarly masculine constructs—peculiarly capable of infallible judgments about their own wants and peculiarly incapable of empathetic knowledge about the wants of others.[38] Classic liberal frameworks take contractual exchanges rather than affiliative relationships as the norm. Such frameworks undervalue the ways social networks construct human identities and the ways individual preferences are formed in reference to the needs and concerns of others. For many women, a nurturing, giving self has greater normative and descriptive resonance than an autonomous, egoistic self.[39]

Critical feminists by no means agree about the extent, origins, or implications of such gender differences. Some concept of autonomy has been central to the American women's movement since its inception, autonomy from the constraints of male authority and traditional roles. How much emphasis to place on values of self-determination and how much to place on values of affiliation have generated continuing controversies that cannot be resolved at the abstract level on which debate has often foundered.[40] Even critical feminists who agree about the significance of difference disagree about its causes and likely persistence. Disputes center on how much importance is attributable to women's intimate connection to others through childbirth and identification with primary caretakers, how much to cultural norms that encourage women's deference, empathy, and disproportionate assumption of nurturing responsibilities, and how much to inequalities in women's status and power.[41]

Yet despite these disagreements, most critical feminists share an

---

37. See JOHN RAWLS, A THEORY OF JUSTICE (1971); Ronald Dworkin, *Liberalism*, in PUBLIC AND PRIVATE MORALITY 113 (S. Hampshire ed. 1978); BRUCE ACKERMAN, SOCIAL JUSTICE IN THE LIBERAL STATE (1980). *See generally* Steven Shiffrin, *Liberalism, Radicalism, and Legal Scholarship*, 30 UCLA L. REV. 1103 (1983); West, *supra* note 36.

38. Robin West, *Economic Man and Literary Woman: One Contrast*, 39 MERCER L. REV. 867 (1988).

39. A. JAGGAR, *supra* note 4, at 21-22; Virginia Held, *Feminism and Moral Theory*, in WOMEN AND MORAL THEORY 111 (E. Kittay & D. Meyers eds. 1987); Susan Moller Okin, *Humanist Liberalism*, in LIBERALISM AND THE MORAL LIFE 39 (N. Rosenblum ed. 1989); Robin West, *Jurisprudence and Gender*, 55 U. CHI. L. REV. 1 (1988).

40. *See, e.g.*, West, *supra* note 39, at 36; Jennifer Nedelsky, *Reconceiving Autonomy: Sources, Thoughts and Possibilities*, 1 YALE J.L. & FEMINISM 7 (1989); *see also* Kathryn Jackson, *And Justice for All? Human Nature and the Feminist Critique of Liberalism*, in WOMEN AND A NEW ACADEMY 122 (J. O'Barr ed. 1989) (arguing that dualistic approaches fail adequately to recognize the interdependence of values such as autonomy and care).

41. Compare the focus on childbirth in West, *supra* note 39, at 2-3, with the emphasis on identification with primary caretakers in NANCY CHODOROW, THE REPRODUCTION OF MOTHERING: PSYCHOANALYSIS AND THE SOCIOLOGY OF GENDER 7 (1978); DOROTHY DINNERSTEIN, THE MERMAID AND THE MINOTAUR 5 (1976); the attention to stereotypes in CYNTHIA FUCHS EPSTEIN, DECEPTIVE DISTINCTIONS (1988); and the focus on power in *Feminist Discourse, Moral*

emphasis on the importance of social relationships in shaping individual preferences. From such a perspective, no adequate conception of the good society can be derived through standard liberal techniques, which hypothesize social contracts among atomistic actors removed from the affiliations that give meaning to their lives and content to their choices.[42]

This feminist perspective points up a related difficulty in liberal frameworks, which critical theorists from a variety of traditions have noted. The liberal assumption that individuals' expressed preferences can be taken as reflective of genuine preferences is flatly at odds with much of what we know about human behavior. To a substantial extent, our choices are socially constructed and constrained; the desires we develop are partly a function of the desires our culture reinforces. As long as gender plays an important role in shaping individual expectations and aspirations, expressed objectives cannot be equated with full human potential. Women, for example, may "choose" to remain in an abusive relationship, but such choices are not ones most liberals would want to maximize. Yet a liberal legalist society has difficulty distinguishing between "authentic" and "inauthentic" preferences without violating its own commitments concerning neutrality and the subjectivity of value.[43]

Similar problems arise with the legal ideology that underpins contemporary liberal frameworks. In its conventional form, liberal legalism assumes that appropriate conduct can be defined primarily in terms of adherence to procedurally legitimate and determinate rules, that law can be separated from politics, and that spheres of private life can be insulated from public intrusion.[44] Critical feminism challenges all of these assumptions on both empirical and normative levels.

The feminist critique joins other CLS work in denying that the rule of law in fact offers a principled, impartial, and determinate means of dispute resolution. Attention has centered both on the subjectivity of legal standards and the gender biases in their application. By exploring particular substantive areas, feminists have underscored the law's fluctuation between standards that are too abstract to resolve particular cases and rules that are too specific to result in principled, generalizable norms.[45] Such explorations have also revealed sex-based assumptions that undermine the liberal legal order's own aspirations.

These limitations in conventional doctrine are particularly apparent

---

Values and the Law—A Conversation, 34 BUFFALO L. REV. 11, 71-72 (1985) (comments of MacKinnon).

42. *See* note 39 *supra.*

43. A. JAGGAR, *supra* note 4, at 40-42; MARK KELMAN, A GUIDE TO CRITICAL LEGAL STUDIES 66-67 (1987).

44. *See* JUDITH N. SHKLAR, LEGALISM (1964); Duncan Kennedy, *Legal Formality,* 2 J. LEGAL STUD. 351, 371-72 (1973); Karl Klare, *Law-Making as Praxis,* 40 TELOS 123, 132 (1970).

45. *See* Clare Dalton, *An Essay in the Deconstruction of Contract Doctrine,* 94 YALE L.J. 997, 1106-08 (1985).

in the law's consistently inconsistent analysis of gender difference. Decisionmakers have often reached identical legal results from competing factual premises. In other cases, the same notions about sexual distinctiveness have yielded opposite conclusions. Identical assumptions about woman's special virtues or vulnerabilities have served as arguments for both favored and disfavored legal treatment in criminal and family law, and for both including and excluding her from public roles such as professional occupations and jury service.[46] For example, although courts and legislatures traditionally assumed that it was "too plain" for discussion that sex-based distinctions in criminal sentencing statutes and child custody decisions were appropriate, it was less plain which way those distinctions cut. Under different statutory schemes, women received lesser or greater punishments for the same criminal acts and in different historical periods were favored or disfavored as the guardians of their children.[47]

The law's traditional approach to gender-related issues has not only yielded indeterminate interpretations, it has allowed broad mandates of formal equality to mask substantive inequality. Part of the problem with "difference" as an organizing principle is that legal decisionmakers do not always seem to know it when they see it. One of the most frequently noted illustrations is the Supreme Court's 1974 conclusion that pregnancy discrimination did not involve gender discrimination or even "gender as such"; employers were simply distinguishing between "pregnant women and non-pregnant persons."[48] So too, although most contemporary divorce legislation promises "equal" or "equitable" property distributions between spouses, wives have in practice received neither equality nor equity. In the vast majority of cases, women end up with far greater caretaking responsibilities and far fewer resources to discharge them.[49]

Such indeterminacies and biases also undermine the liberal legalist distinction between public and private spheres. From a critical feminist

---

46. See Rhode, Definitions of Difference, supra note 6.

47. Territory v. Armstrong, 28 Haw. 88 (1924) (upholding greater statutory penalties for males than females convicted of adultery); Wark v. Maine, 266 A.2d 62, 64-65 (Me. 1970) (upholding greater statutory penalties for males than females convicted of escape from penal institutions), cert. denied, 400 U.S. 952 (1970); Ex parte Gosselin, 141 Me. 412, 421, 44 A.2d 882, 885-86 (1945) (upholding greater statutory penalties for females than males convicted of misdemeanors such as intoxication); Commonwealth v. Daniel, 210 Pa. Super. 156, 232 A.2d 247 (1967), rev'd, 430 Pa. 642, 243 A.2d 400 (1968) (invalidating statute that gave judges greater discretion to consider exonerating circumstances for males than females convicted of robbery). For changes in custody provisions, see Fran Olsen, The Politics of Family Law, 2 LAW & INEQUALITY 1, 12-19 (1984).

48. Geduldig v. Aiello, 417 U.S. 484, 497 n.20 (1974); see also General Elec. Co. v. Gilbert 429 U.S. 125 (1976).

49. LENORE J. WEITZMAN, THE DIVORCE REVOLUTION (1985); Herma Hill Kay, Equality and Difference: A Perspective on No-Fault Divorce and Its Aftermath, 56 U. CIN. L. REV. 1, 60-65 (1987); Deborah L. Rhode & Martha Minow, Reforming the Questions, Questioning the Reforms: Feminist Perspectives on Divorce Reform, in DIVORCE REFORM AT THE CROSS ROADS (S. Sugarman & H. Kay eds. 1990) (forthcoming).

view, the boundary between state and family is problematic on both descriptive and prescriptive grounds. As an empirical matter, the state inevitably participates in determining what counts as private and what forms of intimacy deserve public protection. Governmental policies concerning childcare, tax, inheritance, property, welfare, and birth control have all heavily influenced family arrangements. As Fran Olsen and Clare Dalton have noted, the same legal decisions regarding intimate arrangements often can be described either as intervention or nonintervention depending on the decisionmakers' point of view. For example, a refusal to enforce unwritten cohabitation agreements can be seen as a means of either preserving or intruding on intimate relationships.[50]

Conventional public/private distinctions present normative difficulties as well. Contrary to liberal legalist assumptions, the state's refusal to intervene in private matters has not necessarily expanded individual autonomy; it has often simply substituted private for public power. Courts' failure to recognize unwritten agreements between cohabitants or to enforce support obligations and rape prohibitions in ongoing marriages has generally enlarged the liberties of men at the expense of women.[51]

Critical feminism does not, however, categorically renounce the constraints on state power that liberal legalism has secured. Rather, it denies that conventional public/private dichotomies provide a useful conceptual scheme for assessing such constraints. As the following discussion of rights suggests, judgments about the appropriate scope of state intervention require a contextual analysis, which takes account of gender disparities in existing distributions of power. In this, as in other theoretical contexts previously noted, we need less reliance on abstract principles and more on concrete experience.

A similar point emerges from one final challenge to liberal legalism. Building on the work of moral theorists such as Carol Gilligan, Annette Baier, and Sarah Ruddick, some commentators have questioned the primacy that this culture attaches to formal, adversarial, and hierarchical modes of dispute resolution.[52] A legal system founded on feminist priorities—those emphasizing trust, care, and empathy—should aspire to less combative, more conciliatory, procedures.

Yet as other feminist critics have noted, an appeal to empathetic values leaves most of the difficult questions unanswered. With whom

---

50. Dalton, *supra* note 45, at 1107; Frances E. Olsen, *The Myth of State Intervention in the Family,* 18 U. MICH. J.L. REF. 835 (1985).

51. *See* MICHAEL D.A. FREEMAN & CHRISTINA M. LYON, COHABITATION WITHOUT MARRIAGE: AN ESSAY IN LAW AND SOCIAL POLICY (1983); DIANA E.H. RUSSELL, RAPE IN MARRIAGE 17-24 (1982); Olsen, *supra* note 50, at 843-58; Marjorie Maguire Shultz, *Contractual Ordering of Marriage: A New Model for State Policy,* 70 CALIF. L. REV. 204 (1982).

52. C. GILLIGAN, *supra* note 26; Annette Baier, *Trust and Antitrust,* 96 ETHICS 231, 247-53 (1986); Sara Ruddick, *Maternal Thinking,* 6 FEMINIST STUD. 342 (1980); *see* Lynne N. Henderson, *Legality and Empathy,* 85 MICH. L. REV. 1574 (1987); Menkel-Meadow, *supra* note 26.

should legal decisionmaking empathize when individual needs conflict?[53] And what procedural protections should be available to monitor those judgments? One risk is that conciliation between parties with unequal negotiating skills, information, and power can perpetuate those inequalities.[54] Judicial systems that have aspired to more nurturing processes, such as juvenile and family courts, have often reinforced patriarchal assumptions and sexual double standards.[55] Norms appropriate to our vision of justice in an ideal state may not be the best way to get us there.

Here again, a critical feminist approach to procedural values demands contextual judgment. To further the substantive objectives that critical feminism seeks, its greatest challenge lies at the pragmatic level; its task is to design frameworks more responsive to the experiences of subordinate groups. A crucial first step is to deconstruct the apparent dichotomy between formalism and informalism that has traditionally structured debate over alternative dispute resolution processes. Since neither approach has adequately responded to women's experiences and concerns, we cannot rest with debunking both possibilities or choosing the least objectionable alternative. Rather, as is true with debates over substantive rights, we need to reimagine the range of procedural options and to challenge the broader system of sex-based subordination that constrains their exercise.

III. RIGHTS

One central difference between critical feminism and other critical legal theory involves the role of rights. Although both bodies of work have challenged liberal legalism's reliance on formal entitlements, feminist accounts, like those of minority scholars, have tended more toward contextual analysis than categorical critique.

Most CLS scholarship has viewed rights-based strategies as an ineffective and illusory means of progressive social change. While sometimes acknowledging the importance of basic political liberties in preserving opportunities for dissent, critical legal theorists have generally presented the liberal rights agenda as a constraint on individual

---

53. Toni Masaro, *Empathy, Legal Storytelling, and the Rule of Law*, 87 MICH. L. REV. 2104 (1989).

54. *See* Janet Rifkin, *Mediation from a Feminist Perspective: Promise and Problems*, 2 LAW & INEQUALITY 21 (1984). For example, the National Center on Women and Family Law maintains that because wives in divorce cases do not have equal financial and social power they cannot assert equal bargaining power in informal settings without representation by counsel. *See* Carol Lefcourt, *Women, Mediation, and Family Law*, 18 CLEARINGHOUSE REV. 266 (1984). Similarly, researchers in domestic violence cases have found that mediation often perpetuates attitudes that perpetuate abuse because it implies that assaultive behavior does not justify criminal sanctions and that parties bear equal responsibility for preventing it. Lisa G. Lerman, *Mediation of Wife Abuse Cases: The Adverse Impact of Informal Dispute Resolution on Women*, 7 HARV. WOMEN'S L.J. 57 (1984).

55. Judith Resnik, *On the Bias: Feminist Reconsiderations of the Aspirations for Judges*, 61 S. CAL. L. REV. 1877, 1926-33 (1988); Rifkin, *supra* note 54.

consciousness and collective mobilization.[56]   Part of the problem arises from the indeterminacy noted earlier.   Feminist commentators such as Fran Olsen have joined other critical theorists in noting that rights discourse cannot resolve social conflict but can only restate it in somewhat abstract, conclusory form.   A rights-oriented framework may distance us from necessary value choices and obscure the basis on which competing interests are accommodated.[57]

According to this critique, too much political energy has been diverted into battles that cannot promise significant gains.   For example, a decade's experience with state equal rights amendments reveals no necessary correlation between the standard of constitutional protection provided by legal tribunals and the results achieved.[58]   It is unlikely that a federal equal rights amendment would have insured the vast array of substantive objectives that its proponents frequently claimed. Supporters' tendencies to cast the amendment as an all-purpose prescription for social ills—the plight of displaced homemakers, the feminization of poverty, and the gender gap in earnings—have misdescribed the problem and misled as to the solution.[59]

A related limitation of the liberal rights agenda involves its individualist premises and restricted scope.   A preoccupation with personal entitlements can divert concern from collective responsibilities.   Rights rhetoric too often channels individuals' aspirations into demands for their own share of protected opportunities and fails to address more fundamental issues about what ought to be protected.   Such an individualistic framework ill serves the values of cooperation and empathy that feminists find lacking in our current legal culture.[60]

Nor are mandates guaranteeing equality in formal rights adequate to secure equality in actual experience as long as rights remain restricted to those that a predominately white upper middle class male judiciary has been prepared to regard as fundamental.   No legal structure truly committed to equality for women would end up with a scheme that affords extensive protection to the right to bear arms or to sell violent pornography, but not to control our reproductive lives.[61]

---

56. Olsen, *supra* note 31; *see* Peter Gabel, *The Phenomenology of Rights-Consciousness and the Pact of the Withdrawn Selves*, 62 TEX. L. REV. 1563 (1984); Mark Tushnet, *An Essay on Rights*, 62 TEX. L. REV. 1363, 1382-84 (1984).

57. *See generally* sources cited in note 56 *supra* and note 66 *infra*; THE POLITICS OF LAW: A PROGRESSIVE CRITIQUE, *supra* note 5; Adelaide Villamore, *The Left's Problems With Rights*, 9 LEGAL STUD. F. 39 (1985).

58. *See generally* Dawn-Marie Driscoll & Barbara J. Rouse, *Through a Glass Darkly: A Look at State Equal Rights Amendments*, 12 SUFFOLK U.L. REV. 1282, 1308 (1978); D. RHODE, JUSTICE AND GENDER, *supra* note 6, at 92.

59. *See* D. RHODE, JUSTICE AND GENDER, *supra* note 6; Catharine A. MacKinnon, *Unthinking ERA Thinking* (Book Review), 54 U. CHI. L. REV. 759 (1987).

60. *See* note 52 *supra;* MICHAEL IGNATIEFF, THE NEEDS OF STRANGERS 13 (1984).

61. *Compare* U.S. CONST. amend. II *and* American Booksellers Ass'n v. Hudnut, 771 F.2d 323 (7th Cir. 1985), *aff'd*, 475 U.S. 1001 (1986), *with* Webster v. Reproductive Health Servs., 109 S. Ct. 3040 (1989), *and* Harris v. McRae, 448 U.S. 297 (1980).

In a culture where rights have been defined primarily in terms of "freedoms from" rather than "freedoms to," many individuals lack the resources necessary for exercising rights to which they are formally entitled. Such problems are compounded by the costs and complexities of legal proceedings and the maldistribution of legal services available to enforce formal entitlements or prevent their curtailment.[62] By channeling political struggles into legal disputes, rights-based strategies risk limiting aspirations and reinforcing dependence on legal decisionmakers.

Yet while acknowledging these limitations, critical feminism has also emphasized certain empowering dimensions of rights strategies that other CLS work discounts. As theorists including Kimberlé Crenshaw, Christine Littleton, Elizabeth Schneider, and Patricia Williams have argued, legal rights have a special resonance in our culture.[63] The source of their limitations is also the source of their strength. Because claims about rights proceed within established discourse, they are less readily dismissed than other progressive demands. By insisting that the rule of law make good on its own aspirations, rights-oriented strategies offer a possibility of internal challenge that critical theorists have recognized as empowering in other contexts.

So too, critiques that focus only on the individualist premises of rights rhetoric obscure its collective dimensions. The dichotomies often drawn between rights and relationships or rights and responsibilities are highly exaggerated. Rights not only secure personal autonomy, they also express relationships between the individual and the community. Just as rights can impose responsibilities, responsibilities can imply rights. Often the concepts serve identical ends: a right to freedom from discrimination imposes a responsibility not to engage in it. Discarding one form of discourse in favor of another is unlikely to alter the foundations of our legal culture. Moreover, for subordinate groups, rights-based frameworks have supported demands not only for individual entitlements but also for collective selfhood. For example, women's right to reproductive autonomy is a prerequisite to their social equality; without control of their individual destinies, women cannot challenge the group stereotypes and role constraints that underpin their subordinate status. Claims of right can further advance collective values by drawing claimants within a community capable of response and de-

---

62. Richard Abel, American Lawyers (1989); Richard L. Abel, *United States: The Contradictions of Professionalism*, 1 Lawyers in Society: The Common Law World 186 (R. Abel & P. Lewis eds. 1988); Stuart A. Scheingold, The Politics of Rights: Lawyers, Public Policy and Political Change 172 (1974); Deborah L. Rhode, *The Rhetoric of Professional Reform*, 45 Md. L. Rev. 274, 281-82 (1986).

63. Kimberlé Williams Crenshaw, *Race, Reform, and Retrenchment: Transformation and Legitimation in Antidiscrimination Law*, 101 Harv. L. Rev. 1331, 1366-69 (1988); Schneider, *supra* note 13; Patricia J. Williams, *Alchemical Notes: Reconstructing Ideals From Deconstructed Rights*, 22 Harv. C.R.-C.L. L. Rev. 401 (1987).

manding that its members take notice of the grievances expressed.[64]

For critical feminism, the most promising approach is both to acknowledge the indeterminate nature of rights rhetoric and to recognize that, in particular circumstances, such rhetoric can promote concrete objectives and social empowerment. Too often, rights have been abstracted from their social context and then criticized as abstract. Yet however manipulable, the rubric of autonomy and equality have made enormous practical differences in the lives of subordinate groups. Undermining the conceptual foundations of rights like privacy, on which women's reproductive choice has depended, involves considerable risks. Even largely symbolic campaigns, such as the recent ERA struggle, can be highly important, less because of the specific objective they seek than because of the political mobilization they inspire. Like the suffrage movements a half century earlier, the contemporary constitutional battle offered women invaluable instruction in both the limits of their own influence and the strategies necessary to expand it.[65]

Whatever its inadequacies, rights rhetoric has been the vocabulary most effective in catalyzing mass progressive movements in this culture. It is a discourse that critical feminists are reluctant to discard in favor of ill-defined or idealized alternatives. The central problem with rights-based frameworks is not that they are inherently limiting but that they have operated within a limited institutional and imaginative universe. Thus, critical feminism's central objective should be not to delegitimate such frameworks but rather to recast their content and recognize their constraints. Since rights-oriented campaigns can both enlarge and restrict political struggle, evaluation of their strategic possibilities requires historically situated contextual analysis.

On this point, feminists join other critical theorists in seeking to build on the communal, relational, and destabilizing dimensions of rights-based arguments.[66] Claims to self-determination can express desires not only for autonomy but also for participation in the communities that shape our existence. If selectively invoked, the rhetoric of rights can empower subordinate groups to challenge the forces that perpetuate their subordination.

IV. ALTERNATIVE VISIONS

One final issue on which critical feminism often parts company with other critical theory involves the construction of alternative visions of the good society. Although both traditions reflect considerable ambivalence about the value of such projects, the focus of concern varies.

---

64. *See* Schneider, *supra* note 13; Martha Minow, *Interpreting Rights: An Essay for Robert Cover*, 96 YALE L.J. 1860, 1875-77 (1987).
65. *See* note 59 *supra*.
66. *See* Staughton Lynd, *Communal Rights*, 62 TEX. L. REV. 1417 (1984); Roberto Mangabeira Unger, *The Critical Legal Studies Movement*, 96 HARV. L. REV. 561, 612-16 (1983).

Most critical theory that has attempted to construct alternative visions assumes away the problems with which feminists have been most concerned or opens itself to the same challenges of indeterminacy that it has directed at other work. Partly for these reasons, feminist legal critics have devoted relatively little attention to idealized programs. Rather, their efforts have centered on identifying the values that must be central to any affirmative vision and the kinds of concrete legal and institutional transformations that such values imply.

A recurrent problem with most progressive utopian frameworks involves their level of generality. Objectives are often framed in terms of vague, seemingly universal aspirations—such as Roberto Unger's appeal to a world free "from deprivation and drudgery, from the choice between isolation from other people and submission to them."[67] Such formulations leave most of the interesting questions unanswered. How are such ideals to be interpreted and implemented under specific circumstances, how are interpretive disputes to be resolved, and how are gender relations to be reconstructed?

In response to such questions, a standard critical strategy is to specify conditions under which answers would be generated. Habermas' ideal speech situation has been perhaps the most influential example. Under his theory, beliefs would be accepted as legitimate only if they could have been acquired through full uncoerced discussion in which all members of society participate. Some critical feminists, including Drucilla Cornell and Seyla Benhabib, draw on similar conversational constructs.[68]

Such strategies are, however, problematic on several levels. One difficulty involves the level of abstraction at which the ideals are formulated. It is not self-evident how individuals with diverse experiences, interests, and resources will reach consensus or how their agreements can be predicted with enough specificity to provide adequate heuristic frameworks. Strategies emphasizing uncoerced dialogue have often assumed away the problems of disparate resources and capacities that parties bring to the conversation. Given the historical silencing of women's voices, many critical feminists have been unsatisfied by approaches that are themselves silent about how to prevent that pattern from recurring.[69]

A related difficulty stems from idealists' faith in dialogue as the pri-

---

67. See Unger, supra note 66, at 651; see also R. UNGER, supra note 9, at 18, 24. For a critical review of such generalized aspirations, see B. HERRNSTEIN SMITH, supra note 33, at 81-114.

68. See Seyla Benhabib, The Generalized and the Concrete Other, in FEMINISM AS CRITIQUE, supra note 4, at 92-94; see also J. HABERMAS, supra note 9; Richard J. Bernstein, Philosophy in the Conversation of Mankind, in HERMENEUTICS AND PRAXIS 54, 82 (R. Hollinger ed. 1985).

69. For discussion of women's silence focusing on law school contexts, see Women in Legal Education—Pedagogy, Law, Theory, and Practice, 38 J. LEGAL EDUC. 147 (1988); Catherine Weiss & Louise Melling, The Legal Education of Twenty Women, 40 STAN. L. REV. 1299 (1988); James R. Elkins, Worlds of Silence: Women in Law School, 8 A.L.S.A.F. 1 (1984).

mary response to social subordination. Alternative visions that proceed as if the central problem were our inability to imagine such alternatives often understate the material conditions that contribute to that inability. Many feminists have no difficulty imagining a world without pervasive sexual violence or the feminization of poverty; the difficulty lies in commanding support for concrete strategies that would make that vision possible.[70] It is, of course, true that we cannot be free from coercive institutional structures as long as we retain an ideology that legitimates them. But neither can we rid ourselves of that ideology as long as such structures limit our ability to challenge it.

In response to this dilemma, critical feminism has tended to focus on particular issues that implicate both material and ideological concerns. Rather than hypothesizing some universal utopian program, feminist legal critics have generally engaged in more concrete analysis that challenges both structural inequalities and the normative assumptions that underlie them. In evaluating particular strategies, critical feminism focuses on their capacity to improve women's social and economic status; to reach those women most in need; and to enhance women's self-respect, power, and ability to alter existing institutional arrangements.[71]

For example, the struggle for comparable pay for jobs of comparable worth presents direct opportunities to increase women's financial security. The campaign has helped reveal the cultural undervaluation of "women's work," has exposed gender and racial bias in employers' own criteria for compensation, and has aided workplace organizing efforts.[72] Pay equity initiatives have also raised broader questions about market principles and social priorities. How should we reward various occupational and worker characteristics and how should those decisions be made? Are we comfortable in a society that pays more to parking attendants than child care attendants, whatever the gender composition of those positions? The struggle for comparable worth could spark a rethinking of the scope of inequality and the ideologies that sustain it.

The feminist focus on concrete issues has avoided an idealized vision that must inevitably change in the course of change. Feminist legal critics have been less interested in predicting the precise role that gender would play in the good society than in undermining its role in this one. Whether sex would ultimately become as unimportant as eye color or whether some sex-linked traits and affiliations would endure is

---

70. B. HERRNSTEIN SMITH, *supra* note 33, at 81, 111; Davis Cole, *Getting There: Reflections on Trashing from Feminist Jurisprudence and Critical Theory*, 8 HARV. WOMEN'S L.J. 59 (1985); Crenshaw, *supra* note 63, at 1387.

71. *See* CHARLOTTE BUNCH, PASSIONATE POLITICS 104, 111 (1986) (advocating similar evaluative criteria and urging feminists to push for reform while rejecting reformism and its premise that gender equality is possible without fundamental social change).

72. *See* D. RHODE, JUSTICE AND GENDER, *supra* note 6, at 368-69, 379-81. *See generally* COMPARABLE WORTH: NEW DIRECTIONS FOR RESEARCH (H. Hartmann ed. 1985).

not an issue on which more speculation seems fruitful.[73] Since what is now problematic about gender relations is the disparity in power, we cannot fully anticipate the shape of those relations in an ideal world where, by definition, such disparities do not exist. At utopian as well as practical levels, critical feminism is unwilling to remain trapped in debates about women's commonality with or difference from men. Its commitment is neither to embrace nor to suppress difference but to challenge the dualism and make the world safe for differences.

Although we cannot know *a priori* what the good society will be, we know more than enough about what it will not be to provide a current agenda. It will not be a society with sex-based disparities in status, power, and security. Nor will it be a society that denies many of its members substantial control over the terms of their daily existence. To realize its full potential, feminism must sustain a vision concerned not only with relations between men and women, but also with relations among them. The commitment to sexual equality that gave birth to the women's movement is necessary but not sufficient to realize the values underlying it. Those values place critical feminism in both tension and alliance with aspirations that other critical legal theory expresses.

---

73. *Compare* Richard A. Wasserstrom, *Racism, Sexism, and Preferential Treatment: An Approach to the Topics*, 24 UCLA L. Rev. 581, 603-15 (1977) (arguing that in the good society, gender will become as inconsequential as eye color) *with* Littleton, *supra* note 6 at 1304-37 (arguing that it is impossible to know what gender differences would survive under new conditions of social existence but that the goal should be to make such differences costless).

Toilets as a Feminist Issue:
A True Story
Taunya Lovell Banks†

THE ESSAY[1]

One can measure the degree of equality between the sexes in America by its public toilets. As a child growing up, I remember that most public toilets for women had pay stalls. It often cost a nickel or even a dime to relieve yourself in a public toilet. There may have been one or even two free stalls, but they often were filthy and usually lacked toilet tissue.

Comparing notes with a male contemporary, I was surprised to learn that there were pay stalls in the men's bathroom, but the urinals were free. Thus, women were penalized because no one had created the "feminine" equivalent of a urinal.[2] If women ventured outside the home and were forced by circumstances to relieve themselves, they had to keep nickels, dimes, and tissue handy. The situation was even worse for women of color

---

† Professor of Law, University of Maryland. I would like to thank Marley Weiss, Mary Coombs, Kathy Abrams, Regina Austin, and Jana Singer for their comments and suggestions on earlier drafts of this article. I also want to thank Robin West, Judy Scales-Trent, Mari Matsuda, Patricia Williams, Lani Guinier, and many others who read earlier drafts, for their words of support and encouragement. I am especially grateful to Richard Delgado, who first thought my initial article worth publishing. Of course, I take full responsibility for the content, shape, and direction of this article, so only my professional reputation is on the line. Finally, I dedicate this article to all the women whose laughter caused me to realize that this article is perhaps deviant, but not a crazy idea.

[1] This is an edited version of an essay which first appeared in Baculus, Publication of the Student Bar Association of the University of Tulsa College of Law, 10 (Oct 1988) (see note 17 and accompanying text).

[2] In fact, someone has invented a device, Le Funelle, a folded and biodegradable paper funnel with handles *and* tissue. The inventor, a woman, claims the device is the answer to women's concerns about contracting diseases from toilet seats. "It is for those times when sitting is simply out of the question, squatting is too difficult, and paper seat covers are either unavailable or too awkward." Gregg Levoy, *Startech: Stand-Up Women*, Omni Mag 114 (Jan 1988). The inventor, Lore Harp, was not successful in marketing her product. Radio stations would not accept the ad because they claimed it violated their program standards; many magazines refused to carry the ad; and drugstores and mass merchants who were afraid that the product might offend customers refused to carry the product. Paul Brown, *Mission Impossible?*, Inc. 109 (Jan 1989). More recently, Kathie Jones obtained a patent for a female urinal called the "She-inal." US Patent 4,985,940 (Jan 22, 1991). Ms. Jones has started a company called Urinette, Inc. to manufacture the urinal. Edward Gunts, *For Relief of Women, "Female Urinal" Considered for New Stadium*, Balt Sun A1 (Jan 25, 1991).

who often found that even when armed with nickels, dimes, and tissue, they were denied access to public toilets—both pay and free.[3] *No wonder many women were reluctant to leave their homes for lengthy activities in public settings. I wonder how many women see the correlation between the difficulties they face at public toilets and the attempt by men to discourage women from participating fully in activities outside the home.*

Even when pay stalls became less common, they were removed first from the men's room and only later, often by law, from the women's bathroom.[4] *But the elimination of the pay toilet did not end discrimination against women in this area. Take, for example, the long lines often seen outside the women's bathroom during intermission at the theatre, concerts, or athletic events. There is rarely even a short line at the men's room.*

One male friend maintains that men simply hold their waste longer than women because men dislike using public toilets. I am not convinced. I believe that the presence of urinals in men's rooms, along with a few stalls, allows these rooms to accommodate more users than women's bathrooms for approximately the same cost of construction. Men would say that this is economic equality. Granted, economic considerations are valid, but I contend that economic claims mask the deep-rooted reasons for inequality of access: men's desire to keep women at home.

There is no valid reason why women should have less access to bathroom facilities than men. Some may maintain that women insist on privacy, which requires building enclosed stalls, whereas men do not. Another male friend of mine suggested that women's bathrooms be constructed with rows of toilets, making the cost similar to that for a bank of urinals. This suggestion ignores the biological differences between men and women. Men use urinals facing inward, whereas women use toilets facing outward; thus, unless the toilets face the wall, women would have less privacy than men under this arrangement.

Would it really be unreasonable to require by law that public restrooms be constructed to accommodate the same number of users? Two possible results of such a measure would be shorter lines for women and

---

[3] Until the mid-1960s toilet facilities in most Southern states were racially segregated. See, for example, *Jones v Marva Theatres*, 180 F Supp 49 (D Md 1960); *King v City of Montgomery*, 42 Ala App 462, 168 S2d 30 (1964) (reversed conviction for trespassing in a coffee shop required by ordinance to maintain separate toilets for each race); *Dawling v City of Norfolk, Va*, 260 F2d 647 (4th Cir 1958). More recently, see *James v Stockham Valves and Fittings Co.*, 559 F2d 310 (5th Cir 1977) (employment discrimination suit reversing the decision of a lower court finding no discrimination where there were claims that the employer maintained racially segregated facilities, including toilets for women, as well as other forms of discrimination).

[4] In 1975, New York prohibited pay toilets by statute. NY Gen Bus Law § 399-A (McKinney 1991). The law was challenged unsuccessfully in *Nik-O-Lok Co. v Carey*, 52 AD2d 375, 384 NYS2d 211, *aff'd*, 40 NY2d 1089, 392 NYS2d 393, 360 NE2d 1076 (1976). For an example of a similar statute, see Va Code § 32.1-201 (1985), which applies to public gathering places, including service stations. However, service stations were excluded from coverage by the legislature in 1988. Va Code § 32.1-198 (1990 Supp). California is more restrictive, mandating free public restrooms only in government agencies. Cal Health & Safety Code § 3980 (West 1990). This provision was added in 1974.

longer lines for men. Either way produces equality. Another possible alternative, the so-called "European model," would make the same bathrooms available to both sexes, just like in private homes. Of course, some might say, and rightfully so, that Americans are too uncivilized, violent, sexist, and puritanical to adjust to unisex bathrooms. Certainly Phyllis Schlafly would agree that Americans would reject unisex bathrooms, even if she would not agree with my reasons.

Unisex bathrooms are an interesting alternative because they would give both sexes equal access to the same number of stalls. Such bathrooms would also result in the elimination of urinals, something that might be hailed by many men. I am sure some men find public urinals offensive. Perhaps my male friend is so uncomfortable in public toilets because he fears that his neighbors at the urinals are covertly comparing their genitals to his, urinal curve notwithstanding. If this is the case, then the men most likely to use public restrooms are either those who are secure enough that they do not care about the size of their genitals or anyone else's, or those men who like to look at men's genitals. Either way, perhaps women should spend more time looking at who is using the men's room.

Even if we resolve the equal access issue, women would still not be equal at the public toilet. I am convinced, based on over forty years of experience, that almost all public toilets are designed by men. These men either hate women or have never paid much attention to women's bathroom needs. I have become adept at contorting my body in ways that will allow me to sit or more likely squat over the toilet bowl.

Men fail to realize that most women, and a few men, have been thoroughly indoctrinated into believing that toilet seats spread all kinds of diseases, including "VD."[5] Thus, I have never been totally convinced that those paper toilet seat covers provided in some toilets or the strips of toilet paper that you use to cover the toilet seat really protect you from all of those diseases. As a result, many of us still squat over rather than sit on public toilet seats.

It is extremely difficult to squat and accurately aim your discharge when the toilet is off center, in the corner, or so close to the stall door that your nose is smashed against it when you squat. There is a bathroom at my school that has been "redesigned" to accommodate the disabled. Some bright man decided that, rather than remove and reposition the stall walls and toilet bowls, he would simply enlarge the space in the last stall to

---

[5] It appears that my fears are justified. Public toilets are full of bacteria, often on toilet seats, faucets, flush and door handles, floors, sinks, toweling, and soap dishes. Anne Cassidy, *Toilet Training for Adults: Learn What You Can Catch In Public Bathrooms*, Redbook 118 (Oct 1987). It is possible, though unlikely, to get herpes or crab lice from sitting on unprotected public toilet seats. However, you are more likely to get a urinary-tract infection or boils from toilet seats or salmonella or shigella from touching handles. Id at 118-19, 198. For an example of implicit judicial acceptance of the idea that venereal diseases are spread by toilet seats, see note 118 and accompanying text.

accommodate a wheelchair. In so doing, he decreased somewhat the space in the neighboring stall and also caused the toilet bowl to be off center. The bowl is very close to one wall, making it difficult, if not impossible, for a large woman to sit comfortably on the seat and requiring us squatters to angle our rears in at forty-five degrees.

A woman would never redesign the bathroom in this way. Of course, if more women were industrial designers, we might have bathrooms designed to accommodate equal numbers of men and women and stalls designed for women's comfort and convenience.[6] Hence another example of inequality perpetuated by the exclusion of women from the workplace.

The final and perhaps most difficult-to-achieve measure of gender equality at the public toilet is guaranteed access to toilet tissue, sanitary pads, and tampons. For years, mothers and grandmothers kept purses stuffed full of tissue because they knew that they would always need tissue when using the toilet, whereas men did not. Failure to provide toilet tissue is arguably a form of sex discrimination, although I am not sure that it would be actionable.

However, at least one court recently concluded that the failure of an employer to provide sanitary restrooms for his female employees constitutes sex discrimination prohibited by Title VII. Specifically, in Lynch v Freeman,[7] *the United States Court of Appeals for the Sixth Circuit ruled that a disparate impact claim could lie where a female construction worker alleged that her employer failed to provide adequate sanitary toilet facilities. She claimed that "the portable toilets were dirty, often had no toilet paper or paper that was soiled, and were not equipped with running water or sanitary napkins."[8] She was fired for using a restroom off the employer's worksite.[9]*

The employer argued that there was no sex-based discrimination since the restroom facilities for men and women were equal.[10] By "equal," the employer meant that the restrooms were unisex. The federal district court ruled in favor of the employer, reasoning that the restroom facilities did not constitute a barrier to equal employment opportunities for women because the women could eliminate any increased health risk from using the toilets by bringing their own toilet paper.[11] *Further, the district court*

---

[6] In fact, Dr. Roger McFadden, a friend and former student of mine, pointed out that there are differences between the male and female pelvis. Women have a wider pelvis (the pelvic arch or outlet is usually at an obtuse angle), while men have a narrower pelvis (the pelvic arch or outlet is usually at an acute angle). Henry Gray, *Anatomy of the Human Body*, 245-47 (Lea & Febiger, 28th ed 1966). Thus, while sitting on the toilet seat, men fit nicely and find it quite comfortable. That is why a man will take a newspaper or book to the bathroom to read while sitting. On the other hand, women find toilet seats uncomfortable because their pelves are wider and hit the seat.

[7] 817 F2d 380 (6th Cir 1987).

[8] Id at 381.

[9] Id at 382.

[10] Id at 387.

[11] Id at 386 (emphasis added).

asserted that the women could protect themselves from dirty toilet seats by covering the seats with toilet paper or by refraining from sitting directly on the seat[12]—the good old squat! The appellate court rejected these arguments.[13]

Men can get very hostile when their bathrooms are threatened, causing one to suspect that men see bathrooms as indices of power. Maybe that explains why corporate executives covet that key to the executive washroom, or even better, the private bathroom. Of course, it could also be the fear of exposing oneself at the public urinal, something that women do not experience because of the exclusive use of stalls in women's bathrooms.

I know of one former law school dean who incurred the wrath of her male faculty members when she converted one of the many bathrooms for men into a facility for women. It mattered not that the men still had many more bathrooms than the women. Even with this change, the women, who constituted approximately one-third of the school population, had only two bathrooms. Nevertheless, the men perceived that they had suffered a great loss. Perhaps the men who complained the most were those who still secretly wished for the "good old days" when women seldom enrolled in law school and were totally absent from the faculty.

The male faculty members at another law school were never troubled by the fact that the one bathroom in the faculty lounge was clearly labeled "men." When asked why female faculty were forced to leave the faculty lounge to share bathroom facilities with women students or staff, one faculty member remarked that the building had been constructed before there were any women on the faculty. Obviously, he felt it appropriate to constantly remind women faculty of this fact, subtly indicating that despite their presence, women still are not welcome, at least at that law school. After some faculty embarrassment, the bathroom was converted to a unisex bathroom by removing the sign and installing a lock—how simple and how equal!

It is time for feminists to realize that access to public toilets is a feminist issue. We must realize that continuing inequality at the toilet reflects this male-dominated society's hostility to our presence outside of the home. This hostility is often most apparent in public settings that traditionally have been closed to women.

Women need to start measuring their degree of equality by public toilets. When the lines are gone, when each stall is clean and always has toilet tissue, when the stalls are reasonably comfortable, and when the dispensing machines are stocked with sanitary supplies, we probably will be much closer to achieving equality between the sexes than we are now. In the meantime, remember the tissue, ladies!

---

[12] Id.

[13] Id at 388. One judge dissented, objecting to what he characterized as a "reasonable accommodation" analysis. Id at 389-91 (Boggs dissenting).

THE STORY

"Well, what about lavatory seats?" [Rachel] suddenly shouted at Gregory
. . . .

"When I sit there . . . I think, this was made for men by other men."[14]

A few years ago, when I could not find a vacant toilet in the Dallas airport while changing planes, I wrote the preceding satirical piece about the problems women have using public toilets[15] in the United States. Writing the article caused me to remember past complaints about public toilet facilities, things I had just accepted without question. I started to seriously question why there is usually a line at the women's but not the men's bathroom. Having never seen the inside of a men's restroom, I spoke to a few men about their facilities. Next, I started monitoring public bathrooms, noticing the number of stalls; whether they were clean; whether there was toilet paper in each stall; whether stall doors swung out or in; and whether stalls for the disabled were really wheelchair accessible. Initially, I penned the title of the article, *Toilets As A Feminist Issue*, tongue in cheek. But I have since concluded that the title is right on point.

A few friends read the final draft and thought it very funny. A male colleague suggested I turn the article into a legal essay by adding some footnotes. I thought briefly about rewriting the piece with a few footnotes but decided the topic was not important enough for a legal journal. Another male colleague said it was fine as long as I intended it as satire, but warned me that I would be ruined professionally if I published the piece in a legal journal.[16] His comments should have prepared me for what was to come, but I was not convinced that equality at the toilet was a threat to "male privilege."

During the summer of 1988, two of my students asked me to write a piece for the school newspaper. On a whim, I gave them the toilet arti-

---

[14] Kathryn Abrams, *Gender Discrimination and the Transformation of Workplace Norms*, 42 Vand L Rev 1183 (1989) (quoting Julian Barnes, *Staring at the Sun* (Knopf, 1st ed 1987)).

[15] I use the term toilet or bathroom in this article to refer to public facilities usually found in gasoline stations, department stores and shopping malls, restaurants, bus and train stations, sports arenas, theaters, auditoriums, schools and universities, and public buildings. These facilities may be referred to in state codes as public toilets, comfort stations, restrooms, bathrooms, lavatories, washrooms, and water closets. These facilities are also referred to as latrines, outhouses, cans, johns, and privies. Writer Anna Quindlen calls female johns "the jane." *Living Out Loud* 36 (Random House, 1988).

[16] Charles Lawrence, in an extremely personal article, describes a dream which forces him to confront his fear of being considered for a permanent teaching position at a prestigious law school. His colleagues cautioned him to edit or make the article "more abstract and theoretical—less concrete and personal." *A Dream: On Discovering the Significance of Fear*, 10 Nova L J 627 (1986). Fortunately, he disregarded their advice.

Too often women and men of color and white women suffer silently in the legal academy thinking that they are alone in their suffering. Belatedly, I realized that we (the "other" or "outsiders") are all hungry for validation of our perceptions and both anxious and ashamed to admit "the privatized damage" we normally keep buried. For a moving personal description of gender bias in law teaching, see Sheila McIntyre, *Gender Bias Within the Law School: "The Memo" and its Impact*, 2 Canadian J Women & L 362 (1987-88).

cle. A shorter version of the original (unpublished) article appeared in the first fall issue of the law school newspaper.[17] On the day the paper was distributed, approximately twenty young white males (ages 22 to 26) became openly outraged, claiming the article was in bad taste. They did not understand what bathrooms have to do with the women's movement. The editors of the newspaper were attacked for printing the article. One even had coffee spilled on him "accidentally" during class. On the other hand, dozens of women of all ages, support staff included, stopped to tell me how much they enjoyed the article. They said it made them laugh, and all too often they added, "and it's so true."

My article was not the most controversial piece in the newspaper, and there were plenty of "trivial" articles.[18] I later learned that several young men had approached the most senior male professor at the law school and asked him to write a response. He declined, saying it was satire, but made a point of telling me he had been asked. This professor also mentioned that an alumnus had called him to ask if the article was serious. Obviously, satire is becoming a lost art form.

Students, colleagues, and friends reported that my article was an agenda item at the weekly meeting of a large local law firm; it was discussed at a faculty meeting of another law school in the state; and it was circulated by a woman law teacher to faculty members at an east coast law school, where some male faculty considered it vulgar or trivial.

None of this distressed me. In fact, I was amused. However, two subsequent events did upset me. The first occurred, ironically, in the women's toilet at the law school. It was crowded, and I mumbled something to myself about toilets. A former student in my constitutional law class who overheard my comment responded that she thought my article on toilets was trivial and not worthy of space in the newspaper. She said there were more important issues and compared the thrust of my article to an incident that occurred at the oil company where she clerked. According to the student, a woman lawyer "caused" the company to close its company gym because it did not have shower and changing facilities for women employees. The company offered to pay the membership fee to a private health club in another building that did admit women, but the woman refused. She insisted that the accommodation be made at her employer's gym. The company subsequently closed the gym. My student blamed the woman for causing so much trouble over such a trivial matter.

---

[17] Taunya Lovell Banks, *Toilets as a Feminist Issue*, Baculus 10 (Oct 1988).

[18] For example, there was a more "controversial" article advocating removal of the divorce process from the judicial system, relying instead on binding mediation. Larry Losoncy, *We Need a Better Mouse Trap*, Baculus 6 (Oct 1988). In addition, there were four articles on sports, two on intramural football alone, covering two full pages, or one-seventh of the paper. Only one, *Torts In Sports: The Marc Buoniconti Case*, Baculus 12 (Oct 1988), was related to a legal topic. Even the Administrative Assistant to the Dean had a small section of "witticisms."

I tried to explain that "trivial" things like equal toilet facilities can operate to deprive women of equal employment opportunities,[19] but the student could not see my point. Obviously, I had failed as a constitutional law teacher. I smiled to myself—she will learn once she has been in the legal profession for a few years.[20] Even with her intelligence, ambition, and "dress for success" suit, she will never fit in at that oil company because she is not a man.[21]

The second incident seems minor, but it deeply wounded me. Shortly after the newspaper was published, I received a large envelope marked "confidential." It came from an African-American man who holds an administrative but non-tenured position on campus. I opened the envelope and found a copy of my article with a note attached which read: "I thought this a rather crude piece. Wasn't there a better way to

---

[19] See notes 86-94 and accompanying text. Traditionally, private men's clubs were places where many important business transactions occurred. The exclusion of women from some of these facilities may violate the law. See *Roberts v U.S. Jaycees*, 468 US 609 (1984); *Board of Directors of Rotary International v Rotary Club*, 481 US 537 (1987); *N.Y. State Club Ass'n, Inc. v City of New York*, 487 US 1 (1988).

[20] Gender bias is still very much alive in the legal profession. Most major law firms hire women as associates, but few become partners. "The message that women are far from fully assimilated into the profession was reinforced in interviews with a score of women who are lawyers and in testimony of more than 60 lawyers before a commission appointed by the American Bar Association to assess the status of women in the profession." Tom Goldstein, *Women in the Law Aren't Yet Equal Partners*, NY Times, B7 (Feb 12, 1988); Nancy Blodgett, *I Don't Think That Ladies Should Be Lawyers*, 72 ABA J 48 (1986). In *Hishon v King & Spalding*, 467 US 69 (1984), a female associate in a large law firm brought a sex discrimination suit under Title VII when the firm failed to consider her for partnership. The Court held that consideration for partnership in a large law firm may constitute a term and condition of employment under Title VII.

Over twenty states have formed commissions to study gender bias in the legal system. Suellyn Scarnecchia, *Gender & Race Bias Against Lawyers: A Classroom Response*, 23 J L Reform 319, 319 n1 (1990). On gender bias in the courts, see *Gender Bias Study of the Court System in Massachusetts*, 24 New Eng L Rev 745 (1990); Ed Bruske, *Sex Bias Pervades Md. Courts, Panel Finds; Discrimination Reported by Litigants, Judicial Candidates Alike*, Wash Post A1 (May 4, 1989); Jennifer Levine, *Preventing Gender Bias in the Courts: A Question of Judicial Ethics*, 1 Georgetown J L Ethics 775 (1988); Sandy Karlan, *Towards the Elimination of Gender Bias in the Florida Courts*, 11 Nova L Rev 1569 (1987); *Report of the New York Task Force on Women In The Courts*, 15 Fordham Urb L J 11 (1986-1987); Rosalie Wahl, *Some Reflections on Women and the Judiciary*, 4 L & Inequality 153 (1986).

[21] Kathryn Abrams asserts that the demand by men that women conform to preexisting norms in the workplace can be viewed as a way of protesting the access of women to the workplace. Abrams, 42 Vand L Rev at 1189 (cited in note 14). But she also notes that most male workers are not conscious of the fact that the accepted workplace norms are partial because they were developed by men for men. Id at 1189-90. But when women try to conform, they are often penalized. See, for example, *Price Waterhouse v Hopkins*, 490 US 228 (1989), where a female partnership candidate in an accounting firm was denied admission as a partner because she was not "feminine enough." The Court ruled that the firm's action constituted sex discrimination under Title VII. "In my view, most women, struggling to survive in hostile environments, often go dead in a variety of ways. Mostly, we make little compromises with our selves: we become silent, withhold our selves, and disengage in situations we care deeply about so that we trade self-respect for what we hope to secure by invisibility and male acceptance." McIntyre, 2 Canadian J Women & L at 371 (cited in note 16). More recently, Vicki Schultz wrote: "Cases involving blue-collar work emphasize the 'masculinity' of the work, drawing on images of physical strength and dirtiness. Cases involving white-collar work focus on the 'femininity' of women, appealing to traits and values associated with domesticity." *Telling Stories About Women And Work: Judicial Interpretations of Sex Segregation In The Workplace In Title VII Cases Raising The Lack Of Interest Argument*, 103 Harv L Rev 1749, 1800-1801 (1990).

make the point? Regrets, ———."[22] I was stunned. Then I realized that he, too, was threatened by the underlying truth of the article. These incidents convinced me that equal public toilets might not be such a trivial matter.

This feeling was confirmed when the next issue of the student paper appeared. There were several letters to the editor about my article. The author of one letter (whose name was withheld upon request) said that the "virtually unanimous response" to my article he or she had heard "has been ridicule and astonishment that a *tenured law professor* doesn't have more serious causes to occupy her time and effort."[23] Four women students wrote that after reading my article they took "an impromptu tour" of the men's toilet and noticed the inequality.[24] A letter by a male second-year student noted that if the tables were turned, men would never take this long to complain about the inequality.[25]

The final letter in that edition was from a fourth-year student who wrote that he was "appalled to think that a fine publication like this would stoop so low as to publish such a completely nonsensical and tasteless article."[26] The student could not believe "that Any Professor would spend his/her valuable time writing about such an irrelevant, tangential topic," and he wondered "who has really thought about the toilet crisis in public places anyway? Leave it to a law school professor to make an issue out of something NOBODY cares about."[27] The editors of *Baculus* informed me that in the unedited version of this letter, the student also called me a "left-wing neo-nazi," but that reference was deleted by those editors.

I thought I had heard the last of the toilet issue, but there were three more incidents. A law professor from another law school in the state referred to me, in my presence, as a "loose cannon." Having just met him, I was surprised. Subsequently, I asked a young white male colleague of mine who knew the professor if he, my colleague, had referred

---

[22] Note (dated Oct 26, 1988) on file with Berk Women's L J. This administrator's action confirms the notion that educated men of color often adopt white male norms in an attempt to gain entry into the hierarchy. Many fail to realize that while they may gain limited access because they are male, their color precludes complete entry because people of color can never gain entry into a system structured to exclude them.

[23] Letter to the Editor, Baculus 14 (Nov-Dec 1988) (emphasis added). The student went on to say: "On one hand, I think Professor Banks goes too far in her claim that inadequate access to ladies' restroom facilities is part of a sinister and deliberate conspiracy to 'keep the women at home.' On the other hand, most of us have gone too far by treating her point as altogether ludicrous.
. . . First, it is undisputed that there is, in fact, a disparity in the equality of access to public restroom facilities. Our own law school is an example of this . . . the men have six stalls and eight urinals while the women have only three stalls—one of which apparently . . . only accommodates an experienced contortionist. This *is* a legitimate problem . . . ." Id.

[24] Dawn Bullen, Jane Feamster, Cindy Phillips and Jacquelyne Rocan, Letter to the Editor, Baculus at 14 (Nov-Dec 1988).

[25] Sean McKee, Letter to the Editor, Baculus at 14 (Nov-Dec 1988).

[26] Kirk Turner, Letter to the Editor, Baculus at 14 (Nov-Dec 1988).

[27] Id.

to me in such a derogatory manner. He replied that he had not used those *precise terms*, but, after all, I wrote "that article about toilets."

A little later, the senior male professor at my school "casually" mentioned that there was graffiti in the men's bathroom offering to buy me a one-way ticket to Baltimore.[28] I felt violated! I also felt betrayed— first, because none of my male "friends" told me, and second, because no one had removed the offending words from the toilet.

Finally, I was approached after class by a student who showed me a copy of the May issue of the American Spectator, a new conservative publication. The following appeared on a page entitled "Current Wisdom":

> In a memorable essay titled "Toilets As A Feminist Issue" Taunya Lovell Banks, professor of Law at the University of Tulsa and a lecturer of both Criminal and Constitutional Law, displays the powers of high ratiocination that would make her a natural collaborator with other distinguished authors of *The Federalist Papers*, if only she were writing in the late eighteenth century and all her readers were drunk by 8:00 a.m.[29]

An excerpt of my article followed. Included on the same page were pieces from the Washington Post, New York Times, San Francisco Chronicle, and Los Angeles Times Magazine. Also included was a handbill from the Women Lawyers Association of Michigan.[30] The tenor of the page was anti-feminist and anti-intellectual.

For reasons not totally unrelated to the article, I decided to leave the school and as a going-away present wrote a follow-up piece detailing state legislative attempts to ensure "toilet parity." That article, *The*

---

[28] Professor Sheila McIntyre discusses anti-feminist graffiti in men's bathrooms at her law school. She refers to this graffiti as pornography because the women faculty were denigrated in sexual terms whereas the male faculty were not. She recounts her feelings walking into a classroom where she knows the men have read the pornographic references about her. McIntyre, 2 Canadian J Women & L at 383-84 (cited in note 16). Although I do not know if the bathroom graffiti reference to me used sexual terms, I had the gut-wrenching feeling that McIntyre described. I felt personally violated in much the same sense that I would feel if my home had been burglarized. One of my male colleagues later admitted seeing sexual references to women faculty in the men's restroom. He also said that the only time he ever saw a reference to a male faculty member, the reference graphically described the alleged sexual preference of this professor. Kathryn Abrams points out that sexual messages in the workplace "have the effect of reminding a woman that she is viewed as an object of sexual derision rather than a credible co-worker." Abrams, 42 Vand L Rev at 1208 (cited in note 14).

[29] *Current Wisdom*, American Spectator 50 (May 1989).

[30] The Women Lawyers Association of Michigan announcement mentioned that the guest speaker for the February meeting was the president of the Metaphysical Association of Flint who would be discussing palmistry and palm reading. The item from the Washington Post was a letter bemoaning Cat Stevens' support of the Ayatollah Khomeini's death sentence for Salman Rushdie. From the New York Times was a piece by J. Anthony Lukas speaking "for the literary nerds of the 'writerly community' " in comparing the Ayatollah's death threat controversy with the Art Institute of Chicago student exhibit "What is the Proper Way to Display a Flag?" controversy. Id.

Also included on the Spectator *Current Wisdom* page was an excerpt from Angela Davis' book, *Women, Culture And Politics*; a Los Angeles Times Magazine article by Susan Littwin about a clash with a male "intruder" in her aerobics class; and short excerpts from the San Francisco Chronicle and that "great American gazette" the Ferndale Enterprise. Id.

Final Flush (Pun Intended), appeared in the last issue of the paper.[31] Although I saw students reading the article, no one said anything to me about it, and the paper received no letters.

Around this time, I received a letter from a law professor in another state saying that he saw the excerpt of my article in the American Spectator and wanted a reprint.[32] He enclosed an article he had written entitled *On Answering The Call Of Nature*.[33] The article decries government regulation as a contributing factor to the disappearance of the public restroom—bans on pay toilets serve to hasten the disappearance of all public toilets.[34] It also blames the difficulty in finding public toilets on the legal obligations imposed by the judiciary on owners and occupiers of buildings accessible to the public.[35]

In June, I noticed a newspaper article about an attempt in the New York state legislature to pass a "toilet parity" law.[36] I reproduced it and posted it on my door. It was still there when I left the school for the last time.

THE SECOND ARTICLE[37]

A few states are taking equality at the toilet seriously. In January 1989, the "restroom equity" act went into effect in California.[38] *The act, the first of its kind, was passed to "end the inequitable delays which women face when they need to use restroom facilities in public places when men are rarely required to wait for the same purpose."*[39] *The measure requires all new or remodeled sports or entertainment facilities, both public and private, to be equipped with the minimum number of toilets recommended by the plumbing industry's uniform code for restrooms.*[40] *The measure recommends that places attracting 200 to 400 women have a minimum of eight toilets for women plus two more per additional 300 women.*[41] *The measure also recommends that these places have three*

---

[31] Baculus at 11 (Apr-May 1989).

[32] Letter (dated Apr 17, 1989) on file with Berk Women's L J.

[33] Ralph Slovenko, *On Answering The Call Of Nature*, 24 Wayne L Rev 1555 (1978).

[34] Id at 1556-57.

[35] Id at 1555-56.

[36] Sam Verhovek, *Toilet Bill: Parity Goal Is Pursued*, NY Times B4 (June 13, 1989). This bill was signed into law on July 11, 1989. *Cuomo Signs Equal-Toilet Bill*, NY Times B2 (July 12, 1989). Ned Zeman, *Women's Room*, Newsweek 4 (Sept 25, 1989).

[37] This section is an edited version of *The Final Flush (Puh Intended)* which first appeared in Baculus 11 (Apr-May 1989).

[38] Cal Health & Safety Code § 3981 (West 1990).

[39] Id. Section 3981 reads: "(a) Publicly and privately owned facilities where the public congregates shall be equipped with sufficient temporary or permanent restrooms to meet the needs of the public at peak hours."

[40] Id. "(b) In conformity with the State Plumbing Code, and except as otherwise provided in this section standards shall be adopted in order to enforce this section . . . ."

[41] Ann Bancroft, *Bill Tackles Long Lines at Women's Restrooms*, UPI NEXIS (Jan 27 AM cycle, 1987).

urinals and three toilets for men.[42]

The California law was introduced by State Senator Art Torres, a Democrat from Los Angeles, who got the idea after several very long waits while his wife stood in line outside of crowded women's restrooms at the Hollywood Bowl, the Rose Bowl, and the Forum, a Los Angeles sports arena.[43] A legislative committee subsequently heard testimony from women who related similar experiences.[44]

On March 1, 1989, Virginia became the second state to legislate for equality at the public toilet.[45] Almost a year earlier, Virginia State House Delegate John A. (Jack) Rollison, a Republican from Woodbridge, introduced a resolution calling for hearings to determine whether the state plumbing code's 50-50 ratio for men's and women's toilets in public buildings was unfair to women.[46] Delegate Rollison cited two recent studies— one from Cornell University[47] and another from Virginia Tech[48]—indicating that a restroom stop takes a woman up to 2.3 times as long as it takes a man.[49]

Rollison proposed that public buildings provide women with at least two toilets for every one designated for men.[50] He argued that there are several reasons why women need more toilets. First, women's public restrooms are underdesigned for their flow.[51] Although the state plumbing code calls for equal restroom space for women and men, urinals occupy less space than toilet stalls, and, as a result, men's restrooms often have more facilities.[52] Second, the elderly and the physically disabled take longer to use the bathroom, and there are more elderly and disabled women in the country than men.[53] In addition, more women take small

---

[42] Russell Snyder, *"Potty Parity" Bill Advances in Senate*, UPI NEXIS (Apr 8 BC cycle, 1987) (*"Potty Parity"*).

[43] Russell Snyder, *"Potty Parity" Bill Whizzes Through Committee*, UPI NEXIS (July 7 BC cycle, 1987).

[44] Snyder, *Potty Parity* (cited in note 42). Yolanda Nava, Senator Torres' wife, told of waiting in line behind 56 other women at the Ahmanson Music Center and how she and a few other women raided a men's restroom. Another woman told of having to relieve herself behind some bushes because the line to the restroom was so long. Id.

[45] *"Potty Parity" Rules Go Into Effect Wednesday*, UPI NEXIS (Feb 28 BC cycle, 1989) (*"Feb 1989 UPI"*).

[46] Donald Baker, *Relief Sought From Restroom Traffic; Va. Delegate Hopes His Bill Will Lead to More Stalls For Women*, Wash Post C6 (Feb 4, 1988).

[47] The Cornell study was conducted by an undergraduate student for the Department of Transportation in Washington State. Larry O'Dell, *Virginia To Study Restroom Equity*, AP NEXIS (May 9 PM cycle, 1988) (*"Virginia Equity Study"*).

[48] John Banzhaf, III, *Final Frontier For the Law?*, Natl L J 13, 14 (Apr 18, 1988). Sandra Rawls at Virginia Polytechnic Institute wrote a doctoral dissertation about behavior patterns in the use of male-female bathrooms. Professor Savannah Day conducted a funded study to determine what people do in public restrooms. Id.

[49] G.L. Marshall, *"Potty Parity" Measure Moves Along*, UPI NEXIS (Oct 17 PM cycle, 1988) (*"Measure Moves Along"*).

[50] Id.

[51] O'Dell, *Virginia Equity Study* (cited in note 47).

[52] Id.

[53] Id.

children to the bathroom than men.[54] *Other factors contributing to longer bathroom stays for women are menstrual periods; urinary tract infections, more common in women than in men, which require more frequent trips to the toilet; pregnancy, which reduces bladder capacity; and, finally, clothing (women have more clothes to manipulate than men do).*[55]

There was no organized opposition to Rollison's proposal despite the fact that it would inflate construction costs in new theatres, concert halls, and sporting arenas (shopping malls are exempt).[56] *New churches, museums, and theatres would also be affected by the new plumbing codes.*[57] *The primary reason for the lack of opposition may be that the measure applies only to new buildings.*[58] *Flushed with success, Rollison next intended to present the Virginia plan for "potty parity" to the national conference of Building Officials and Code Administrators during its March 1989 meeting.*[59]

Most observers agreed that public toilets in many older buildings and stadiums, as constructed, were inadequate for women and reduced their enjoyment of public events. However, at least one critic claimed that taking mirrors out of women's bathrooms would substantially shorten women's bathroom stays.[60] *Nevertheless, one of these critics conceded that women probably need 15 to 20 percent more bathroom stalls than men do due to biological differences.*[61]

Other states have not been so progressive. In 1988, the male members of the Illinois House Executive Committee voted 7 to 3 to defeat the Equitable Rest Rooms Act that would have required three bathroom stalls in women's bathrooms for every two urinals in men's bathrooms.[62] *In 1987, the Oregon State House killed a bill that would have required more toilets for women in public restrooms.*[63]

---

[54] Id.

[55] G.L. Marshall, *Restroom Parity Examined*, UPI NEXIS (Oct 17 PM cycle, 1988); *Quirks in the News*, UPI NEXIS (Oct 17 PM cycle, 1988).

[56] Marshall, *Restroom Parity Examined* (cited in note 55).

[57] *Feb 1989 UPI* (cited in note 45).

[58] John Harris, *Va. Potty Parity No Longer Bathroom Humor; State Panel Orders Increase of 50% in Women's Restrooms*, Wash Post B1 (Nov 22, 1988).

[59] *Feb 1989 UPI* (cited in note 45).

[60] Id. In reply, one reader responded: "The suggestion that the long lines could be reduced by the removal of all these mirrors is not frivolous. I am familiar with a private girls' school where this is done, and it shortened the time spent by each individual in the restroom by at least 50 percent.

We do not need legislation to solve this problem. All we need is the elimination of all accessories in these places that encourage the expression of female vanity while people are waiting in line to use the facility. (signed) Charlotte Halstead," (letter responding to *Potty Parity* article), Wash Post D6 (Nov 27, 1988).

Both the original critic and the reader overlook the fact that women are standing in line to use the toilets, not the mirrors! Both expressions evidence a disdain for women and rely heavily upon stereotypical notions of women for support.

[61] Id.

[62] *But Aren't You Always Supposed to Give Seats to Ladies?*, Student Lawyer 19 (Dec 1988) ("*Give Seats to Ladies*").

[63] UPI NEXIS (June 17 BC cycle, 1987).

The so-called "potty parity" measures received considerable national attention. For example, California Senator Torres received letters from across the state, the nation, and the world.[64] *A woman approached him and said, "Thank you, senator. I've waited 60 years for this bill."*[65] *The Virginia bill's progress generated an essay in the National Law Journal*[66] *and was followed for several months by National Public Radio. The December 1988 issue of Student Lawyer noted the defeat of the Illinois measure.*[67]

Just think, if Virginia Delegate Rollison is successful, "potty parity" may become the norm. However, until those potties are constantly stocked with toilet paper, remember the tissue, ladies and gentlemen.

TOILETS AND FEMINISM

From a feminist perspective, my experiences with toilet inequity illustrate the extent to which males' epistemological power defines equality. Bathrooms are not an issue for them; therefore, bathrooms are not an issue, period. But toilet inequity is just one of many instances where men tend to ignore women's problems because they are not a part of a man's world.

Historically, courts have recognized that equality is an illusive term. It may mean the same treatment or treatment without regard to differences;[68] substantial equality in the sense that certain inequalities are acknowledged, but not considered constitutionally important;[69] or, when they are important, taking conscious action to remedy past inequalities.[70] The problem with so-called "neutral" equality concepts is that often women and men are not similarly situated, and thus these concepts

---

[64] Jerry Gillam, *Anti-Gridlock Bill, Carrying Fines of $50 to $500, Signed By Governor*, LA Times A29 (Sept 19, 1987).

[65] Id.

[66] Banzhaf, Natl L J at 13 (cited in note 48). The author ended the piece:

"If the Restroom Equity Bill does nothing else, it may help to free us from constraints and assumptions accepted for so long without even a second thought. At the very least, it provided one law professor with the inspiration for a somewhat tongue-in-cheek article finalized on April Fools' Day!" Id at 14, 17.

[67] *Give Seats to Ladies*, Student Lawyer at 19 (cited in note 62).

[68] See, for example, *Mississippi University for Women v Hogan*, 458 US 718 (1982) (exclusion of male from nursing program at state college for women unlawful); *Brown v Board of Education*, 347 US 483 (1954) (racially separate, but "substantially" equal public school facilities violate the equal protection clause).

[69] See, for example, *Geduldig v Aiello*, 417 US 484 (1974) (exclusion of pregnancy from state disability insurance coverage not unlawful); *San Antonio Independent School District v Rodriguez*, 411 US 1 (1973) (different expenditures for students in poor school districts upheld). But, compare *Michael M. v Superior Court*, 450 US 464 (1981) (gender specific statutory rape statute upheld); *Rostker v Goldberg*, 453 US 57 (1981) (statutory exemption of women from military registration upheld).

[70] See, for example, *Johnson v Transportation Agency*, 480 US 616, 631 (1987) (upholding the validity under Title VII of a voluntary affirmative action plan for women who were underrepresented in traditionally segregated job categories, citing *United Steelworkers of America v Weber*, 443 US 193, 197 (1979)).

reflect men's and not women's needs.[71]

Numerous examples come to mind. Traditionally, women's clothiers refused to make free alterations, while men's clothes were routinely altered without charge.[72] One proffered justification is that the cost of alteration is built into the price of men's, but not women's, clothes. Undoubtedly, this way of thinking has roots in stereotypical notions about the traditional roles of women and men. Historically, many women learned to sew and made or altered their own clothes, whereas men, without willing mothers or wives, had others alter their clothes. Alterations were seen as a problem for men only. Even as social conditions and women's roles changed, no thought was given to their problems.

A similar problem arises when women are charged more than men for laundering shirts. The explanation is that laundry presses are designed for men's shirts, not women's. Since women's shirts require more labor, laundries charge more.[73] The result is plain inequality. Formal equality would at least require all shirts that fit the press to cost the same. This would include some, but not all, women's as well as men's shirts. But *real* equality would require asking why the press was designed only for men's shirts, or why there is not another, smaller press for women's shirts. From the perspective of equal price for equal value, all simple, unruffled shirts should cost the same to launder.

Another area of unequal treatment is health care—a matter most people do not consider trivial. Yet physicians, mostly male or male-trained, historically discounted medical complaints made by their female patients.[74] As a result, illnesses like Premenstrual Syndrome (PMS) and

---

[71] As Kathryn Abrams points out: "Even the successful attacks on the exclusion of women have failed to reach many attitudes about the differences between men and women, attitudes that continue to shape the institutions in which women now find themselves. Challenging the pervasive influence of these norms is the next feminist task." Abrams, 42 Vand L Rev at 1185 (cited in note 14).

[72] See, for example, Gail Anderson, *Women Hemmed in by Alteration Fees*, 68 ABA J 669 (1982) (sex discrimination charge filed against a Chicago department store which charged women but not men for altering pants); Larry Bodine, *Policy Tailored for "Pink Collar" Challenge*, Natl L J 39 (Jan 12, 1981) (sex discrimination suit for charging women but not men for tailoring garments).

[73] A suit was filed against a Los Angeles cleaners for charging more for women's blouses than for men's shirts. Mary Ann Galante, *The Long Sleeve of the Law*, Natl L J 63 (Sept 24, 1984).

[74] See, for example, Gena Corea, *The Hidden Malpractice: How American Medicine Mistreats Women* 78-89 (Harper & Row, updated ed 1985). Abigail Trafford, writing in the Washington Post, recounts the reaction of women to an article by a woman who tried to find a physician who would take her symptoms seriously. It took five years before a physician told her she had advanced Hodgkin's disease, a cancer of the lymphatic system. Trafford points out that traditional stereotypes persist, notably the impression that heart disease is a man's disease. The result of this history of sexism in medicine is that women tend to be treated less aggressively than men and are less likely to be recommended for coronary bypass surgery. Abigail Trafford, *Sexism in Medicine*, Wash Post (Health Sec) 9 (May 31, 1988).

Women, unless covered under employer group health policies, may pay more for individual health coverage. Id. Published with Trafford's article was a page of letters from other

post-partum depression have only recently been taken seriously.[75] Common medical studies have often completely excluded women from tested sample populations.[76] As a result, "women are often treated according to scientific protocols that have been done only on men,"[77] even though it is likely that women would have distinct biological responses.[78] Women also have been excluded from drug clinical trials, with most studies restricted to middle-aged men.[79]

With toilets, the formal equality requirement might be met through

---

women recounting similar incidents. *Doctors Listen Less to Female Patients*, Wash Post (Health Sec) 8 (May 31, 1988).

Another medically-related instance when male-centered norms work to the disadvantage of women is learning disabilities. Reading disabilities are biologically-based and were long thought to be more prevalent among boys than girls. Recent studies indicate that this assumption is incorrect. Sally Shaywitz, Bennett Shaywitz, Jack Fletcher, Michael Escobar, *Prevalence of Reading Disability in Boys and Girls*, 264 JAMA 998 (1990); Patricia M. Phipps, *The LD Learner Is Often a Boy—Why?*, 17 Academic Therapy 425 (1982); Ellen D. Rie, Herbert E. Rie, *Reading Deficits and Intellectual Patterns Among Children with Neurocognitive Dysfunctions*, 3 Intelligence 383 (1979). Two of the earlier studies also found that girls with reading disabilities are less likely than boys to be identified, Rie, 3 Intelligence at 383, and when finally identified are often more severely impaired, Phipps, 17 Academic Therapy at 429. The most recent study concluded that the gender disparity in identification of learning disabled children reflects teacher bias in ascertaining the condition. The researchers found that classroom teachers, who do the bulk of identification, are more likely to identify and refer students as reading disabled who are more active, more inattentive, less dexterous, and who have problems in behavior, language, and academics. Children who were researched and identified as learning disabled, almost an equal number of girls and boys, had more problems in attention, motor skills, language, and academics, but not in activity level or behavior. The researchers conclude that most boys may simply be more active than most girls and that academic difficulty is a more reliable basis for referral. Shaywitz, et al, 264 JAMA at 1001-02.

[75] Women have described PMS symptoms to health care providers for thousands of years. As early as 1931, two medical researchers described the condition and suggested possible approaches to treatment, but only within the past decade have physicians become more cognizant of the need for better understanding and treatment. There is persistent disagreement as to whether PMS should be defined as an emotional or a physical disorder. Howard Osofsky, *Efficacious Treatments of PMS: A Need for Further Research*, 264 JAMA 387 (July 18, 1990).

[76] "Most of the research on protective qualities of aspirin was performed on 22,071 men, and like so many medical studies, no women. And a study measuring the links between high cholesterol, lack of exercise, smoking and heart disease likewise featured 12,866 men—and no women." Leonard Abramson, *Uncaring Health Care For Women*, Balt Sun A9 (June 5, 1990). In 1987, the National Institutes of Health spent only 13.5 percent of their research budget on women's health. Id.

[77] Sally Squires, *A Look at Research Involving Women*, Wash Post 29 (Dec 12, 1989) (quoting Sally Rynne, a health care consultant in Evanston, Illinois).

[78] Evlin Kinney, Joanne Trautmann, Jay Gold, Elliot Vesell & Robert Zelis, *Underrepresentation of Women in Drug Trials: Ramifications and Remedies*, 95 Annals Intern Med 495, 498 (1981).

[79] Squires, Wash Post at 29 (cited in note 77) (citing fear of potential harm to the fetus; monthly menstrual cycle fluctuations; different risks for men and women); Kinney, et al, Annals Intern Med at 495 (cited in note 78) (FDA regulations placed restrictions on using women with childbearing potential). I hasten to point out that such middle-aged men have also been overwhelmingly white; people of color have also been underrepresented in clinical drug trials. Craig Svensson, *Representation of American Blacks in Clinical Trials of New Drugs*, 261 JAMA 263 (1989).

Women have been excluded from such trials because their inclusion would make the trials larger and more costly. However, researchers commonly cited concern about women's reproductive organs as the overriding reason. In 1987, the National Institutes of Health advisory committee on women's health issues recommended that women always be included in NIH-sponsored clinical trials unless researchers could present scientific reasons for their exclusion. Squires, Wash Post at 29 (cited in note 77).

an equal allocation of money for the construction of bathrooms, or alternatively, through a requirement that men's and women's bathrooms occupy identical square footage.[80] Other options might include the provision of an equal number of toilets for women and men, even if this means spending more money and allocating more space for women's toilets. This approach, however, ignores the fact that women, due to biological and cultural differences, need more toilets than men do.[81]

At a superficial level, the equal toilet facilities problem resembles the "equal cost versus equal benefits" problem under Title VII and the Equal Pay Act.[82] But the issue is different here because the greater cost for women's benefits is tied to methods of benefit calculation and culturally developed differences in benefit utilization rates rather than merely to any biological differences between the sexes. To better ensure equality for women, "benefits" must be defined from the recipients' perspective to provide equal "value."[83]

What these examples have in common is that they write women out of existence by defining the problem in terms of its male aspects. Thus, toilet inequality is yet another example of how so-called "neutral" equality principles are, in fact, not neutral.[84] The law's tendency to ignore or

---

[80] Virginia state laws already mandate equal space for women's and men's public toilets. They also require an equal number of stalls for women and men. See notes 46 and 52 and accompanying text.

[81] See notes 48, 53, 54, and 55 and accompanying text.

[82] In *City of Los Angeles Dept. of Water & Power v Manhart*, 435 US 702 (1978), the Supreme Court held that section 703(a)(1) of the Civil Rights Act of 1964, commonly known as Title VII, prohibited employers from requiring female employees to make larger contributions than male employees to an employer-operated pension fund. The employer argued that since women as a group live longer than men, male employees would be subsidizing female employees if all employees made equal contributions to the fund. The Court indicated that the weakness in this argument was in treating women as a group rather than as individuals, some but not all of whom live longer than men. *Manhart*, 435 US at 716-17. This argument holds true for all individuals, regardless of gender. More recently, in *Arizona Governing Committee For Tax Deferred Annuity and Deferred Compensation Plans, et al v Norris*, 463 US 1073 (1983), the Court struck down a compensation plan offered by the state which paid women lower monthly retirement benefits than men who had made the same contributions. As had the City of Los Angeles Department of Water and Power in *Manhart*, Arizona had relied on the argument that women, as a group, live longer than men.

[83] On the surface, the value issue may seem analogous to the comparable worth argument, raised unsuccessfully under Title VII, that sex discrimination exists if employees in job classifications occupied primarily by women are paid less than employees in job classifications occupied primarily by men when these jobs, despite their dissimilarities, are of equal value to the employer. The problem with the comparable worth argument lies in deciding what to compare to determine equal value. However, unlike comparable worth, present in the toilet issue are objective criteria to determine value. Toilets are provided for both women and men; the focus in determining value is simply an issue of quantity. For a discussion of comparable worth issues, see Judith Brown, Phyllis Baumann & Elaine Melnick, *Equal Pay for Jobs of Comparable Worth: An Analysis of the Rhetoric*, 21 Harv CR-CL L Rev 127 (1986); Paul Weiler, *The Wages of Sex: The Uses and Limits of Comparable Worth*, 99 Harv L Rev 1728 (1986); Norman Vieira, *Comparable Worth and the Gunther Case: The New Drive for Equal Pay*, 18 UC Davis L Rev 449 (1985); Martha Chamallas, *Exploring the "Entire Spectrum" of Disparate Treatment Under Title VII: Rules Governing Predominantly Female Jobs*, 1984 U Ill L Rev 1.

[84] See, generally, Patricia Williams, *The Obliging Shell: An Informal Essay On Formal Equal Opportunity*, 87 Mich L Rev 2128 (1989). Williams writes that "Blacks and women are

trivialize these issues illustrates how male-centered formal equality doctrines fail to address many important problems in women's lives.

This notion that male needs are universal is reflected in an EEOC guideline to Title VII which arguably could be construed to prohibit an employer from providing more toilets for female than for male employees.[85] The result is not true equality: such formal equality fails to recognize that parity would require that facilities be constructed to accommodate equally the real, but different, needs of each sex. These differences and needs should be taken into account, especially where women are shown to suffer some economic detriment, like unequal access to employment because of inadequate bathroom facilities.

Employment cases involving women and access to the toilet cover a wide range of issues. One of the earliest cases imposed a duty of care on employers who provided women employees with toilets on the job site.[86] The employer provided a toilet, but the stall door could not be secured from inside, and a female employee mangled her hand trying to hold the door closed.[87] The issues presented were whether the employer was negligent in maintaining the toilet and whether the female employee was contributorily negligent.[88] The court held that the employer had a duty to maintain a toilet that could be safely closed and that, in the emergency situation in which the employee found herself, her actions did not amount to contributory negligence.[89]

But the *Lynch* case, mentioned previously,[90] is more typical of cases reaching the courts today. Such cases involve employers who harass women working in blue collar jobs (from which they were once excluded) by restricting access to the toilet.[91] There are also race-based employ-

---

objects of a constitutional omission which has been incorporated into a theory of neutrality." Id at 2142.

[85] 29 CFR § 1604.2(b)(4) (1990) prohibits employers from providing special benefits to female employees, including "special . . . physical facilities for women . . . ." These guidelines were aimed at so-called women's protective laws enacted by many states in the early part of the twentieth century. Inconsistent state protective laws in two states were challenged under § 1604.2(b)(4). The Missouri Attorney General issued an opinion stating that Title VII preempted a state law requiring employers to provide a suitable number of seats for women employees. 31 Op Atty Gen No 287 (Mo Dec 21, 1973). A Title VII challenge to a New York law which included "separate water closets" as a special benefit was not resolved. Op Atty Gen 43, 47-48 (NY Nov 13, 1972). However, another EEOC guideline on sex discrimination states that an "employer may not refuse to hire men or women, or deny men or women a particular job because there are no restroom or associated facilities, unless" the employer can demonstrate that providing these facilities would be unreasonable. 41 CFR § 60-20.3(e) (1989).

[86] *Cook v Lewis K. Liggett Co.*, 127 Fla 369, 173 So 159 (Fla 1937).

[87] Id at 371-72.

[88] Id at 373.

[89] Id at 374, 375-76.

[90] *Lynch v Freeman*, 817 F2d 380 (6th Cir 1987). See text accompanying notes 7-13.

[91] In *Kilgo v Bowman Transportation, Inc.*, 789 F2d 859 (11th Cir 1986), the court affirmed a magistrate's finding that a trucking company's refusal to provide separate sleeping accommodations, showers, and toilets for women over-the-road-tractor-trailer drivers because of a policy against women driving with men other than their husbands constituted unlawful sex discrimination. Id at 874-75. In *Hall v Gus Construction*, 842 F2d 1010 (8th Cir 1988), the

ment discrimination cases involving segregated toilet and locker facilities.[92]

The employment discrimination cases illustrate how differences, such as biology and race, are used to discourage entry into traditionally white male domains and how "trivial" issues, like access to toilets, are used to oppress subordinated groups. This oppression can take two forms. The first occurs when access to the toilet is used as a pretext for denying employment, or where an employer intentionally adopts a facially neutral policy because of, rather than in spite of, its adverse impact on all women or men of color. This is blatant discrimination. A second, more subtle form of oppression occurs when the disparate treatment, from the victim's perspective, causes exclusionary effects. For example, an employer provides a toilet, but no toilet tissue, as in *Lynch*. This would constitute discrimination from a woman's perspective whereas a man, like the employer in *Lynch*, might simply respond that women employees should bring their own toilet tissue.[93]

So-called "difference" feminists,[94] while rejecting formal equality, do not agree on what differences between women and men the law should take into account when defining equality, nor on how the law should respond to these differences. Some argue that limited exceptions to formal equality should be made for substantial physical differences.[95] Others argue that we must first determine the real sources of these differences and how they operate.[96] Still other feminists argue that the law

---

court affirmed a magistrate's finding that two women traffic controllers at a road construction site were constructively discharged because of a continuing pattern of sexual harassment which created a hostile and abusive work environment. The magistrate had found that as part of this harassment the women were denied use of the company truck to go to town for a bathroom break and were observed by male crew members through surveying equipment when they had to relieve themselves in a ditch. Id at 1012, 1018. See also Leonard Buder, *Hearing Faults Building Field On Wide Bias*, NY Times B4 (Mar 13, 1990) reporting that women in the construction industry told New York City officials about the widespread gender bias still in the industry. In addition to sexual harassment, women complained of "having insufficient toilet and changing facilities on the job . . . ."

[92] See, for example, *James v Stockham Valves & Fittings Co.*, 559 F2d 310 (5th Cir 1977). Here the employer persisted, more than ten years after the enactment of Title VII of the 1964 Civil Rights Act, in maintaining racially segregated toilets, cafeteria seating, drinking fountains, locker rooms, and showers. Id at 319-21.

[93] 817 F2d at 386.

[94] Professor Kathryn Abrams uses this term to describe feminists who advocate redefining equality principles in ways that recognize and equally value differences between women and men. Abrams, 42 Vand L Rev at 1193 (cited in note 14). See Catharine MacKinnon, *Feminism Unmodified—Discourses On Life and Law* 32-45 (Harvard Press, 1987) (*"Feminism Unmodified"*); Martha Minow, *The Supreme Court, 1986 Term—Foreword: Justice Engendered*, 101 Harv L Rev 10 (1987); Christine Littleton, *Equality and Feminist Legal Theory*, 48 U Pitt L Rev 1043 (1987); Ruth Colker, *Anti-Subordination Above All: Sex, Race, and Equal Protection*, 61 NYU L Rev 1003 (1986); Ann Scales, *The Emergence of Feminist Jurisprudence: An Essay*, 95 Yale L Rev 1373 (1986).

[95] Some feminists, also called accommodationists, argue for limited exceptions to formal equality principles for some sex-based physical differences like pregnancy. See Herma Hill Kay, *Equality and Difference: The Case of Pregnancy*, 1 Berk Women's L J 1 (1985); Sylvia Law, *Rethinking Sex and the Constitution*, 132 U Pa L Rev 955 (1984).

[96] See MacKinnon, *Feminism Unmodified* at 38-39 (cited in note 94).

should consider biological differences between women and men.[97] This approach would address most of the toilet parity concerns women face in an employment context, but it ignores any cultural differences between women and men which affect women's freedom in public places outside the workforce.[98] Therefore, a fourth group of difference feminists argues that cultural as well as biological differences should be considered.[99] However, this fourth approach is also fraught with problems, the very least of which is determining which cultural attributes should be considered.[100]

This discussion does not attempt to resolve the argument among difference feminists. Instead, I use toilet inequity to illustrate that current male-centered equality models often fail to achieve full equality for women because they fail to reconcile legally significant biological or bio-cultural differences between women and men. Powerful men traditionally define what is trivial, and issues like toilet parity are not things which make a difference in *their* lives. Thus, the issue of toilet parity is a gateway to other issues considered trivial or nonissues from an androcentric perspective.

TOILETS AND EQUALITY—BEYOND FEMINISM

In truth, formal equality rhetoric is used as a cover for many other things. For example, at one level toilet parity is really a controversy over economic resources. In the employment context, the concern is over who will bear the cost of incorporating women into the workforce.[101] Outside the workplace, the concern is who will bear how much cost in the public arena.[102] In and outside the workplace women are the "add-ons"—we are blamed and often penalized for not fitting into a male-designed world;[103] and we are not allowed to engage in self-help methods

---

[97] See Robin West, *Jurisprudence and Gender*, 55 U Chi L Rev 1 (1988).

[98] For example, women, not men, usually take small children to the toilet, and women's clothing makes it more difficult to use the toilets quickly. See notes 54-55 and accompanying text. These are cultural, not biological, differences.

[99] Minow, 101 Harv L Rev at 10 (cited in note 94); Littleton, 48 U Pitt L Rev at 1043 (cited in note 94); Colker, 61 NYU L Rev 1003 (cited in note 94).

[100] For criticisms of this approach see Abrams, 42 Vand L Rev at 1193-95 (cited in note 14); Joan Williams, *Deconstructing Gender*, 87 Mich L Rev 797, 813-21 (1989).

[101] This same concern is a factor in resistance to so-called affirmative action efforts. The courts openly express concern for measures that unduly trample the rights of innocent third parties, primarily white males. See *United Steel Workers of America v Weber*, 443 US 193, 208 (1979) (upholding union-bargained affirmative action training programs which reserved 50% of openings for blacks until their numbers were commensurate with the percentage of blacks in the local labor force as permissible under Title VII of the Civil Rights Act of 1964).

[102] During the discussion of the Virginia toilet parity law, one newspaper editorial noted: "The objections to the bathroom bill are limited to this: More bathrooms of any sort will cost more. The more serious problem for the bill is that so many people—to be specific, so many men—refuse to take it seriously." *The Bathroom Bill* (Editorial), Fairfax J A14 (Oct 19, 1988).

[103] Maryland State Senator Barbara Hoffman introduced legislation that would require any public or private building built after July 1, 1990 to have as many toilets for women as for men. John Frece, *Restroom Legislation Intends Equal Opportunities in New Buildings*, Balt Sun A1 (Feb

to rectify the lack of forethought regarding our need to eliminate our waste. For example, Denise Wells was fined $200 and escorted out of a concert in Houston for using the men's bathroom because the line at the women's bathroom was "unbearably long."[104]

Denise Wells' problem stemmed from city officials' assumption that more men than women attend sporting events and concerts, and thus men need more toilets.[105] The city code was changed after a study challenged the validity of the initial assumption, but the fact remains that even if fewer women did frequent these public places, we would still need more bathrooms than men do.[106] Formal equality, as protected by the American judiciary, cannot accommodate differences, be they physical or cultural.[107] The courts consistently measure equality in male terms from a liberal, eurocentric perspective—assimilate or remain different, the "other," in the eyes of the law.

2, 1990). The Senate Finance Committee defeated the bill 7-2 during the absence of Senator Catherine I. Riley, co-sponsor with Hoffman of the bill and chairperson of the Committee. The Committee claimed it was "unworkable." Mark Bomster, *Panel Flushes "Potty Parity,"* Balt Evening Sun D3 (Feb 23, 1990).

[104] Lisa Belkin, *Seeking Some Relief, She Stepped Out Of Line*, NY Times A6 (July 21, 1990). A Houston city ordinance makes it unlawful to knowingly and intentionally enter any public restroom designated for the opposite sex. Id (citing Houston City Ordinance 72-904 (1972): "It shall be unlawful for any person to knowingly and intentionally enter any public restroom designated for the exclusive use of the sex opposite to such person's sex . . . in a manner calculated to cause a disturbance."). Another woman was also fined. Ms. Wells encountered long lines (30 or more women) during her two attempts to use the women's restroom. Ironically, both the mayor and chief of police in Houston are women. Id.

[105] Id. Thus, until 1985, Houston plumbing codes for large public gathering places allowed a higher number of combined toilets and urinals in men's bathrooms than in women's bathrooms. Id.

[106] Id.

[107] The courts consistently uphold educational decisions that reinforce the "Americanization" process which heavily influenced the formative stages of public education in the late 1800s and early 1900s. The original aim of Americanization efforts was "to assimilate and to amalgamate [European immigrants] as part of our American race" by forcing them to adopt Anglo-Saxon culture and values as superior. H. Prentice Baptiste, Jr., *Multicultural Education and Urban Schools From a Sociohistorical Perspective: Internalizing Multiculturalism*, 6 J Ed Equity & Leadership 295, 295-366 (1986) (quoting E. Cubberly, *Changing Conceptions of Education* (Riverside Educational Mimeographs, 1909)). Today, eurocentric culture and values are presented as superior to other cultures and values, a form of cultural imperialism.

One notable example of American cultural intolerance is the treatment of bilingual education. In *Lau v Nichols*, 414 US 563 (1974), the Supreme Court held that Title VI of the Civil Rights Act of 1964 required English instruction for Chinese children who spoke no English. These children were considered linguistically disadvantaged. Following *Lau*, there was concern that the decision conflicted with the mandate of *Brown v Board of Education*, 347 US 183 (1954), that schools be racially integrated because racial isolation of children of color, when enforced by law, disadvantages those children, as opposed to disadvantaging all children. The policy of racial integration reinforces efforts to force assimilation of American culture on children from different cultural backgrounds. See Comment, *Bilingual Education and Desegregation*, 127 U Pa L Rev 1564, 1565-67 (1979). (However, the student author believes that a pluralistic approach to this issue is not incompatible with the goals of integration.) In *Martin Luther King, Jr. Elementary School Children v Ann Arbor School District*, 473 F Supp 1371 (ED Mich 1979), the court treated "black English" as a separate language and ordered school teachers to learn the language to help students overcome the language barrier. In each instance, the school children's failure to speak standard English is viewed as a sign of inferiority. They are not encouraged to learn English as a second language, but to forego their "home" language for "superior" standard English.

At another level, the refusal to consider biological and cultural differences when measuring equality reflects the extent to which formal equality models permit the continued subordination of all women and men of color. Full-scale recognition of biological and cultural differences in measuring equality could result in a radical restructuring of American society in ways that go beyond gender and include race, ethnicity, sexuality, physical ability, and even class.[108] Because toilets are essential to human dignity in our culture, they are a good place to start.

Feminist and civil rights attorney Flo Kennedy contends that restricting access to bathrooms is an easy way to make people feel that they are other.[109] In 1973, Harvard Divinity School "reluctantly agreed that a limited number of women could sit for entrance exams,"[110] but the administration refused to let the women use the only bathroom in the building. Instead, they were offered facilities across the street, a 15 minute trip—time which few women were willing to lose.[111]

More recently, several male Naval Academy midshipmen carried a female midshipman, Gwen Marie Dreyer, into a bathroom, handcuffed her to a urinal, and photographed her.[112] Dreyer resigned.[113] Oddly enough, Jane Good, the civilian dean of advising and counseling, remarked that while women midshipmen are admitted to the Academy, "we're not confident about assimilation and acceptance."[114]

It is no accident that Gwen Dreyer was cuffed to a urinal and not to a toilet. As one news reporter noted: "A urinal is used for elimination, and only by men. Handcuffing a woman to one is symbolism of the high-

---

[108] This form of cultural pluralism would reflect an "open society in which a variety of cultures, value systems, and lifestyles not only coexist but are nurtured." Delmo Della-Dora & James E. House, *Education For an Open Society* 3 (Association for Supervision and Curriculum Development, 1974).

[109] Irene Davall, *To Pee or Not To Pee: Celebrating Women's History*, XV On The Issues 20, 21 (Summer 1990). "A man can urinate in urinals even when the stalls require change, or he can go off to some corner and inconspicuously pee. Whereas a woman always has to pay in public places unless she chooses to use the sink or that one free toilet that either has no door or no paper or a puddle or something just to remind you you're a n—r." Id. (I refrain from using the racially derogatory term Flo Kennedy used because I have come to believe, like Mari Matsuda, that use of racial hate words, even in a scholarly context, still hurts people of color and legitimizes these terms. For a more complete discussion of this concept, see Mari Matsuda, *Public Response To Racist Speech: Considering The Victim's Story*, 87 Mich L Rev 2320 (1989).

[110] Davall, XV On The Issues at 20 (cited in note 109).

[111] Id. The women at Harvard, assisted by African-American lawyer Flo Kennedy, demonstrated in colorful and graphic fashion.

[112] Felicity Barringer, *Harassment Case Shakes Annapolis*, NY Times A22 (May 20, 1990).

[113] The males are still midshipmen. The male midshipmen admitted that the woman struggled during the incident, but they remarked that she smiled or laughed during the incident and therefore was not offended. The female midshipman reported that she was smiling to get through the incident; she was trying to fit into a male-defined and -dominated world. Mary Cantwell, *Annapolis and Karen Finley*, Balt Even Sun A8 (May 29, 1990). The Naval Academy has since issued an order that any future hazing or physical or emotional abuse of a midshipman is punishable by expulsion. Jay Merwin, *Navy to Crack Down on Abuse*, Balt Even Sun B1 (May 29, 1990).

[114] Barringer, NY Times at A22 (cited in note 112).

est, and the lowest, order."[115] To assimilate is to become like white males and deny one's self, one's culture.[116] Total acceptance is impossible in androcentric America because it requires elimination of differences, like gender and color, which are immutable. Therefore, formal equality can only result in the continued subordination of oppressed groups.

The toilet incidents at Harvard Divinity School and the Naval Academy reflect men's continuing hostility toward women trying to enter traditionally male structured and dominated occupations. In each instance, the toilet was used to reinforce the notion that women are unwanted, unassimilated, and alien to that environment. Both examples support Flo Kennedy's claim about the use of the toilet by white men to oppress others. The basic nature of the need to eliminate waste, and the humiliation entailed in having to overcome obstacles to meet this need, make toilets the ideal choice, conscious or unconscious, for those bent on excluding outsiders from white male preserves.

African-Americans of both sexes also have experienced similar incidents.[117] However, the issue becomes more complex when race is added. With white women, the argument centers on biological and/or cultural differences, but with people of color, the argument is more openly derogatory of difference.

The City of Memphis tried to justify its refusal to integrate toilet facilities at the newly-desegregated public library by claiming that there were valid health reasons for racially separate toilets. The city relied on the allegation that African-Americans in that county had a higher incidence of venereal disease than whites.[118] The notion is that people of

---

[115] Cantwell, Balt Even Sun at A8 (cited in note 113).

[116] Despite the often articulated myth of America as a melting pot, suggesting an intermingling of various cultures, or cultural democracy, what occurred was acculturation, the adoption of different cultural patterns. However, for many, acculturation did not result in real assimilation—acceptance by and into the dominant groups' institutions and infrastructures—only a loss or devaluation of the outsider's own culture and values. See note 107.

The denial of culture, race, or gender may result in serious mental and/or emotional consequences. See Matsuda, 87 Mich L Rev at 2337 n88 (cited in note 109) (citing Joseph Baldwin, *African Self-Consciousness and the Mental Health of African-Americans*, 15 J Black Studies 177 (1984); Minow, 101 Harv L Rev at 67-68 (cited in note 94); Lorna Dee Cervantes, *Poem for the Young White Man Who Asked Me How I, An Intelligent Well-Read Person Could Believe in the War Between Races*, in Marta Sanchez, *Contemporary Chicana Poetry* 90 (California Press, 1985); William Grier, Price Cobbs, *Black Rage* (Basic Books, 1968)).

[117] See, for example, *McLaurin v Oklahoma State Regents*, 339 US 637, 640 (1950), where McLaurin, an African-American graduate student admitted to the previously segregated University of Oklahoma, was forced to attend classes in racially segregated classrooms and assigned a racially segregated bathroom and place in the University cafeteria. The Court held that these conditions were unconstitutional. More recently, a male African-American cadet at The Citadel in Charleston, South Carolina resigned after racially motivated hazing. *5 Citadel Cadets Indicted on Minor Charge in Racial Hazing*, NY Times Y15 (Oct 8, 1987). In addition, the wave of racial abuse of African-American and other students of color on American college campuses sends the same message. See Matsuda, 87 Mich L Rev at 2333 n71 (cited in note 109).

[118] *Turner v Randolph*, 195 F Supp 677, 679-80 (WD Tenn 1961); see Cassidy, Redbook at 118 (cited in note 5).

color are "unclean." The same idea was conveyed in a separate incident in 1985 when a "Spanish-Filipino" woman was subjected to sexist and racist comments from a fellow passenger when she tried to use a restroom in the first class section of an airplane.[119]

In *Turner*, the Tennessee federal district court rejected the city's claim, saying instead that people who use the library, whatever their race, are not likely to have venereal diseases.[120] Illiteracy rates are higher among poor people, and so there is a subtle class bias implicit in the court's ruling. That court's class bias works against all poor people as well as people of color. The court suggests that only poor people are unclean. While poverty is not limited to people of color, a disproportionate percentage of people living in poverty are people of color. Thus, the court's perpetuation of this class bias only reinforces, perhaps unconsciously, the notion that people of color are unclean and diseased, as well as poor.

There are other examples of the toilet's use as a means to oppress subordinated groups. Patricia Williams recounts the story of a transsexual student's search for a bathroom at her law school.[121] Neither women nor men law students wanted to share a bathroom with a person attempting to define her own sexual identity in a nontraditional way. Their discomfort with difference led them to ignore the fundamental and universal need of all individuals to eliminate their waste. The students' actions only reinforced the otherness of the transsexual student.

The class bias reflected in both the airline passenger's comment and the Tennessee judge's opinion continues today. The poor are routinely oppressed by being denied access to public bathrooms. American businesses by law and custom are permitted to restrict use of their bathrooms to paying customers.[122] Still others, including fast food businesses, have

---

[119] *Woman Wins Award in Airliner Fracas Over Restroom*, UPI NEXIS (Jan 30 PM cycle, 1987). When she tried to enter the restroom, a male passenger seated in first class shoved her and yelled a variety of vulgar, sexist, and racist comments, including "ch—k slut" and "whore." Id (expletive deleted). He continued: "Get out of first class where you don't belong. Someone like you would dirty the first class bathroom." Id. When the male passenger refused to apologize, insisting he had done nothing wrong, the woman, a news employee at a television station, sued and was awarded $8,000 by the court. *Vaccaro v Stephens*, 1989 US App LEXIS 5864 at *6 (9th Cir 1989), appeal dismissed, 879 F2d 866, 1989 US App LEXIS 10268 (9th Cir 1989) (unpublished disposition).

[120] *Turner*, 195 F Supp at 680. "In fact, in the absence of proof, one would be led to believe that venereal disease would not be expected to occur at any appreciable extent among that segment of the population, whether white or Negro, using the facilities and services afforded by the public libraries of the city." Id.

[121] Williams, 87 Mich L Rev at 2144-46 (cited in note 84).

[122] For example, Maryland does not require that commercial establishments provide public restrooms, and even allows these businesses to deny access to employee bathrooms by customers in most instances. Md Health-Gen Code Ann §§ 24-209, 24-210 (1989). Maine requires eating establishments licensed for 13 or more seats to "provide at least one toilet facility for the use of its *customers*" (emphasis added), a requirement that does not apply in certain circumstances when other toilet facilities are available elsewhere. 22 Me Rev Stat Ann § 1686 (1989).

even stopped providing customers bathrooms to avoid providing facilities for poor and homeless men, women, and children.[123] Our response to the homeless is to "decry the fact that [the homeless] use the rest rooms, shut the rest rooms, and then be outraged that they defecate and urinate in the streets."[124]

Perhaps only people who have been denied access by law to bathrooms can fully understand the impact both on body and dignity of this form of discrimination. As an African-American child in Washington, D.C. in the 1950s and as a lawyer in Mississippi in the late 1960s, I experienced this form of oppression. In the South you had to plan ahead if you might need to use a toilet away from home. If you did not plan ahead, you faced possible humiliation—either because you had to crouch in the grass behind some bushes or trees exposing your most private parts, or because you had to urinate in your pants.[125] The availability of a bathroom, even one marked "colored women," was a luxury. Too often African-Americans traveling south by train had to use the fields near train stops to relieve themselves. Even now, I have not forgotten my experiences, nor the habits developed and still with me to cope with the denial. As long as the law continues to be defined by moneyed white men and based on male-centered Eurocentric norms, the outsiders of American society have no chance at full equality, an equality that recognizes and values difference.[126]

POSTSCRIPT

In retrospect, it is not surprising that my initial article caused such a stir, but the reasons for the reactions are complex. My reference to male genitals and the issue of men wanting (perhaps) to see and to be seen raised in some men deep-seated and profound fears of sexual inadequacy or homosexuality. And, in this sense, male cries of triviality are denials of those fears.

In addition, bathrooms are the only admittedly "gendered" institu-

---

[123] It is almost impossible to find a fast food restaurant in New York City with a bathroom available for customer use. In addition, I have stopped at a few McDonald's in other cities which do not have bathrooms for customers.

[124] Richard Conniff, *In Washington: A Guide to Discomfort Stations*, Time 13 (Oct 3, 1988) (quoting the late political activist for the homeless, Mitch Snyder). "What's happened is that the number of homeless has mushroomed, and we haven't come to grips with that . . . . When street people started to use part of a Metro station in Farragut West as a nighttime rest room last year, the Metro responded by fencing off the station at night." Snyder suggested, "Why not install a public restroom?" They replied that it was "a terrible idea." Id at 13-14.

[125] In her novel *Sula*, Toni Morrison graphically portrays the dilemma of African-American women traveling through the South during the Jim Crow era. Toni Morrison, *Sula* 23-24 (Allen Lane, 1974).

[126] "[A]s long as what is male-defined and male-centered about law remains unacknowledged, unexplored, and unexpressed, women's interests, experiences, and perspectives will be excluded, devalued, and subverted. . . ." McIntyre, 2 Canadian J Women & L at 373-74 (cited in note 16).

tions in law school.[127] My article was a direct attack on this institution, the one place in law school where men are secure from women.[128] If the hierarchy of legal education reinforces or reproduces negative attitudes toward women, it is not surprising that there is anti-feminist graffiti in the men's room.[129] What is unfortunate, and yet reflects American society, is that these same male graffiti-writers will be some of the lawyers, legislators, and judges of tomorrow. These men, if unchallenged, will continue to reproduce a legal hierarchy of exclusion and subordination that harms women.

It is also not surprising that there were personal attacks on me. These attacks reflect hostility toward me as an authority figure. First, I am a woman writing about women's issues. Second, as an African-American woman, my opinions are even less "credible."[130] Only white male views are "neutral," valued, and accurate, and only if they are white male-centered, writing all others out of the picture where they differ from men. My views are doubly "biased" because I am a woman and an African-American with vision which perceives us all.

Some white male students were especially angry because my status as a "tenured full professor" gave me a certain amount of "credibility" even my gender and race could not fully diminish. In the law school hierarchy, a tenured professor outranks a student, even when the student is a white man and the professor an African-American woman. My criticism of toilet inequality as an example of male privilege carried more weight than it might have if I were merely a student or untenured assistant professor.

I wish my experiences were unique. Insensitivity and indifference to all women, men of color, poor men, and other societal outsiders continues, especially in law school. Unfortunately, the incidents I just described could happen at almost any law school in the United States.[131]

---

127 I took this phrase from Christine Boyle's article, *Teaching Law as if Women Really Mattered, or, What About the Washrooms?*, 2 Canadian J Women & L 96, 102 n30 (1986).

128 In all fairness, this argument cuts both ways. Women's public toilets are places of retreat for women as well. Anna Quindlen calls them "settings for the free exchange of ideas." Quindlen, *Living Out Loud* at 36 (cited in note 15). Marilyn French in her novel *The Women's Room* (Summit Books, 1977) uses the toilet as both a place of retreat and a setting for the free exchange of liberating ideas.

129 See discussion of this issue in note 28 and accompanying text.

130 McIntyre, 2 Canadian J Women & L at 400 n42, 401 (cited in note 16).

131 In the fall of 1988, condom machines were installed in the bathrooms of the library at my current institution as part of a university-wide study. This action did not go unnoticed. One third year male wrote to the law school newspaper that the library bathrooms were inappropriate places for condom machines. (letter from Richard Ingrao) The Raven 4 (Jan 1, 1989).
    One woman student wrote in response: "In general I agree with the editorial . . . however, . . . an issue remains to be addressed . . . . The installation and maintenance of condom dispensers reminds female students of the administration's refusal to fill tampon/feminine napkin machines. These machines in the library ladies' rooms are left empty. One bears a note which reads: 'The University provides no mechanism for filling these machines. However outrageous that may seem, the Library staff has exhausted all possible avenues for solving this problem . . . .' I rarely run into a bathroom and realize that I absolutely must have a

Tolerance for differences is a lesson too seldom taught in law schools these days.

condom. Yet I do, from time to time, have an immediate need for a tampon. The presence of a filled condom machine next to an empty tampon machine makes the predicament not only comical but insulting. (signed) A Female, 3D." The Raven at 13 (Feb 27, 1989).

ARTICLES

Nasty Law or Nice Ladies?
Jurisprudence, Feminism,
and Gender Difference

Judith A. Baer

ABSTRACT. This article examines the premises of the emerging field of feminist jurisprudence and critically reviews some basic works in this field. While feminist legal scholars agree that law, both as an institution and as an academic enterprise, contains an inherent male bias, they differ among themselves in their explanations of how this bias arose and what its effects are. Several of these scholars emphasize gender differences, rather than male domination, in their critiques of law. This article examines the underlying premises characteristic of what it labels "difference jurisprudence." The analysis concludes, first, that difference jurisprudence has no adequate theory of gender difference, and, second, that the existing scholarship rests on premises which are dangerous to sexual equality.

Judith A. Baer is affiliated with Texas A&M University. A version of this paper was presented at the 1990 annual meeting of the Southwestern Social Science Association, Hyatt Regency, Fort Worth, TX, March 29-31.

Women & Politics, Vol. 11(1) 1991

"Legal thinking is nasty," I said to Gina.
                                    —Scott Turow, *One L*

Sigh no more, ladies.
Time is male
and in his cups drinks to the fair.
Bemused by gallantry, we hear
our mediocrities over-praised,
indolence read as abnegation,
slattern thought styled intuition,
Every lapse forgiven, our crime
only to cast too bold a shadow
or smash the mold straight off.

                                    —Adrienne Rich
                        Snapshots of a Daughter-in-Law

The emergence of feminist jurisprudence is part of the "flowering in feminist thought" which characterized the 1980s (Mansbridge 1986, 197). As feminism has permanently changed the arts, the sciences, and the humanities, it has also made its presence felt in the law. Legal scholars have built on the feminist contributions in other disciplines and on conventional legal and political theory to invent and practice a jurisprudence which is grounded in women's character and experience.

That last phrase is as close as this essay will come to a definition of "feminist jurisprudence." I do not attempt greater precision because the field is in the process of defining itself. At present, feminist jurisprudence is usually a label which scholars apply to their own work.[1] The authors who so label their work do not comprise a monolithic group; as this essay will show, the field of feminist jurisprudence is diverse and disputatious. What these scholars have in common, however, is as important as what divides them.

THE FOUNDATIONS OF FEMINIST JURISPRUDENCE

Feminist jurisprudence, as self-identified, shares some basic underlying premises with such cognate subdisciplines as feminist psychology, epistemology, and political philosophy. These premises may be either explicit or implicit. First, the field under discussion has a fundamental and unrecognized male bias. Men founded and developed the discipline, once monopolized it, continue to dominate it, identify its chief concerns in ways that come out of their experience and reflect their interests, and select and socialize its practitioners to carry on the male tradition.

Second, sex differences exist which are significant enough to make male-oriented scholarship inadequate as knowledge. Men and women are different, not only in their physical characteristics but in psyche, personality, experience, and existential reality: in their ways of being in the world. Acceptance of this premise does not force the scholar to take sides on the old "nature versus nurture" controversy. In fact, feminist theory lacks a coherent position on whether these differences are inherent or acquired, and how, if the latter, they are acquired. Whatever the source of gender differences, feminist scholarship holds that any psychology, epistemology, or political philosophy failing to take these differences into account produces theories that are seriously deficient as explanations of whatever they purport to explain.

A third premise characteristic of feminist scholarship is that the primary contribution women can make to knowledge is consciously to produce scholarship that incorporates their specific female experience and viewpoints. This sort of scholarship carries inherent risks, because it rejects the conventional assumption, present in law as in other fields, that scholarship is neutral and objective. Insisting that traditional scholarship has an unrecognized male orientation, feminist scholars seek to provide, not the exact opposite of this approach, but an explicit and deliberate female orientation.[2]

Substituting the word "law" in the last few paragraphs where appropriate provides a partial description of feminist jurisprudence; it is to law what feminist political science is to political science, feminist psychology is to psychology, etc. But the concerns of feminist jurisprudence go beyond scholarship, because law is more than an academic discipline. Law is also a social institution, a manifestation of power. Feminist jurists study both positive law and legal philosophy. When Catharine MacKinnon, for instance, analyzes pornography, she addresses both First Amendment law and the existing scholarly literature on freedom of expression (1989, chap. 11).

Her application of a feminist critique to both aspects of law is typical of this new jurisprudence. The critique itself, like the content of most feminist legal scholarship, is the subject of vigorous dispute within this contentious field.

What feminist jurists disagree on is as important as those premises on which they agree. While these scholars share the presumption that law is male, they have different views of how and why law is male. One group of authors provides the juristic version of what has been labelled "difference theory." Influenced by feminist psychology and epistemology, most powerfully by Carol Gilligan's landmark work *In a Different Voice*, authors like Robin West (1988), Lucinda Finley (1986), and Suzanna Sherry (1986) maintain that law places women at a disadvantage because it derives from predominantly male ways of knowing and thinking. Other feminist jurists, influenced by Marxist scholarship and the Critical Legal Studies movement, assert that male bias in law results specifically from men's subjection of women (e.g., Copelon 1989; MacKinnon 1987, 1989; Schneider 1986; Taub and Schneider 1982).

These two orientations do not comprise the whole field of feminist jurisprudence. Several authors take neither of the positions I have described; their work resists categorization along these lines (see, e.g., Littleton 1987; Minow 1985, 1987; Olsen 1983; Scales 1986). Nor do the two approaches split into an absolute dichotomy. The authors in the first group do not deny that men have power over women; for their part, jurists who emphasize male dominance do not insist that women and men reason, know, and exist alike. But the distinction is clear enough to justify assigning the label "difference jurisprudence" to the works in the first group. Difference jurists interpret male dominance through gender difference, while other scholars do the opposite. Difference jurists regard male dominance as the root of law that disfavors women by ignoring gender differences, rather than regarding non-physical gender differences as the result of male dominance.

This essay is an examination of the foundations and underlying premises of difference jurisprudence. I find much to praise in the scholarship that provides the foundations of difference jurisprudence, but the analysis is critical and, on balance, unfavorable. The school of feminist jurisprudence that emphasizes sex differences rather than male dominance rests on explanations of those differences that are of highly dubious validity. However radical it appears, difference jurisprudence is inherently conservative. Difference jurisprudence, in its present state, poses a threat to women's equality and autonomy.

SEEING THE WORLD AS MALE: CONVENTIONAL THEORY AND THE FEMINIST RESPONSE

By the time feminism was making its presence felt in academia, most scholars had abandoned the claim that the great ideas of the Western tradition were the products of abstract thought divorced from the concrete experience of the thinkers. For example, Marxists, whose concepts scholars often borrow even in capitalist societies, had argued that "philosophical theories may put forth as a necessary truth that which is in fact merely an historically conditioned contingency" (Murphy 1986, 636). The step, by analogy, from an argument like this to an assertion that some supposed truths may be the result of physically conditioned contingencies, like the sex of the philosopher, is a short one. Feminists have even turned this kind of insight back on Marxists; an example is MacKinnon's implication that the strongest determinant of a woman's class position is not her relationship to production but her relationship to a man (1989, 47-48).

The Male Bias of Traditional Thought

Feminist scholars start from the recognized fact that the giants of the Western tradition — the interpreters of our world, at least those whose names and work have survived to the present — have been men. Feminist jurists start from the same observation about law. These scholars have been no more successful than anyone else, ever, in explaining, to universal satisfaction, why this work has been men's work. Were these divisions of labor loosely derived from differences in reproductive function; did the more powerful sex reserve this relatively cushy job for itself while assigning grubbier tasks to the subordinate sex; or both? The fact that we cannot really explain *why* theory is a male preserve, however, does not preclude the possibility of starting a worthwhile analysis from the fact *that* theory has been men's work.

No one seriously suggests that any of these intellectual or legal founding fathers began their work with the thought: "I am male; I shall construct a theory that only a man could create." The male bias that pervades so many of these works appears to result, instead, from the authors' habits of deriving ostensibly universal truths from their individual, and therefore male, viewpoint. Philosophy and law both provide many examples of connections between theory and gender. Some of these examples are overtly, even blatantly, sexist. Aristotle's argument in Book 1 of the *Politics* that men are superior to women, and Sigmund Freud's theory of penis envy (1927, 133-42, 1964) come to mind, along with Justice Joseph Bradley's insistence in *Bradwell v. Illinois* (1872, 140-42) that a state may exclude women from the legal profession so that they may fulfill their destiny as wives and mothers. By the time large numbers of women were beginning academic and legal careers, none of these ideas was widely believed, nor did any state restrict bar admission to men. But apprentice scholars soon began to perceive that the male bias in the disciplines was far deeper and more pervasive than overt sexism.

We need go no further than the two authors I have already mentioned, whose influence on the scholarly enterprise is hard to exaggerate, to find this orientation. First, reconsider the *Politics*: not its defense of patriarchy and natural slavery, but the pre-eminent place among human activities that Aristotle assigns to philosophy and public life. How much of this theory has to do with the intrinsic value of these activities, and how much with the fact that the author was one of the infinitesimal number of human beings who have ever lived who had the time and leisure to pursue such activities? This group excludes the vast majority of men, but it has excluded even more women than men. Very, very few women have ever had much opportunity either to engage in government or to philosophize about it; the rare exceptions must often wrench that time and leisure away from other demands on them in ways that male philosophers have not had to confront. Most women have led lives that gave them more experience with homemaking, child care, and family life than Aristotle got; had women done philosophy, they might have looked at things differently. Aristotle's ranking of human endeavors neither originated nor ended with him; Plato before him, John Locke after him, and Hannah Arendt still later than Locke, similarly valued human activities. This hierarchy elevates the public and academic sphere, both traditional male preserves, while it devalues home and family life, the activities in which women have engaged (Plato, Books V and VI; Locke 1690; Arendt 1958).

Even if we abandon penis envy—as mainstream psychology has long since—Freud's psychoanalytic theory of personality development provides a clear instance of what one critic called "sexual solipsism" (Friedan 1963, chap. 5). Freud's theory that the superego develops around the Oedipus complex and the fear of castration rests on a presumption that the male body is the human norm. It did not take long for some of Freud's women students to begin constructing theories from female physiology: theories, for example, which posited male "womb envy." But Freud's work has survived longer, and been read more widely, than that of the dissidents; Freud, like Aristotle, became part of the intellectual tradition that aspiring scholars must master. One ultimate result of the primacy of Freudian theory in psychology was that "a problem in theory became cast as a problem in women's development" (Gilligan 1982, 7).[3]

The Feminist Critique of Male-Centered Theory

Once feminists posited a connection between existing theory and maleness, there ensued a rich intellectual game that has fruitful possibilities (see, e.g., Hirschmann 1989). Any existing part of the received intellectual tradition can be revealed and challenged as male. Thomas Hobbes' argument that "a perpetual and restless desire of power after power, which ceaseth only in death" (1962, 80) is part of human nature? Marxists have suggested that Hobbes elevated the greed produced by capitalism to a universal truth; might he not also have characterized as universally human that which was specifically and contingently male? Or consider liberal individualism, as represented, for instance, by John Stuart Mill (1859). Does not this philosophy, which posits the human being as separate from every other human being, contradict the reality of human reproduction? Might not the theory's emphasis on conflict between society and the individual implicitly disregard reality as experienced by women immersed in family life? Or what about a theory based on such presumptions about the range of choice available to human beings, and the nature of mother-child relationships, revealed in a statement like the following:

> Economic analysis suggests that a parent may, over some range, trade custodial rights for money. Although this notion may offend some, a contrary assumption would mean that a parent with full custody would accept no sum of money in return for slightly less custody, even if the parent were extremely poor. Faced with such alternatives, most parents would prefer to see the child a bit less and be able to give the child better housing, more food, more education, better health care, and some luxuries. (Mnookin and Kornhauser 1979, 964)

This legal model presumes that individuals aggressively assert their rights, that they will trade, barter, and exchange, that they are rational maximizers. Mothers of young children, however, do not typically behave in this manner when they negotiate with former husbands for custody (see Chambers 1984; Chesler 1986; Polikoff 1982, 1983; Weitzman 1986). Nor, for that matter, do fathers who relinquish custody "rationally" exchange money for the assurance of their children's welfare. The rational choice model is based on public (and, therefore, traditionally male) behavior. Trying to explain post-divorce parental behavior in rational choice terms, then, illustrates the inadequacies of a male-based model to explain the behavior of either men or women. This kind of legal thinking seems nasty indeed (see Olsen 1983). Ann Scales speaks for many feminist legal scholars when she writes:

Feminists have tried to describe for the judiciary a theory of "special rights" for women which will fit the discrete, non-stereotypical, "real" differences between the sexes. And herein lies our mistake: We have let the debate become narrowed by accepting as correct those questions which seek to arrive at a definitive list of differences. In so doing, we have adopted the vocabulary, as well as the epistemology and political theory, of the law as it is. (1986, 1375)

The article quoted just above this passage is a perfect illustration of the dangers inherent in feminist reliance on "the vocabulary . . . of the law as it is." One possible reaction to that paragraph is that it could only be the product of a male mind. The discovery that two men did in fact write those words may be gratifying to the feminist jurist, but building a theory on notions of sexual differences derived from these or any other texts is a dangerous enterprise. The problem of infinite regression looms as one formidable obstacle to this sort of theorizing. Since all philosophers were human beings and had individual lives, all ideas can be traced to subjective and contingent experience. If we read the classics of the received tradition, we can find examples of ideas that appear to be contingent on male experience. But if male bias explains everything, sooner or later male bias explains nothing—unless we have a coherent and consistent theory of how men think that is different from our theory of the way women think. And that theory does not exist. The theories of gender difference which do exist are not adequate.

Feminists can argue that certain theories posited as universal truths are in fact gender-conditioned contingencies, but these assertions cannot be shown to be true, any more than a Marxist can show that the greed that Hobbes observed resulted from capitalism. We cannot really claim to know that female contemporaries of Aristotle or Hobbes would have constructed different theories. Such women would, after all, have had to have led very privileged lives to have done philosophy at all; they might have looked at domestic duties from the disdainful standpoint of one who has escaped them, or cast a critical, detached eye upon less fortunate beings struggling for power. Freud, unlike either Aristotle or Hobbes, did have women students; while some of these psychoanalysts rejected his theories, others enthusiastically embraced them. Both liberalism and rational choice have women adherents, some of whom call themselves feminists. The obstacles these scholars have confronted consist, not in the dissonance of male-centered scholarship to their reality, but, in their exclusion by a sexist academic establishment. Any claim that traditional theory is ill-adapted to women's existential reality has to confront the fact that women have shown that they can produce, within male-defined disciplines, psychology, epistemology, political theory, and jurisprudence that is every bit as good as men's scholarship.[4] A critic could argue that these women have been stifled by male influence and, therefore, suffer from a kind of false consciousness, but that charge leads us down the twin blind alleys of infinite regression and selective interpretation: when a woman theorist agrees with me, she is thinking like a woman; when she disagrees, she is thinking like a man.

We do not even know whether, or to what extent, the classic works were the exclusive product of male minds. Research on art, music, and literature has uncovered several instances of work attributed to a man that was actually the work of a woman. One of several possible answers to the old question, "Why are there no great woman artists/novelists/musicians?" is that, "there were, but some man attached his name to their work"; and we should recall Virginia Woolf's statement, "Anonymous was a woman" (1929).[5] There is one famous instance of a philosopher acknowledging his wife's equal partnership. That author was John Stuart Mill, whose *On Liberty* is a classic of the liberal individualism which feminists now challenge! Yet Mill, in dedicating the book to the memory of Harriet Taylor Mill, wrote, "Like all that I have written for many years, it belongs as much to her as to me." It is entirely possible that other "great works" were likewise not based on the male experience only.

Our ability to find flaws in the presumption that scholarship is male-centered, however, is no reason to abandon the effort to create new women-centered theory. Difference theorists may proceed from shaky assumptions, but the only way to judge whether feminist scholarship can make a contribution to our knowledge is to try to derive theory from women's experience and evaluate the results.

The evidence that is in, so far, demonstrates, without doubt, that women scholars, studying women's experiences, have added to our knowledge. We know so much, in 1990, of which we had no idea in 1970, that we can justifiably suspect that the received tradition is excessively male. Nevertheless, the difference theory we now have rests on assumptions and interpretations for which validity is highly suspect and that are inherently dangerous to women's interests.

The *"Different Voice"* in Jurisprudence

How are men and women different from each other? We know that they have different bodies; the fact that they lead different lives — in other words, are assigned different social roles — is only slightly less obvious. Beyond these physical and social differences, we also perceive many ways in which men and women seem to act, think, and feel differently; casual empiricism suggests that personality differences may exist. Common perceptions of such differences make the work of feminist difference theorists more plausible to the reader; they describe behavior that we can recognize. What we do not yet know or understand, is, first, whence these personality differences arise — in particular whether they are natural or conventional — and, second, whether such differences are healthy or unhealthy for human beings.

Deriving theories of sex differences from anatomical and physiological differences is a common practice of the received tradition, which has paid rather less attention to the equally evident physical similarities. Thus, the fact that women bear children becomes important not only because it is a physiological gender difference but because society assigns a greater importance to this difference than to the fact, for example, that men and women have similar brains. Conventional theory typically explains role differences in terms of sexual differences; women's domestic responsibilities and relative exclusion from public life are seen as derived from their childbearing function.

The feminist theories of gender difference which have emerged since the mid-1970s reject the conventional assumption that the male body, mind, or experience represents the norm from which the female body, mind, or experience is a deviation. Feminist difference theorists differ as to whether gender difference is due primarily to physical differences, to role differences, or to a combination of the two. But the feminists share one feature of their thought with one another and with conventional theorists: this work is being grounded on the premise that sexual differences are more important than sexual similarities.

Difference jurisprudence has, essentially, two theories of gender difference. The most influential explanation, so far, is that associated with Carol Gilligan as derived essentially from Nancy Chodorow: male and female psychology differs because of a combination of physical difference and role assignment. The second explanation, developed in a specifically legal context by Robin West, emphasizes physiology, specifically sexuality and reproductive functions.

Carol Gilligan:
Women's Psychology and Moral Theory

In a Different Voice is, without question, one of the foremost contributions to psychological theory produced in this century. Carol Gilligan has produced a work that no scholar can ignore and from which every reader can learn. Gilligan's thesis is that women derive from their life experience a morality fundamentally different from that of men: while men's moral development emphasizes "rights and noninterference," women's psychology is "distinctive in its greater orientation toward relationships and interdependence," valuing "attachment" to others rather than "separation" from them (1982, 2, 151). This argument represents both a major contribution to the psychology of moral development and a radical departure from existing theories, which were largely derived from studies of male subjects.

Gilligan supports her thesis with data that she herself generated. She draws on psychological studies that she conducted during the 1970s. She has amassed a substantial collection of material that shows women doing their moral reasoning differently from men. Throughout her remarkably concise book, she quotes her subjects' own words. She writes of these women, "The standard of moral judgment that informs their assessment of self is a standard of relationship, an ethic of nurturance, responsibility, and care" (1982, 159).

Both Gilligan's words and those of her subjects resonate powerfully for any woman acquainted with the literature on moral development. The reaction her book produces among women is almost universal recognition. At some level, the differences seem to exist. The association of care and nurturance with women conforms to our experience as human beings. These values are undeniably important and healthy, indeed necessary, for individuals and for society. Yet male-dominated psychology has de-emphasized them, thereby implicitly devaluing those who have them. Gilligan's discovery of a "different voice" brings a promise of sexual equality.

If Gilligan is right, her conclusions represent a challenge not only to psychological theory but to the philosophy of liberal individualism and to law based wholly or partly on that philosophy. A theory which juxtaposes society and the individual, in opposition to each other, cannot adequately deal with women if they are enmeshed in relationships and connections in the way Gilligan describes. But feminist scholars know the dangers of basing general theories on the limited amount of empirical observations that one individual can make in one career (see Kerber et al. 1986, 310-316). Indeed, feminists may be more aware of these dangers than most scholars are, because theories detrimental to women have been developed in that way.

How does Gilligan develop her theory? A frequently quoted passage recounts the different responses of two eleven-year-olds, Jake and Amy, to this classic ethical problem: is a man justified in stealing a drug which he cannot afford to buy, in order to save his wife's life? Jake's unequivocal "yes," advocating a principled decision to break a rule, fits onto the highest level of Lawrence Kohlberg's "stages of moral development," the dominant paradigm in the field when Gilligan wrote. By contrast, Amy's answer implicitly rejects the terms of the question: "If he stole the drug, he might save his wife then, but if he did, he might have to go to jail, and then his wife might get sicker again, and he couldn't get more of the drug . . . They should really just talk it out and find some other way to make the money.'' She perceives "not a math problem involving humans but a narrative of relationships that extends over time" — not to mention the fact that her answer indicates better knowledge of the way medicine works than Jake displays (Gilligan 1982, chap. 2).

When Gilligan participated in a symposium at Buffalo Law School in 1984, Carrie Menkel-Meadow described Amy's approach as "typical of a 'bad' law student: Amy 'fought the hypo.' [i.e., the hypothetical question]" (1985, 50). But Jake handled the question exactly as a law student is supposed to do. The "hypo" typifies the kind of "nasty" legal thinking that Turow describes: not only does it posit an adversary relationship between society and the individual, but it also "involved being suspicious and distrustful" — of everything, that is, except the terms and rules of legal education (1977, 6). Amy's solution is nicer: talk it over, find an alternative. It is tempting to conclude from this discussion that law, as taught to aspiring practitioners, has a male bias, and that what the legal system needs is more female moral reasoning.

At the same symposium in Buffalo, the co-moderator commented, "Now I understand at a new level why I felt so uncomfortable in law school" (1985, 1). No matter where women's morality comes from, or how healthy it is, society's simultaneous assignment of relational morality to women and exclusion of it from public discourse has made law a preserve of values contingently associated with men. Gilligan's work led the speaker, by then a senior law professor, to the insight that this phenomenon was a problem with law, not a problem with her as a woman.

As a political scientist, I regard law as a subfield of my discipline; I can attest that the valuable moral perspective that develops from women's assigned roles is missing from both the curriculum and the ambience of political science. But I had another equally strong response to *In a Different Voice*. Reading it, I thought: "Now I understand why the clerk at the convenience store unloads his personal problems on me, a total stranger; why I have such a hard time getting a morning's work done without interruption, while my male colleagues are undisturbed; why, if I 'listen with the third ear' to my students' requests and complaints, I can almost hear the refrain, 'mommy, mommy, mommy.'"[6] My experiences, which are far from unique, reflect an ethic of care that arises not from women's psyches but from the demands that other people make on women. The difficulty with Gilligan's work may be a problem inherent in the study of psychology; by focusing on individuals' accounts, she misses the extent to which individuals are constrained by outside expectations.

Some quotations from Gilligan's subjects reveal a darker side of the female ethic that she herself does not seem to notice. Emily, for example, decides not to go to a medical school far from home because this act would hurt her parents. There is no indication that they need her in any special way, just that "my parents have a right to see me a certain way, at certain times." Since Emily was a college student at the time, she had not yet confronted the inevitable tension between this "right" and the demands which medical school (let alone medical practice) makes on one's time and energy. Her future is in jeopardy because she perceives her parents as having rights, while "my motivation was sort of selfish" (1982, 140-43).

This vignette sounds, not like a different voice at all, but like the same old voice. The psychiatrist Joseph Rheingold wrote back in 1964 that *"Woman is nurturance,"* and, "When women grow up" free of "subversion by feminist doctrine" and "enter upon motherhood with a sense of altruistic fulfillment, we shall attain the goal of a good life and a secure world in which to live it" (714, emphasis in the original). A few years later, David Bakan, a philosopher, described women as characterized by "communion" with others while men sought "agency," which "manifests itself in the formation of separations" (1966, 14-15). Gilligan is not even the first woman to write like this; Gina Lombroso, in 1923, labelled women as "alterocentric" while men were "egocentric."[5] (Gilligan, incidentally, cites none of these works.) When men and pre-feminist women express such ideas, feminists rightly reject them. Why are they suddenly palatable when a self-described feminist bases them on equally problematic evidence?

Many of Gilligan's critics have refused to accept her evaluation of women's ethic of care as natural and healthy. Catharine Mac-

Kinnon's opinion of Gilligan's psychology is indicated both by what she writes and by the fact that each of her two books published since 1982 mentions Gilligan exactly once. "It is enlightening," MacKinnon writes, "that affirming the perspective that has been forced on women is rather widely taken as progress toward taking women seriously" (1989, 52).[7] Women's morality may emphasize nurturance and care because a male supremacist society forces upon women the duties of nurture and care. Far from being benign, the different moral voice may be an unhealthy adaptation to male dominance.

Yet most thoughtful feminists are reluctant to dismiss attachment, caring, and nurturance as maladaptive. This ethic can, obviously, be carried to extremes, but the fact that society assigns women these duties does not make caring and nurturance inherently bad. Most of us recognize them as good, and are reluctant to accept the conventional implication that separation and independence are superior values. Gilligan is quite right on two crucial points. First, this society ranks the "disconnector" virtues above the "connector" virtues; second, the latter are associated with women. But Gilligan's uncritical accounts of her subjects' reasoning raise more questions than they answer. For Gilligan to make a case that behavior like Emily's is natural and healthy for women rather than a product of learned self-devaluation, she must provide an underlying theory of sexual differences that rests on a presumption of sexual equality.

Gilligan's difference theory is derived from the psychoanalytic theory of Nancy Chodorow, expounded in her 1978 book, *The Reproduction of Mothering*. Chodorow, like Freud, starts with infancy and early childhood, but her interpretations of essentially the same facts are diametrically opposed to his. She traces sex differences in personality to common childhood experiences combined with physical differences. Because, as Chodorow's first sentence states, "Women mother," infants and children experience a woman as the primary caregiver and socializer. This experience affects boys and girls differently because the reciprocal relationship between mother and child differs with the child's sex. Mother perceives a daughter as being like her, but a son as being different. A girl sees herself as being like mother, while a boy perceives that he is different from mother. Thus, a girl's most significant relationship is with a person with whom she identifies, while a boy relates to someone he distinguishes from himself. Attachment is built into a girl's development, while a boy's experience emphasizes separation.[8]

Even if Chodorow is right, we could still assert that the results are unhealthy and that what we need to do is to make men more responsible for child care and women less so. Chodorow herself is open to this possibility; she is more critical of present arrangements than Gilligan is. But we do not even need to make this kind of argument unless the theory can be shown to be correct. Chodorow draws on a vast collection of scholarship that, interpreted without Freudian bias, can support her thesis. But the problem with psychoanalytic theory is that it depends on data that simply do not interpret themselves; one needs to start with a theory in order to make much use of them. The facts with which Chodorow starts are hardly matters of controversy: yes, women take care of children; and yes, girls' bodies are more like those of their caregiver than boys' bodies are. But the theory that Chodorow and Gilligan construct from these facts discounts other potentially important facts.

What would have to be true for male and female personalities to develop as Chodorow posits? Children would have to become familiar with adult bodies at an early age. They probably do; even in households with a less than relaxed attitude toward nudity, differences in size between children and adults facilitates immature observation. Familiarity with men's bodies as well as with those of women would facilitate this kind of psychic development. Boys can better appreciate mother's difference from them, and girls her similarity, if they have access to an adult body different from hers. Although mother usually spends more time with children than father does, most children have enough contact with men to learn that adult male bodies differ from adult female bodies.

Cradled in adult arms, infants are close to breasts, beards, and voices; held in laps, they are near genitals. Toddlers, who are more or less at crotch height relative to adults, have a convenient vantage point. Anyone who spends much time with young children knows that they are enthusiastic explorers of others' bodies as well as of their own. The little girl learns that mother, like her, has a vulva, vagina, and clitoris, while the little boy perceives that he lacks these parts but has a penis and testicles, which mother lacks.

The little boy, then, perceives that his mother's body looks, sounds, feels, and smells differently from his own. To that extent, the theory works. But does he see his father's body as essentially similar to his? Adults' bodies look, sound, feel, and smell differently from children's bodies, even those of the same sex. The little girl, likewise, sees that mother has the same genital parts that she does. But they do not look the same. And mother also has breasts and pubic hair (not to mention body hair in general; shaving the legs is not a universal female custom), both of which the little girl lacks.

How do we know that age differences are perceived by children as being less important than sex differences? Can the little girl, in any meaningful sense, see her mother as more like her than different from her, while the boy is drawing just the opposite conclusion? Might it not even be possible that a little girl perceives her mother's body as not much more like her own body than her small brother's is? The difficulty with difference theories based on childhood perceptions is that they tend to focus on the physical differences which adults consider important: sexual distinctions rather than those based on age. But we do not really know that children perceive things this way. Children might well have just the opposite idea; boys and girls alike may see themselves as little and weak, surrounded by big, strong, and powerful adults, whatever their sex. Children's psychosexual development may depend as much on adult-child differences as on male-female differences. If they do, psychoanalytic theories of development are defective. And if the theory on which Gilligan depends is wrong, her psychology of sexual differences is inadequate.

Gilligan has failed to provide a satisfactory argument that sex differences in personality rest on anything other than sex-role socialization, which may not be healthy or desirable at all. Gender differences in moral reasoning may well result from a little old-fashioned social learning: as girls grow up, they learn that society expects different things from men and women and adopt the modes of thought and behavior that win them the approval of adults. If that is the way in which sexual differences develop, there is nothing particularly praiseworthy about them. We need to look elsewhere for a satisfactory difference theory.

Robin West:
Women's Physiology and Legal Theory

Robin West, a law professor, does not set her theory of gender differences in opposition to that of Gilligan and Chodorow. Far from rejecting their analysis, she discusses both scholars favorably and at length. She reads Gilligan's work to support her own "connection thesis" that "women are actually or potentially materially connected to other human life. Men aren't" (1988, 14). This thesis is compatible with Gilligan's and Chodorow's, but it is distinct from theirs. West grounds her difference theory not on the effects of childrearing practices but squarely on physiology.

"Virtually all modern American legal theorists," West writes, accept "the 'separation thesis' of what it means to be a human being: a 'human being,' whatever else he is, is physically separate from all other human beings." West's "he" is deliberate:

The modern, increasing use of the female pronoun in liberal and critical legal theory, although well-intended, is empirically and existentially false. For the cluster of claims that jointly constitute the "separation thesis" . . . while "usually true" of men, are patently untrue of women. Women are essentially, necessarily, inevitably, invariably, always, and forever . . . connected to life and to other human beings during at least four recurrent and critical material experiences: the experience of pregnancy itself; the invasive and "connecting" experience of heterosexual penetration; the monthly experience of menstruation, which represents the potential for pregnancy; and the post-pregnancy experience of breast-feeding. Indeed, perhaps the central insight of feminist theory in the last decade has been that women are "essentially connected," not "essentially separate," from the rest of human life, both materially, through pregnancy, intercourse, and breast-feeding, and, existentially, through the moral and practical life. If by "human beings," legal theorists mean women as well as men, then the "separation thesis" is clearly false. (1988, 1-3)

Now, physical sex differences provide a much firmer foundation for difference theory than childrearing practices do. Prominent among representative works in this area are Elshtain 1981; Gilligan 1982; Harding 1986; and Rich 1976, 1979. The physiological functions to which West refers are natural, permanent, and exclusively female. They refer to experiences that no man has, and that only women have. If we accept the idea that our experience effects our existential reality, it would seem at least plausible that the sexes are, indeed, different in the ways West describes.

The more closely we analyze these "critical material experiences," however, the less adequate they become as foundations for West's theory. Three of the four, sexual intercourse, pregnancy, and breast-feeding, involve a physical relationship with another person, who may be male. Why is the male penetrator, the unborn male child, or the breast-fed baby boy not materially connected to the woman? West's assumption that relationships are unilateral rather than reciprocal is bad logic.

If fetuses and infants perceive the material connections between mother and themselves—with the same brains that, however immature, are presumed to recognize mother's voice and to perceive the difference between breast and bottle—then we could assert that both males and females are "actually or potentially materially connected to human life" and that the separation thesis is false for all human beings. However, such a theory would have to argue convincingly that these connecting experiences are more important to psychosexual development than those experiences which make human beings conscious of their separation from others. In developing her difference theory, West fails to accomplish this task with respect to women.

Even if we consider the critical functions unilaterally, from the woman's viewpoint, they are insufficient bases for a theory of personality. West's unqualified language implies that her four critical material experiences are common to all or virtually all women. In fact, this generalization holds for only one of them, menstruation, and for only part of a woman's life cycle. Menstruation is a phenomenon of relatively half the life of a woman who lives out her normal life span in Western industrial societies. Furthermore, the connection West posits between menstruation and fertility is a connection made by the intellect. It is not at all clear that women's concrete experience of menstruation has anything to do with material connection to other human beings.

The other three experiences, while probably common to a majority of women who have ever lived, are far from common to all women. Heterosexual intercourse is not a characteristic experience either for lesbians or for celibate women. Heterosexually active women need not always experience intercourse primarily as "penetration"; think, for instance, of "enclosing" or "receiving." The number of women who experience pregnancy is smaller than the number who experience heterosexual intercourse; the number of women who breast-feed is smaller still. West has thus committed an error similar to the one she attributes to mainstream legal theorists: if by "women" she means those for whom her connection thesis is true, then women who do not perform any, some or all of these functions are not women.

One necessary feminist response to this argument, at least from women who have not undergone any, some, or all of these "critical material experiences," is precisely analogous to the appropriate response of a gay scholar to heterosexist theory or a black scholar to white supremacist theory. We should reject it as bigoted, intentionally or not, just as West rejects mainstream legal theory as sexist. Beyond this political objection, we can make the same criticism of this kind of work that we make of scholarship that draws conclusions about women from information about only white women or only middle-class women. It is exclusive rather than inclusive, contingent rather than universal.

Another necessary feminist response to West is not analogous with but identical to other critiques of exclusive scholarship: West's work is heterosexist and white supremacist. She clearly excludes lesbians — indeed, any women who do not have sex with men — from her theory. Her racial exclusiveness is less obvious, but Angela Harris (1990, 604) has argued persuasively that West is guilty of "white solipsism": her thesis that gender is the primary determinant of personal identity, and therefore more important than race, is true only for white women.[9]

Another difficulty confronted by the scholar who would build a theory of gender differences on these experiences is that, in the normal course of events, none of them happens until a girl is several years old. Although psychology does not maintain that *only* early childhood experience counts in human development, general agreement exists among psychological theorists that much if not most personality formation occurs before puberty. Therefore, a woman's formative years are not influenced by the experiences that West sees as crucial to women's sense of self.

West's "connection thesis," then, has four critical defects. First, it rests on faulty logic; second, it treats as universal phenomena female experiences that are not in fact typical of all women; third, its politics are exclusive; and, finally, it makes psychosexual development contingent on experiences that do not occur until the second decade of life. Since West's theory is weak, her criticism of mainstream legal theory cannot be accepted on its own terms. We have seen that her difference theory rests on logical, psychological, demographic, chronological, and political errors. Moreover, the conclusions she draws from the incontrovertible fact of gender-specific material experiences are problematic. We all know that only women, and no men, menstruate, give birth, breast-feed, and are penetrated in heterosexual intercourse. The difficulty consists in determining what we can infer from these facts.

Are sexual differences important? To varying degrees, yes; no one seriously denies, for instance, that having a baby affects a woman's self-definition. But we do not need to assert that all exclusively female material experiences are trivial in order to question West's inference that they are *critical* determinants of women's existential reality, and that they are more crucial than the experiences that men and women share. Do we know, for instance, that menarche has a greater effect on a girl than does the transition from elementary to junior high school, or that having sex with a man changes her more than leaving her parents' home, going to college, or getting a full-time job? West commits the same error that Aristotle, Freud, and so many other theorists have made in thinking about women; she presumes that what is different is what is most important.

Emphasizing sexual differences has served a crucial function in traditional theory: rationalization of the status quo. If women are different from men, they do not need and should not want the rights and privileges that men enjoy; if bearing children is the most important thing women do, it makes sense to confine women to the domestic sphere and to assign them the duties of care and nurturance. It's not male supremacy or, worse yet, patriarchy; it's everybody doing what's best for him or her. West's connection thesis lends itself to the same misuse: if women are materially connected to others and men aren't, won't women be better off caring for other human beings?

Worse, feminist theory that emphasizes physical differences leaves women defenseless against a powerful ongoing threat to their personhood: the currently popular "fetal rights" movement. At present, lawmakers are seriously considering measures that would allow the state to lock up pregnant women who use drugs or alcohol during pregnancy. We can concede that liberal theory, premised on the separation thesis, is inadequate to deal with this problem without sanctioning the invasions of liberty now being recommended in some quarters. But criminalizing women's behavior in the interests of the fetus only rejects the part of the separation thesis which emphasizes individual *freedom*; liberal theory's assumptions about individual *responsibility* are left intact. Only the mother has responsibility for the child's welfare, before or after birth. The old libertarian principle, "that government governs best which governs least," discourages intervention to help but permits intervention to punish. If society is to deal with threats to fetal health without oppressing women, we need an ethic of connection and care that includes men and institutions, not just women. Difference jurisprudence, having concentrated on women's exclusion from male-centered legal theory, has no adequate response to this kind of coercion. For opposite positions on this issue, compare Pollitt 1990 with Dorris 1989.

CONCLUSION:
DIFFERENCE JURISPRUDENCE IN PRACTICE

A theory's ability to stimulate further inquiry is as valid a test of the theory as is its ability to withstand critical scrutiny. The serious flaws in Aristotelian, Hobbesian, and Freudian theory are old news by now, but they do not detract from the extraordinary contributions that all three made to the scholarly enterprise. Likewise, the defects of feminist difference theory need not deprive it of any generative (what scholars used to call "seminal") value. Since West's article was published in 1988, this kind of judgment is premature with respect to her contribution. But difference theory in general and Carol Gilligan's work in particular have generated a body of jurisprudence that can be examined.

We can even get a crude idea of what the state of scholarship would be if feminist difference theory had never existed. The critique of individualism that West makes explicit, and that Gilligan permits the reader to infer from her thesis, has been made independently of their work. It is not even fundamentally a feminist critique. Both Philip Slater in the 1970s and Robert Bellah in the 1980s argued that individualism encourages people to separate themselves from others in pathological ways: that what Slater calls the "disconnector virtues" destroy intimacy and relationship. Slater specifically describes the virtues of care, nurturance, and attachment as qualities society attributes to women (Slater 1970, 1974, 26; Bellah 1985).[10]

Sara Ruddick's essay, "Maternal Thinking," reads remarkably like an application of "different voice" theory to a specific human enterprise. Ruddick maintains that "a mother engages in a discipline [in which] she asks certain questions rather than others; she establishes certain criteria for the truth, adequacy, and relevance of proposed answers; and she cares about the findings she makes and can act on." So engaged, a mother becomes "a mentalist rather than a behavioralist, and she assumes the priority of personhood over action." Ruddick's call for "a theory of justice shaped by and incorporating maternal thinking" echoes Gilligan's efforts to elevate women's morality to an equal status with that of men. But Ruddick produced this original and important thesis without reference to Gilligan or difference theory. "Maternal Thinking" was published in 1980 (1983, 214, 219, 226).[11]

Neither feminist jurisprudence nor its critiques of conventional theory is dependent on feminist difference theory. But what happens when scholars announce their intention to build on difference theory to construct their own theses? A look at several representative results illustrates the inherent dangers of difference theory. For instance, psychologist Sydney Callahan draws on Gilligan's work in constructing her argument for what she, Callahan, calls "pro-life feminism." Callahan argues that establishing a right to abortion is a rejection of "woman's biologically unique capacity and privilege" and "a responsible commitment to the loving nurture of specific human beings" in favor of "male aggression and destruction" (1988, 147, 143). But Callahan's "privilege" in fact becomes a duty; and if women have duties that men do not share, they are not equal to men.

Suzanna Sherry's 1986 article, "Civic Virtue and the Feminine [sic] Voice in Constitutional Adjudication," raises some hackles by its title alone; there was a time not so long ago when "feminine" and "feminist" were viewed as contradictions. Sherry's long, uncritical discussion of *In a Different Voice* indicates unambiguously what her intellectual roots are. Her celebration of what she regards as the unique judicial voice of Sandra Day O'Connor, the only woman ever to sit on the United States Supreme Court, is problematic on its face. A belief in the possibility of a woman-centered jurisprudence does not require us to regard any contemporary woman jurist as its exemplar. O'Connor is, after all, a product of Turow's "nasty," male-biased legal education. Feminist jurisprudence will not stand or fall on her ability to distinguish herself from her male peers.

But Sherry's assumption that O'Connor must be an original jurist is less troubling than what the professor chooses to praise in the judge's so-called "feminine perspective." O'Connor's preference for a "republican community [which] may, indeed must, reward individual virtue" over "an egalitarian community of autonomous individuals [which] must not . . . is consistent with the feminine rejection of individual rights except where they implicate community membership." Sherry praises O'Connor's willingness "to allow communities to discriminate among members on the basis of their past willingness to suppress their own selfish desires for the benefit of the community" (1986, 601). There is that word "selfish" again; it echoes Gilligan's Emily in her ranking her parents' interests above her own. This is the kind of outlook which male supremacist societies have urged upon women for years. Here, the demand to "put the community first" is not at least female-specific. But does it really call for celebration when the powerful urge individuals to subordinate themselves to the collectivity?

Lucinda Finley's essay, "Transcending Equality Theory," was published in 1986, the same year as Sherry's article. Finley's search for "a way out of the maternity and the workplace debate," concludes, unexceptionably if derivatively, on this note: "If we supplement our existing conception of rights with a concept of responsibility arising from our interconnectedness," we can arrive at "workplace policies that make it possible for both women and men to combine their work lives with involvement in the family" (1182). On the way to this conclusion, however, Finley lets the search for a "different voice" get out of hand. Responding to another jurist's androgynous vision, she writes:

> I sense that we will have lost something very fundamentally human in such a world of no "real" [sexual] differences. My sense of loss stems from the feeling that I as a woman want to be able to revel in the joy and virtually mystical specialness of having a baby. What I do not want is to be punished for this wonderful gift at the same time. (1986, 1139)

Now, we might conclude from this prose, appearing in the *Columbia Law Review*, that Finley has inadvertently made a powerful case against student-edited publications. An experienced editor might have warned against this excess. It is hard to expect much original thought in conjunction with such hackneyed sentiment and such pedestrian observation. The real difficulty, though, is that the only motherhood that Finley has had any opportunity to observe can hardly warrant her idealized description. As Ruddick reminds us, "Throughout history most women have mothered in conditions of military or social violence and often in extreme poverty. They have been governed by men, and often increasingly by managers and experts of both sexes, whose policies mothers neither shape nor control" (1980, 220). Therefore, what is Finley getting so excited about?

That law has, so far, been a male preserve is an incontrovertible truth. That this same, male-developed law ignores or discounts women's reality is at least plausible. But difference jurisprudence has yet to produce either an adequate theory of gender differences or an explanation of the ways in which male legal thinking has excluded women. These gaps in theory might not be so troubling if difference jurisprudence worked out better in practice than it does in theory. Unfortunately, difference jurisprudence as practiced has a tendency to result in conclusions that embody uncritical acceptance of the status quo: a different voice, perhaps, but the same words. Theories of gender difference have not given rise to a woman-centered jurisprudence that avoids the errors of the male tradition it claims to replace. What is lacking, so far, is an understanding of gender difference that incorporates an understanding of power, and that admits the possibility of contingent rather than universal differences. With such a theory, we may be able to approach nasty law with alternatives other than the perspectives of nice ladies.

NOTES

1. By "feminist jurisprudence," I do not mean any of the following: all legal scholarship done by people who label themselves feminists; all legal scholarship done by women; only legal scholarship done by women; or all legal scholarship about gender-related topics.

2. Prominent among representative works in this area are Elshtain 1981; Gilligan 1982; Harding 1986; and Rich 1976, 1979.

3. Prominent dissenters from Freudian psychoanalytic theory included Horney 1926, and Thompson 1942. For feminist critiques of Freud, see Chodorow 1978, chap. 9; Beauvoir 1952, chaps. 2, 12; and Weisstein 1970.

4. See Arendt 1958. For criticism of Arendt, see Elshtain 1981. On Freud, see, e.g., Deutsch 1944; Lundberg and Farnham 1947. For liberal theory and rational choice, see McElroy, ed. 1982; Rowland and Schwartz-Shea 1989; Levi 1988.

5. For instances of men taking credit for work done by women, see Milford 1970; Morgan 1977, 189-201; Plath 1975. How do we know that the same phenomenon was not present in philosophy or law?

6. The phrase is Theodor Reik's (1948).

7. See also 1987, 38-39, and "Feminist Discourse," especially 26-28. For other critiques of Gilligan, see e.g., Kerber et al. 1986; Lerner 1988, 52; Schneider 1986; Squier and Ruddick 1983; Wendell 1987; Westcott 1986, 141.

8. Chodorow 1978, Part II; Gilligan 1982, chap. 1. For a theory similar to Chodorow's which emphasizes social rather than psychoanalytic theory, see Dinnerstein 1976.

9. Harris asserts that women of color typically describe themselves as "black," "Asian," etc., while women rarely (in her experience, never) describe

themselves as white. I wonder, however, whether this insight really shows that race is not central to a white woman's identity. Is our self-perception—who we think we are—necessarily a reflection of who we really are?

10. Gilligan obviously could not have cited Bellah, but neither does she refer to Slater's books, though both were available to her. West cites neither author.

11. The essay was originally published in *Feminist Studies*, 6, #2(Summer 1980). The version from which I quote appears in Trebilcot, ed. 1983.

REFERENCES

Arendt, Hannah. 1958. *The Human Condition* Chicago: University of Chicago Press.

Aristotle. *Politics*.

Bakan, David. 1966. *The Duality of Human Existence*. New York: Rand-McNally.

Beauvoir, Simone de. 1952. *The Second Sex*. Ed. and Trans. by H.M. Parshley. New York: Alfred A. Knopf.

Bellah, Robert et al. 1985. *Habits of the Heart*. New York: Harper & Row.

Callahan, Sydney. 1988. "Abortion and the Sexual Agenda: A Case for Prolife Feminism." In *Abortion and Catholicism: The American Debate*, eds. Patricia Beatty Jung and Thomas A. Shannon. New York: Crossroad Publishing Company.

Chambers, David L. 1984. "Rethinking the Substantive Rules for Custody Disputes in Divorce." *Michigan Law Review* 83(December): 480-569.

Chesler, Phyllis. 1986. *Mothers on Trial: The Battle for Children and Custody*. New York: McGraw-Hill.

Chodorow, Nancy. 1978. *The Reproduction of Mothering*. Berkeley: University of California Press.

Copelon, Rhonda. 1989. "Beyond the Liberal Idea of Privacy: Toward a Positive Right of Autonomy." In *Judging the Constitution*, eds. Michael W. McCann and Gerald L. Houseman. Glenview, IL: Little, Brown, and Company.

Deutsch, Helene. 1944. *The Psychology of Women*. New York: Grune and Stratton.

Dinnerstein, Dorothy. 1976. *The Mermaid and the Minotaur*. New York: Harper Colophon Books.

Dorris, Michael. 1989. *The Broken Cord*. New York: Harper & Row.

Elshtain, Jean Bethke. 1981. *Public Man, Private Woman*. Princeton, NJ: Princeton University Press.

"Feminist Discourse, Moral Values, and the Law—A Conversation." 1985. *Buffalo Law Review* 34: 11-87.

Finley, Lucinda. 1986. "Transcending Equality Theory: A Way out of the Maternity and the Workplace Debate." *Columbia Law Review* 86(October): 1118-82.

Freud, Sigmund. 1964. "Femininity." *New Introductory Lectures in Psychoanalysis*. Trans. by James Strachey. New York: W.W. Norton.

Freud, Sigmund. 1927. "Some Psychological Consequences of the Anatomical Distinction Between the Sexes." *International Journal of Psychoanalysis* 7: 133-42.

Friedan, Betty. 1963. *The Feminine Mystique*. New York: W.W. Norton.

Gilligan, Carol. 1982. *In a Different Voice*. Cambridge, MA: Harvard University Press.

Harding, Sandra. 1986. *The Science Question in Feminism*. Ithaca: Cornell University Press.

Harris, Angela P. 1990. "Race and Essentialism in Feminist Legal Theory." *Stanford Law Review* 42(February): 581-616.

Hirschmann, Nancy J. 1989. "Freedom, Recognition, and Obligation: A Feminist Approach to Political Theory." *American Political Science Review* 83 (December): 1227-44.

Hobbes, Thomas. 1651 (1962). *Leviathan*, ch. 11, ed. Michael Oakeshott. New York: Collier Books.

Horney, Karen. 1926. "The Flight from Womanhood." *International Journal of Psychoanalysis* 6: 324-39.

Kerber, Linda K. et al. 1986. "On In A Different Voice: An Interdisciplinary Forum." *Signs* 7(Winter): 304-33.

Lerner, Harriet G. 1988. *Women in Therapy*. New York: Harper & Row.

Levi, Margaret. 1988. *Of Rule and Revenue*. Berkeley: University of California Press.

Locke, John. 1690. *Two Treatises on Government*.

Lombroso, Gina. 1923. *The Soul of Woman*. New York: E.P. Dutton.

Lundberg, Ferdinand, and Marynia F. Farnham. 1947. *Modern Woman: The Lost Sex*. New York: Grosset and Dunlap.

MacKinnon, Catharine A. 1987. *Feminism Unmodified*. Cambridge, MA: Harvard University Press.

MacKinnon, Catharine A. 1989. *Toward a Feminist Theory of the State*. Cambridge, MA: Harvard University Press.

Mansbridge, Jane J. 1986. *Why We Lost the ERA*. Chicago: University of Chicago Press.

McElroy, Wendy, ed. 1982. *Freedom, Feminism and the State*. Washington, DC: Cato Institute.

Milford, Nancy. 1970. *Zelda*. New York: Harper & Row.

Mill, John Stuart. 1859. *On Liberty*.

Minow, Martha. 1985. "'Forming Underneath Everything that Grows': Toward a History of Family Law." *Wisconsin Law Review* 4: 819-88.

Minow, Martha. 1987. "Justice Engendered." *Harvard Law Review* 101(November): 10-95.

Mnookin, Robert H. and Lewis Kornhauser. 1979. "Bargaining in the Shadow of the Law: The Case of Divorce." *Yale Law Journal* 88: 950-97.

Morgan, Robin. 1977. *Going too Far*. New York: Random House.

Murphy, Jeffrie G. "Marxism and Retribution." In *Philosophy of Law*, 3rd ed., eds. Joel Feinberg and Hyman Gross. Belmont, CA: Wadsworth Publishing Company.

Olsen, Frances. 1983. "The Family and the Market: A Study of Ideology and Legal Reform." *Harvard Law Review* 96(May): 1497-1578.

Plato. *The Republic*.

Plath, Sylvia. 1975. *Letters Home*. Ed. and Intro. Aurelia Schober Plath. New York: Harper & Row.

Polikoff, Nancy. 1982. "Why Mothers are Losing: A Brief Analysis of Criteria Used in Child Custody Determinations." *Women's Rights Law Reporter* 7 (Spring): 235-43.

Polikoff, Nancy. 1983. "Gender and Child Custody Determinations." In *Families, Politics, and Public Policy*, ed. Irene Diamond. New York: Longman.

Pollitt, Katha. 1990. "'Fetal Rights': A New Assault on Feminism." *The Nation* 250, #12(March 26): 409-18.

Reik, Theodor. 1948 (1983). *Listening with the Third Ear: The Inner Experience of a Psychoanalyst*. New York: Farrar, Straus, and Giroux.

Rheingold, Joseph. 1964. *The Fear of Being a Woman*. New York: Grune and Stratton.

Rhode, Deborah L. 1990. "Feminist Critical Theories." *Stanford Law Review* 42(February): 617-38.

Rich, Adrienne. 1976. *Of Woman Born: Motherhood as Experience and Institution*. New York: W.W. Norton.

Rich, Adrienne. 1979. *On Lies, Secrets, and Silence*. New York: W.W. Norton.

Rowland, Barbara M. and Peregrine Schwartz-Shea. 1989. "Empowering Women: Self, Autonomy, and Responsibility." Prepared for delivery at the 1989 annual meeting of the American Political Science Association, Atlanta, GA, August 31-September 3.

Ruddick, Sara. [1980] 1983. "Maternal Thinking." In *Mothering: Essays in Feminist Theory*, ed. Joyce Trebilcot. Totowa, NJ: Rowman and Allenheld.

Scales, Ann M. 1986. "The Emergence of Feminist Jurisprudence: An Essay." *Yale Law Journal* 95(June): 1373-1403.

Schneider, Elizabeth. 1986. "The Dialectic of Rights and Liberties: Perspectives from the Women's Movement." *New York University Law Review* 61(October): 589-652.

Scott, Joan W. 1988. "Deconstructing Equality-versus-Difference: Or, the Uses of Poststructuralist Theory for Feminism." *Feminist Studies* 14(Spring): 33-50.

Sherry, Suzanna. 1986. "Civic Virtue and the Feminine Voice in Constitutional Adjudication." *Virginia Law Review* 72(April): 543-616.

Slater, Philip. 1970. *The Pursuit of Loneliness*. Boston: Beacon Press.

Slater, Philip. 1974. *Earthwalk*. Garden City, NY: Doubleday.

Taub, Nadine, and Elizabeth Schneider. 1982. "Perspectives on Women's Subordination and the Role of the Law." In *The Politics of Law: A Progressive Critique*, ed. David Kairys. New York: Pantheon Books.

Thompson, Clara. 1942. "Cultural Pressures in the Psychology of Women." *Psychiatry* (August 1942): 331-39.

Squier, Susan and Sara Ruddick. 1983. "Review of In a Different Voice." *Harvard Education Review* 53(August): 338-42.

Turow, Scott. 1977. *One L.* New York: G.P. Putnam's Sons.

Weisstein, Naomi. 1970. "'Kinder, Kuche, Kirche' as Scientific Law: Psychology Constructs the Female." In *Sisterhood is Powerful*, ed. Robin Morgan. New York: Random House.

Weitzman, Lenore. 1986. *The Divorce Revolution*. New York: Basic Books.

Wendell, Susan. 1987. "A 'Qualified' Defense of Liberal Feminism." *Hypatia* 2 (Summer): 83.

West, Robin. 1988. "Jurisprudence and Gender." *University of Chicago Law Review* 55(Winter): 1-72.

Westcott, Marcia. 1986. *The Feminist Legacy of Karen Horney*. New Haven: Yale University Press.

Woolf, Virginia. 1929. *A Room of One's Own*. New York: Harcourt, Brace, and Company.

CASE

Bradwell v. Illinois. 1872. 83 U.S. 130.

From Practice to Theory, or What is a White Woman Anyway?

Catharine A. MacKinnon†

And ain't I a woman?
Sojourner Truth[1]

Black feminists speak as women because we are women . . . .
Audre Lorde[2]

It is common to say that something is good in theory but not in practice. I always want to say, then it is not such a good theory, is it? To be good in theory but not in practice posits a relation between theory and practice that places theory prior to practice, both methodologically and normatively, as if theory is a terrain unto itself. The conventional image of the relation between the two is first theory, then practice. You have an idea, then act on it. In legal academia you theorize, then try to get some practitioner to put it into practice. To be more exact, you read law review articles, then write more law review articles. The closest most legal academics come to practice is teaching—their students, most of whom will practice, being regarded by many as an occupational hazard to their theorizing.

The postmodern version of the relation between theory and practice is discourse unto death. Theory begets no practice, only more text. It proceeds as if you can deconstruct power relations by shifting their markers around in your head. Like all formal idealism, this approach to theory tends unselfconsciously to reproduce existing relations of dominance, in part because it is an utterly removed elite activity. On this level, all theory is a form of practice, because it either subverts or shores up existing deployments of power, in their martial metaphor. As an approach to change, it is the same as the conventional approach to the theory/practice relation: head-driven, not world-driven. Social change is first thought about, then acted out. Books relate to books, heads talk to heads. Bodies do not crunch bodies or people move

---

† Catharine A. MacKinnon is Professor of Law at the University of Michigan Law School. This paper benefitted from the comments of members of the Collective on Women of Color and the Law at Yale Law School.
1. BLACK WOMEN IN NINETEENTH-CENTURY AMERICAN LIFE: THEIR WORDS, THEIR THOUGHTS, THEIR FEELINGS 235 (Bert J. Loewenberg & Ruth Bogin eds., 1976).
2. AUDRE LORDE, SISTER OUTSIDER 60 (1984). The whole quotation is "Black feminists speak as women because we are women and do not need others to speak for us."

people. As theory, it is the de-realization of the world.

The movement for the liberation of women, including in law, moves the other way around. It is first practice, then theory. Actually, it moves this way in practice, not just in theory. Feminism was a practice long before it was a theory. On its real level, the women's movement—where women move against their determinants as women—remains more practice than theory. This distinguishes it from academic feminism. For women in the world, the gap between theory and practice is the gap between practice and theory. We know things with our lives, and live that knowledge, beyond anything any theory has yet theorized. Women's practice of confrontation with the realities of male dominance outruns any existing theory of the possibility of consciousness or resistance. To write the theory of this practice is not to work through logical puzzles or entertaining conundra, not to fantasize utopias, not to moralize or tell people what to do. It is not to exercise authority; it does not lead practice. Its task is to engage life through developing mechanisms that identify and criticize rather than reproduce social practices of subordination and to make tools of women's consciousness and resistance that further a practical struggle to end inequality. This kind of theory requires humility and it requires participation.

I am saying: we who work with law need to be about the business of articulating the theory of women's practice—women's resistance, visions, consciousness, injuries, notions of community, experience of inequality. By practical, I mean socially lived. As our theoretical question becomes "what is the theory of women's practice," our theory becomes a way of moving against and through the world, and methodology becomes technology.

Specifically—and such theory inhabits particularity—I want to take up the notion of experience "as a woman" and argue that it is the practice of which the concept of discrimination "based on sex" is the legal theory. That is, I want to investigate how the realities of women's experience of sex inequality in the world have shaped some contours of sex discrimination in the law.

Sex equality as a legal concept has not traditionally been theorized to encompass issues of sexual assault or reproduction because equality theory has been written out of men's practice, not women's. Men's experiences of group-based subordination have not centered on sexual and reproductive abuse, although they include instances of it. Some men have been hurt in these ways, but they are few and are not usually regarded as hurt because they are men, but in spite of it or in derogation of it. Few men are, sexually and reproductively speaking, "similarly situated" to women but treated better. So sexuality and reproduction are not regarded as equality issues in the traditional approach.[3] Two intrepid, indomitable women, women determined to write the practice of their lives onto the law, moved the theory of sex equality to include

---

3. I detail this argument further in *Reflections on Sex Equality Under Law*, 100 YALE L.J. 1281 (1991).

these issues.

In her case, *Meritor Savings Bank v. Vinson*,[4] Mechelle Vinson established that sexual harassment as a working environment is sex discrimination under civil rights law. Her resistance to her supervisor Sidney Taylor—specifically, her identification that his repeated rape, his standing over her in the bank vault waving his penis and laughing, were done to her because she was a woman—changed the theory of sex discrimination for all women. In her case, *California Federal Savings and Loan Association v. Guerra*,[5] Lillian Garland established that guaranteeing unpaid leaves for pregnant women by law is not discrimination on the basis of sex, but is a step in ending discrimination on the basis of sex. Her resistance to her employer, the California Federal Savings and Loan Association, in its refusal to reinstate her in her job after a pregnancy leave; her identification of that practice as illegal treatment of her because she was a woman, gave sex equality law a decisive spin in the direction of promoting equality, away from its prior status quo-mirroring regressive neutrality. The arguments that won these cases were based on the plaintiffs' lives as women, on insisting that actual social practices that subordinated them as women be theoretically recognized as impermissible sex-based discrimination under law. In the process, sexual assault and reproduction became sex equality issues, with implications for the laws of rape and abortion, among others.

So what is meant by treatment "as women" here? To speak of being treated "as a woman" is to make an empirical statement about reality, to describe the realities of women's situation. In this country, with parallels in other cultures, women's situation combines unequal pay with allocation to disrespected work, sexual targeting for rape, domestic battering, sexual abuse as children, and systematic sexual harassment; depersonalization, demeaned physical characteristics, use in denigrating entertainment, deprivation of reproductive control, and forced prostitution. To see that these practices are done by men to women is to see these abuses as forming a system, a hierarchy of inequality. This situation has occurred in many places, in one form or another, for a very long time, often in a context characterized by disenfranchisement, preclusion from property ownership (women are more likely to be property than to own any), ownership and use as object, exclusion from public life, sex-based poverty, degraded sexuality, and a devaluation of women's human worth and contributions throughout society. This subordination of women to men is socially institutionalized, cumulatively and systematically shaping access to human dignity, respect, resources, physical security, credibility, membership in community, speech, and power. Comprised of all its variations, the group women can be seen to have a collective social history of disempowerment, exploitation and subordination extending to the present. To be treated "as a

---

4. Meritor Sav. Bank v. Vinson, 477 U.S. 57 (1986).
5. California Fed. Sav. & Loan Ass'n v. Guerra, 479 U.S. 272 (1987).

woman" in this sense is to be disadvantaged in these ways incident to being socially assigned to the female sex. To speak of social treatment "as a woman" is thus not to invoke any abstract essence or homogeneous generic or ideal type, not to posit anything, far less a universal anything, but to refer to this diverse and pervasive concrete material reality of social meanings and practices such that, in the words of Richard Rorty, "a woman is not yet the name of a way of being human . . . ."[6]

Thus cohering the theory of "women" out of the practice of "women" produces the opposite of what Elizabeth Spelman has criticized as a reductive assumption of essential sameness of all women that she identifies in some feminist theory.[7] The task of theorizing women's practice produces a new kind of theory, a theory that is different from prior modes of theorizing in form, not just content. As Andrea Dworkin said quite a long time ago, women's situation requires new ways of thinking, not just thinking new things.[8] "Woman" as abstraction, distillation, common denominator, or idea is the old way of thinking, or at most a new thing to think, but it is not a new way of thinking. Nor is thinking "as" a woman, as one embodiment of a collective experience, the same as thinking "like" a woman, which is to reproduce one's determinants and think like a victim.

Some recent work, especially Elizabeth Spelman's, could be read to argue that there is no such thing as experience "as a woman" and women of color prove it.[9] This theory converges with the elevation of "differences" as a flag under which to develop diverse feminisms.[10] To do theory in its conventional abstract way, as many do, is to import the assumption that all women are the same or they are not women. What makes them women is their fit within the abstraction "woman" or their conformity to a fixed, posited female essence. The consequence is to reproduce dominance. While much work subjected to this criticism does not do this,[11] one can trace it, surprisingly, in the works

---

6. Richard Rorty, *Feminism and Pragmatism*, 30 MICH. Q. REV. 231, 234 (1991) ("MacKinnon's central point, as I read her, is that 'a woman' is not yet the name of a way of being human—not yet the name of a moral identity, but, at most, the name of a disability.").

7. ELIZABETH V. SPELMAN, INESSENTIAL WOMAN: PROBLEMS OF EXCLUSION IN FEMINIST THOUGHT 158-59 (1988).

8. "[O]ne can be excited *about* ideas without changing at all. [O]ne can think *about* ideas, talk *about* ideas, without changing at all. [P]eople are willing to think about many things. What people refuse to do, or are not permitted to do, or resist doing, is to change the way they think." ANDREA DWORKIN, WOMAN HATING 202 (1974).

9. SPELMAN, *supra* note 7, at 164-166, 174, 186. Spelman defines "essentialism" largely in terms of central tenets of radical feminism, without being clear whether the experience "as a woman" she identifies in radical feminism is a social or a biological construct. Having done this, it becomes easy to conclude that the "woman" of feminism is a distilled projection of the personal lives of a few comparatively powerful biological females, rather than a congealed synthesis of the lived social situation of women as a class, historically and worldwide.

10. Spelman implies that "differences" not be valorized or used as a theoretical construct, *id.* at 174, but others, building on her work and that of Carol Gilligan, CAROL GILLIGAN, IN A DIFFERENT VOICE (1982), do.

11. The philosophical term "essentialism" is sometimes wrongly applied to socially-based theories that observe and analyze empirical commonalities in women's condition. *See, e.g.*, Angela P. Harris, *Race and Essentialism in Feminist Legal Theory*, 42 STAN. L. REV. 581, 590-601 (1990). One can also take

of Simone DeBeauvoir and Susan Brownmiller.
DeBeauvoir, explaining why women are second class citizens, says:

> Here we have the key to the whole mystery. On the biological level a
> species is maintained only by creating itself anew; but this creation
> results only in repeating the same Life in more individuals. . . . Her
> [woman's] misfortune is to have been biologically destined for the
> repetition of Life, when even in her own view Life does not carry
> within itself its reasons for being, reasons that are more important than
> Life itself.[12]

Here women are defined in terms of biological reproductive capacity. It is
unclear exactly how any social organization of equality could change such an
existential fact, far less how to argue that a social policy that institutionalized
it could be sex discriminatory.

Susan Brownmiller argues the centrality of rape in women's condition in
the following terms:

> Man's structural capacity to rape and woman's corresponding structural
> vulnerability are as basic to the physiology of both our sexes as the
> primal act of sex itself. Had it not been for this accident of biology,
> an accommodation requiring the locking together of two separate parts,
> penis and vagina, there would be neither copulation nor rape as we
> know it. . . . By anatomical fiat—the inescapable construction of their
> genital organs—the human male was a natural predator and the human
> female served as his natural prey.[13]

Exactly how to oppose sexual assault from this vantage point is similarly
unclear. Do we make a law against intercourse? Although both theorists have
considerably more to offer on the question of what defines women's condition,
what we have in these passages is simple biological determinism presented as
a critical theory of social change.

The problem here, it seems to me, does not begin with a failure to take
account of race or class, but with the failure to take account of gender. It is
not only or most fundamentally an account of race or class dominance that is
missing here, but an account of male dominance. There is nothing biologically
necessary about rape, as Mechelle Vinson made abundantly clear when she
sued for rape as unequal treatment on the basis of sex. And, as Lillian Garland
saw, and made everyone else see, it is the way society punishes women for

---

an essentialist approach to race or class. In other words, a theory does not become "essentialist" to the
degree it discusses gender as such nor is it saved from "essentialism" to the degree it incorporates race
or class.

12. SIMONE DEBEAUVOIR, THE SECOND SEX 64 (H.M. Parshley ed. & trans., 1971).
13. SUSAN BROWNMILLER, AGAINST OUR WILL: MEN, WOMEN, AND RAPE 4, 6 (1976).

reproduction that creates women's problems with reproduction, not reproduction itself. Both women are Black. This only supports my suspicion that if a theory is not true of, and does not work for, women of color, it is not really true of, and will not work for, any women, and that it is not really about gender at all. The theory of the practice of Mechelle Vinson and Lillian Garland, because it is about the experience of Black women, *is* what gender is about.

In recent critiques of feminist work for failing to take account of race or class,[14] it is worth noting that the fact that there is such a thing as race and class is assumed, although race and class are generally treated as abstractions to attack gender rather than as concrete realities, if indeed they are treated at all. Spelman, for example, discusses race but does virtually nothing with class.[15] In any event, race and class are regarded as unproblematically real and not in need of justification or theoretical construction. Only gender is not real and needs to be justified. Although many women have demanded that discussions of race or class take gender into account, typically demands these do not take the form that, outside explicit recognition of gender, race or class do not exist. That there is a diversity to the experience of men and women of color, and of working class women and men regardless of race, is not said to mean that race or class are not meaningful concepts. I have heard no one say that there can be no meaningful discussion of "people of color" without gender specificity. Thus the phrase "people of color and white women" has come to replace the previous "women and minorities," which women of color rightly perceived as not including them twice, and embodying a white standard for sex and a male standard for race. But I hear no talk of "all women and men of color," for instance. It is worth thinking about that when women of color refer to "people who look like me," it is understood that they mean people of color, not women, in spite of the fact that both race and sex are visual assignments, both possess clarity as well as ambiguity, and both are marks of oppression, hence community.

In this connection, it has recently come to my attention that the white woman is the issue here, so I decided I better find out what one is. This creature is not poor, not battered, not raped (not really), not molested as a child, not pregnant as a teenager, not prostituted, not coerced into pornography, not a welfare mother, and not economically exploited. She doesn't work. She is either the white man's image of her—effete, pampered,

---

14. I am thinking in particular of SPELMAN, *see supra* note 7, and Marlee Kline, *Race, Racism, and Feminist Legal Theory*, 12 HARV. WOMEN'S L.J. 115 (1989), although this analysis also applies to others who have made the same argument, such as Harris, *supra* note 11. Among its other problems, much of this work tends to make invisible the women of color who were and are instrumental in defining and creating feminism as a movement of women in the world, as well as a movement of mind.

15. This is by contrast with the massive feminist literature on the problem of class, which I discuss and summarize as a foundational problem for feminist theory in TOWARD A FEMINIST THEORY OF THE STATE (1989). Harris, *supra* note 11, discusses race but does nothing with either class or sexual orientation except invoke them as clubs against others. See, for example, *id.* at 588, n.26 and accompanying text.

privileged, protected, flighty, and self-indulgent—or the Black man's image of her—all that, plus the "pretty white girl" (meaning ugly as sin but regarded as the ultimate in beauty because she is white). She is Miss Anne of the kitchen, she puts Frederick Douglass to the lash, she cries rape when Emmett Till looks at her sideways, she manipulates white men's very real power with the lifting of her very well-manicured little finger. She makes an appearance in Baraka's "rape the white girl,"[16] as Cleaver's real thing after target practice on Black women,[17] as Helmut Newton's glossy upscale hard-edged, distanced vamp,[18] and as the Central Park Jogger, the classy white madonna who got herself raped and beaten nearly to death. She flings her hair, feels beautiful all the time, complains about the colored help, tips badly, can't do anything, doesn't do anything, doesn't know anything, and alternates fantasizing about fucking Black men with accusing them of raping her. As Ntozake Shange points out, all Western civilization depends on her.[19] On top of all of this, out of impudence, imitativeness, pique, and a simple lack of anything meaningful to do, she thinks she needs to be liberated. Her feminist incarnation is all of the above, and guilty about every single bit of it, having by dint of repetition refined saying "I'm sorry" to a high form of art. She can't even make up her own songs.

There is, of course, much to much of this, this "woman, modified," this woman discounted by white, meaning she would be oppressed but for her privilege. But this image seldom comes face to face with the rest of her reality: the fact that the majority of the poor are white women and their children (at least half of whom are female); that white women are systematically battered in their homes, murdered by intimates and serial killers alike, molested as children, actually raped (mostly by white men), and that even Black men, on average, make more than they do.[20] If one did not know this, one could be taken in by white men's image of white women: that the pedestal is real, rather than a cage in which to confine and trivialize them and segregate them from the rest of life, a vehicle for sexualized infantilization, a virginal set-up for rape by men who enjoy violating the pure, and a myth with which to try to control Black women. (See, if you would lie down and be quiet and not move, we would revere you, too.) One would think that the white men's myth that

---

16. LeRoi Jones, *Black Dada Nihilismus*, in The Dead Lecturer 61, 63 (1964).

17. "I became a rapist. To refine my technique and *modus operandi*, I started out by practicing on black girls in the ghetto . . . and when I considered myself smooth enough, I crossed the tracks and sought out white prey." Eldridge Cleaver, Soul on Ice 14 (1968). "[R]aping the white girl" as an activity for Black men is described as one of "the funky facts of life," in a racist context in which the white girl's white-girlness is sexualized—that is, made a site of lust, hatred and hostility—for the Black man through the history of lynching. *Id.* at 14-15.

18. Helmut Newton, White Women (1976).

19. Ntozake Shange, Three Pieces 48 (1981).

20. In 1989, the median income of white women was approximately one-fourth less than that of Black men; in 1990 it was one-fifth less. U.S. Bureau of the Census, Current Population Rep., Ser. P-60, No. 174, Money Income of Households, Families, and Persons in the United States: 1990 104-05 (tbl. 24) (1991).

they protect white women was real, rather than a racist cover to guarantee their exclusive and unimpeded sexual access—meaning they can rape her at will, and do, a posture made good in the marital rape exclusion and the largely useless rape law generally. One would think that the only white women in brothels in the South during the Civil War were in *Gone With the Wind*.[21] This is not to say there is no such thing as skin privilege, but rather that it has never insulated white women from the brutality and misogyny of men, mostly but not exclusively white men, or from its effective legalization. In other words, the "white girls" of this theory miss quite a lot of the reality of white women in the practice of male supremacy.

Beneath the trivialization of the white woman's subordination implicit in the dismissive sneer "straight white economically-privileged women" (a phrase which has become one word, the accuracy of some of its terms being rarely documented even in law journals) lies the notion that there is no such thing as the oppression of women as such. If white women's oppression is an illusion of privilege and a rip-off and reduction of the civil rights movement, we are being told that there is no such thing as a woman, that our practice produces no theory, and that there is no such thing as discrimination on the basis of sex. What I am saying is, to argue that oppression "as a woman" negates rather than encompasses recognition of the oppression of women on other bases, is to say that there is no such thing as the practice of sex inequality.

Let's take this the other way around. As I mentioned, both Mechelle Vinson and Lillian Garland are African-American women. Wasn't Mechelle Vinson sexually harassed as a woman? Wasn't Lillian Garland pregnant as a woman? They thought so. The whole point of their cases was to get their injuries understood as "based on sex," that is, because they are women. The perpetrators, and the policies under which they were disadvantaged, saw them as women. What is being a woman if it does not include being oppressed as one? When the Reconstruction Amendments "gave Blacks the vote," and Black women still could not vote, weren't they kept from voting "as women?" When African-American women are raped two times as often as white women, aren't they raped as women? That does not mean their race is irrelevant and it does not mean that their injuries can be understood outside a racial context. Rather, it means that "sex" is *made up of* the reality of the experiences of all women, including theirs. It is a composite unit rather than a divided unitary whole, such that each woman, in her way, is all women. So, when white women are sexually harassed or lose their jobs because they are pregnant, aren't they women too?

The treatment of women in pornography shows this approach in graphic relief. One way or another, all women are in pornography. African-American women are featured in bondage, struggling, in cages, as animals, insatiable. As Andrea Dworkin has shown, the sexualized hostility directed against them

---

21. This is an insight of Dorothy Teer.

makes their skin into a sex organ, focusing the aggression and contempt directed principally at other women's genitals.[22] Asian women are passive, inert, as if dead, tortured unspeakably. Latinas are hot mommas. Fill in the rest from every demeaning and hostile racial stereotype you know; it is sex here. This is not done to men, not in heterosexual pornography. What is done to white women is a kind of floor; it is the best anyone is treated and it runs from Playboy through sadomasochism to snuff. What is done to white women can be done to any woman, and then some. This does not make white women the essence of womanhood. It is a reality to observe that this is what can be done and *is* done to the most privileged of women. This is what privilege as a woman gets you: most valued as dead meat.

I am saying, each woman is in pornography as the embodiment of her particularities. This is not in tension with being there "as a woman," *it is what being there as a woman means*. Her specificity makes up what gender *is*. White, for instance, is not a residual category. It is not a standard against which the rest are "different." There is no generic "woman" in pornography. White is not unmarked; it is a specific sexual taste. Being defined and used in this way defines what being a woman means in practice. Robin Morgan once said, "pornography is the theory, rape is the practice."[23] This is true, but Andrea Dworkin's revision is more true: "Pornography is the theory, pornography is the practice."[24] This approach to "what is a woman" is reminiscent of Sartre's answer to the question "what is a Jew?" Start with the anti-Semite.[25]

In my view, the subtext to the critique of oppression "as a woman," the critique that holds that there is no such thing, is dis-identification with women. One of its consequences is the destruction of the basis for a jurisprudence of sex equality. An argument advanced in many critiques by women of color has been that theories of women must include all women, and when they do, theory will change. On one level, this is necessarily true. On another, it ignores the formative contributions of women of color to feminist theory since its inception. I also sense, though, that many women, not only women of color and not only academics, do not want to be "just women," not only because something important is left out, but also because that means being in a category with "her," the useless white woman whose first reaction when the going gets rough is to cry. I sense here that people feel more dignity in being part of any group that includes men than in being part of a group that includes that

---

22. ANDREA DWORKIN, PORNOGRAPHY: MEN POSSESSING WOMEN 215-16 (1981).

23. ROBIN MORGAN, GOING TOO FAR 169 (1978).

24. Personal communication with Andrea Dworkin. *See also* ANDREA DWORKIN, MERCY 232, 304-07. (1991).

25. "Thus, to know what the contemporary Jew is, we must ask the Christian conscience. And we must ask, not 'What is a Jew?' but '*What have you made of the Jews?*'

The Jew is one whom other men consider a Jew: that is the simple truth from which we must start. In this sense . . . it is the anti-Semite who *makes* the Jew." JEAN-PAUL SARTRE, ANTI-SEMITE AND JEW 69 (George J. Becker trans., 1948).

ultimate reduction of the notion of oppression, that instigator of lynch mobs, that ludicrous whiner, that equality coat-tails rider, the white woman. It seems that if your oppression is also done to a man, you are more likely to be recognized as oppressed, as opposed to inferior. Once a group is seen as putatively human, a process helped by including men in it, an oppressed man falls from a human standard.[26] A woman is just a woman—the ontological victim—so not victimized at all.

Unlike other women, the white woman who is not poor or working class or lesbian or Jewish or disabled or old or young *does not share her oppression with any man*. That does not make her condition any more definitive of the meaning of "women" than the condition of any other woman is. But trivializing her oppression, because it is not even potentially racist or class-biased or heterosexist or anti-Semitic, does define the meaning of being "anti-woman" with a special clarity. How the white woman is imagined and constructed and treated becomes a particularly sensitive indicator of the degree to which women, as such, are despised.

If we build a theory out of women's practice, comprised of the diversity of all women's experiences, we do not have the problem that some feminist theory has been rightly criticized for. When we have it is when we make theory out of abstractions and accept the images forced on us by male dominance. I said all that so I could say this: the assumption that all women are the same is part of the bedrock of sexism that the women's movement is predicated on challenging. That some academics find it difficult to theorize without reproducing it simply means that they continue to do to women what theory, predicated on the practice of male dominance, has always done to women. It is their notion of what theory is, and its relation to its world, that needs to change.

If our theory of what is "based on sex" makes gender out of actual social practices distinctively directed against women as women identify them, the problem that the critique of so-called "essentialism" exists to rectify ceases to exist. And this bridge, the one from practice to theory, is not built on anyone's back.

---

26. I sense a similar dynamic at work in the attraction among some lesbians of identification with "gay rights" rather than "women's rights," with the result of obscuring the roots in male dominance of the oppression of both lesbians and gay men.

Ain't I a Feminist?

Celina Romany[†]

I want to recover my faith in feminism during the 1990's. The feminism that gave me the strength to understand the story of a woman born and raised in a colony who migrates to the metropolis, feminism as a liberation project. The feminism which launches a multi-faceted attack on legal institutions that perpetuate substantial inequities.

The current state of feminist legal theory makes me wonder if I am still a feminist. The feminism I see myself associated with has a capital F. That which aims at eradicating the various forms of oppression that affect all women, a project overlooked by "small-town" feminism. I am willing to risk being outside current postmodern theoretical trends by supporting capital letters. My capital letters connote expansion, breadth and inclusion. Far from claiming privileged access to truth with a capital T, feminism with a capital F thrives in a room with a great view of narratives about intersections.

Feminist legal theorists belong to a norm-forming group involved in what Robert Cover has described as the creation of new legal meanings.[1] As he suggested, we need to examine the juris-generative operation of such a group and how the process of creating new legal meanings depends on sustaining narratives. Narratives that define both the vision of the juris-generative group and its location in making its work a viable alternative.

Today, I'd like to critique the feminist narratives that sustain the creation of feminist legal theory as new legal meaning. My principal claims are: 1) that the feminist narrative deployed as a foundation with its monocausal emphasis on gender falls short of the liberation project feminism should be about: the emancipation of all women, 2) that feminism so defined cannot adequately address the shortcomings of liberal legalism and 3) that postmodernism, although helpful in counteracting feminist essentialism by giving space and voice to a multiplicity of accounts, nevertheless lacks a material analysis of macrostructures of inequality and thus lacks translation potential for social change.

Feminist legal theory needs to allow room for the destabilization of gender as both a conceptual and practical tool of analysis. Feminist legal theory moves

---

† Celina Romany is Associate Professor of Law at City University of New York (CUNY) Law School. This piece is a close adaptation of the speech she gave on the panel *Broadening the Definition of Feminism* at the *Conference Feminism in the 90s: Bridging the Gap Between Theory and Practice*. I dedicate this article to those Puerto Rican Feminists who struggle against all forms of colonialism.

1. Robert Cover, *Foreword: Nomos and Narrative*, 97 HARV L. REV. 4 (1983).

in the right direction when it pursues the humanist project of agency and subjectivity and attempts to redefine subjectivity to redress gross gender-related exclusions. Yet, it needs to move beyond. The feminism with a capital F which I want to recover in the context of legal theory is that which redefines subjectivity in light of the key variables of subject formation: race, ethnicity, class and gender. A feminist theory of subjectivity can adequately elaborate an alternative vision to the liberal self by showing the centrality of the political and cultural history in which the subject is born; a context of personal and social de-legitimation. Through this route, the elaboration of feminist subjectivity can plausibly seize the deep meanings of difference, subordination and oppression. By not filling this gap, we only catch a glimpse of meaning and experience exclusion. Universalist assumptions deny intersubjectivity any opportunity to liberate us from the appropriation and objectification of *others*, to pave the way for a real recognition of differences and commonalities and to serve as a reminder that "the *other* is just as entitled as I am to her/his humanity expressed in her/his cultural reality."[2]

What is the special claim of feminism in challenging core assumptions of liberalism? The emergence of what is currently characterized as many feminisms or postfeminism makes the project of identifying its unique contribution to the challenge of liberalism much more difficult. The liberal system which is so fond of binary oppositions contained in the separate public/private arenas is endorsed by the allegedly neutral, objective and procedurally fair rule of law. In spite of the different twists and turns of feminism, we can recognize that both methodologically and substantively it has put on the table the subordination, oppression, and second-class citizenship brought about by the devaluation of the personal and the so-called domestic sphere. It gave personal experience epistemological standing, offering counternarratives which have served as critiques of the values and assumptions lying beneath our social and political organization, social contract included. It challenged male norms. As Teresa de Lauretis correctly points out, feminism defined subjectivity as the very site of the material inscription of the ideological.[3]

However, such material inscription of the ideological has insisted on the preeminence of gender subordination at the expense of other forms of oppression, missing a basic point. If feminism was to be about freedom for all women, it had to consequently address multiple experiences—not an easy task both for theoretical generalizations and for political strategy. There are historical and sociological explanations for the essentialism of the woman standpoint. First, there is the interplay of practice and theory: the cross-

---

2. *See* Marnia Larzreg, *Feminism and Difference: The Perils of Writing as a Woman on Women in Algeria,* 14 FEM. STUD. 81, 98 (1988).
    3. Teresa de Lauretis, *Feminist Studies/Critical Studies: Issues, Terms and Contexts, in* FEMINIST STUD./CRITICAL STUD. 1 (Teresa de Lauretis ed., 1986).

fertilization between the political practice generated by the feminist movement and its theoretical conceptualizations. bell hooks and other women of color have done excellent work in documenting the schism existing between women of color and white women in the context of the feminist movement, and the influence of color and class composition on these conceptualizations.[4] Second, there is a history of frustration brought about by the political left's inability to grasp the centrality of gender subordination, as shown by the many indictments against feminists' alleged misunderstanding of a class analysis.

Although solidarity, empathy, altruism, and collective attachments are dimensions increasingly explored through the acquisition of a feminist consciousness, the power dynamics generated by institutions creating and perpetuating the cultural and psychological manifestations of racism and classism are left intact. The elaboration of theoretical arguments exclusively resting upon gender sustains the narratives emerging from such feminist consciousness. Race, ethnicity, and class are viewed as diluting the thrust of gender oppression. The biggest irony is that just as gender is dismissed by reductionist Marxist critiques, race, ethnicity, and class are assigned by essentialist feminism to maximum security and isolated confinement. They are allowed to join the general prison population only for good behavior: when the race, ethnicity and class categories learn to stay where they belong, when their subsidiary explanatory power is understood, when basic rules of grammar are comprehended and the auxiliary nature of the conjunction "and" is fully grasped. Bear in mind the by now familiar descriptions: gender *and* race, gender *and* class, gender *and* ethnicity.

I have critiqued elsewhere the essentialist and universalist character of feminist theorists,[5] with their substitution of the view from nowhere with the view from womanland. I have specifically targeted the work of Carol Gilligan and her reliance on Nancy Chodorow's essentialist account of reproduction and motherhood. My critique has focused on those feminist legal theorists who have uncritically and enthusiastically adopted some of her limited findings as the basis of their work. Likewise I have critiqued radical feminists' reductionist accounts of sexual oppression. Four examples follow.

1) Robin West, in trying to reconcile or at least understand the "fundamental contradiction" between cultural feminists largely defined by Gilligan and radical feminists largely defined by MacKinnon, asserts that women want to mother in spite of the compulsory nature of institutional motherhood and that women strive for intimacy even though they are oppressed

---

4. *See generally* BELL HOOKS, FEMINIST THEORY: FROM MARGIN TO CENTER (1984); TALKING BACK: THINKING FEMINIST, THINKING BLACK (1989); YEARNING: RACE, GENDER AND CULTURAL POLITICS (1990); AIN'T I A WOMAN (1981, 1984).

5. Celina Romany, The Intersection of Race, Gender and Class in the Critique of the Liberal Self, presentation at the Critical Legal Studies Conference (1988) (unpublished manuscript on file with the *Yale Journal of Law and Feminism*).

by it.[6] She uses Gilligan in a structuring way although Gilligan's work is more of a descriptive mechanism than a theoretical model. Thus, West ends up using a Gilliganesque model without rigorously examining the assumptions behind her positing of gender-specific characteristics.[7]

2) Martha Minow provides a sensitive discussion of the dilemma of difference, yet she also implicitly integrates Gilligan into her analysis when she concludes that by acknowledging and struggling against one's own partiality and by making an effort to understand the reality of others we will all move towards comprehending reciprocal realities.[8] In proffering such advice, Minow risks falling into a Gilliganesque model of problem solving, i.e. an examination of competing values and views. But where does her acknowledgement of differences take us? Were she to develop the power imbalances underlying "reciprocal realities," she could perhaps escape the criticism that simply talking to each other does not necessarily mean that we can hear one other.[9]

---

6. *See* Robin West, *Jurisprudence and Gender*, 55 U. CHI. L. REV. 1 (1988).

7. Other feminist jurisprudence scholars also make gender-based assumptions without sufficient analysis of the complex factors shaping gender. *See* Christine Littleton, *Restructuring Sexual Equality*, 75 CAL. L. REV. 1279, 1296-97 (1987). Even Elizabeth Schneider, who acknowledges the critique of Gilligan's work for "its insensitivity to race and class differences, and its disregard of historical context," believes that it is possible to set aside the problematic elements of Gilligan's analysis and assumptions. She concludes that "for my purposes, however, the significant aspect of her work is her insight into the way in which rights claims can be an aspect of psychological and social transformation—a moment in a dialectical process of change—and the way in which rights claims asserted as part of that process might be different." Elizabeth Schneider, *The Dialectic of Rights and Politics: Perspectives from the Women's Movement*, 61 N.Y.U. L. REV. 589, 617 (1987).

8. Martha Minow, *The Supreme Court 1986 Term-Foreword: Justice Engendered*, 101 HARV. L. REV. 10, 76 (1987).

9. Catharine MacKinnon has critiqued Carol Gilligan in this regard for not taking into account powerlessness in her work. In an informative conversation between several prominent figures in feminist jurisprudence, the following exchange between Catharine MacKinnon and Carol Gilligan illustrates this problem in a discussion of Menkel-Meadow's hypothetical mediation session between Jake and Amy:

CM: Power is socially constructed such that if Jake simply chooses not to listen to Amy, he wins; but if Amy simply chooses not to listen to Jake, she loses. In other words, Jake still wins because that is the system. And I am trying to work out how to change that system, not just how to make people more fully human within it.

CG: Your definition of power is his definition.

CM: That *is* because the society is that way, it operates on his definition, and I am trying to change it.

CG: To have her definition come in?

CM: That would be part of it, but more to have a definition that she would articulate that she cannot now, because his foot is on her throat.

CG: She's saying it.

CM: I know, but she is articulating the feminine. And you are calling it hers. That's what I find infuriating.

CG: No, instead I am saying she is articulating a set of values which are very positive.

3) Catharine MacKinnon's critique of Gilligan also adopts the essentialist standpoint of the silenced woman, without elaborating the multi-layers of oppression vividly represented by women of color. For MacKinnon, there is no female subjectivity, as women are defined by men. In effect collapsing all forms of oppression, she views sexuality as a "pervasive dimension of social life, one that permeates the whole, . . . a dimension along which other social divisions, like race and class, partly play themselves out."[10] Her totalizing theory of social reality based on sexual oppression does not admit to a concept of identity, and therefore, cannot account for the multilayered experience of women of color.[11] Symptomatically, even in her acknowledgment of the contribution of writings of women of color, in her most recent book, MacKinnon implies that these works lack a theoretical framework and, as such, others will have to build upon those writings in the coming years.[12] The experience of women of color seems to be viewed as the anecdotes that will unfold, with the passage of time, grand theoretical discoveries in sync with MacKinnon's overarching theory of sexual oppression.

4) Carrie Menkel-Meadow has explicitly used Gilligan as a starting point for her discussion of women's lawyering process. Despite the limitations of Gilligan's description of women's experience, Menkel-Meadow uses Gilligan's description to structure her analysis of the way in which women's values can inform their lawyering process. She assumes that if parties speak "directly to each other, they are more likely to appreciate the importance of each other's needs."[13] However, Menkel-Meadow's observations fail to explore the effect of power imbalances on mediated solutions. She has also discussed the

---

CM: Right, and I am saying they are feminine. And calling them hers is infuriating to me because we have never had the power to develop what ours really would be.
Ellen C. DuBois, et al., *Feminist Discourse, Moral Values and the Law: A Conversation*, 34 BUFF. L. REV. 11, 74-75 (1985). *See also* Ann C. Scales, *The Emergence of Feminist Jurisprudence: An Essay*, 95 YALE L.J. 1373, 1381 (1986) (arguing against lawyers' simplistic use of Gilligan's work to graft women's different voices onto rights-based system).
    10. CATHARINE MACKINNON, TOWARD A FEMINIST THEORY OF THE STATE 130 (1989).
    11. Marlee Kline's excellent critique of MacKinnon points out the tension in MacKinnon's work between her recognition of the multiplicity of race and class differences that exist among women and her emphasis on women's gender commonality. As Kline states "[e]ven where MacKinnon provides an in-depth analysis of the particular experiences of women of color, she does not allow those experiences to challenge the premise of her theory. . . . Thus, it is not surprising that about half of MacKinnon's examples of the particular experiences of women of color in *Feminism Unmodified* refer to racism only in the context of pornography or rape. The other examples of the particular experiences of Black women and First Nations women are confined to brief comments or footnotes." (citations ommitted). Marlee Kline, *Race, Racism and Feminist Legal Theory*, 12 HARV. WOMEN'S L.J. 115, 138-39 (1989). Kline further argues that MacKinnon's "construction of the feminist project [is] limited in its capacity to capture the complex impact of racism in the lives of women of color" and "neither the differences in interest and priority that exist between white women and women of color nor the unequal power relationship between the groups are confronted or dealt with in her work." *Id.* at 140-41.
    12. MACKINNON, *supra* note 10.
    13. Carrie Menkel-Meadow, *Portia in a Different Voice: Speculations on a Women's Lawyering Process*, 1 BERKELEY WOMEN'S L.J. 39, 51 (1985). *See also* Carrie Menkel-Meadow, *For and Against Settlement*, 33 U.C.L.A. L. REV. 485 (1985); Janet Rifkin, *Mediation from a Feminist Perspective: Promise and Problems*, 2 LAW & INEQ. J. 21 (1984).

"epistemology of exclusion." She remarks: "It has become too easy, I think, for those who have been excluded by the 'white male club' to be lumped together in exclusions. One bit of knowledge we have gained from feminist knowledge is the contextual particularity of our experiences."[14]

In support of this principle, however, she cites Gilligan, who has notably failed to particularize realities in terms of race. She later states: "Thus the knowing that comes from exclusion is based not on intrinsic characteristics, but rather on perverse oppositional knowledge that may be necessary for survival and adaptation to exclusion. The parallels to exclusion based on race and class should therefore be obvious."[15] Menkel-Meadow fails to spell out what she calls the "obvious" implications of this model for a subject considered to have a race and class as well as a gender. Furthermore, she concludes that although exclusion may create certain characteristics, we needn't reject those characteristics.[16] This position has dangerous implications for a truly feminist lawyering process in that a socially-constructed definition of women's skills and values becomes the norm for all women.[17]

* * * * *

Do feminist legal theory's sustaining narratives have the breadth required to challenge different strands of oppression within liberal legalism, as experienced by all women? Can this work, as Robert Cover suggested, offer a viable alternative? Think about the critique of rights, their affirmative and negative character, ascription of rights, the instrumental value of rights, the nature of adjudication, core principles such as property, the exchange of commodities (personal included), demarcations of the public and private, boundaries for state intervention and non-intervention, the discrimination principle, conflicts among different sources of discrimination, and reflect on the limited potential a gender-essentialist analysis has for a thorough analysis of these core institutions.

I am skeptical of the ability of a feminist legal theory based on exclusive gender narratives to deal with the overall challenge. Essentialist narratives overload feminism as a key tool in the critique of the liberal project and utterly fail to offer a comprehensive critical framework for liberal legal institutions. The paradigm selection process (the architectural design, selection of building materials, objectives, aesthetics) is informed by that limited experience. At

---

14. Carrie Menkel-Meadow, *Excluded Voices: New Voices in the Legal Profession Making New Voices in the Law*, 42 U. MIAMI L. REV. 29, 31 (1987) (footnote omitted).

15. *Id.* at 43.

16. *See also* Littleton, *supra* note 7, at 1296-97 (1987) (advocating "acceptance" model to grapple with difference which is attentive to "consequences of gendered difference, and not its sources").

17. *See, e.g.,* EEOC v. Sears Roebuck & Co., 628 F. Supp. 1264 (N.D. Ill. 1986), *aff'd*, 839 F. 2d 302 (7th Cir. 1988).

their best these narratives offer partial critiques with partial and insular results: small-town feminism generating small-town feminist theory and politics.

To the extent that a racial/ethnic/class "minority perspective" gets incorporated into the feminist redefinition of subjectivity, the latter's critique of rights and fairness also undergoes revision. The normative intuitions that are to guide such an analysis are "different." As the "minority" critique of critical legal studies scholarship points out, the evaluation of rights stems neither from what a critical legal scholar would describe as an alienating experience originating from the fear of connection, nor from what a feminist legal scholar would characterize as a gender experience of connection that spells solidarity and responsibility to others in lieu of atomized individualism. The intersection of race and gender in the redefinition of subjectivity and intersubjectivity points to a different legal consciousness. Rights that "separate" individuals also trace boundaries of mutual respect in such separation and (no matter what amount of false consciousness is involved) can strengthen identities.

If feminism, and feminist legal theory in particular, is to remain a liberation project, it needs to come to grips with its cognitive distortions and self-idealized universal discoveries. Feminism needs to put forth sustaining narratives that capture the centrality of intersections in the intersubjective formation of identities. In the meantime, we could use a heavy dose of modesty, giving pretentiousness a deserved vacation and publicly announcing the incorporation of the project as "Feminism, Limited."

Postmodernism has been recruited in an effort to counter the essentialist dimension of the woman standpoint. Although I am sympathetic to the efforts of those (in particular the work of Nancy Fraser and Linda Nicholson)[18] who are are trying to match feminism and postmodernism through the magic of supplementation (a match not necessarily made in heaven), I am highly skeptical of satisfactorily concrete outcomes. The postmodern fallibilistic and decentering approach moves away from a unitary concept of the woman standpoint and opens up the door for alternative accounts of difference. However, this new entrance leads us into a meeting of discourses rather than to an encounter of those differences at the very concrete level of power differentials and unequal distribution of privileges.

Discourse, the understudy for representation, supplants representation once it is discarded as an obsolete and decadent way of apprehending reality.[19] I

---

18. Nancy Fraser & Linda Nicholson, *Social Criticism Without Philosophy: An Encounter Between Feminism and Postmodernism, in* UNIVERSAL ABANDON? THE POLITICS OF POST MODERNISM 83 (Andrew Ross ed., 1988).

19. Although postmodern feminists have attempted to move away from some of postmodernism's main tenets, the social critique of power differentials remains inadequate and the primacy of discourse remains significantly unaltered. *See* FEMINISM/POSTMODERNISM (Linda J. Nicholson ed., 1990); JEAN-FRANCOIS LYOTARD, THE POSTMODERN CONDITION (1984); STEPHEN A. TYLER, THE UNSPEAKABLE: DISCOURSE, DIALOGUE AND RHETORIC IN THE POSTMODERN WORLD (1988); F. Jameson, *Postmodernism or the Cultural Logic of Late Capitalism,* 146 NEW LEFT REV. 53 (1984).

am highly suspicious of discourse accounts, especially when I run into the postmodernist discussion of colonialism, a paradigm for marginality with which I am quite familiar. There is nothing outside the text in the realm of discourse, there is no point from which opposition forms. As Benita Parry accurately points out in her critique of Gayatri Spivak's work, the move is one to place "incendiary devices within the dominant structures of representation and not to confront these with another knowledge;"[20] the subaltern voice is deemed irretrievable; counternarratives of resistance are labeled as reverse discourse.

Linda Nicholson and Nancy Fraser talk about adopting a fallibilistic approach which "would tailor its methods and categories to the specific task at hand, using multiple categories when appropriate and foreswearing the metaphysical comfort of a single 'feminist method' or 'feminist epistemology.'"[21] Their approach "would be more like a tapestry composed of threads of many different hues rather than one woven in a single color."[22] Not much is said, however, as to the relinquishment of privileges necessary for the multi-colored, multi-class composition of the weavers' labor force. I have levelled the same critique against those who, like Roberto Unger, in the elaboration of "context-smashers narratives" guided by empathy and solidarity, need to resort to the trinity of love, faith, and hope.[23]

When I attempt to figure out if there is life after postmodernism, the recurrent image I have is one where I stand in the middle of a ballroom, paralyzed, surrounded by dancers experiencing the *jouissance* generated by dances of heterogeneous and fragmented accounts. Paralysis skyrockets my anxiety because I love to dance and thought I knew a lot about dancing . . .

* * * * *

Ain't I a Feminist? I am a feminist with a broad and expansive liberation project. I advocate a broadening of horizons to show that the humanist project of subjectivity and agency need not be trashed but rather redefined. We have to expose those legal institutions which delay and obstruct the creation of conditions for strengthening identities, thereby enabling them to engage in dialogues which further refine our subjective perceptions and which serve as spaces for the creation of new narratives that are able to sustain the paradigm choices guiding the formation of new legal meanings.[24]

Autonomy and subjectivity have a lot of appeal to Third World women. Feminist scholars and feminist legal theories should pay more attention to the

---

20. Benita Parry, *Problems in Current Theories of Colonial Discourse,* 9 OXFORD LITERARY REV. 27, 43 (1987).
21. Fraser & Nicholson, *supra* note 18, at 101.
22. *Id.* at 101-02.
23. Celina Romany, Book Review, 54 U.P.R. L. REV. 587 (1985) (reviewing ROBERTO UNGER, PASSION: AN ESSAY ON PERSONALITY (1984)).
24. Cover, *supra* note 1.

work of Third World cultural theorists, who expose the intimate connections between political and national history and the constitution of the subject, stress the importance of revealing marginality conditions which bring about non-identity,[25] and grasp the meaning of the "border [which] houses the power of the outrageous, the imagination needed to turn the historical and cultural tables."[26] As the writings of Guillermo Gomez-Pena, George Yudice, and Juan Flores describe, "the view from the border enables us to apprehend the ultimate arbitrariness of the border itself, of forced separations and inferiorizations."[27]

Juan Felipe Herrera's poem *"What if suddenly the continent turned upside down?"* says it best:

What if the U.S was Mexico?
What if 200,000 Anglosaxicans
were to cross the border each month
to work as gardeners, waiters,
3rd chair musicians, movie extras,
bouncers, babysitters, chauffers,
syndicated cartoons, feather-weight
boxers, fruit-pickers & anonymous poets?
What if they were called waspanos,
waspitos, wasperos, or wasbacks?
What if we were the top dogs?
What if literature was life, eh?[28]

---

25. Abdul R. JanMohamed & David Lloyd, *Introduction: Minority Discourse—What is to be Done?*, 7 CULTURAL CRITIQUE 5, 16 (1987).

26. Juan Flores & George Yudice, *Living Borders/Buscando America: Languages of Latino Self-Formation*, 24 SOC. TEXT 57, 80 (1990).

27. *Id.*

28. *Id.* at 79.

Postscript

Some time ago I read a paper in which I attempted to describe what it meant to be the concrete embodiment of the abstract conversation of feminists at a feminist conference: my invisibility. I said:

I looked around and saw that notwithstanding my unique location, the only Latina in the room, eye contact was avoided so as to reinforce my social invisibility. The experience is not exactly new. Yet, as at other times, I somehow nurtured hopes and expectations that my presence, or for that matter the presence of any other woman of color, could stir some interest in addressing the multi-facetedness of oppression. While following and observing the dynamics in that room, I asked myself how many of those participants actually had a person of color as a good friend or lover. I knew that a high percentage of those who had children have at least had close contact with that woman of color which allowed them to pursue their professional careers and personal realization: the domestic servant. At a more distant level many had come into contact with them in the lower ladders of service. In fact, at that same conference we were served food by one of them.

Therefore my presence in that room served the dual purpose of reminding them of their previous limited contacts with women of color, evoking feelings of distance and separation, and generating a good deal of curiosity as to my presence in that group. By talking of the need to find commonalities while asserting differences, I became the concrete embodiment of their abstract conversation. At one point an assertive student—why is it that students usually have the ability to generate honest confrontations?—directly gazed at me and asked the facilitators to discuss how those alluded differences were integrated into their feminist works. Loving and hating that student for her directness which was an open invitation for my intervention, I realized that the secure, yet uncomfortable, position of *observadora* was coming to an end.

That student had spoiled my otherwise successful "observer approach" in American feminist conferences. Since the rage and indignation were, as usual, very much inside myself, it was easier than I thought to accept her invitation. My accent, my color, the Caribbean rhythm in my words felt "different." The established feminist authorities assented with their heads to my thoughts. Yet in their faces you could see their inability to grasp, apprehend my feelings and emotions. They were too distant, I was too "other." Their otherness as women allowed them to walk with me half-way. But only half-way.

Marisa, one of my students at CUNY, after having read that paper, wrote:

Dear Celina:

What was it like becoming the concrete embodiment of their abstract conversation? What was it like to become the personification of theory? Why were they too distant? Why were you too other? You wrote that "their otherness as women allowed them to walk with me half-way, but only half-way." Is there just one path? Many paths? A straight line, a direction? Is that direction involved with purpose? Or is it a continuum, reflecting each of our lives? I think you hedge on page 8 when you refer to your rage and indignation. Is it that this "genre" of writing does not allow for visceral truthfulness/primitive truthfulness? Level with me and talk about that rage and indignation.

What is it like being invisible? Being made invisible by the discourse, by deconstruction, by academia? Being invisible in a world you've chosen to be in; in a world you thrive in? Don't you see the paradox, the dichotomy, the schism? You passed the professional rituals—but still you are invisible. You seek to become truly visible in evaluating social structures based upon experiencing oppression as a way of being.

So why is this core forced into hiding? It is forced externally (I realize you talk about internalization and complicity yet I want to dwell in the external). The externality of tentacles and arms which have the ability to enter human flesh—which have the ability to penetrate and wound—the tension at the moment of penetration . . . once inside, the tentacles divide and turn themselves into open hands which reach out for and search for living essences, the heart, the brain-they reach and squeeze hard. The essences aren't destroyed, they merely escape and hide, hide behind the heart and mind and continue to exist within the grip of those tentacles, because the essences of life have gone into hiding so that the whole organism can survive. These essences live themselves in a shallow pool of water—crystal clear, walled in by purple flowers that are always in bloom, which grow to enormous heights as the grip becomes stronger.

What does your space look like? You see my space, I don't know if it is a space for feminist legal scholars, but it is mine. Where is yours?

I realized I was truly visible to Marisa.

FEMINIST THEORY IN LAW: THE DIFFERENCE IT MAKES

Martha Albertson Fineman*

INTRODUCTION

This essay is a consideration of the feminist project in law and two contemporary legal feminist approaches to the historical construction of women as "different"—a characterization that has had implications in regard to the way in which women are understood as objects and subjects of law. These competing feminist responses are based on similar conclusions about women's uneasy relationship to law as well as to other institutions of power in our society. They differ, however, in their analyses of the nature and extent of the difference between women and men and the conceptual and theoretical implications of differences.

Until fairly recently, legal feminism was primarily an equality-based strategy, which assumed no legally relevant differences between men and women. This emphasis was perhaps determined by the many ways in which the law historically both facilitated and condoned women's exclusion from the public (therefore, overtly powerful) aspects of society. Difference was the rationale and the justification for this exclusion which was based on the belief that women's unique biological role demanded their protection from the rigors of public life. It was no surprise, therefore, that when significant numbers of women began to make inroads into public institutions such as the law, they sought to dismantle the ideology which had excluded them—assimilation became the goal and equality the articulated standard.

Recently, some feminists have called attention to the fact that "equality" tends to be translated as "sameness of treatment" in American legal culture and, for that reason, actually operates as a conceptual obstacle to the formulation and implementation of solutions to the unique economic and

* Martha Albertson Fineman is the Maurice T. Moore Professor of Law at Columbia University in the City of New York. She is a 1975 graduate of the University of Chicago Law School. In 1984 she developed the Feminism and Legal Theory Project at the University of Wisconsin Law School. The project is now located at Columbia Law School and is devoted to fostering interdisciplinary feminist work on law and legal institutions.

I wish to thank Mindy Dutton for her valuable assistance on this article.

societal problems women encounter.[1] These "post-egalitarian feminists" urge a reconsideration and reconstruction of differences—this time from a feminist perspective. Those feminists who now want to move beyond equality and establish affirmative theories of difference recognize that initial adherence to an equality concept was necessary in taking the first steps to change the law and legal institutions. The lesson some of us have learned from the results of the past several decades of equality feminism, however, is that a theory of difference is necessary in order to do more than merely open the doors to institutions designed with men in mind. Arguing for a theory of difference questions the presumed neutrality of institutions, calling into question their legitimacy because they are reflective of primarily male experiences and concerns. In that way, a theory of difference has the potential to empower women.

This essay begins with a consideration of the development of the current debate over differences which continues to characterize much of legal feminist writing. I attempt to address some of the limitations I think feminists encounter when law is the subject about which they write. In the latter half of this essay I expand on a notion of "gendered life" which I first began to develop in an earlier article.[2] I am developing this concept in order to facilitate a discussion of differences that is both grounded in concrete and empirical experiences of significant numbers of women as well as reflective of the dominant ideological presentation of women as constructions of our culture and its institutions.

The idea of a gendered life is *not* the same as asserting the notion of "essential" femaleness. The concept of a gendered life is based on the belief that most differences between the sexes are socially manufactured, not inherent. This realization, however, should not obscure the overwhelming nature of the task faced by feminists seeking change in social and cultural representations of women. Changing society is not an easy task. In fact, in some ways it might be *easier* were differences the result of nature or biology. In that instance technology might prove of assistance.[3] Culture and

---

[1] See, e.g., Martha Albertson Fineman, The Illusion of Equality: The Rhetoric and Reality of Divorce Reform (1991); Diana Majury, Strategizing in Equality, in At the Boundaries of Law: Feminism and Legal Theory 320 (Martha Albertson Fineman & Nancy Sweet Thomadsen eds., 1991); Isabel Marcus, Reflections on the Significance of the Sex/Gender System: Divorce Law Reform in New York, 42 U. Miami L. Rev. 55 (1987).

[2] Martha L. Fineman, Challenging Law, Establishing Differences: The Future of Feminist Legal Scholarship, 42 Fla. L. Rev. 25 (1990).

[3] Altering the biological capacities of men so that they could carry a fetus might be the only way to evoke significant change in other areas. Many people reflect on the fact that American men are assuming more responsibilities for children. How

male interest in children is expressed, however, may reinforce rather than dismantle existing power relationships. I believe this is illustrated by three clippings I occasionally distribute to my family law classes. These clippings represent to me three competing models of the "new father."

The first clipping is a letter to Ann Landers in which an expectant mother confessed that while she considered herself "lucky" in comparison to the women who complained about their husbands not paying much attention to their newborns, she was "concerned." The soon-to-be Mom wrote: "Larry doesn't want me to breast-feed our child because he wants to play a significant part in the care of our newborn. He recently read that if the father isn't involved in the feeding of the infant, bonding won't take place. I've always believed that breast is best, but I certainly don't want to deny my husband the opportunity to bond with our baby." Ann responded: "It's wonderful that your husband is so eager to be part of the baby's early life. But a breast-fed child has a decided advantage . . . [y]our husband can hold the child after he feeds. He can burp, cradle, coo and establish bonding in this way." Ann Landers, Wisconsin State Journal, Feb. 18, 1988, § 3, at 6.

The second clipping announces the development of something called "Dr. Goldson's Baby Bonder." The device is described by Barbara Roessner thus: "[A man's] chest is cloaked in a biblike garment with breast-shaped protuberances into which ordinary baby bottles have been inserted." She quotes from the advertisement: "Something new for the mouths of babes . . . . Now, nursing can be done by anyone for just $19.95. . . . Breast-feeding isn't just women's work anymore." Barbara Roessner, Device to Let Fathers 'Breast-Feed' May Be the Latest Sign of the Times, The Capital Times (Madison, Wis.), Mar. 15, 1988, at 8.

The most radical (and technology-dependent) vision of the new father, however, was offered by the British magazine *New Society*. The magazine reported scientists as saying that "the technology exists to enable men to give birth." The Associated Press followed up on this story with interviews and reported:

> Male pregnancy would involve fertilizing a donated egg with sperm outside the body. The embryo would be implanted into the bowel area, where it could attach itself to a major organ. The baby would be delivered by Caesarean section. . . .
>
> . . . .
>
> The embryo creates the placenta, so theoretically the baby would receive sufficient nourishment.

The question of whether or not there would be a market for this technology is an interesting one. It was dismissed by one fertility researcher with the comment "Nobody has tried it—and why would they? . . . It's bizarre and fanciful." Others, however, saw the potential for a limited market: "[C]andidates for male pregnancy might be homosexuals, transsexuals or men whose wives are infertile." Mr. Mom: Scientists Say Men Could Give Birth, Wisconsin State Journal, May 9, 1986, § 1, at 2.

These three stories represent three possible male adaptations to the existence of a biologically based difference between men and women that actually favors women in regard to the establishment of a claim to children. In the first story the male response is to force the woman to deny the implications of difference, even at the possible cost of harm to the child. She is coerced into conforming her conduct to the male's physical limitations so that she does not garner any advantage.

society are not easily manipulated and change occurs slowly if at all. Even what appears to be progress is often the superficial adjustment of institutions undertaken only to maintain old hierarchies in the face of challenges.[4]

Finally, I suggest that the concept of a "gendered life" can be helpful in urging cooperation among women across our differences in areas where social and cultural definitions of "Woman" operate to potentially oppress us all. The notion of women's experiences is problematic when consideration is given to the differences among women. This aspect of the debates about difference is currently of particular interest to the legal feminist community. This last section of the essay is ultimately a plea that the feminists who are engaged in writing theory about law not "unique" ourselves out of existence as an analytic category—as "women."[5] My argument is based on the assumption that as feminist women we have an

---

The second story, in my opinion, represents an even more insidious response, however. The male merely makes a superficial adjustment—dons an obviously artificial imitation (almost a caricature) of maternity while not altering the reality of his physical situation. Such subversion disguises the fact that a move from breast to bottle has occurred at the same time that it asserts on an ideological level the erroneous notion that breast-feeding is nothing special—an activity that can be duplicated by some wire, material, strings, and a great deal of smoke and mirrors. This example of resort to gimmicks in order to assume away any significance inherent in a biological difference may be tempting to advocates of equality. It has the potential to backfire, however. What may occur is the devaluation and minimization of an important biological, social, and cultural event (breast-feeding) in order for us to pretend that fathers can "breast-feed."

The third story illustrates my point that technology can in some circumstances eliminate differences. While it is true that this story involves gestation, not breast-feeding, the hope is that once this step is accomplished the subsequent nurturing may be expedited. Surely for the advocate of equality, the direction—elimination of differences—is the right one. The goal is assimilation, although this time it is the conformity of the male to the female norm in regard to procreation. As the comments quoted above indicate, however, even if the technology exists, the cultural and societal arrangements make it unlikely that anyone other than those who have no woman to do their bearing for them will ever use it.

[4] For an explication of this in the context of family law rules, see, e.g., Fineman, *supra* note 1.

[5] The term "uniqueing" was used by eminent Native American scholar Rennard Strickland to describe the factionalization of the Native American community among tribal lines that prohibited their working together for common aims and purposes against the common foe. Conversation with Rennard Strickland (Dec. 8, 1991). Feminist writing in law is increasingly fractionalized in style, with sweeping generalizations and characterizations of "other" groups of women as the guarantee of entry and audience in the debate. Such condemnations serve a variety of functions. At the outset, they establish a need for the specific views advanced by the writer through the process of labeling the "other" group (usually

important and unrepresented perspective with which to assess and critique the law. It is further based on the assertion that as privileged women we have the obligation to help other women who suffer in their gendered lives in our culture but have no access to legal institutions and discourse.

THE FEMINIST PROJECT IN LAW

The answer to the question "What is the feminist project in law?" changes over time as either the law or circumstances change or as perceptions of the problems alter. At any one time there are many feminist projects in law. The designation of what are the most pressing feminist projects varies with the feminists consulted; some are concerned primarily with issues of legal knowledge and the production of doctrine, others with women's opportunities within the profession. In my own work I have been interested in the impact of law on women's lives—the role of law in the construction and perpetuation of a gendered social existence.

It is important to emphasize that when *law* is the object of analysis, there are somewhat unique methodological and conceptual constraints that operate upon feminist endeavors. The feminist project in law, of course, is defined in the first instance by the characteristics of law and legal institutions. Feminist responses to law are shaped by our perceptions about law and its role and function in society.[6] In particular, because I view law as a system of allocation of power and believe that legal discourse both reflects and constitutes the consequences of power in our society, my attention has been directed to the processes whereby explicitly coercive rules are generated and implemented. I have specifically focused on family law. This choice was prompted in part by my belief that the family is the most gendered institution in our society, and therefore, one that should receive serious feminist scrutiny.

My consideration of family law has given me pause because it is apparent that the generation and implementation of legal rules quite often

those who have been writing in the area) as unrepresentative—as really little better than the dominant group in society. The condemnations also create distance between the "other" women and the writer (and the group that the writer claims to represent based on a shared characteristic). The distance lessens the scholarly necessity for the writer to credit or even acknowledge the contributions and/or accomplishments of the other women. Furthermore, the process of condemnation enables the writer to assert herself as an authority for the faction of women identified in this process.

[6] This means, of course, that the differences among various legal systems will be of significance in the development of feminist legal theory(ies) and limit the nature of a comparative perspective.

proceed in haste, without adequate reflection. Rules typically are made in response to political and social pressures—adopted for their symbolic rather than their pragmatic characteristics and contents. Even the best intentioned legal actors will find themselves with imperfect and incomplete information, yet required to make decisions which will have significant, immediate impacts on people's lives.

There are also limitations on theorizing that one must acknowledge when law is the object of study. Most significantly for a feminist is the explicit reliance in law on the process of classification.[7] The law is a system of rules and/or norms, many of which are designed to have universal application, all of which have potential application beyond any specific set of circumstances. Therefore, the process of lawmaking relies on the generation of broad generalizations about groups or classes of things and people at the legislative level. On the individual case level, law is also a process of classification—courts make decisions using analogies and distinctions within the context of precedent and stare decisis, tying "like things" together in a web of consistent and coherent doctrine.

Classification, inevitable though it might be, is nonetheless a process that is susceptible to criticism because it invariably will both include inappropriate cases and exclude appropriate ones.[8] As classification involves

---

[7] Classification is the process applied to facts whereby they are given legal meaning. Claims under the Equal Protection Clause of the Fourteenth Amendment provide a familiar example of this classification process. State action, which itself distinguishes between groups of actors, is analyzed at a level of scrutiny dependent upon the classification of the state action in question. Where a law classifies people according to their race, "such classifications are subject to the most exacting scrutiny." Palmore v. Sidoti, 466 U.S. 429, 432 (1984). Where the distinction is based on gender, however, the law is given an intermediate level of scrutiny. See, e.g., Mississippi Univ. for Women v. Hogan, 458 U.S. 718 (1982). Race and gender are separate bases for classification.

The extent to which the process of classification pervades all legal analysis is evident in the very research tools that are used by lawyers, judges, and other legal scholars. Classification is the process whereby the diverse and broad range of factual circumstances that might become the subjects of legal scrutiny are channeled into discrete categories, ultimately susceptible to the application of rules and norms operating on such categories of facts—rules and norms which can be referenced in key word indices and treatises on specific subject matter.

[8] However, the creation of fixed categories with concrete legal implications has often been a feminist (and other) objective in law reform. Classification in this regard is seen as an alternative to more amorphous processes such as "balancing," "weighing," or other devices to implement judicial discretion—fixed rules are seen as preferable to unrestrained judicial bias. See Fineman, supra note 1, ch. 3, for a discussion of this phenomenon in the context of rules governing the distribution of property at divorce.

line drawing and assessments of similarity and difference, it seems clear that both as a process and in terms of fashioning responses, classification should be understood to be of a political nature. It will generate controversy. Murray Edelman has noted:

> The character, causes, and consequences of any phenomenon become radically different as changes are made in what is prominently displayed, what is repressed, and especially in how observations are classified. Far from being stable, the social world is therefore a chameleon, or, to suggest a better metaphor, a kaleidoscope of potential realities, any of which can be readily evoked by altering the ways in which observations are framed and categorized. Because alternative categorizations win support for specific political beliefs and policies, classification schemes are central to political maneuver and political persuasion.[9]

In addition to the problems inherent in classification, and whatever its institutional manifestations, problems exist because law must operate in a "practical" or pragmatic manner. Decisions must be made even if the processes are imperfect and the results unpopular. Given the demands made upon it and its limitations, one might conclude that the legal system works pretty well. But from a feminist perspective, focused on the material and legal position of women in our society, the nature and operation of the coercive power of law is cause for concern. Our critiques have an air of urgency (perhaps desperation) because the power of the system is so explicitly and immediately threatening to women.

The fact that the law relies so heavily on classification has meant that some part of the feminist project in law historically and contemporarily has been focused on the question of "differences." The assertion of differences has always been a basis for distinctions in legal treatment. The negative aspects of difference occupied feminist legal theorists' attention until fairly recently. Increasingly, however, and I would argue with evolving sophistication and complexity, feminist legal theorists are considering differences from an affirmative and creative perspective. Differences can be empowering—providing opportunity, not stigma. This assertion is made without the intent to obscure the fact that a focus on differences holds potential dangers for women. I do, however, believe the problems are not the same as they were even ten years ago. Our way of thinking about differences and the value we attach to them has evolved over time, and the feminist project in law should respond to these changes.

---

[9] Murray Edelman, Category Mistakes and Public Opinion 1 (1992) (unpublished manuscript, on file with author).

The Initial Project—Women Into Law

At the turn of the century, the early feminist project in law was fairly clearly defined by the explicit nature of doctrinal assumptions about differences. Because of their perceived biological or "natural" attributes, women were considered appropriately excluded from the practice of law and other positions of public power. They were relegated to the private or family "sphere." In his much quoted concurring opinion in *Bradwell v. Illinois*, the Supreme Court case which upheld an Illinois prohibition on women practicing law, Justice Bradley explained that the civil law

> as well as nature herself, has always recognized a wide difference in the respective spheres and destinies of man and woman. . . . The natural and proper timidity and delicacy which belongs to the female sex evidently unfits it for many of the occupations of civil life. The constitution of the family organization, which is founded in the divine ordinance, as well as in the nature of things, indicates the domestic sphere as that which properly belongs to the domain and functions of womanhood.[10]

In the rhetoric of the *Bradwell* case as well as in other "protective" doctrines, women's perceived differences from men operated to exclude women from the "public" or market sphere—to set them apart, outside of the main avenues to power and economic independence.

These exclusionary consequences of differences led many feminist legal scholars and practitioners who finally did make it into the profession to argue for equality in terms of sameness of treatment as a matter of moral and legal right.[11] Assimilation was the goal, and difference was

---

[10] Bradwell v. Illinois, 83 U.S. (16 Wall.) 130, 141 (1872) (Bradley, J., concurring).

[11] In a classic article on the subject, Wendy Williams expresses the concerns of those advocating for an equality model. While noting the "instinct to treat pregnancy as a special case," Williams warns:

> [T]he same doctrinal approach that permits pregnancy to be treated *worse* than other disabilities is the same one that will allow the state constitutional freedom to create special *benefits* for pregnant women. The equality approach to pregnancy . . . necessarily creates not only the desired floor under the pregnant woman's rights but also the ceiling . . . . If we can't have it both ways, we need to think carefully about which way we want to have it.
>
> My own feeling is that, for all its problems, the equality approach is the better one. The special treatment model has great costs.
>
> . . . .
>
> . . . At this point we need to think as deeply as we can about what we want the future of women and men to be. Do we want equality of the

suspect as easily translated into a basis for discrimination. Any arguments for consideration of differences were assailed as harboring the inevitable potential for exclusion and differentiation that harmed women. Feminist reformers attacked existing classifications and categories based on gender and favored a gender-neutral paradigm of equality that linguistically assumed and asserted sameness between men and women. The most ambitious of such symbolic reforms was the movement for the Equal Rights Amendment[12] to the Federal Constitution that, although it ultimately failed on a national level, mothered changes in some state constitutions forbidding distinctions based on sex.[13] The momentum for gender neutrality also produced other results, generating significant statutory and case law alterations in family law as well as in other doctrinal areas.[14] In general, it was clear to legal feminists in the 1960s and 1970s that the best way to ensure that perceived differences between men and women were not used to disadvantage women was to refuse to recognize any differences as legally relevant.

Differences and Perspectives

Contemporary circumstances suggest there may be significant problems with a continued overarching feminist denial of relevant differences between men and women.[15] Increasingly, there is recognition that a neu-

---

sexes—or do we want justice for two kinds of human beings who are fundamentally different?

Wendy W. Williams, The Equality Crisis: Some Reflections on Culture, Courts, and Feminism, 7 Women's Rts. L. Rep. 175, 196, 200 (1982).

[12] H.R.J. Res. 208, 92nd Cong., 2d Sess. (1972).

[13] Eighteen states and territories have constitutional amendments which specifically mandate sexual equality under the law. Alaska Const. art. I, § 3; Colo. Const. art. II, § 29; Conn. Const. art. I, § 20; Haw. Const. art. I, § 3; Ill. Const. art. I, § 18; La. Const. art. I, § 3; Md. Const. Decl. of Rts. art. 46; Mass. Const. pt. 1, art. I; Mont. Const. art. II, § 4; N.H. Const. pt. 1, art. II; N.M. Const. art. II, § 18; Pa. Const. art. I, § 28; P.R. Const. art. II, § 1; R.I. Const. art. I, § 2; Tex. Const. art. I, § 3a; Utah Const. art. IV, § 1; Va. Const. art. I, § 11; Wash. Const. art. XXXI, § 1; Wyo. Const. art. I, § 3, art. VI, § 1.

[14] See, e.g., Fineman, supra note 1; Marcus, supra note 1.

[15] For example, the rhetoric surrounding the equality debate has raised questions in the context of adoptions. Unmarried fathers are employing equality models to attack the rules that treat them differently than the child's mother in terms of due process and substantive rights when a child is to be placed for adoption. See Caban v. Mohammed, 441 U.S. 380 (1979) (single father who had lived with his children for five years may block adoption of children by withholding consent); Quilloin v. Walcott, 434 U.S. 246 (1978) (natural father who had never exercised custody over or legitimated the child could not object to adoption). See

tral equality model serves as an artificial limit on the feminist project in law, which is increasingly defined as the affirmative use of law to address the social inequities women experience in our society as the result of their gendered roles as wives and mothers. It has proved difficult to suggest remedies for unequal circumstances within an equality paradigm which emphasizes sameness of treatment and is suspicious of accommodation of differences. This revelation has been prompted in part by the recent evolution of feminist "perspective" scholarship.

The term "perspective scholarship"[16] encompasses an ever-growing body of work connected by the fact that it challenges the traditional notion that law is a neutral, objective, rational set of rules, unaffected in content and form by the passions and perspectives of those who possess and wield the power inherent in law and legal institutions. In some regards, perspective scholarship is merely the most recent expression of a critical scholarly movement known as "legal realism," which during the 1920s and 1930s called into question the prevailing idea of law as an autonomous system of rules and principles. The early legal realists stressed the factual context of cases, not abstracted legal principles.[17] They urged the use of extra-legal material—such as that produced by social scientists—to aid in resolving the social and political issues that found their way into courtrooms and legislatures.[18]

Perspective scholars begin with the same initial skepticism about the objectivity and neutrality of law and legal institutions as the legal realists.

also Lehr v. Robertson, 463 U.S. 248 (1983), (refusing to strike as unconstitutional a law that provided different procedures and rights to fathers of nonmarital children up for adoption than to mothers). In *Lehr* the Court found it significant that the father had not maintained a relationship with the child since her birth, quoting with approval Justice Stewart's dissent in *Caban*: "'The mother carries and bears the child, and in this sense her parental relationship is clear. The validity of the father's parental claims must be gauged by other measures. By tradition, the primary measure has been the legitimate familial relationship he creates with the child by marriage with the mother. . . . In some circumstances the actual relationship between father and child may suffice to create in the unwed father parental interests comparable to those of the married father.'" Id. at 260 n.16 (quoting Caban, 441 U.S. at 397 (Stewart, J., dissenting)).

[16] Kimberle Crenshaw traces the ideal (and unreal) concept of "perspective-lessness" (an analytic stance that law has no specific cultural, political, or class characteristics) and the growing challenges to the ideal in the context of arguments for a race-conscious approach to specific legal issues. Kimberle Williams Crenshaw, Foreword: Toward a Race-Conscious Pedagogy in Legal Education, 11 Nat'l Black L.J. 1 (1989).

[17] See, e.g., Laura Kalman, Legal Realism at Yale 9–10 (1986).

[18] Id. at 17–18.

They also look to the social, cultural, and political, in addition to the legal, to provide a context for understanding the operation and impact of law in our society. The perspective scholar's definition of "law" is broad, and law is to be discovered in actions as well as in words—in the interpretation and implementation of rules as well as in their formal doctrinal expression. Law is not only something "out there"—an independent body of principles— but a product of society, acted upon and responsive to political and cultural forces. For this reason, it is as essential to understand societal and cultural forces as it is to decipher doctrine in order to understand "the law."

Perspective scholarship adds the explicit consideration of diverse perspectives to the realist, law-in-society tradition. Perspective scholarship is based on the premise that certain groups historically have been unrepresented in law and their exclusion has led to biases—an incompleteness or deficit in contemporary legal analysis and legal institutions. Furthermore, perspective scholars argue the corresponding contention that historically excluded groups have different, perhaps unique, views and experiences that are relevant to the issues and circumstances regulated and controlled by law. Perspective scholarship adds nuance to the traditionally rather monotone canvas of law. It adds the possibility of color and texture to the legal palette by introducing diverse and often divergent viewpoints based on the social and cultural experiences of race, gender, class, religion, and sexual orientation, for example. It makes more complete and more complex our consideration of the questions "what is law?" and "what are the roles and functions of law in our society?"

Questioning Neutrality

Indeed, the lessons learned from perspective scholarship have led some feminist legal scholars to assert that gender neutrality may ultimately be as oppressive to the interests of women as was the creation of differences exemplified by the *Bradwell* opinion.[19] In family law in particular this is clear, since women, as members of the gendered categories of wives and mothers, have borne the burdens of intimacy in our society. The presence of children creates dependency not only because the children are themselves dependent, but also because the person who assumes primary care for them is dependent on social and other institutions for accommodations so that such care can be delivered. However, institutions in our society do not facilitate the care of children, and sacrifices are expected in career plans and other goals if one is to have children. The same is true in regard to caring for the elderly or any dependent adult with whom one is

---

[19] See supra text accompanying note 10.

intimate and therefore feels responsibility. Typically it is women who bear the costs of the expectations associated with such intimate relations in our society. Women are not compensated for bearing these costs, and in the make-believe world of equality they are, in fact, penalized.

Neutral treatment in a gendered world or within a gendered institution does not operate in a neutral manner. There are more and more empirical studies that indicate that women's relative positions have worsened in our new ungendered doctrinal world.[20] Ignoring differences in favor of assimilation has not made the differences in gender expectations disappear. They operate to disadvantage women as the material implications of motherhood, for example, are realized in the context of career development and opportunity. Furthermore, even for women choosing to forgo gendered roles and to accept the male worker standard as the norm, entry into previously male-dominated institutions does not guarantee equality. Many such women encounter incremental obstacles to their advancement as glass ceilings and other impediments appear.

In the context of considering the limitations of assimilation as a goal, it is also important to remember that law is a conservative discipline, resistant to change. This is relevant given that the issue in the *Bradwell* case itself was the exclusion of women from the practice of law. This historic exclusion signals that there are significant problems for women's adherence to an equality or neutrality model. Law as an institution—its procedures, structures, dominant concepts, and norms—was constructed at a time when women were systematically excluded from participation. Insofar as women's lives and experiences were the subjects of law, they were of necessity translated into law by men. Even social or cultural institutions that women occupy exclusively, such as "motherhood," as legally significant categories initially were what I call "colonized categories"—defined, controlled, and given legal content by men. Male norms and male understandings fashioned legal definitions of what constituted a family, who had claims and access to jobs and education, and, ultimately, how legal institutions functioned to give or deny redress for alleged (and defined) harms. Existing concepts and categories have not been easily dismantled.

Women were, of course, politically active during the *Bradwell* era, and some sought to implement their views into law. Florence Kelley and

---

[20] This is true economically, as demonstrated by recent statistics. See, e.g., Victor R. Fuchs, Women's Quest for Economic Equality (1988). It is also true when legal results such as awards of custody in contested cases are considered. See Fineman, supra note 1, at 90 & n.35. For the latest statistics regarding divorce and the poverty of children, see Jason DeParle, Child Poverty Twice as Likely After Family Split, Study Says, N.Y. Times, Mar. 2, 1991, § 1, at 8.

others from the National Consumer's League, for example, attempted to introduce a "female standard" into employment law.[21] These early women reformers believed that the only way to achieve equality was through the legal recognition and accommodation of women's differences. Unfortunately, they had to rely on men to be the translators and transmitters of their views. This was a process fraught with peril; male legal actors such as Felix Frankfurter, comfortable with and in control of "Law," shaped and reshaped their feminist clients' ideas until they were no longer recognizable as such.[22] Difference was ultimately translated as inferiority, resulting in stigma and exclusion.

The desire to establish that there is a feminist or difference perspective that merits positive accommodation in law has not abated. Increasingly there is feminist resistance to the assimilation model which was the dominant approach after the *Bradwell* era. Contemporary attention to differences is grounded in the notion that law must take into account that there are significant differences between men and women in the ways in which they experience the world and that modification of specific doctrine is necessary to remedy power imbalances and to correct existing biases in laws that reflect only male norms and experiences.

An important distinction between our own era and that of *Bradwell* is, of course, that feminists are no longer dependent upon the Frankfurters of the world for the translation of our ideas. Women now occupy professorships, are members of the bar, and make up almost half of law classes. A few of us are even legislators and judges.[23] While the full integration of the profession is far from complete (especially at the most powerful levels), feminist women can at least give our own legal voice to our ideas. The current debate about differences is an example of what can happen when such voices are heard.

DIFFERENCES INTO LAW: THE CURRENT DEBATES

Any contemporary consideration of differences must first address the question of what are the legally relevant differences between men and

---

[21] For a documentation of this process in regard to the litigation involving industrial equality, see Sybil Lipshultz, Social Feminism and Legal Discourse, 1908–1923, in At the Boundaries of Law: Feminism and Legal Theory, supra note 1, at 209.

[22] Id.

[23] As of 1988 approximately 42% of those enrolled in law school were women. A Review of Legal Education in the United States, Fall 1988, 1988 A.B.A. Sec. Legal Educ. & Admission to B. 65. The Census Bureau reports that as of 1989, 22.3% of all lawyers and judges were women. U.S. Bureau of the Census, Statistical Abstract of the United States 395 (1991).

women. It is now generally, though not universally, conceded that narrowly defined reproductive roles represent a "significant" difference worthy of some legal accommodation, but there are questions as to whether anything else should be considered relevant.

The whole question of differences between men and women has generated a lot of debate in general outside of law, and unanswerable questions have arisen concerning causation and the respective roles of "nature" and "nurture." In other disciplines some feminists are concerned with definitively establishing that it is society and culture that construct gender roles and that there are no fundamental biological distinctions that produce differences between women and men.[24] I do not consider these debates to be of central importance to the feminist *legal* project—I believe engaging in them will only syphon energy needed for more immediate concerns. Law has a concrete, immediate impact on women's lives and legal feminists do not have the luxury of indulging in esoteric debates about the location of differences. My own position, if pushed, has been that, regardless of how fashioned, differences matter.[25] Upon the respective reproductive roles of the sexes are built social and cultural assumptions and expectations. These social and cultural constructs have significant material consequences that cry out for legal redress and remedy. Differences in this regard are "real." They are manifest, and are harmful to women.

The realization that differences exist, however, does not resolve much for a legal audience—in fact, it generates further questions. For example, what legal significance should any differences between men and women have—should, or must, they be accommodated? In law this is a question of remedies. A second set of legal questions concerns the possibility of law

---

[24] For a discussion of the feminist debate over social construction of gender versus female essentialism, see Linda Alcoff, Cultural Feminism Versus Poststructuralism: The Identity Crisis in Feminist Theory, 13 Signs 405 (1988).

[25] Even if differences are considered to be socially rather than biologically constituted, nothing is resolved. Feminists who dawdle over this point seem to assume that social construction is easier to handle or alter than biological differences. I disagree. In fact, if it were merely biology, technology and medical innovations might be enlisted in the construction of an androgynous future. See supra note 3. Society is not easily manipulated. To state that something is socially constructed, in my opinion, is to concede that it is powerful and resistant to change. We all, even those of us who are critically inclined, must operate within our culture. None of us may totally escape it—to some extent it defines us all. The point is that differences, however constructed, have real material effects on women, and, for me, this means that the task of feminist legal theorists is to consider in what ways the law can remedy inequities that have occurred and that continue to operate to disadvantage women.

as a tool of reconstruction—can the law be used to eliminate some of the constructed differences, to assist in the project of fashioning an egalitarian, genderless world? Many legal feminists find themselves occupied in answering these questions. Increasingly more of us are concluding that the unequal and inequitable position of women can only be remedied through pervasive legal accommodation of difference.[26] Thus, for many American feminist legal scholars, there has been a move away from equality as one of *the* organizing principles of legal thought.

The Concept of a Gendered Life

In an earlier work I argued for the concept of "gendered lives" in order to legitimate differences based on the idea of a women's perspective rooted in the shared potential for a variety of experiences that are gendered in our culture.[27] In a world in which gender is more than semantics, feminist legal theory *cannot* be gender-neutral, nor can it have as its goal equality in the traditional, formal legal sense of that word. Feminist theory *must* be woman-centered, gendered by its very nature because it takes as its raw building material women's experiences. Since women live gendered lives in our culture, any analysis that begins with their experiences *must* of necessity be gendered analysis.[28] Addressing the real material consequences of women's gendered life experiences cannot be accomplished by a system that refuses to recognize gender as a relevant perspective, imposing "neutral" conclusions on women's circumstances.

In this earlier work I argued that this concept of gendered life begins with the observation that women's existences are constituted by a variety of experiences—material, psychological, physical, social, and cultural, some of which may be described as biologically based, while others seem more rooted in culture and custom. The actual *or* potential experiences of rape, sexual harassment, pornography, and other sexualized violence women may suffer in our culture shape individual experiences. So, too, the potential for reproductive events such as pregnancy, breast-feeding, and abortion have an impact on women's constructions of their gendered lives. I addressed the question of superficial similarities with the concession that while some gendered experiences are events that are shared with

---

[26] See supra text accompanying notes 19–23.

[27] Fineman, supra note 2, at 37.

[28] See Catharine A. MacKinnon, Feminism, Marxism, Method and the State: An Agenda for Theory, 7 Signs 515, 530–41 (1982) (discussing human sexuality as a gendered experience), 535 (discussing feminism as "the theory of women's point of view") (1982).

men, there is often a unique way in which these events are generally or typically lived or experienced by women as contrasted with men in our culture. I used the example of aging as a life event falling in this category, stating that "while both men and women age, the implications of aging from both a social and economic perspective are different for the genders in our culture."[29]

This concept of gendered life is my attempt to create a way to argue that a concept of differences is necessary to remedy socially and culturally imposed harms to women. Notice that the formulation of the differences debate is distinguishable from that of Justice Bradley's opinion in the *Bradwell* decision. In *Bradwell* differences were based on biology, nature, and, ultimately, on God, and they operated as an exclusionary device to limit women's participation. The contemporary difference argument by contrast is grounded in empirical realizations, in experiences, and in society and culture, and is an affirmative position, arguing for remedies, for differentiated treatment to rectify existing pervasive social and legal inequality.

An example of this type of sensitivity to differences is found in a recent employment discrimination case.[30] In that case, Judge Beezer (a Reagan appointee on the Ninth Circuit) adopted a "reasonable woman" standard for the assessment of allegations of sexual harassment:

> [W]e believe that in evaluating the severity and pervasiveness of sexual harassment, we should focus on the perspective of the victim. If we only examined whether a reasonable person would engage in allegedly harassing conduct, we would run the risk of reinforcing the prevailing level of discrimination. Harassers could continue to harass merely because a particular discriminatory practice was common . . . .

---

[29] Fineman, supra note 2, at 37. On the economics of aging for women, see Paul E. Zopf, American Women in Poverty 109–11 (1989).

[30] Ellison v. Brady, 924 F.2d 872 (9th Cir. 1991). However, the particular aspect of protectiveness evidenced in *Bradwell* may still be detected in court cases. See, e.g., International Union, UAW v. Johnson Controls, Inc., 886 F.2d 871 (7th Cir. 1989), where the court sitting *en banc* upheld a company policy which banned women of child-bearing years from occupying particular positions of employment because of evidence that the exposure to lead incident in those positions would cause severe birth defects if a woman were to become pregnant. While this was later overruled by the Supreme Court, International Union, UAW v. Johnson Controls, Inc., 111 S.Ct. 1196 (1991), the Court did not reject the basic premise of the lower court—that is, that all women should be viewed as potential mothers—but instead emphasized the woman's right to make choices regarding childbearing and pregnancy.

. . . .

. . . [B]ecause women are disproportionately victims of rape and sexual assault, women have a stronger incentive to be concerned with sexual behavior. . . . Men, who are rarely victims of sexual assault, may view sexual conduct in a vacuum without a full appreciation of the social setting or the underlying threat of violence that a woman may perceive.[31]

The majority opinion adopted a reasonable woman standard in the recognition of the fact that women experience at least some aspects of the world differently than men. Judge Beezer was opposed to a purely subjective test and indicated that the "objective" reasonable woman standard was fashioned "[i]n order to shield employers from having to accommodate the idiosyncratic concerns of the rare hyper-sensitive employee."[32] He noted that the court found it necessary to "adopt the perspective of a reasonable woman primarily because we believe that a sex-blind reasonable person standard tends to be male-biased and tends to systematically ignore the experiences of women."[33] The court reversed the trial judge's finding that the woman, who had received "love letters" from a male colleague that she found frightening, had failed to state a prima facie case of hostile environment sexual harassment.

On a very significant level, the opinion in this case is a victory for feminist legal theorists who emphasize the different ways in which men and women in our culture experience events. Feminist legal writers' works are found in the text of the opinion.[34] Even more important, certain relevant aspects of women's gendered lives were not systematically ignored and male experiences were not adopted as the norm. In referencing the "real" world context of sexual violence toward women, Judge Beezer recognized that such reality can shape an individual woman's reception of amorous and insistent unwanted declarations of affection.

---

[31] Ellison, 924 F.2d at 878–79 (citations omitted).

[32] Id. at 879.

[33] Id.

[34] Judge Beezer cites the following feminist writing in the area of sexual harassment:

> Ehrenreich, Pluralist Myths and Powerless Men: The Ideology of Reasonableness in Sexual Harassment Law, 99 Yale L.J. 1177, 1207–1208 (1990) (men tend to view some forms of sexual harassment as "harmless social interaction to which only over-sensitive women would object"); Abrams, Gender Discrimination and the Transformation of Workplace Norms, 42 Vand. L. Rev. 1183, 1203 (1989) (the characteristically male view depicts sexual harassment as comparatively harmless amusement).

Id. at 878–79.

But, before feminists do too much celebrating,[35] we should be aware that the opinion also reflects an aspect of the difference debate with which feminist legal scholarship continues to struggle on a basic conceptual level. At the same time that Judge Beezer affirms that there are relevant legal differences between the social and cultural experiences of men and women, he assumes that a reasonable woman standard can be applied in the context of the fact-finding process. The opinion does make note of the

---

[35] Winning the battle is not winning the war. Compare *Ellison* with Scott v. Sears, Roebuck & Co., 798 F.2d 210 (7th Cir. 1986), in which the court found that repeated propositions by a supervisor, slapped buttocks, and sexual comments from coworkers did not poison the work environment, and Rabidue v. Osceola Refining Co., 805 F.2d 611 (6th Cir. 1986), cert. denied, 481 U.S. 1041 (1987), in which a majority held that sexually explicit and derogatory remarks about women and pin-ups in the office did not seriously affect the female plaintiff's psychological well-being.

Another ominous note in regard to the progress being made in the sexual harassment area was the treatment that Professor Anita Hill received in her appearances before the Senate Judiciary Committee in conjunction with her allegations against Supreme Court nominee Clarence Thomas. Whether one believes that Hill was sexually harassed or not, it is clear that the manner in which her credibility was assessed reflected male bias and an ignorance of women's experiences even though the experience of sexual harassment is essentially a gendered event.

Throughout the Hill/Thomas hearings the nation watched (and overwhelmingly nodded agreement) as a woman was judged by an all-male panel and a predominantly male media who repeatedly raised questions as to why she would continue her employment with Thomas in the first instance and maintain contact with him after she left the Justice Department if she had in fact been sexually harassed. Senator Orrin Hatch, in particular, seemed to feel it was unbelievable that Hill did not do something drastic if things were as she reported.

I find it incredible that these men could think Hill's inaction was of any significance. Even if they choose to ignore the argument that many women in this position fail to act, their own experiences with (nonsexual) harassment from superiors who had power over them should have provided some insight into the dilemma someone in Hill's position would face. No doubt in their professional lives—as law students, as young associates in law firms or junior governmental officials—they have suffered humiliation, indignities, or insults at the hands of powerful supervisors, yet continued their employment and actively fostered continued contact for the future references and opportunities the person in the explicit position of power would supply.

The Senators and the male media did not place Hill's experience of sexual harassment in the context of "normal" power hierarchical relationships with which they might have had some basis for identification and empathy, however. Instead, and perhaps because the indignities and humiliation she suffered were sexual in nature, what transpired was the application of the tired, old, traditional, patriarchal male vision of female virtue and how it should be expressed—"death before dishonor."

possibility of relevant differences among women, but banishes any doubt that generates in the interests of protecting the employers from the "idiosyncratic concerns of the rare hyper-sensitive employee." Any potential differences among female perspectives are not the occasion for withholding a gender-specific new standard given the need that, the court concludes, exists for "[a] gender-conscious examination of sexual harassment [that] enables women to participate in the workplace on an equal footing with men."[36] While the distinction may be considered welcome and even necessary, the question arises whether recognition of this aspect of difference alone is enough. What about the "dilemma" presented by the recognition that there are relevant differences among women?[37]

Differences Among Women

The thorny theoretical question of what are the relevant differences among women and how they should be recognized and accommodated in feminist discourse has been one of the most hotly debated recent issues in the difference debates.[38] While I think feminists in general are to be commended for their concern with differences among women and their desire not to indulge in essentialism, I am concerned that recent developments seem to have paralyzed many—silencing or restricting voices as women determine that they cannot speak for anyone other than those women with whom they share major non-gender characteristics, such as class, sexual preference, or race.

Some writers have even gone so far in accommodating differences among women that they assert that there is no category of "woman" upon which we can build theory and/or assign social, cultural, or political considerations or consequences.[39] Others question whether we can speak even for ourselves—challenging the concept of "self," and asserting there are no unitary beings that exist over time, in space, to whom one can

---

[36] Ellison, 924 F.2d at 879.

[37] Martha Minow develops the various aspects of the "dilemma," which she describes as "[t]he risk of recreating difference by either noticing it or ignoring it," in her new book. Martha Minow, Making All the Difference: Inclusion, Exclusion, and American Law 40 (1990).

[38] See, e.g., Fineman, supra note 2; Angela P. Harris, Race and Essentialism in Feminist Legal Theory, 42 Stan. L. Rev. 581 (1990); Deborah L. Rhode, Feminist Critical Theories, 42 Stan. L. Rev. 617 (1990); Joan C. Williams, Deconstructing Gender, 87 Mich. L. Rev. 797 (1989).

[39] For a further exposition of this view, see Patricia A. Cain, Feminism and the Limits of Equality, 24 Ga. L. Rev. 803, 838–41 (1990).

pretend to give coherent voice.[40] We are, thus—either in a group, a cluster, or as an individual—deconstructed.[41] I have a lot of problems with the politics and implications of these discourses.

It is important to remember in the context of *legal* feminism that as the questioning of "categories" (in fact, the questioning of the whole process of categorization) goes on, society has generated, and continues to recreate and act upon, universalized, totalizing cultural representations of women and women's experiences. Even those critical of cultural constructions of essentialist images of women must recognize the force these images hold. None of us completely escapes the dominant images of the society within which we operate. Interpretation of life events, the processes whereby events are given meaning, is not an atomistic, individualistic procedure. Social action and interaction, as well as dominant cultural images, significantly contribute to individual interpretation of and reaction to events. Furthermore, the law utilizes and facilitates the construction of these totalizing social and cultural images.

Consider the institution of motherhood, for example. I have argued elsewhere that *all* women must care about social and legal constructions of motherhood, because, although we may make individual choices not to become a mother, social construction and its legal ramifications operate independent of individual choice.[42] As is demonstrated by a case like *Johnson Controls*,[43] women will be treated as mothers (or potential mothers) because "Woman" as a cultural and legal category inevitably encompasses and incorporates socially constructed notions of motherhood in its definition.[44] In addition, it is important to note that although the social and legal construction of motherhood occurs in a variety of different contexts, there is a common image of "mother" which emerges. A comparison of images of single motherhood which emerge in both poverty and in divorce discourses, for example, demonstrates that concepts and totalizing

---

[40] See id. at 806–10.

[41] Robin West has voiced a powerful critique of this deconstruction fetish as manifested in law. See Robin West, Feminism, Critical Social Theory and Law, 1989 U. Chi. Legal F. 59, 84–89. See also Drucilla Cornell, The Doubly-Prized World: Myth, Allegory and the Feminine, 75 Cornell L. Rev. 644 (1990).

[42] Martha L. Fineman, Images of Mothers in Poverty Discourses, 1991 Duke L.J. 274, 276–77.

[43] International Union, UAW v. Johnson Controls, Inc., 886 F.2d 871 (7th Cir. 1989), rev'd, 111 S. Ct. 1196 (1991).

[44] See Martha Albertson Fineman, Intimacy Outside of the Natural Family: The Limits of Privacy, 23 Conn. L. Rev. 955 (1991), for a discussion of how law uses the "natural family" as its ideological paradigm, thus incorporating socially constructed ideals of family.

"ideals" tend to cross over.[45] The ideas (and ideals) forged in one context constrain and direct the debates in another.[46] Motherhood as a totalizing, culturally defined institution is applied across race and class lines. She is objectified—heterosexual, ideally married, chaste, self-sacrificing, etcetera— a rather statistically improbable and oppressive construct. This process of objectification is inevitable, although the form of the image may be up for reconstruction:

> It is the *expression* of ideas that makes it possible to hold them, think about them, react to them, and spread them to others. There must be an image, as articulated in art, in words, or in other symbols. The notion that an idea can somehow exist without objectification in an expression of any kind is an illusion, though the expression may take the form of a term or image in one's own mind: i.e., as a contemplated exchange with others.[47]

The assertion that there is a totalizing tendency represented in the social and legal construction of women as "Women" suggests there is a basis for women working together across their differences. This rather hopeful twist on the oppressive extent of gender stereotyping is premised on its utility for unifying different groups of women. Using the concept of gendered lives that I earlier developed to distinguish women's from men's lived experiences in our culture, it is possible to see some unifying potential in the very extensiveness of the cultural stereotype. The existence of the social construction suggests that, while few could legitimately dispute that characteristics such as race, class, and sexuality are significant to one's experiences, it is an error for women to proceed as though these differences were *always* relevant. I earlier listed characteristics I considered relevant in addition to race, class, and sexual orientation. For example, I believe that

> age, physical characteristics (including "handicaps" *and* "beauty" or the lack thereof), religion, marital status, the level of male identification (which is independent of both marital status and sexual preference—what Gerda Lerner has referred to as "the man in our head"[48]), birth order, motherhood, grandmotherhood, intelligence,

---

[45] See Fineman, supra note 42, at 275.
[46] Id. at 276.
[47] Edelman, supra note 9, at 11.
[48] From conversations between Gerda Lerner and the author. By the term "man in our head," reference is made to the masculinist culture and society that defines for us what is right and wrong, good and evil, male and female—a male voice of authority that is internalized and operates as a social control. For a general discussion of male hegemony over that which is defined socially as "universal truth," see Gerda Lerner, The Creation of Patriarchy 219–29 (1986).

rural or urban existence, responsiveness to change or ability to accept ambivalence in one's personal life or in society, sources of income (self, spouse or state), degree of poverty or wealth, and substance dependency, among others[49]

shape existence in both how individual women experience the world and how others, particularly those in power, relate to them. Women also have characteristics or clusters of characteristics related to the gendered aspects of their lives that have social and legal significance and, therefore, give women a basis for cooperation and empathy across their differences.

CONCLUSION

Note that the concept of a gendered experience is an attempt simultaneously to open a space for women's perspective in law as distinct from men's, and to provide the occasion for unity among women over some specifics of their lives. Because gendered experiences focus us on specific experiences, hopefully they can avoid perpetrating an idealized, universal notion of "Woman." Attention to the force that an imposed (and in that sense, therefore, "common") socially constructed concept of gender exercises upon aspects of all women's lives also presents an opportunity for diverse women to participate in resisting that imposition. Women can coalesce across differences to work together on the project of defining for ourselves the implications and ramifications of the gendered aspects of our lives. In other words, I'm interested in exploring whether it is possible to have an *affirmative* politics of difference that defines groups and classifications tenuously, whereby group identification is recognized as politically necessary, but is also seen, in the words of Marion Young, as "ambiguous, relational, shifting," without "clear borders" that bind people in all circumstances for all time.[50] Women need not be considered to be inevitably either in opposition to or having little in common with other women

---

[49] Fineman, supra note 2, at 39–40 (footnote omitted).

[50] I. Marion Young, Justice and the Politics of Difference 171 (1990). Young argues that in this way women of different races, classes, and sexual preferences can seize the power of naming their differences as women without being frozen into essentialist categories. Differences can be understood and accommodated in the context of specificity, variation, and heterogeneity. She defines this as "relational understanding" of difference. The relevance of differences depends on context and shift in the contexts.

because of non-gender group differences. Women will converge to organize around overlapping experiences.[51]

My hopes for a development of the concept of gendered lives as a creative way to address both distinct aspects of the differences debate may be too optimistic. I am convinced, on the other hand, that the renewed interest in difference in feminist legal theory that has occurred during the last decade is positive because it reaffirms that our struggle over content and meaning in law is inherently political and that perspectives count. I recognize that the focus on difference is fraught with potential pitfalls, particularly if used to divide women, diluting our collective potential as a group to challenge male defined and controlled gendered notions of law that systematically disadvantage women in a variety of contexts. I defend my attempt here by stating only that this paper is the beginning of my search for pragmatic ways for legal feminists to work with law, recognizing its gendered nature *and* the need for the contexts supplied by considerations of differences.

---

[51] A gendered experience approach is also consistent with the philosophy underlying feminist methodology since it focuses on the concrete, not the abstractions of women's lives. In feminist theory, methodology is step-by-step a part of theory. For the most part, feminist methodology is about making theory more concrete, bringing in stories and other ways of identifying and describing women's experiences as they exist and as they have been left out of the legal system. Angela Harris refers to shifting methodology as a way to get around dangerous gender essentialism. See Harris, supra note 38. Deborah Rhode turns to it as a way to assure that critical theory does not become so abstract as to remove itself from women's experiences. See Rhode, supra note 38. Methodology, not always explicitly as such, includes literature (Adrienne Rich is as quoted as any legal scholar) and psychology (note the role of Carol Gilligan's book, In a Different Voice: Psychological Theory and Women's Development (1982)) as a way of bringing in women's experiences seemingly excluded from traditional legal rhetoric.

Katharine Bartlett argues that feminist method is feminist theory. Her recommended method of "positionality" suggests that truth shifts according to position but that feminists must try to posit this contingent truth—yet be willing to change. Bartlett says that asking the "woman question" is what starts feminist method; she then discusses the importance of "practical reasoning" and consciousness-raising. She criticizes both Robin West and Catharine MacKinnon for what she calls "standpoint epistemology" because it cannot adequately describe or follow feminist knowing. These epistemologies rely too heavily on essentialism to take account of real knowledge. She also criticizes postmodern—deconstructionist—method because it cannot move past its own sense of contingency to recommend reform. Bartlett says her argument for "positionality" recognizes the contingency of a truth but allows the feminist reformer to embrace a truth long enough to advance reform and explore experience. Katharine T. Bartlett, Feminist Legal Methods, 103 Harv. L. Rev. 829 (1990).

Whiteness and Women, In Practice and Theory: A Reply To Catharine MacKinnon

Martha R. Mahoney[†]

I. INTRODUCTION

As a white woman, I want to respond to Catharine MacKinnon's recent essay subtitled "What is a White Woman Anyway?"[1] I am troubled both by the essay's defensive tone and by its substantive arguments.[2] MacKinnon's contribution to feminism has emphasized the ways in which gender is constructed through male domination and sexual exploitation, and the profound structuring effect of male power on women's lives. This emphasis on what is done to women creates conceptual problems in understanding race and particularly in understanding whiteness. Defining gender by what is done to women makes it hard to see the many ways in which women act in our own lives and in the world. Dominance and privilege tend to seem normal and neutral to the privileged. To overcome this tendency, white people need to see aspects of our actions in the world that are particularly difficult for us to see. The difficulty in seeing women as social actors interacts with the difficulty that white people have in seeing whiteness and its privileges.

Other feminists have criticized MacKinnon's work for the extent to which her emphasis on sexual oppression displaces attention to racism,[3] and for treating race as additive or incremental to the "essential" oppression of women.[4] Her emphasis on the ways in which women are constructed as the

† Associate Professor, University of Miami School of Law. I am particularly grateful to Lisa Iglesias for talking through the inception of this essay with me. Blanca Silvestrini helped me start thinking about race as a cultural construct. Thanks also to Jeanne Adleman, Fran Ansley, Ken Casebeer, Mary Coombs, Adrienne Davis, Rachel Godsil, Lynne Henderson, Val Jonas, Sharon Keller, Jayne Lee, Chris Littleton, Bill Mahoney, Joan Mahoney, Judith Mahoney Pasternak, Sharon Oxborough, Rob Rosen, Steve Schnably, Jonathan Simon, Susan Stefan, and Stephanie Wildman, none of whom are responsible for my conclusions or any errors that remain.

1. Catharine A. MacKinnon, *From Practice to Theory, or What is a White Woman Anyway?*, 4 YALE J.L. & FEMINISM 13 (1991) [hereinafter MacKinnon, *Practice to Theory*].
2. MacKinnon has a distinguished stature in American feminism. In part, this reflects the strength of her work on sexual harassment, rape, and pornography, and her achievements as a teacher and activist, and, in part, the particular attention she has received in the media. *See, e.g.,* Fred Strebeigh, *Defining Law on the Feminist Frontier*, NY TIMES MAG., Oct. 6, 1991, at 29. This focus on MacKinnon's work creates the possibility that, unless responded to, her position will be seen as *the* position of white feminists. *Cf.* CATHARINE A. MACKINNON, *Desire and Power, in* FEMINISM UNMODIFIED 46, 49 (1987) [hereinafter MACKINNON, *Desire and Power*] ("you will notice that I equate 'in my view' with 'feminism'. . . ."); CATHARINE A. MACKINNON, *On Collaboration, in* FEMINISM UNMODIFIED, *supra*, 198-205 (asserting that women who disagreed with her proposed anti-pornography ordinance were not "feminists").
3. Marlee Kline, *Race, Racism and Feminist Legal Theory*, 12 HARV. WOMEN'S L.J. 115 (1989).
4. Angela Harris, *Race and Essentialism in Feminist Legal Theory*, 42 STAN. L. REV. 581 (1990).

objects of male power has been criticized for its tendency to overlook resistance to power or to treat as inauthentic interests women perceive as our own.[5] My essay focuses on the interaction of these issues and their consequences in MacKinnon's feminist theory.[6] Understanding the social construction of race[7] requires a vision of women as differentiated social actors.

White women urgently need ways of understanding and working on race and racism that are not liberal—neither based on liberal guilt, nor liberal as the term is used in critical theory (as in liberal legalism, with its emphasis on individualism and intent). Like MacKinnon and many other feminists, I believe feminist theory must be built from the diverse practice of many women. I emphasize in this practice women's creativity and struggles to survive under oppression as well as our experience of oppression. I also suggest that a sharp split between theory and practice hides the ways in which race as an ideology affects the development of pluralist feminist theory.[8]

In her recent response to critiques of essentialism, MacKinnon states that the method of building feminist theory out of the necessarily diverse practice of women inherently includes the particularity and diversity of women's experience. The problem, she argues, is that academic women start with

---

5. *See infra* note 26.

6. I do not believe MacKinnon's work is racist; as Angela Harris also points out, MacKinnon is anti-racist. Harris, *supra* note 4, at 585. MacKinnon does not ignore race when describing the oppression of women. Her former students tell me that MacKinnon shows real commitment to and respect for women of color in her teaching, and I believe them. However, I also believe that we are all affected by the racist society in which we live, and that the invisibility of privilege to the privileged is one reason most white feminists have not given the same depth of thought to our own race that we have to our own gender. This shared racist culture is why racism can be called "a public health problem," Charles R. Lawrence, *The Id, The Ego, and Equal Protection: Reckoning with Unconscious Racism*, 39 STAN. L. REV. 317 (1987), and a "societal illness," Trina Grillo & Stephanie Wildman, *Obscuring the Importance of Race: The Dangers of Making Comparisons Between Racism and Sexism (or Other-Isms)*, 1991 DUKE L.J. 397, 398. To get at the ways in which this system has been internalized differently by whites and by people of color, bell hooks uses the term "white supremacy" rather than "racism." BELL HOOKS, *Overcoming White Supremacy: A Comment, in* TALKING BACK: THINKING FEMINIST, THINKING BLACK 112, 112-13 (1989).

7. In this essay, I have chosen not to capitalize the terms "black" and "white." In discussing the social construction of race and of whiteness as a racial category, nonparallel capital letters appeared to me and to the editors of this journal to reproduce the problem of treating "white" as an invisible norm. Capitalizing the term "black" shows respect for a particular culture and history that goes beyond skin color. *See, e.g.,* CATHARINE A. MACKINNON, *Not by Law Alone: From a Debate with Phyllis Schlafly, in* FEMINISM UNMODIFIED, *supra* note 2, at 238 n.12; Kimberle Williams Crenshaw, *Race, Reform and Retrenchment: Transformation and Legitimation in Antidiscrimination Law*, 101 HARV. L. REV. 1331 (1988). However, capitalizing "white" does not comparably recognize history and culture. When discussing particular examples, this essay sometimes uses the black/white paradigm of race that has been important to the construction of whiteness. On the need to "interrogate whiteness," see BELL HOOKS, *Critical Interrogation, in* YEARNING: RACE, GENDER, AND CULTURAL POLITICS 51, 54-55 (1990). For a thoughtful new work undertaking the project of interrogating whiteness, see RUTH FRANKENBERG, WHITE WOMEN, RACE MATTERS: THE SOCIAL CONSTRUCTION OF WHITENESS (1993). On the convention of footnotes explaining choices regarding racial terms, see Kendall Thomas, *Rouge et Noir Reread: A Popular Constitutional History of the* Angelo Herndon *Case*, 65 S. CAL. L. REV. 2599 n.2 (1992).

8. *Cf.* BELL HOOKS, *Feminist Theory: A Radical Agenda, in* TALKING BACK: THINKING FEMINIST, THINKING BLACK, *supra* note 6, at 35, 37 (criticizing courses on feminist theory that treat writings by working class women of color as "experiential" and writings by white women as "theoretical").

theory, not practice.[9] The practice of women is the experience of oppression. Discrimination based on sex is the legal theory that embodies the practice of experience as a woman.[10] She cites landmark women's equal-rights cases on sexual harassment and pregnancy leave in which the plaintiffs were African-American women to show that these plaintiffs, Mechelle Vinson and Lillian Garland, were oppressed "as women."[11]

MacKinnon believes that much of the discussion of the privilege of white women is based on denying the existence of oppression as women. Critiques of white feminists reflect a reluctance to identify with white women, a reluctance based on seeking identification with men, a greater source of social power.[12] "White woman" is a term in which the modifier "white" discounts the oppression embodied in the category "woman."[13] MacKinnon resists this discounting: if "white" means "not oppressed," she answers that women *are* oppressed.[14] The way that white women are constructed and treated is "a particularly sensitive indicator of the degree to which women, as such, are despised."[15] What is done to white women is a "floor" for what is done to all women. What is done to women of color is more, added, and worse.[16]

Finally, the structure of MacKinnon's argument tracks her substantive emphasis on the objectification of women. She analyzes the ways in which women of various races appear in pornography[17]—inherently, a framework of inauthenticity in which women are actresses playing roles created by men, and not social actors in our own lives and in the world. In an extended, ironic, rhetorical passage, MacKinnon examines the "problem" of the white woman as objectified through what she calls a "white man's image" and a "Black man's image."[18]

---

9. MacKinnon, *supra* note 1, at 13-14.
10. *Id.* at 14-16.
11. *Id.* at 14-15, 17-18.
12. MacKinnon believes these critiques show that:
   [M]any women, not only women of color and not only academics, do not want to be "just women," not only because something important is left out, but also because that means being in a category with "her," the useless white woman whose first reaction when the going gets rough is to cry. I sense here that people feel more dignity in being part of any group that includes men than in being part of a group that includes that ultimate reduction of the notion of oppression, that instigator of lynch mobs, that ludicrous whiner, that equality coat-tails rider, the white woman. It seems that if your oppression is also done to a man, you are more likely to be recognized as oppressed, as opposed to inferior.
Id. at 21-22.
13. *Id.* at 19.
14. *Id.* at 19-20.
15. *Id.* at 22.
16. *Id.* at 21. The metaphor of a "floor" to oppression invokes the concept of additive oppressions that has been criticized by many feminists. *See, e.g.*, ELIZABETH V. SPELMAN, INESSENTIAL WOMAN: PROBLEMS OF EXCLUSION IN FEMINIST THOUGHT 123-25 (1988); Frances Lee Ansley, *A Civil Rights Agenda for the Year 2000: Confessions of an Identity Politician*, 59 TENN. L. REV. 593, 601 (1992); Harris, *supra* note 4, at 595-97; Deborah King, *Multiple Jeopardy, Multiple Consciousness*, 14 SIGNS 42, 47 (1988) (criticizing "additive" models of race and gender oppression and calling for an interactive model of understanding the oppression facing women of color).
17. MacKinnon, *supra* note 1, at 20-21.
18. MacKinnon writes:
   [I]t has recently come to my attention that the white woman is the issue here, so I decided I better

MacKinnon is a complex writer, hard to critique without caricature. She not only describes women as objects of a process of social construction, but also sometimes refers to women as authentic actors or acknowledges women's "visions," "history," "culture," and "resistance."[19] Her relentless insistence on seeing the harm to women is often a response to pervasive social and legal ideology that pretends away oppression.[20] Both parts of MacKinnon's concept of feminism, however—defining gender by what is done to women, and centering the definition of what is done to us around sexual exploitation—tend to ignore creativity and struggle in women's experience that have been particularly emphasized as important to women of color.[21] MacKinnon makes the implicit assertion that, to work together as women, what we really need to learn is our shared sexual exploitation as women.

All women struggle to understand the world and to construct lives under conditions of male domination. But race is also a social construction, one in which the participation of white people is often peculiarly invisible to ourselves. A crucial part of the privilege of a dominant group is the ability to see itself as normal and neutral.[22] This quality of being "normal" makes

---

find out what one is. This creature is not poor, not battered, not raped (not really), not molested as a child, not pregnant as a teenager, not prostituted, not coerced into pornography, not a welfare mother, and not economically exploited. She doesn't work. She is either the white man's image of her—effete, pampered, privileged, protected, flighty, and self-indulgent—or the Black man's image of her—all that, plus "the pretty white girl" (meaning ugly as sin but regarded as the ultimate in beauty because she is white). She is Miss Anne of the kitchen, she puts Frederick Douglass to the lash, she cries rape when Emmett Till looks at her sideways, she manipulates white men's very real power with the lifting of her very well-manicured little finger. She makes an appearance in Baraka's "rape the white girl," as Cleaver's real thing after target practice on Black women, as Helmut Newton's glossy upscale hard-edged distanced vamp, and as the Central Park Jogger, the classy white madonna who got herself raped and beaten nearly to death. She flings her hair, feels beautiful all the time, complains about the colored help, tips badly, can't do anything, doesn't do anything, doesn't know anything, and alternates fantasizing about fucking Black men with accusing them of raping her. As Ntozake Shange points out, all Western civilization depends on her. On top of all of this, out of impudence, imitativeness, pique, and a simple lack of anything meaningful to do, she thinks she needs to be liberated. Her feminist incarnation is all of the above, and guilty about every single bit of it, having by dint of repetition refined saying "I'm sorry" to a high form of art. She can't even make up her own songs.
Id. at 18-19.

19. *Id.* at 14; CATHARINE A. MACKINNON, *Difference and Dominance: On Sex Discrimination, in* FEMINISM UNMODIFIED, *supra* note 2, at 39 [hereinafter MACKINNON, *Difference and Dominance*] ("Women have done good things, and it is a good thing to affirm them . . . I think women have a history. I think we create culture."). *See also* CATHARINE A. MACKINNON, TOWARD A FEMINIST THEORY OF THE STATE 47, 80, 92, 101-02, 153 (1989) [hereinafter MACKINNON, FEMINIST THEORY OF THE STATE] (discussing the possibility of resistance, transformative action, or sexual self-assertion for women). These references are not fully developed in her work, and the only women who "resist" in her recent essay are those who sue over sex discrimination. MacKinnon herself has said that it is a mystery "[h]ow sisterhood became powerful when women were powerless." CATHARINE A. MACKINNON, *The Art of the Possible, in* FEMINISM UNMODIFIED, *supra* note 2, at 3, *discussed in* Christine A. Littleton, *Feminist Jurisprudence: The Difference Method Makes*, 41 STAN. L. REV. 727, 783 (1989).

20. *See* Frances Olsen, *Feminist Theory in Grand Style*, 89 COLUM. L. REV. 1147, 1176 (1989) (reviewing MACKINNON, FEMINISM UNMODIFIED, *supra* note 2).

21. *See, e.g*, Harris, *supra* note 4, at 613 ("black women have had to learn to construct themselves in a society that denied them full selves"); Regina Austin, *Sapphire Bound!*, 1989 WIS. L. REV. 539, 541 ("Minority women do amazing things with limited resources, are powerful in their own communities.").

22. *See generally* SPELMAN, *supra* note 16; *cf.* Kimberle Williams Crenshaw, *Demarginalizing the Intersection of Race and Sex: A Black Feminist Critique of Antidiscrimination Doctrine, Feminist Theory*

whiteness and the racial specificity of our own lives invisible as air to white people, while it is visible or offensively obvious to people defined outside the circle of whiteness. Part of the construction of race is the way that, when used by whites, the word "race" comes to mean otherness—often, in this society, blackness--while whiteness become transparent and neutral. Inescapably, race is not merely "another" form of oppression that happens to women of color, but a part of the experience of all women.

We cannot understand race without seeing women as subjects and recognizing women as differentiated actors. If race is not simply to mean "otherness" or "blackness"—if *all* people have a "race" that is part of the social construction of race—then we must critically examine the participation of white women as actors in society. This inquiry involves looking both at women and how we understand ourselves, and at whiteness and how white people understand (or fail to understand) ourselves.

This essay first argues that, because MacKinnon defines gender as constructed of domination, she has difficulty grappling with the complex experience of women as oppressed actors. I then discuss race as a social construction, drawing upon recent insights in anthropology and critical race theory. To look at the particular experiences of white women as differentiated actors in the world, I shift the analytical framework away from pornography to other areas in which women historically have been oppressed: housework, access to money and credit, and the experience of single motherhood.

The final section of my essay discusses the tensions between the way MacKinnon seeks to show the oppression of women "as such" by pointing to the example of privileged white women, and her goal of building theory that reflects the diversity of women's experience. Despite the goal of building theory from diversity, this reductionist approach to proving oppression tends to reproduce a white norm. Also, the dichotomy between theory and practice fails to reckon with the ways in which some aspects of the practice of white feminists are invisible to ourselves. The liberatory project therefore demands a willingness to hear things, including things about ourselves, that we do not ordinarily see for ourselves. It also demands that we change what we do and find ways to work with what we learn, treating identity as something developed and experienced in working toward transformation as well as in the experience of oppression.

---

and Antiracist Politics, 1989 U. CHI. LEGAL F. 138, 151 (in discrimination cases, race and sex are significant only as they disadvantage victims; privilege is implicit and not perceived). MacKinnon eloquently describes this with regard to gender:

> The male epistemological stance, which corresponds to the world it creates, is objectivity: the ostensibly noninvolved stance, the view from a distance and from no particular perspective, apparently transparent to its reality, it does not comprehend its own perspectivity, does not recognize what it sees as a subject like itself, or that the way it apprehends its world is a form of its subjugation and presupposes it.

MACKINNON, FEMINIST THEORY OF THE STATE, *supra* note 19, at 121-122.

II. Defining People By What Is Done To Them, And Feminism By What Is Done To Women, And The Taking Of Sex As What Is Done To Us

For a decade, MacKinnon has explained feminism by analogy to Marxism:

> Sexuality is to feminism what work is to marxism: that which is most one's own, yet most taken away. . . . As the organized expropriation of the work of some for the benefit of others defines a class, workers, the organized expropriation of the sexuality of some for the use of others defines the sex, woman.[23]

This does not precisely claim to describe the nature of woman for all time, but for this theory: "That which most makes one the being the theory addresses [is] that which is most taken away by what the theory criticizes. In each theory you are made who you are by that which is taken away from you by the social relations the theory criticizes."[24]

Who you are is therefore based on what is done to you. Harm defines gender. This has proven both valuable and controversial within feminism. A one-sided description of women's experience as constructed of oppression may be a necessary choice because admitting greater complexity and discussing agency in women could be co-opted into belittling or dismissing the reality and depth of oppression.[25] However, this one-sidedness may make difficult identifying any authentic women's action or vision.[26] Even if not read literally,[27] MacKinnon's emphasis on women as the objects of the constructive force of male power puts a tilt in her work that has crucial consequences when she turns to discussion of race.

The analogy MacKinnon uses to define gender is a partial misdescription

---

23. MACKINNON, FEMINIST THEORY OF THE STATE, *supra* note 19, at 3.

24. MACKINNON, *Desire and Power*, *supra* note 2, at 48.

25. Olsen, *supra* note 20, at 1176.

26. This question of women's agency and authenticity has been addressed by many feminist authors. *See, e.g.*, MACKINNON, FEMINIST THEORY OF THE STATE, *supra* note 19; CAROL SMART, FEMINISM AND THE POWER OF LAW (1989); Kathryn Abrams, *Ideology and Women's Choices*, 24 GA. L. REV. 761 (1990); *Feminist Discourse, Moral Values and the Law: A Conversation*, The 1984 James McCormick Mitchell Lecture, 34 BUFF. L. REV. 11, 75 (1984) [hereinafter *Feminist Discourse*] (confrontation between Mary Dunlap and MacKinnon over concepts of women's subordination); Lucinda Finley, *The Nature of Domination and the Nature of Women: Reflections on Feminism Unmodified*, 82 NW. U. L. REV. 352 (1988) (reviewing MACKINNON, FEMINISM UNMODIFIED, *supra* note 2); Lynne Henderson, *Law's Patriarchy*, 25 LAW & SOC'Y REV. 411, 424-30 (1991) (reviewing ZILLAH R. EISENSTEIN, THE FEMALE BODY AND THE LAW (1988)); Littleton, *supra* note 19; Stephanie M. Wildman, *The Power of Women*, 2 YALE J.L. & FEMINISM 435 (1990) (reviewing MACKINNON, FEMINIST THEORY OF THE STATE, *supra* note 19), *discussed in* DRUCILLA CORNELL, BEYOND ACCOMMODATION (1990).

27. Olsen, *supra* note 20, at 1173-77, argues that MacKinnon's "grand theory" is presented in unambiguous terms in order to render it politically mobilizing and effective. Olsen believes MacKinnon makes a reasonable political choice to counter a social tendency to see sexuality as "natural and largely unproblematic"; MacKinnon answers this tendency to "treat women as agents whose agency needs merely to be appreciated" with emphasis on the systematic violence that denies women the opportunity to develop any voice or desires of their own.

of Marxism.[28] Of course, much of Marxist analysis defines workers through their social role in capitalist society. But capitalism appears as one stage in a larger historical picture that begins with the human struggle for survival, locating the creation of human products in the effort to sustain life. MacKinnon recognizes this too,[29] but, in her theory, what women do to survive humanly is constructed only *against* what men do to women.[30] When Marxist theory finds that capitalism makes working people into workers is possible only because of a previous analytical step in which labor created wealth—a claim about the dignity and potential of the oppressed.

It is this underlying positive claim that generates a transformative vision and has made portions of Marxist thought compatible with aspects of liberation theology. The lamp shining on the page you are reading, the page, the chair upon which you sit, the food you ate at your most recent meal, your clothes, and your shoes, the metal of the fillings in your teeth—and the vehicle that got you here, the stop signs that make traffic coherent, and the pavement on the streets—are suddenly revealed as the fruit of the work of people. It is not just that these are commodities, it is that someone made them. Your own work is part of this entire picture. Through your efforts to do your work, and to protect yourself as you do it, you are "naturally" one with the others who created these things.

Marxist theory generally organizes its vision of society around roles played in the production and exchange of commodities. But the deepest claim of Marxism is not its adoption of what Marx called the viewpoint of the commodity—the stance from which the relations of production construct workers—but its underlying vision of the primacy and dignity of labor in human life, couched in terms of historical development. Social transformation is based on identifying the oppressor and identifying that which is taken through oppression based on a positive vision of the worker and the nature of work, not merely a vision of the evil of exploitation. Class consciousness means recognizing not only that you are jointly oppressed as workers, but also that you have shared potential. Your efforts to survive will lead you (now the plural you) to try to free yourselves from the chains of oppression that bind you to exploitation—will lead toward freedom. It is consciousness lit by the

---

28. I do not wish to argue for Marxism as opposed to feminism, to assign analytical primacy to either class or gender, or to evaluate the contributions of Marxist feminist writings to feminism or Marxism. Rather, I believe the flaw in MacKinnon's analogy illustrates a problem internal to her theory and helps to demonstrate the consequences of her understanding of race.

29. "In marxist theory, we see society fundamentally constructed of the relations people form as they do and make those things that are needed to survive humanly." MACKINNON, *Desire and Power, supra* note 2, at 48.

30. See, for example, the discussion of consciousness-raising in MACKINNON, FEMINIST THEORY OF THE STATE, *supra* note 19, at 83-105. Being a woman means living within the meanings created through social oppression. Transformation consists of developing consciousness (lived knowing) of that oppression as it is manifested in women's lives. "Realizing that women largely recognize themselves in sex-stereotyped terms, really do feel the needs they have been encouraged to feel . . . often actually choose what has been prescribed, makes possible the realization that women at the same time do not recognize themselves in, do not feel, and have not chosen this place." *Id.* at 102.

merged value of your actual social contribution today and your shared role in the future. The fundamental liberatory claim of Marxism is therefore addressed to the worker: The world is rightfully yours, you have nothing to lose but your chains, what you do is the basis of human development—reclaim it.

MacKinnon's vision of feminism has no parallel claim about women. Gender itself is constructed of domination—the taking of women's sexuality—and constructs social relations and individual experience. When women develop shared transformative consciousness, it is "lived knowing"[31] of unity built through oppression, but lacks a positive claim about sexuality and the many other ways in which women participate in the creation of the world.[32] This void is particularly significant because sexuality is central to her theory. Group consciousness without any positive liberatory vision inevitably means a group or class made only of shared harm and implies no positive vision of shared experience, interest, or potential.[33]

MacKinnon makes arguments about women and race by analyzing the roles women play in pornography. These arguments are conceptually similar to the ways in which Marxist analysis adopts the viewpoint of the commodity.[34] The difference between the roles of the oppressed classes in the production of pornography and in the production of other commodities demonstrates the difference between Marxism and MacKinnon's definition of feminism. Workers are actors in producing commodities in ways that reflect a productive social role and liberatory potential. In contrast, women are actresses, not actors, in pornography, which is men's construction and objectification of women's sexuality and which implies no vision of a liberatory or transformative potential

---

31. *Id.* at 95.

32. The insistence on seeing present exploitation is a common thread between MacKinnon's analysis and Marxism. But unlike Marxism, which includes a liberatory potential for the worker, MacKinnon's work focuses not on creating authentic female sexuality but on liberating women from exploitive male constructions of sexuality. She is primarily concerned with rejecting concepts of female sexual autonomy that mask existing sexism, *id.* at 153. One difference between sexuality and work is that the women who are sexually exploited are often described as desiring the exploitation. *See infra* note 34.

33. By analogy, it is a prison camp, not a village, nor the complex world of both resistance and oppression that social historians have described among slaves—although as Mary Coombs has reminded me, there is resistance even in prison camps. Telephone Interview with Mary Coombs (Mar. 1993). MacKinnon recognizes struggle but is mainly concerned with how some women feminists and others do not, and with how women can become a sex "for itself," MACKINNON, FEMINIST THEORY OF THE STATE, *supra* note 19, at 102-05, reflecting her focus on seeing through oppression rather than examining present duality (including strength) in women's lives and struggles.

34. MacKinnon makes an analogy between male domination and the perception of the commodity as "an objective thing rather than as congealed labor." Because women have been the objects of this process of male power and social construction, feminist consciousness consists of identifying the "objective" point of view as male. MACKINNON, FEMINIST THEORY OF THE STATE, *supra* note 19, at 122. The common thread between Marx and MacKinnon is their focus on the socially constructed nature of apparently natural categories. Social perception of the commodity as a naturalized thing is part of what supports capitalism; Marx identified in the commodity the social relationships between labor and capital. The naturalization of women's role and the perception that women were unproblematically persons acting in natural ways are props of gender oppression; MacKinnon argues that male power constructs women as objects. But these insights lead in different rhetorical directions. While Marx emphasized social relationships hidden in objects (commodities), MacKinnon has fought to show the objectifying process of domination hidden in what society called unproblematically human, through emphasizing power rather than struggle.

in women.[35]

Other feminists have pointed to the problems with MacKinnon's emphasis on women as objectified by male power.[36] Christine Littleton explored the difficulty of finding within MacKinnon's vision of feminism a way to establish a shared position as women that could be both authentic (based on our own experience) and critical (not itself created by or perpetuating men's domination).[37] Littleton argues that MacKinnon's method, with its emphasis on consciousness-raising as a means of both exploring and transforming women's experience, is her greatest contribution. She concludes that MacKinnon treats the seeing of oppression as itself a transformative and political act, creating the impetus to disengage from oppression.[38] MacKinnon's most recent book takes this approach, movingly describing[39] the transformative work of feminist consciousness-raising groups.[40]

Some feminists who developed the method of consciousness-raising emphasized action against oppression as an integral part of the process.[41] MacKinnon's view of transformative consciousness, in contrast, seems largely internal to women's groups and to individual women. It implies no necessary

---

35. *See infra* text accompanying notes 112-15 (discussing the problems in understanding race when pornography is the paradigm of women's oppression).

36. Angela Harris's critique has been cited mainly for her argument about essentialism, but Harris also criticized overemphasis on the objectification of women as being inconsistent with the way women of color know themselves to have strength, creativity, and success at survival under oppression. Harris, *supra* note 4, at 612-14. Lucinda Finley questioned whether MacKinnon overlooked women's strength and creativity by implying that *all* women were in male-dominated society was what what men created through oppression. Finley, *supra* note 26, at 379. Drucilla Cornell took literally MacKinnon's emphasis on women as the objects of social construction and counterposed the possibility of a less determined reconstruction of the feminine. Cornell treats MacKinnon's work as unambiguous about the way women are constructed as the objects of male power. CORNELL, *supra* note 26, at 123. "In MacKinnon's feminist recasting of Marxist materialism, to be female is to be the one who is fucked. 'Man fucks woman; subject verb object.'" *Id.* at 119 (quoting MACKINNON, TOWARD A FEMINIST THEORY OF THE STATE, *supra* note 19, at 124). Cornell criticizes MacKinnon for seeing only the "frame" in which women are placed, not "beyond to the current frame." CORNELL, *supra* note 26, at 141.

37. Littleton, *supra* note 19, at 782-84.

38. *Id.* at 752-54, 782. *Cf.* CORNELL, *supra* note 26 ("Put very simply, MacKinnon's central error is to reduce feminine 'reality' to the sexualized object we are for *them* by *identifying* the feminine totally with the 'real world' as it is seen and constructed through the male gaze").

39. *See, e.g.,* MACKINNON, FEMINIST THEORY OF THE STATE, *supra* note 19, at 87:

The point of the process was not so much that hitherto-undisclosed facts were unearthed or that denied perceptions were corroborated or even that reality was tested, although all these happened. It was not only that silence was broken and that speech occurred. The point was, and is, that this process moved the reference point for truth and thereby the definition of reality as such. Consciousness-raising alters the terms of validation by creating community through a process that redefines what counts as verification. This process gives both content and form to women's point of view.

40. *Id.* at 101-02.

41. *See, e.g.,* Elizabeth Schneider, *The Dialectic of Rights and Politics*, 61 N.Y.U. L. REV. 589, 601-04 (1986) (on the relationship between women's experience, feminist theory and political action); *id.* at 642-48 (rights claims against the harms of battering and sexual harassment grew out of looking at women's experience, became transformative movements, and changed societal perception of what constituted suitable material for legal and social discourse). One early feminist book on rape treated consciousness-raising, speaking out, theoretical analysis, and feminist action as successive stages of feminist work, but added: "But in reality these are not separate steps at all, but a complex experience of growing awareness and involvement." NEW YORK RADICAL FEMINISTS, RAPE: THE FIRST SOURCEBOOK FOR WOMEN 4 (1974).

interaction between consciousness and practice and requires no interaction with the world.

Although transformation is part of MacKinnon's account of consciousness-raising, all sense of women as transformative actors disappears when MacKinnon turns to answering critiques of essentialism in her discussion of white women. I believe this reflects the extent to which she has anchored her theory to the vision of women as objects of sexual exploitation. Defining women by the taking of our sexuality could be a privatizing vision. MacKinnon's analysis explodes this—especially through her emphasis on pornography—into a collective, cultural harm that affects all women. She is correct in many ways: our lives and relationships are not truly severable from cultural distortion and the expropriation of our sexuality. But this is not otherwise a vision with any sense of shared experience of acting in the world. Defining women by what is done to us asserts women's shared experience based on these harms.[42] Centering theory on the taking of sexuality hides other forms of oppression[43] and other shared aspects of our lives.[44]

I am not arguing that transformative theory necessarily requires any single core positive claim that will underlie liberatory struggle.[45] But centering theory around a core *negative* claim such as sexual exploitation has its own consequences for transformative vision and organization. Christine Littleton has suggested that accepting partial authenticity and the inevitability of partial inauthenticity in women's lives, choices, and struggles could allow us to oppose oppression without anchoring ourselves to a fundamental claim about gender that leads to a vision defined by inauthenticity.[46] Or, we could arrive at a transformative vision based on an "objective" claim about the structure of the world as Marxism does, or spiritually (including humanism), or through

---

42. This overlooks many questions upon which transformative struggle depends: whether shared harm (to the extent that women perceive it as shared) will be a sufficient basis for women to decide what to do about oppression, how to act together, or whether in fact to act together.

43. Marlee Kline has pointed out that the emphasis on sexual exploitation reflects and reinforces the centrality of white feminist theorists to feminist theory. Kline, *supra* note 3, at 142-43 ("MacKinnon's assertion that the content of feminist practice supports her insistence on the centrality of sexuality to feminism is tautological. She appears to accept white feminist practice as coincident with feminism rather than challenging the limits of white feminist practice when applied to or used as a basis for explaining the oppression of women of color.").

44. For example, emphasizing the taking of sexuality tends to downplay or ignore other shared or collective harms suffered by women—like the ways in which harm to children becomes harm to women through our love and responsibility for them—and the shared experiences of struggle and survival that are part of race, ethnicity, and class.

45. "Grand theory" in general may have both strengths and weaknesses for feminist work. *See* Martha L. Fineman, *Challenging Law, Establishing Difference: The Future of Feminist Legal Scholarship*, 42 FLA. L. REV. 25 (1990); *cf.* Olsen, *supra* note 20 (defending grand theory).

46. Interview with Christine Littleton (Nov. 1992). Perhaps we could accept as partly authentic the consciousness of women who perceive themselves as agents in their lives, rather than treating women's task as solely the recognition of inauthenticity. For example, I have argued that women's perceptions of agency in their own lives are both true and false. Martha R. Mahoney, *Legal Images of Battered Women: Redefining the Issue of Separation*, 90 MICH. L. REV. 1, 25 (1991) [hereinafter *Legal Images*]; Martha R. Mahoney, *EXIT: Power and the Idea of Leaving in Love, Work, and the Confirmation Hearings*, 65 S. CAL. L. REV. 1283, 1308 ("this strong sense of agency reflects both sound self-knowledge and denial of the impact of structures of power").

the reconstruction of the "feminine" and the expansion of the possibilities for love.[47]

Many feminists continue to explore ways to value the work women have done[48] and the wisdom and love women have developed despite and because of conditions of oppression, without defining women by the roles we have traditionally played or implicitly accepting the constraints under which women have lived and worked.[49] MacKinnon has incisively criticized positive views of relational reasoning and valorization of "difference" in women because women have no choice about being caring.[50] Without re-creating a view of motherhood as authentically "womanly" or the paradigmatic role for women, feminists still face the question of valuing the work women do, much of which involves care for dependent others.[51] Feminist legal theory has grappled with women's responsibility for children and for emotional life through debates about connectedness, nurturance, and an ethic of care.[52] If we devalue and overlook much of the work women do, we will encounter further difficulty in seeing the connections between the work women do and the social construction of race, which has been built partly around this work.[53]

MacKinnon's discussion of white women is rhetorically structured to track her emphasis on the objectification of women and the centrality of sexuality to her theory. She argues against straw persons, ironically stating that the

---

47. CORNELL, *supra* note 26, at 205 ("Affirmed as the feminine, the threshold might be the opening to a new alliance. . . . Ontology of gender identity, then, has been deconstructed not just to expose the normative injunction that lies at its base, but to protect the possibility of a different destiny.").

48. A recent article points to the importance of the racial differentiation of this work. Evelyn Nakano Glenn, *From Servitude to Service Work: Historical Continuities in the Racial Division of Paid Reproductive Labor*, 18 SIGNS 1 (1992). Martha Fineman discusses the importance of reorganizing family law to recognize the inevitability of dependency and the derivative dependency of caregivers, rather than the sexual ties between adults. Martha A. Fineman, *Intimacy Outside of the Natural Family: The Limits of Privacy*, 23 CONN. L. REV. 955 (1991).

49. *See, e.g.,* Mary Becker, *Maternal Feelings: Myth, Taboo, and Child Custody*, 1 S. CAL. REV. L. & WOMEN'S STUD. 133 (1992). Becker points out that it has been difficult for feminists to deal with the profound ways in which women love their children. *Id.* at 159-67. Although social insistence on motherhood as *the* natural role of women has been destructive to women, the opposite development, ignoring women's passionate love for and commitment to children, is also destructive. *Id.* at 159. *See also* CORNELL, *supra* note 26, at 21-78 (discussing "the maternal and the feminine"); *see generally* ADRIENNE RICH, OF WOMAN BORN (1976).

50. MACKINNON, FEMINIST THEORY OF THE STATE, *supra* note 19, at 51.

51. *See, e.g.,* Martha Fineman, *Dominant Discourse, Professional Language, and Legal Change in Child Custody Decisionmaking*, 101 HARV. L. REV. 727 (1988) (discussing the devaluation of primary caregiving, which involves both love and physical work, in an attempt to create gender-neutral standards of parenting); *see also* Martha A. Fineman, *The Neutered Mother*, 46 U. MIAMI L. REV. 653 (1992).

52. *See, e.g.,* Robin West, *Jurisprudence and Gender*, 55 U. CHI. L. REV. 1 (1988). But see Celina Romany, *Ain't I a Feminist?*, 4 YALE J.L. & FEMINISM 23 (1991), for a critique of West, Menkel-Meadow and others for over-relying on Carol Gilligan. This literature on "connectedness" has been the main account of love in feminist legal theory, at least until the recent proliferation of work on motherhood. MacKinnon and others have criticized the sentimentalization and incorporation of roles that are forced upon women. *See, e.g., Feminist Discourse, supra* note 26; MACKINNON, *Difference and Dominance, supra* note 19, at 38-39. *See also* Joan C. Williams, *Gender Wars: Selfless Women in the Republic of Choice*, 66 N.Y.U. L. REV. 1559 (1991) [hereinafter *Gender Wars*] (emphasizing the impact of Gilligan on feminist theory and critiquing the ideology of domesticity).

53. *See infra* text accompanying notes 73-85 (discussing race as a social construction), and particularly notes 117-29 (on housework and the racial structure of reproductive labor).

white woman must be either the "white man's image" or the "Black man's image," listing stereotypes attributed to these images, and then pointing out that the stereotypes are not true. First, this argument makes a crucial omission: despite a brief appearance by Ntozake Shange, hidden in the middle of a passage focused on the "Black man's image," MacKinnon omits the possibility that the white woman could be defined from the viewpoint of the woman of color.[54] Also, MacKinnon's version of the "white man's image" is profoundly class-bound: her description of the "pretty, pampered, protected, flighty" woman ignores the also-subordinated, hard-working helpmeet who is the ideal woman in some working class and farming cultures.

Her "Black man's image" is a caricature that invokes racist stereotypes of black people as well as distortions of white women. "She [the white woman] makes an appearance in Amiri Baraka's 'rape the white girl.'"[55] This quotation is out of context.[56] The violence in the poem is in response to racist violence against black people, including sexual exploitation by whites.[57] The poem expresses not only rage itself but also anguish and despair over the murderousness of this rage—feelings that are missing from MacKinnon's brief excerpt.

The excerpt appears in the middle of a stanza: "Rape the white girls. Rape/ their fathers. Cut the mothers' throats."[58] In the poem, the objects of rape

---

54. I am grateful to Elizabeth Iglesias for pointing this out to me. Interview with Elizabeth Iglesias (Feb. 1993). I had noticed only that Ntozake Shange was oddly placed in this paragraph because she is not a man. Once Professor Iglesias mentioned the omission of women of color, I found the omission glaring and obvious, but even as of the second draft of this essay, I had not seen it for myself. *See infra* text accompanying notes 90-99 and 163-66 (on the difficulty for whites in perceiving white privilege). Part of white privilege is failing to notice the omission of those who do not share this privilege.

55. MacKinnon, *Practice to Theory, supra* note 1, at 19; this passage is quoted in full *supra* note 18.

56. I do not intend to write a defense of Baraka here. Rather, I want to challenge the particular use of these words from his poem. The citation is also ahistoric. THE DEAD LECTURER was published when Amiri Baraka still used the name LeRoi Jones—MacKinnon's text therefore says "Baraka" and cites to "Jones." *Id.* He changed his name in 1968. *See* AFRO-AMERICAN POETS SINCE 1955, 23 (Trudier Harris & Thadious M. Davis, eds., 1985). The consciousness reflected in the changed name is the product of a historical period that also saw the growth of the modern women's liberation movement. Citing to "Baraka" acknowledges this poet's chosen name but indirectly implies that "rape the white girl" is a statement contemporary with that name and consciousness.

57.   Black dada nihilismus, choke my friends
        in their bedrooms with their drinks spilling
        and restless for tilting hips or dark liver
        lips sucking splinters from the master's thigh.
LEROI JONES, *Black Dada Nihilismus, in* THE DEAD LECTURER 61, 63 (1964).

58.   From Sartre, a white man, it gave
        the last breath. And we beg him die,
        before he is killed. Plastique, we

        do not have, only thin heroic blades. . . .
        . . . .
                . . . A cult of death,

        need of the simple striking arm under
        the streetlamp. The cutters, from under
        their rented earth. Come up, black dada

are both "girls" and "their fathers." Sexual violence and domination are exercised over men (by treating them like women—raping them) as well as over "girls." White women are not only "girls" to be raped but are (at least ambiguously) also "mothers" whose throats are to be cut. I am not arguing that rape is legitimated by calling it an expression of racial outrage, or made gender-neutral by directing it against men as well as women. However, complexity is lost in MacKinnon's quotation. In the context of the poem, the line seems less about the black man's image of white women than it did in MacKinnon's article. Her quotation puts white women at the center again.[59]

In associating "rape the white girl" with the black man's image of the white woman, MacKinnon unconscionably invokes the rape image that is an important part of American racism. The black man's image of the white woman is equated with the image of the object of intended rape—a false description.[60] This misrepresentation is especially troubling because MacKinnon invokes a somewhat different version of race/gender rape myths, with obvious irony, with regard to white women. The statement that the white woman "alternates fantasizing about fucking Black men with accusing them of raping her" appears in the middle of a section on how white women fling their hair, don't work, and don't do anything. This description is clearly intended to be read as a false image of white women.[61] But the quotation from Baraka makes white-woman-as-rape-object seem authentically the image held by black men. Her only other citation to a black man is to Eldridge Cleaver, a rapist defending his rape of black women as preparation for his rape of white women.[62] These attributions to black men make "rape the white girl" appear to represent the black male image of white women more authentically than the other images in the rest of this passage.[63]

The structure of MacKinnon's arguments may in part be a product of the influence of the field of law itself. Much of her energy has gone into

---

nihilismus. Rape the white girls. Rape
their fathers. Cut the mothers' throats. . . .
. . .
(may a lost god damballah, rest or save us
against the murders we intend
against his lost white children
black dada nihilismus

Id. at 63-64.

59. Grillo & Wildman, *supra* note 6, at 401-04 (describing as "taking back the center" and "stealing the center" the moves by which white people make white experience the subject of discussion and attention in response to critiques by people of color).

60. *See, e.g.,* BELL HOOKS, *Reflections on Race and Sex, in* YEARNING: RACE, GENDER, AND CULTURAL POLITICS, *supra* note 7, at 57-61 (describing and criticizing the historical narrative "invented by white men . . . about the overwhelming desperate longing black men have to sexually violate the bodies of white women," *id.* at 58, as well as the "sexist paradigm that suggests rape of white women by black men is a reaction to racist domination," *id.* at 61).

61. MacKinnon, *Practice to Theory, supra* note 1, at 19; *see also supra* note 18 for full quotation.

62. *Id.* at 19 n.17 (quoting ELDRIDGE CLEAVER, SOUL ON ICE 14 (1968)).

63. For a searching discussion of feminism, racism, and rape, see Erin Edmonds, *Mapping the Terrain of Our Resistance: A White Feminist Perspective on the Enforcement of Rape Law,* 9 HARV. BLACKLETTER J. 43 (1992).

expanding and recasting sex discrimination law, which requires that "sex" be the reason for the oppression.[64] The demands of legal rhetoric encourage a tilt toward what is done to women. Even though legal action is a complex mix of both social control and adjustments to social struggle, the structure of legal argument encourages an all-agent or all-victim construction in which one either does or is done to, and women have gender oppression done to us.[65]

MacKinnon finds essentialism in Simone de Beauvoir's statement that women are "biologically destined for the repetition of Life, when even in [women's] own view Life does not carry within itself its reasons for being, reasons that are more important than Life itself."[66] She criticizes de Beauvoir for "defin[ing] [women] in terms of biological reproductive capacity" and emphasizes the difficulty of translating such a view into arguments about sex discrimination: "It is unclear exactly how any social organization of equality could change such an existential fact, far less how to argue that a social policy that institutionalized it could be sex discriminatory."[67] Her critique of Susan Brownmiller's "even more biologically destined" view of rape—"[b]y anatomical fiat . . . the human male was a natural predator and the human female served as his natural prey"—also emphasizes the difficulty of handling essentialism in law.[68]

One danger in allowing legal concepts of discrimination to set the framework of social interpretation within which we try to understand women's lives is that this framework renders invisible or uninteresting many aspects of creativity, struggle, and multiple interests. MacKinnon has fought to expand the concept of sex discrimination to make possible claims about sexual harassment and pornography in order to bring law closer to addressing the harms that women experience. But the legal concept of "discrimination based

---

64. *See generally* Judy Scales-Trent, *Black Women and the Constitution: Finding Our Place, Asserting Our Rights*, 24 HARV. C.R.-C.L. L. REV. 9 (1989). *Cf.*, Crenshaw, *supra* note 22, at 150-52.

65. A powerful and troubling example is the development of expert testimony regarding battered-woman syndrome and learned helplessness to account for the behavior of battered women who kill in self-defense. *See, e.g.*, Elizabeth Schneider, *Describing and Changing: Women's Self-Defense Work and the Problem of Expert Testimony on Battering*, 9 WOMEN'S RTS. L. REP. 193 (1986) (treating battered women as all agent or all victim). *See also* Mahoney, *Legal Images, supra* note 46, at 4, 28-43 (describing how the effect of the demands of forensic testimony in self-defense cases influences cultural and psychological concepts of battered women).

66. MacKinnon, *Practice to Theory, supra* note 1, at 17 (quoting SIMONE DE BEAUVOIR, THE SECOND SEX 64 (H.M. Parshley ed. & trans., 1971)).

67. MacKinnon, *Practice to Theory, supra* note 1, at 17. I believe de Beauvoir is describing a tension based on women's capacity for reproduction rather than asserting that women are in fact destined for reproduction. De Beauvoir's work has been described as having contradictory aspects in terms of essentialism. *See* SPELMAN, *supra* note 16, at 57-79.

68. MacKinnon, *Practice to Theory, supra* note 1, at 17 ("Exactly how to oppose sexual assault from this vantage point is similarly unclear. Do we make a law against intercourse?") Of course, many feminist concepts of equality do not depend on the difference between biology and the social construction of gender. *See generally* MARTHA MINOW, MAKING ALL THE DIFFERENCE: INCLUSION, EXCLUSION, AND AMERICAN LAW (1990); Martha Fineman, *Feminist Theory in Law: The Difference It Makes*, 2 COLUM. J. GENDER & L. 1 (1991); Christine A. Littleton, *Reconstructing Sexual Equality*, 75 CAL. L. REV. 1279 (1987); Martha Minow, *The Supreme Court, 1986 Terms—Foreword: Justice Engendered*, 101 HARV. L. REV. 10 (1987).

on sex" tends to place struggle against the oppression of women into the framework of liberal legal contest. If, as MacKinnon says, "discrimination 'based on sex'" is the legal theory embodying the "practice" of "experience 'as a woman,'"[69] then the passions and struggles of women's lives are inevitably whittled into concepts of "equality" and "discrimination" that imply some existence of a liberal norm of equality.[70]

MacKinnon is committed to and concerned with substantive equality, not merely with its legal forms. In a recent article, she begins to develop a vision of substantive equality on which to ground a theory of sex discrimination.[71] But the liberal legal notion of sex discrimination—which MacKinnon has shown to reproduce male norms, standards, and vision—still tends to make departure from the liberal norm the point of argument. First, the liberal concept asserts that there really is equality (except for women) out there somewhere. Then, it focuses our attention on what departs from that norm. The rhetorical demands of liberal legal argument can exercise a pull on MacKinnon's theory despite the depth of her critique.[72]

MacKinnon's work on sexual harassment, rape, and pornography has helped to expand social and legal recognition of harm to women, revealing the violence involved in subjugation and subordination, the sexualization of dominance and subordination, and their pervasive social effects. She has shown real genius at articulating harm to women. But to engage in transformative struggle within the legal system or outside it, articulating the harm is only part of the fight. We must discuss it in ways that do not continually put white women back at the center of the definition of harm. Only then can we develop both theory and a transformational struggle, based on the understanding, needs, and struggles of all women.

III. RACIAL CONSTRUCTION
AND WOMEN AS DIFFERENTIATED ACTORS

What is race? Race is also a social construct, a concept having no natural truth, no truth separate from historical development,[73] and possibly no truth comprehensible separately from domination. The term has meant different things in this country over time,[74] and its social and cultural meanings

---

69. MacKinnon, *Practice to Theory, supra* note 1, at 14.

70. As Kimberle Crenshaw has shown, the requirement that discrimination be "based on sex" has developed in law in ways that erase or directly disadvantage women of color. Crenshaw, *supra* note 22, at 150-52.

71. Catharine A. MacKinnon, *Reflections on Sex Equality Under Law*, 100 YALE L.J. 1281 (1991).

72. Crenshaw, *supra* note 22, at 167. This is why feminists so frequently cite AUDRE LORDE, *The Master's Tools Will Never Dismantle the Master's House, in* SISTER OUTSIDER 110 (1984) (emphasizing that working within legal doctrine affects feminist analysis).

73. *See, e.g.*, Michael Banton, *The Idiom of Race: A Critique of Presentism, in* RESEARCH IN RACE AND ETHNIC RELATIONS 21 (Cora Bagley Marret & Cheryl Leggon eds., 1980).

74. *Id.* at 22.

continue to shift and change within our own time.[75] In law as well as elsewhere in society, as Neil Gotanda has recently shown, the term "race" has been used to stand for several different concepts.[76] Even the Supreme Court, when faced with the question directly, had to recognize that "race" was a troublesome and contingent category that shifted over time.[77]

Race is a social construct. However, to say that something is socially constructed does not mean that it is not real or that we can just stop doing it.[78] And even if race is a set of beliefs and cultural meanings subject to change, it is not "just" an idea. The question is, What does it mean for race to be socially constructed. Race is not only skin color. Social rules and, at times, legal rules have determined racial identification as black when people are phenotypically white,[79] and some dark-skinned groups are not consistently socially defined as black in this country. The existence of the concept of "passing for white"—the word "passing"—is itself evidence that color is not race.

"Race" is partly about culture: some European cultures (as shown in recent events in Eastern Europe) have experienced something like racism from people with different cultures but similar skin-color. Race is partly about skin color: in the United States "race" has been anchored to an obsession with skin color and phenotype. And it is insistently about domination: the dominant group or culture uses its power to attempt to define and dominate the "other."[80]

---

75. MICHAEL OMI & HOWARD WINANT, RACIAL FORMATION IN THE UNITED STATES, FROM THE 1960s TO THE 1980s 11-13 (1985) (describing racial theory as being "shaped by actually existing race relations in any given historical period," always subject to contestation, and identifying a transition in the 1920s from biological and social Darwinian views of race to an ethnicity-based paradigm which was in turn challenged in the 1960s by class- and nation-based paradigms of race).

76. See Neil Gotanda, A Critique of "Our Constitution is Colorblind," 44 STAN. L. REV. 1, 4 (1991); see also Lawrence H. Tribe, The Puzzling Persistence of Process-Based Constitutional Theories, 89 YALE L.J. 1063, 1074 (1980).

77. St. Francis College v. Al-Khazraji, 481 U.S. 604, 608-13 (1987); Shaare Tefila Congregation v. Cobb, 481 U.S. 615, 617-18 (1987) (discussing whether Arabs and Jews were "distinct races" and thus "within the protection of" civil-rights statutes). Confronted by the indeterminacy of the concept of "race," the Court decided that the important question today is what legislators thought race was when the statutes were enacted. St. Francis and Shaare Tefila therefore stand for the proposition that the relevant social construction for civil rights law today is the archaic one.

78. Cf. Barbara Jeanne Fields, Slavery, Race and Ideology in the United States of America, 181 NEW LEFT REV. 93 (1990). Fields describes the indeterminate nature of race and the functioning of race as an ideology. She concludes, however, that the problem is the creation and re-creation of "race" in the present time by people as diverse as members of the Klan and "spokesmen for affirmative action." Id. at 117-18. MacKinnon has criticized a similar concept of indeterminacy, sometimes associated with the concept of social construction, by describing the powerful force of gender oppression as having "all the indeterminacy of a bridge abutment hit at sixty miles per hour." MACKINNON, FEMINIST THEORY OF THE STATE, supra note 19, at 123.

79. Race is built around skin color, yet skin color is not really determinative of race. Not all dark-skinned people are "black" and not all light-skinned people are "white." See OMI & WINANT, supra note 75, at 57 (describing Susie Guillory Phipps' challenge of a Louisiana law that quantified the racial identification of "black" as being anyone with at least one-thirty-second "Negro blood"); Judy Scales-Trent, Commonalities: On Being Black and White, Different, and the Same, 2 YALE J.L. & FEMINISM 305 (1990).

80. Some authors see "whiteness" as a claim of genetic purity. See, e.g., Gotanda, supra note 76, at 27. The concept of whiteness, however, is malleable in some ways: whites may acknowledge close familial relationship with some Native Americans while still perceiving themselves as "white." When I lived in Louisiana, I heard people who self-confidently considered themselves white say, "My grandmother

Perhaps dominance is actually the key here. The official rules that define "race" in America have been the white rules, even though the meaning of race has been contested in many ways,[81] and even though African-American culture has had a great, though generally unacknowledged, impact on white culture and perhaps on concepts of race as well.

If dominance/subordination is what turns "culture" into "race," does this then define the oppressed person or group as the mere object of the process of social construction?[82] White use of the term "race" is based on definitions of the "other" which imply a normal, neutral, objective, culture-less stance to whiteness.[83] This does not mean that white culture actually fully succeeds in defining the "other." The complex interactions of African-American self-assertion in black culture have a long history in the United States; white appropriation, commercialization, and transformation of parts of that culture have a complex history as well.[84] Nor does it mean only that whites concoct the dominant social definition of "other," imposing on society as much as possible our vision of the world, including our vision of people of color. Whites also define whiteness, albeit in ways that we cannot fully see, and then impose that vision on the world as much as we can.[85] If this process does not entirely persuade the rest of the world that our vision is "truth," it surely protects our own perceptions.

Anthropologist Renato Rosaldo describes "culture" as something one does not perceive oneself as having. Culture is something that is seen in someone else.[86] According to Rosaldo, culture is perceived in inverse proportion with power: the less full citizenship one possesses, the more "culture" one is likely

---

was a full-blooded Cherokee"—always a grandmother, always a Cherokee.

81. Consistent with an emphasis on domination/racism, Peter Jackson quotes Kevin Brown's suggestion that white academics with an interest in race focus on "analyses of white society, i.e., of racism." Peter Jackson, *The Ideology of "Race" and the Geography of Racism, in* RACE AND RACISM: ESSAYS IN SOCIAL GEOGRAPHY 3 (1987) (quoting Kevin Brown, *Race, Class and Culture: Towards a Theorization of the "Choice/Constraint" Concept, in* SOCIAL INTERACTION AND ETHNIC SEGREGATION 185, 198 (P. Jackson & S.J. Smith eds., 1981)).

82. In fact, the African-American experience demonstrates (even more keenly than debates between cultural and radical feminists) the importance of the struggle for a positive ground within oppressed culture. *See, e.g.,* Thomas, *supra* note 7, at 2615 (describing culture as "the site in which African-Americans have historically sought to make sense of, and respond to, their experience in the United States").

83. Feeling culture-less may lead you to crave the "Other" to transform yourself, as bell hooks has recently pointed out about contemporary white culture's interest in black culture. BELL HOOKS, *Eating the Other: Desire and Resistance, in* BLACK LOOKS: RACE AND REPRESENTATION 21 (1992). But this does not mean that you really *are* without culture, only that your own (dominant) culture is invisible to you and the "Other" sought for variety.

84. *Id.* at 21-28 (on commodification and exploitation of ideas of blackness and the "Other").

85. This does not mean that those defined outside the circle of whiteness cannot see whiteness, or are not actors in profound and important ways. There is not just one reality of race to be seen by anyone. But what we see and what we fail to see are integral parts of privilege, and whites can afford not to see much about whiteness at all. *Cf.* BELL HOOKS, *Representations of Whiteness in the Black Imagination, in* BLACK LOOKS: RACE AND REPRESENTATION, *supra* note 83, at 165; *see also* text accompanying note 157 *infra.*

86. RENATO ROSALDO, CULTURE AND TRUTH: THE REMAKING OF SOCIAL ANALYSIS (1988). *Cf.* Mari Matsuda, *Voices of America: Accent, Antidiscrimination Law, and a Jurisprudence for the Last Reconstruction,* 100 YALE L.J. 1329 (1991) (indicating that we hear accents in others but not in ourselves).

to have.[87] What we ourselves do and think is the way we are, normal and neutral, like the air we breathe, transparent to us—not "culture."[88] Rosaldo uses an example drawn from Francis FitzGerald's work on the people of Sun City, Arizona. Residents repeatedly remarked upon the lively, accepting atmosphere in which nobody cared about your background. They saw great diversity among themselves but failed to note that the men were virtually all retired professionals, the women virtually all housewives, most of the residents Protestant, Republican, white, and conservative.[89]

In a reflective working paper, Peggy McIntosh explores the ways in which it is difficult for people who are privileged to see or understand their privilege.[90] Realizing that even men who are committed to women's liberation have difficulty seeing their own male privilege, McIntosh began consciously seeking to understand the ways in which she had been taught to accept life structured around privilege that she had also been taught not to see. To begin the project of learning to see, she listed forty-six ways that she identified the daily effects of white privilege in her life. McIntosh says she found all of these effects of privilege extremely subtle and forgot them repeatedly until she wrote them down.

The list includes things that happen because she is white and things that do not happen because she is white. It includes the ability to go shopping alone, pretty well assured that she will not be followed or harassed;[91] the ability to use checks, credit cards or cash as she chooses without her skin color working against the appearance of financial reliability; the ability to arrange to protect her children most of the time from people who might not like them, and the fact that she does not need to educate her children to be aware of systemic racism for their own daily physical protection.[92] She can arrange her activities so that she will never have to experience feelings of rejection owing to her race,[93] and she can speak in public to a powerful male group without putting her race on trial.[94]

McIntosh conceptualizes her white privilege as an invisible, "weightless knapsack of special provisions, assurances, maps, tools, guides, codebooks, passports, visas, clothes, compass, emergency gear, and blank checks."[95] Her

---

87. *Id.* at 198-99.
88. *Id.* at 198.
89. *Id.* at 203.
90. PEGGY MCINTOSH, WHITE PRIVILEGE AND MALE PRIVILEGE: A PERSONAL ACCOUNT OF COMING TO SEE CORRESPONDENCES THROUGH WORK IN WOMEN'S STUDIES (Wellesley College Center for Research on Women Working Paper No. 189, 1988). For a thoughtful exploration of whiteness and transparency, see Barbara J. Flagg, *"Was Blind, But Now I See": White Race Consciousness and the Requirement of Discriminatory Intent,* 91 MICH. L. REV. 953 (1993).
91. MCINTOSH, *supra* note 90, at 5. *Cf. infra* note 127 (discussing security personnel in department stores).
92. *Id.* at 6.
93. *Id.* at 9.
94. *Id.* at 7.
95. *Id.* at 2.

knapsack includes both unearned assets (things that should be entitlements of humanity and that everyone should have in a just society, but which in fact are awarded to the dominant race) and unearned power that is systematically conferred (those things that are damaging in human terms even as they bring advantage and are associated only with dominance, such as the freedom not to be concerned about the needs, culture, or reality of others). There is a social, physical analogue to this invisible knapsack, namely, the invisible conveniences structured into the development of American cities: location of transit and other municipal services, and even the plotting of streets, have often been planned to serve white neighborhoods and preserve their whiteness.[96]

Part of white privilege, therefore, is not seeing all we have and all we do,[97] and not seeing how what we do appears to those defined into the category "other." Whites cannot just opt out of the process of formation of this racial consciousness that takes the form of unconsciousness.[98] This can be painful. For example, note the feeling of exclusion that arises when white college students notice that black students all sit together—but don't also notice that the white students all sit together. And whiteness can re-create itself without the conscious will to exclude, as when people interview and hire through friends and acquaintances and find desirable candidates to be others like themselves.[99]

This country is both highly segregated and based on a concept of whiteness as "normal." It is therefore hard for white people to see whiteness both when we interact with people who are not socially defined as white and when we interact with other white people, when race doesn't seem to be involved. White women see ourselves as acting as individuals rather than as members of a culture in part because we do not see much of the dominant culture at all. Our own lives are therefore part of a racialized world in ways we do not see. This happens when we interact with people of color thinking we are acting as individuals but are in fact acting as part of a white pattern. It also happens when we interact with other white people in ways that seem attached to individuality, humanity, or personhood, but that are not consistently accorded to people who are not white. These interactions with other white people are a circumstance that arises with some frequency because of urban, occupational, and social segregation.

---

96. I am grateful to Jonathan Simon for reminding me of this point. Telephone Interview with Jonathan Simon (May 1993).

97. Cf. Crenshaw, supra note 22, at 151 (only downward departures from equality are noticeable in legal cases on discrimination; white privilege does not see itself).

98. In his critique of the intent requirement in equal-protection cases, Charles Lawrence points out that much racism is unconscious. Lawrence, supra note 6. The process of the construction of race that I am describing here is not just individual racism (conscious or unconscious), but the selective unconsciousness about race in which whiteness is not visible to whites even though whites are extremely conscious of non-whiteness. Nor is it possible to solve the painful consciousness of race by deciding not to recognize it. Gotanda, supra note 76, at 16-23 (describing the myth and impossibility of nonrecognition of race in American society).

99. Rodney Thaxton, Racism & Its Use of Myths, MIAMI HERALD, May 17, 1992, at C1.

This is where the difficulty of seeing whiteness intersects the idea that gender is defined by what is taken from us. Both contribute to perpetuating the invisibility to ourselves of our particular experience of privilege as white women. Seeing only harm hampers our vision of women as actors. Further, seeing women's work in social reproduction (cleaning, cooking, caring, and more) as inherently inauthentic contributes to denying dignity in this work;[100] treating it as unimportant hides the ways in which reproductive labor has been racially structured in our society as a result of the effort to minimize its oppressiveness.[101]

Women's consistently gendered participation in the world takes place in many ways. We bear the children and, for the most part, we raise them. We work at home, in businesses, or both: either we simply do both sorts of work, or our work merges the home with the market (as in some forms of piecework, telephone solicitation, childcare for pay, and cosmetics sales). Our work is reproduction and production, sex and labor, sex as labor, and combinations of them all.

The lines between women's individual lives, emotionality, and work are often blurred.[102] Emotional work—the commodification of care that is part of the task of social workers, waitresses, flight attendants, and sex workers—is a crucial part of service work as well as a way to sell for wages skills that women cultivate as part of social roles.[103] Also, women have been responsible in many ways for the emotional and spiritual glue that holds life together. Care and love involve both sentiment and work. It is particularly the province of women to create care and love and to create from whatever materials are at hand a supportable or pleasant environment—both a domestic environment, including responsibility for others,[104] and a community environment, including church congregations, PTAs, and so on—within which people are cared for and loved, and human growth transpires.

Even if women feel some of these interests as our own,[105] we live out

---

100. BELL HOOKS, *Re-thinking the Nature of Work*, *in* FEMINIST THEORY FROM MARGIN TO CENTER, 95, 102-05 (1984).

101. *See* Glenn, *supra* note 48, at 7.

102. On false distinctions between family and the rest of society, *see generally* Frances Olsen, *The Family and the Market: A Study of Ideology and Legal Reform*, 96 HARV. L. REV. 1497 (1983).

103. *See, e.g.*, ARLIE RUSSELL HOCHSCHILD, THE MANAGED HEART: COMMERCIALIZATION OF HUMAN FEELING (1983).

104. In addition to child care, women have care of the aging forced upon us. "The average American mother spends seventeen years caring for children and eighteen years caring for elderly parents, both her own and her husband's." Williams, *supra* note 52, at 1598. Despite the oppressive nature of this assignment to women of care and services, we may well find it important that those who bore and raised us receive adequate care—in which case we need to find a way to value the physical and emotional work involved. It is not clear how care can or should be valued without sentimentalizing or perpetuating oppression, given the oppressive social assignment of this work to women and the ways it has been internalized among women, but failing to value it leaves us unable to answer the complexity of these questions of love, care, and responsibility.

105. Distinctions between choice and constraint also blur. *See generally* Williams, *supra* note 52; Abrams, *supra* note 26 (discussing social images of choice and determinism). The sensation of choice under conditions of oppression can be false consciousness, but MacKinnon, in emphasizing what women are

the effort to achieve them in an oppressive world. Women may want children, raise them gladly, and love them dearly, yet find maternal roles both enforced and restricted, and find possibilities constrained—not only for ourselves, but because motherhood means raising children in an oppressive world. We may want sex and be sexual, yet find our sexual expression coerced and distorted and its consequences hurtful.[106] If we want love or family, and harm and pain make us stop seeking them, this adjustment is obviously not neutral but an active state of withdrawal from which we may again try to venture later on.[107]

Stephanie Wildman recently called on MacKinnon to deepen her work to include motherhood.[108] Wildman is correct about the importance of children in the lives of the majority of women. But motherhood is not easily incorporated into MacKinnon's vision because it is in some tension with her emphasis on what is done to women.[109] Pregnancy, in contrast, is consistent with her emphasis on women as the objects of male domination, in part because it is a consequence of sexual intercourse with a man, and fits with a vision of woman's-body-done-to-by-a-man.[110] But raising children is both

programmed to want undervalues the complexity that many women experience. Her focus precludes authenticity when what women pursue is something society has assigned to women, including the bearing and rearing of children, heterosexual sex, and long-term caring relationships with aging parents. *See* MACKINNON, FEMINIST THEORY OF THE STATE, *supra* note 19, at 102.

106. *See* Littleton, *supra* note 19, at 772 (criticizing the way in which MacKinnon collapses the categories of "use" and "abuse" by men), and Finley, *supra* note 26, at 378-84 (criticizing MacKinnon's emphasis on the sexual victimization of women).

107. *See, e.g.,* MARY ANN DUTTON, EMPOWERING AND HEALING THE BATTERED WOMAN 65-70 (1992) (discussing difficulties women have after abuse, including loss of sense of personal safety, difficulties with trust, and difficulties with relationships).

108. Wildman, *supra* note 26, at 446-47.

109. MacKinnon is against forced motherhood, because we should be able to want our children, but emphasizes women's lack of ability to choose whether to have sex or to choose to use contraception rather than the contradictions women face when we want children. CATHARINE A. MACKINNON, *Not by Law Alone: From a Debate with Phyllis Schlafly, in* FEMINISM UNMODIFIED, *supra* note 2, at 28-29.

110. Defining women by the taking of our sexuality also fails to address the ways in which women's actions in the world meet with interactive oppression: we can't work because we lack adequate or even inadequate child care; we can't earn enough to live decently by caring for the children or aging parents of others; we are excluded from work altogether not only as women but as members of communities that do not have adequate work for women or men; we "choose" whether or not to continue pregnancies based on whether or not we fear loss of jobs or have inadequate income to support children we are now raising. Some of the most brutal recent oppression of women in this country has occurred in the area of welfare "reform," built around this multiple participation in the world and exclusion from work and care. Women rearing children on inadequate incomes without men are stigmatized for having children and punished by the deprivation of income in the event they have additional children. *See generally,* Martha A. Fineman, *Images of Mothers in Poverty Discourses,* 1991 DUKE L.J. 274.

The term "welfare" is so often identified with black women that it is common to see "welfare" used as a "code word" for "black." *See, e.g.,* Monte Piliawsky, *Racial Politics in the 1988 Presidential Election,* 20 BLACK SCHOLAR 30 (1989). While this hides both the unemployment of white women and the productivity of black working women, the oppression is not symmetrical because of the particular stigma perpetrated by linking the concepts of black and unemployed/unemployable. In recent welfare-reform discourses, all the functions that society calls "womanly"—heterosexual sex, child rearing, home care—are treated as if dysfunctional for women on welfare. This is especially ironic since the oppression of women of color has historically included holding up a white ideal of female domesticity to women whose lives always required them to work extensively outside the home. *See, e.g.,* Patricia Hill Collins, *The Meaning of Motherhood in Black Culture and Black Mother-Daughter Relationships, in* DOUBLE STITCH: BLACK WOMEN WRITE ABOUT MOTHERS & DAUGHTERS 42, 43-44 (Patricia Bell-Scott et al. eds., 1991).

creative and oppressed. Understanding motherhood therefore requires a vision of women as actors in the world—shaping children's lives, struggling to meet the tasks society hands them with the resources available—as well as trapped with children in a system of male domination.

In MacKinnon's vision of feminism, pornography is a central and useful paradigm of the oppression of women.[111] Consistent with the focus on the construction of women's sexuality by men, it is a "taking" of women's sexuality: women are objectified and sexually used in the production process, in the artifact of pornography, and (individually and culturally) as an effect of the consumption of pornography. In describing the harm of pornography, MacKinnon's work has had the positive effect of linking the women whose images are used in making pornography with the women who are directly and immediately affected by its consumption, and these women with all women through its impact on society and culture.

Making pornography the framework within which to examine the oppression of women of many races and ethnic groups, however, inevitably limits the scope of feminist analysis. MacKinnon seems to treat whiteness as specific and to avoid equating the experience of white women with that of all women; she asserts that in pornography whiteness is not "unmarked" but "a specific sexual taste."[112] Asian, Latina, black, white, Jewish, disabled, all become subsets of women in pornography, variously stereotyped as particular sexual tastes.[113] What is done to white women appears particular because vicious acts of sexual exploitation against white women are described and then identified as the least that is done to all women.[114]

Making pornography the paradigm locates the process of racial construction entirely outside of the actions of women. Choosing an example in which all women are objectified and sexually used hides the ways in which women interact with each other and the ways that, as we struggle to survive and construct lives in the world under conditions of oppression, a racially constructed society shapes our actions and our lives by race. Making pornography the paradigm also ensures that sexual exploitation of all women will again seem the central discovery. Therefore, the paradigm of pornography implicitly provides support for the equation of whiteness with the least-bad-things-done-to-women,[115] rather than treating whiteness as part of a complex world of power, privilege, oppression, and struggle.

To better understand women as actors differentiated by race, I want to look at areas outside pornography where women have historically been oppressed

---

111. This paradigm seems particularly useful for a feminist theory that defines women as those from whom sex is taken.

112. MacKinnon, *Practice to Theory*, *supra* note 1, at 21.

113. *Id.* at 20-21 (describing pornographic images of African-American women as animals, enslaved, caged and insatiable; Asian women as passive, tortured and inert; Latinas as "hot mommas").

114. *Id.* at 21 ("What is done to white women is a kind of floor; it is the best anyone is treated and it runs from Playboy through sadomasochism to snuff").

115. *Id.* ("This is what privilege as a woman gets you: most valued as dead meat.")

and have tried to solve the problems posed by that oppression: housework, and access to money and credit. First, I would like to shift the paradigm of oppression to housework, beginning with the part of this story that is about meeting fundamental needs—the part that parallels "humanly struggling" in Marxism: it is pleasant to live in a clean house; it is necessary for health to live in a house that is not extremely dirty; houses do not clean themselves.[116] Housework is therefore a human need—one that is oppressively assigned to women. Domestic services (as well as sexual access) are often brutally enforced within marriages and in social expectation.

To accomplish having a clean house and to cope with the oppressive assignment of household work to women, some women employ other women to do significant amounts of household work.[117] The historical and contemporary relationships of white women and women of color with regard to housework are noted only ironically and in passing in MacKinnon's essay.[118] White women have employed women of color in the privatized, isolated context of the individual white woman's home. With some justification, MacKinnon might emphasize the framework of oppression here: these services are oppressively assigned to women, and most white women do the housework for their own households and have no resources to do otherwise. Also, sexual predations by white men against women of color in white homes[119] were not committed by white women, were committed against white women household workers, and caused pain to white women as well as women of color.

But many women of color have worked for many white women over time. Historically, the domestic employment of women of color by white women has been culturally important to many women of color, and women of color have fought hard to keep their daughters from going into household employment.[120] This racial employment relationship was known as important in the experience of women of color in ways that were not comparable or symmetrical for white women. First, relatively economically privileged white women were the ones who more often employed domestic workers.[121] The world in which many white women employ women of color to do housework

---

116. I know this, because I've been waiting all my life and they haven't started yet.

117. In a recent article, Evelyn Nakano Glenn analyzes the way that the activities of *social reproduction* (purchasing household goods, preparing and serving food, laundering and repairing clothing, maintaining furnishings and appliances, and care for children and the elderly) have been organized by race and ethnicity in the United States. Glenn, *supra* note 48, at 6-19 (on the racial structure of private domestic work) and 19-31 (on the racial division of public reproductive labor).

118. "Miss Anne of the kitchen . . . complains about the colored help . . . can't do anything, doesn't do anything . . . ." MacKinnon, *Practice to Theory, supra* note 1, at 19.

119. *See, e.g.,* Barbara Omolade, *Black Women, Black Men, and Tawana Brawley—The Shared Condition,* 12 Harv. Women's L.J. 11, 14 (1989) (quoting Gerda Lerner, Black Women in White America: A Documentary History 156 (1973)).

120. Glenn, *supra* note 48, at 18-19.

121. At particular historic times, white women have more commonly hired women of color as domestic help and benefitted from the oppressive labor structures that kept women of color available for work at such low wages. *Id.* at 6-11.

will be generally invisible to the many white women who never employ (and whose mothers never employed) household help.[122] Second, white women who did employ household help could generally maintain the almost magical invisibility of dominance to itself—household workers, not their white employers, were the issue for white women.

Privileged identity requires reinforcement and maintenance, but not seeing the mechanisms that reinforce and maintain privilege is an important component of privilege. In responding to MacKinnon's discussion of white women, Cathy Powell emphasized the subordination of women of color in the labor market, and recounted the experience of her grandmother, a black woman who had little contact with white women while growing up in a family that survived on subsistence farming, "until she later moved to New York where she worked as a domestic for a wealthy white family. She has told me how degrading this experience was in both gender and racial terms."[123] Although employment of people of color to perform domestic service has been important to white dominance,[124] it seems unlikely that women from the wealthy white family would tell their grandchildren about the employment of the black domestic worker as an important part of their experience of their race and gender. These different learned cultural truths—and the power that backs them—have made it possible for white women not to see the ways in which women of color have experienced employment interactions with white women.

In an essay in Alice Childress's book *Like One of the Family*, a domestic worker describes a white woman who fiercely clutches her purse whenever the black housekeeper is anywhere on the premises.[125] Mildred, the narrator, makes a pointed response by leaving on an errand without her own purse, then racing back anxiously and grabbing her purse theatrically—she also protests directly.[126] This white woman's behavior is so patently ugly, so viciously racist, that it is almost too easy an example of racist interaction. It shows her hostility, her fear, and her privilege to act on them offensively. It is consistent with a picture of black people as dishonest, with white women who grab their purses tighter when a black man walks by on the street, with many vicious racist stereotypes.

---

122. Some white women have historically done housework for others; most white women today do not hire household help. This difference in visibility and social understanding of one's experience is part of what we mean when we say "minority": a "minority" experience happens to fewer people, as well as having less social visibility and power. *Id.* at 9, 33; JACQUELINE JONES, LABOR OF LOVE, LABOR OF SORROW: BLACK WOMEN, WORK, AND THE FAMILY FROM SLAVERY TO THE PRESENT 74 (1985); BETTE WOODY, BLACK WOMEN IN THE WORKPLACE: IMPACTS OF STRUCTURAL CHANGE IN THE ECONOMY 52-53 (1992).

123. Letter from Cathy Powell, *Open Letters to Catharine MacKinnon*, 4 YALE J. L. & FEMINISM 189 (1991).

124. Glenn, *supra* note 48, at 9, 32.

125. ALICE CHILDRESS, *The Pocketbook Game, in* LIKE ONE OF THE FAMILY: CONVERSATIONS FROM A DOMESTIC'S LIFE 26 (1956).

126. *Id.* at 27 ("Later, when I was leavin' she says real timid-like, 'Mildred, I hope that you don't think I distrust you because . . .' I cut her off real quick. . . . 'That's all right, Mrs E . . . I understand. 'Cause if I paid anybody as little as you pay me, I'd hold my pocketbook too!").

But the white woman could conceivably have seen herself as motivated not solely by race or not by race at all. She could think, maybe without self-delusion, that she would also grab her purse when a white household worker came in—and not think about whether she would learn to hide her purse to avoid embarrassing that white woman. She could think these things and not see where she fit in a world of white women who treat black women as potentially dishonest, and white people who treat black people as dishonest and dangerous (like security personnel who follow black people through stores to monitor against shoplifting).[127] She could protect her purse without seeing where she fit in a world of white power which creates different job paths for black women and white women, so that black women were for many years forced into domestic work by exclusion from many other forms of employment. Especially important, she could act without seeing where she fit among the several simultaneous white employers of that particular black woman, including the white women who said they just "loved" the maid and claimed she was "like one of the family,"[128] and the white woman who tried to extract extra unpaid work by juggling work days and pay schedules,[129] and all the others.

Those attributes of whiteness were invisible to that white woman. She could possibly think to herself, "I never let anyone else (strangers, delivery people, maybe even neighbors) stay in the room with my purse." But she also never let anyone else have the mobility in her home without trust or closeness that many domestic workers have, an intimacy in the flotsam of household activities and the jetsam of bodily functions: old letters, food wrappers, Tampax, and the myriad things that turn up in laundry and garbage.

Each white woman who tightens the grip on her purse when a black man approaches on the street, or who acts uneasy when a black person enters an elevator,[130] may see herself as acting as an individual in response to a dangerous other, but she is part of a pattern to those defined outside the circle of whiteness. These examples, however, still have aspects of what we usually

---

127. *See, e.g.*, Lena Williams, *When Blacks Shop, Bias Often Accompanies Sale*, N.Y. TIMES, Apr. 30, 1991, at A1 (describing the pervasiveness of discriminatory treatment of black people in stores and other public places, including the experiences of Julianne Malveaux, a professor at the University of California at Berkeley, who was accused of switching tags on a dress at Saks Fifth Avenue in New York; Cedric Holloway, a 20-year-old black man who was arrested at gunpoint while he read brochures about money-market accounts in his car outside a bank in Florida; and Daniel Lamaute, a business consultant who narrowly escaped arrest by police at an airport in Denver).

128. CHILDRESS, *supra* note 125, at 1-3.

129. ALICE CHILDRESS, *I Hate Days Off*, in LIKE ONE OF THE FAMILY: CONVERSATIONS FROM A DOMESTIC'S LIFE, *supra* note 125, at 97-98.

130. Searching for an anecdote about women of color riding in an elevator who are treated with fear and hostility by white women, I found in works by African-American women several anecdotes in which elevators were described as the site of tense or hostile racial interactions. *See, e.g.*, Peggy C. Davis, *Law as Microaggression*, 98 YALE L.J. 1559 (1989); Jewelle Gomez, *Repeat After Me: We Are Different, We Are the Same*, 14 N.Y.U. REV. L. & SOC. CHANGE 935 (1986). *Cf.* WILLIAMS, THE ALCHEMY OF RACE AND RIGHTS, 76 (1991) (hypothetical illustrating a race-reversed version of the Bernard Goetz case, in which a black man in an elevator shoots some white men because he feels threatened by them).

call racism. In each case, the white woman is acting on her sense of black people and reacting to black people. Privilege also often exists for the white woman as an individual (for example, being waited on promptly in stores, or not being assumed to be a representative of her race) when she need not see the event as a matter of "race" at all.[131]

One of the most important characteristics of whiteness in modern society is the way in which white people can have little contact with people of color. We live in a society that is profoundly geographically segregated. Many white people live predominantly white lives without being more than intermittently conscious of "choosing" whiteness—or may live this way without ever consciously choosing whiteness if instead the person is choosing a "good neighborhood." The cultural values surrounding this segregation—the set of values in which white neighborhoods and "good" neighborhoods come together—are part of the oppression of people of color, and these values are also part of the construction of race itself.[132]

Therefore, part of the experience of white women in this racially constructed society is that we may live where we have minimal interactions with people of color. Then the issue is one of the social construction of race: how living this way shapes white women and shapes a cultural phenomenon of whiteness. This can be particularly important because of our feeling of vulnerability as women, which leads to a quest for safety that we cannot really achieve and tends to reinforce emphasis on "good neighborhoods" and "safe areas." Since we cannot sort away from men and the dangers they pose, we may accept social markers that treat "safety" as equivalent with whiteness, reflecting and reinforcing racism.

Women have historically lacked access to money and property, and equal access to credit was a component of the modern women's movement. (The recent introduction of commercials for dual-signature travelers checks shows how long a struggle this has been.) Once money, checking accounts, or credit cards have been secured, however, their usefulness and the experience of using them differentiates by race.

Imagine a line of women with checkbooks in hand at a cash register. The white woman writes a check or pulls out her credit card and charges a purchase. Black women often encounter much more difficulty in ordinary commercial transactions,[133] and the black woman who comes to the cash

---

131. Peggy McIntosh mentions a related phenomenon: she was raised to see herself as an individual and not as part of a culture. McIntosh, *supra* note 90, at 4.

132. The concept of "white" as employed, employable, and competent is in part a product of the access to employment in white neighborhoods; the concept of black as unemployed/unemployable follows patterns of urban development that segregated urban areas by race, deprived black neighborhoods of jobs, and then defined these neighborhoods as filled with unemployables known by their blackness. *See generally* WILLIAM JULIUS WILSON, THE TRULY DISADVANTAGED (1987); Martha Mahoney, Note, *Law and Racial Geography: Public Housing and the Economy in New Orleans*, 42 STAN. L. REV. 1251 (1990).

133. *See, e.g.*, Williams, *supra* note 127, describing the experience of actress and television producer Debbie Allen, who found a white clerk in a Beverly Hills store unwilling to show her merchandise and certain that, because she was black, she could not afford anything in the store.

register next has her identity and her credit card questioned. In the first transaction, the woman cashing the check is actually experiencing life as a white woman—but from her vantage point, all she did was cash a check, not conduct a racial transaction.[134] And in the second transaction, the woman who has trouble cashing the check is actually experiencing life as a black woman. She is more likely to know it as a racial transaction, or constantly be forced to suspect it or to ignore the issue of why this happened this time—and all these levels of consciousness are part of that experience of a black woman cashing a check.[135] Part of the first transaction was the white woman's whiteness—and that is the invisible part. Both of these transactions are part of the construction of race, but white people have difficulty seeing exchanges with other white people as race-charged.

As a white single mother, my parenting was socially suspect (as when my daughter's second-grade teacher commented that it was fortunate that she had a new friend, because the new girl's home had "structure," which he explained meant "two parents").[136] Compared with black single mothers I knew, however, my suspect competence seemed less policed (white neighbors in mostly white university communities did not call the authorities when my children cried at night, and accidents to my children were less likely to be treated as possible abuse). My children were less likely to be seen as "streetwise" for curiosity or insight (no one who knew all the children thought mine more intelligent or more sheltered).[137] Questions about family were structured to imply less insult ("do the children see their father?" as against

---

134. *Cf.* McIntosh, *supra* note 90, at 6 (white privilege in using checks). In my seminar, after reading the McIntosh working paper on white privilege, black students sometimes tell check or credit stories of their own; for example, an African-Caribbean woman had experienced rejection of her check by a store clerk despite showing a driver's license and her American Express Card. But white students have not had stories to tell about check cashing, presumably because what they experienced seemed not "privilege" but business as usual.

Also, there is the "rules were made to be broken" phenomenon. My sister, Joan Mahoney, uses a drive-through banking window at which a sign announces that drivers' licenses must be presented to the teller. She does not send her license in and has never been asked to show it, even when receiving cash from tellers she did not know. As a white woman driving a late model Toyota Camry, her race and class insulate her from the operation of "rules" which can be "impartially" invoked any other time. Telephone Interview with Joan Mahoney (Jan. 1993). On commercial interactions, see also Ian Ayres, *Fair Driving: Gender and Race Discrimination in Retail Car Negotiations*, 104 HARV. L. REV. 817 (1991).

135. There is a parallel here to situations in which white women walking down the street clutch their purses when a black man approaches. Many white women tell me in conversation that they clutch their purses when any man who is not perceptibly elderly approaches. Even if these women accurately perceive their own patterns of behavior (and do not underestimate the times they fail to notice white men on the street, for example) their actions have social meanings created by the actions of others and of society. To white men walking down the street, these actions are usually not part of a pattern of fearful-acting white women nor a pattern of social treatment of these men as dishonest, dangerous, criminal. To black men walking down the street, the women's actions are part of those patterns *and* part of a social script about the dangers of black men to white women.

136. He may have implicitly meant two white parents, or else he had not noticed her other friend who had two black parents, a construction contractor and a schoolteacher, present in the home and active around the school.

137. Black women live with the necessity to educate their children about racism. This has a powerful, particularized impact on the relationships between black women and their children. Collins, *supra* note 110, at 52-57.

"do the children know their father?").

My status as a white single parent pursuing graduate and professional education was sometimes seen as noble (for example, some attorneys saw going to law school while raising children as heroic, although the secretaries in their firms who worked while raising children were not considered heroes). I fought to establish my analytical abilities against an aura of maternal worthiness which dominant society does not usually perceive simultaneously with the perception of keen intelligence. The maternal image was not affected by the risk of being seen as too strong, part of a pattern of social dysfunction or unhealthy matriarchy in my community.[138] The struggle to win recognition of ability is different where there is a race-privileged presumption of intelligence rather than a racial slur on intelligence.[139]

The fact that I experienced oppression does not constitute proof that women who are single mothers experience oppression (the experience of women of color would be sufficient proof) nor was it the "floor" of oppression for single mothers (for example, I had less financial resources than some single mothers and more than many). Rather, both my experience and my friends'[140] experiences were particular to the social construction of our identities.[141] But mere recognition of diversity of experience does not fill in the picture: I did not see myself as a "white single mother," and I believe the privilege of not noticing one's race as a single mother is absent for black women.[142] My status had no common race-specific phrase. Nothing brought to my attention that portion of how I was treated which was in accord with societal norms. The opposite was true: although my whiteness was invisible, many events and interactions showed me that I faced stigma and struggle. Most important, nothing would have told me that I was experiencing "privilege," and nothing would have shown me that whiteness was part of the picture, had I not been simultaneously hearing the experience of women of color. Like the white woman cashing a check, I would know only whatever it took for me to get there, and I would take the money and go.

---

138. *See* Austin, *supra* note 21, at 566-67.

139. Also, neighbors did not respond to my academic successes with rumors about my sex life. I am not saying that these things do not happen to white women, but that they did not happen to me. This is consistent with women of different races and ethnicities being differently constructed in cultural imagination, a point made by MacKinnon and also by Harris, *supra* note 4, and SPELMAN, *supra* note 16, among others.

140. For white people discussing race, mention of friendship has acquired a bad name. It reeks of a 1950s liberalism in which the claim that "some of my best friends are black" is a way of saying "I am not racist." But what I have learned about race has come mostly from friends, from listening to the few women of color with whom I have been close share their thoughts and feelings, and from watching their lives unfold alongside my own. I believe that discounting the transformative potential in friendship perpetuates the societal devaluation of any love that is not heterosexually sexual and the devaluation of affection between women generally.

141. As students, we shared to some extent in class privilege.

142. Though again there are likely to be quite different constructions of "single mother" in the social construction of different cultural groups.

IV. WHAT IS A WHITE WOMAN ANYWAY? V.
WHAT SHOULD WHITE WOMEN DO?

MacKinnon's reductive method of identifying the oppression of women insistently reproduces a white norm: strip out all "other" forms of oppression, identify the woman who is "not poor or working class or lesbian or Jewish or disabled or old or young," and this white woman who "does not share her oppression with any man"[143] experiences oppression from men, which becomes a "particularly sensitive indicator of the degree to which women, as such, are despised."[144] She argues that this does not make white women's condition "any more definitive of the meaning of 'women' than the condition of any other woman is." Rather, "trivializing" the oppression of this woman (oppression that is not racist, anti-Semitic, or otherwise-oppressed) is "anti-woman."[145]

There are two problems here. First, identifying women as differentiated actors is not the same as trivializing the oppression of women. MacKinnon recognizes additional hardships and burdens and the particular oppression of women of color, differentiating women by degrees and types of oppression. She agrees white women are less oppressed. But she hears discussion of racial privilege in white women as "trivializing" or denying gender oppression,[146] which then seems "anti-woman." Counterposing "privileged" and "oppressed," creating a sharp dichotomy of woman as oppressed or not oppressed, creates a false distinction that reflects the problems of the additive approach to oppression criticized by other feminists, in which various distinct sorts of oppression are seen as added together (gender plus race), rather than reckoning with the complexity of interlocking systems of power.[147] Also, the additive approach tends to make relations among women invisible or unimportant, when they are part of the construction of race and require attention fundamental to transformative struggle.

Second, although I am sure MacKinnon does not mean to take white women as typical women, this method still asserts there is some core truth to gender oppression arrived at by taking away "other" oppressions. There follows the implication that the woman with other-features-that-also-face-oppression stripped away can be fairly or usefully understood as "woman" in

---

143. MacKinnon, *Practice to Theory, supra* note 1, at 22 (emphasis omitted).
144. *Id.*
145. *Id.*
146. This perception is reflected in the ironic subtitle of her essay, *What is a white woman anyway?* and in the tone that marks the passages on white women, quoted *supra* notes 12 and 18.
147. See discussion, *supra* note 16, of feminist criticism of the additive treatment of oppression. The conceptual problem here is that "oppressed" should not be treated as the opposite of the category "privileged." The opposite of "oppressed" is "free"—or, given a history and contemporary reality of oppression and struggle, "liberated." Privilege is a concept that can describe many types of hierarchy and subordination, not consistently interchangeable with either "not-oppressed" or "oppressor." The white woman cashing a check is privileged though she may experience economic oppression herself. *See supra* text accompanying notes 133-35. I am grateful to Christine Littleton for her clarifying insight on this point.

her oppression and not as contingent and particular, not peculiarly white, middle-class, Christian, and so on.[148]

MacKinnon seeks to hold onto this reductive method of determining the existence of oppression "as a woman," the oppression of women "as such," and simultaneously to hold onto the principle that building theory out of the necessarily diverse practice of women will make feminist theory incorporate the diversity of women and the multiplicity of women's experience. She thinks she can have both reduction and diversity because she looks at the experience of women by focusing on what is done to women. As a social thinker, she can grasp the social construction of race as well as gender, but the resulting view of white women is in tension with her concepts of gender as constructed by what men see and do. Only if woman is defined by what is done to her—only if "that which is most one's own [is that which is] taken away"[149] and "you are made who you are by that which is taken away from you by the social relations the theory criticizes"[150]—can we reach this view in which "woman" is not a historically and socially specific actor but a being from which all "other" oppression has been stripped away and some oppression remains.

It is this view which leads MacKinnon to confuse discussions of privilege in white women with the concept of white-woman-not-oppressed. Although it is not entirely clear to whom MacKinnon is responding in her article, she seems to read recent works that emphasize the diversity and particularity of women's experience as denials of the experience of women's oppression. Angela Harris,[151] Kimberle Crenshaw,[152] Elizabeth Spelman,[153] and other feminists who have criticized the tendency of some white feminists to center feminist theory around the experience of white women,[154] have not denied that women are oppressed on the basis of gender, that white women experience gender oppression, or that gender oppression is an important issue. Rather, these are feminist assertions that the experience of being a woman of color

---

148. This approach has some similarity to the self-described "suburban women" who discovered that comfort only hid their "essential powerlessness and oppression," of whom MacKinnon wrote that the "place of consciousness in social construction is often most forcefully illustrated in the least materially deprived women, because the contrast between their economic conditions and their feminist consciousness can be so vivid." MACKINNON, FEMINIST THEORY OF THE STATE, *supra* note 19, at 92. Despite the diversity of many consciousness-raising groups, *id.* at 84-85, the "suburban women" were historically specific people. If a camera focused on a 1970s CR meeting in one of those suburban homes had risen up and pulled away in an aerial shot of the neighborhood, the viewer would have seen suburbs built during the 1950s and 1960s that were created as white areas by governmental and social processes (for example, lending policies originally systematized by the federal government that effectively barred lending in areas where people of color lived, and cumulative individual acts of housing discrimination) and in which women were captured by an ideology of domesticity as historically specific as the later advent of the ideology of the professional Supermom. The experience subjected to that set of consciousness-raising discussions was in fact white and middle class—not just suburban nor merely "not otherwise oppressed."
149. MACKINNON, FEMINIST THEORY OF THE STATE, *supra* note 19.
150. MACKINNON, *Desire and Power, supra* note 2, at 48.
151. Harris, *supra* note 4.
152. Crenshaw, *supra* note 22.
153. SPELMAN, *supra* note 16.
154. Edmonds, *supra* note 63; Grillo & Wildman, *supra* note 6; Kline, *supra* note 3.

cannot be described in any way that sees only what is done to women, that what happens to white women cannot be usefully described without further examination as what happens to "women," and that focus on the sexual exploitation of women hides both racist oppression and the strength, struggles, and multiple interests of women of color. MacKinnon anchors herself to the reductive end of this problem when she chooses to treat criticism as denying oppression in women and answers with the argument that women are oppressed and the proof is that bad things have been and are done to white women.[155]

MacKinnon's dichotomy between practice and theory also helps to hide whiteness in women. Her concept of "practice" is effectively limited to what is done to women, not what we do—or only what we do in response to what is done to us, instead of what we do and attempt, individually and together, for ourselves. This confuses "treatment as a woman" with "experience as a woman"—a complex matter which involves both how we are treated and how we try to live. Practice must mean more than how we are treated.

Her concept of "practice" is also limited by the way she distinguishes it from the "theory" which should be built from practice. By engaging in abstract discussions, feminist legal theory has indeed missed some of the keen reality of women's oppression, but that does not mean that a raw "practice" of women completely uninformed by "theory" exists.[156] In consciousness-raising groups, some women were reading the feminist theory that existed at the time,[157] some were writing theory (and journals and poems), and some were listening to each other's experience and their own as they told it (and forming friendships with each other, falling in love with each other, going to demonstrations together, organizing women's classes at local schools, and doing all the many things women in those groups did). Practice as a woman is informed by oppressive theory or affected by liberatory theory—it isn't pure, raw, unmediated experience.

The theory/practice split is particularly important to understanding race, because race itself is culture and ideology, not a natural truth. White people will think racially as whites without thinking "about race," because we tend to equate "race" with "not-white." We will not understand that we are thinking racially when we are not thinking about people of color. This will be part of our practice as white women because it will shape what we do, though it will be very difficult for us to see.

So if we are building theory out of the practice of women, white women need to reckon with the ways in which some of our practice will not be

---

155. This explains why MacKinnon could interpret critiques emphasizing differentiation among women as concerned only with oppression that men also suffer.

156. Schneider, *supra* note 41 (describing interaction of theory and practice).

157. MacKinnon herself refers to the reading of feminist theory in many consciousness-raising groups. MacKINNON, FEMINIST THEORY OF THE STATE, *supra* note 19, at 85. Many more women in consciousness-raising groups were reading theory outside those groups and carrying ideas in with them as part of their processing of experience.

addressed in our theory because it is not visible to us. This is a problem which cannot be answered by arguing that women really are oppressed as women. Rather, if we want liberation as women (including liberatory theory), we need to explore the experience and needs of *all* women. In this process, we will need to hear accounts of women's experience in which whiteness itself may become visible in ways we find uncomfortable.[158] The meaning of whiteness will therefore need to be examined and challenged.

A white woman lives the tension between ongoing oppression and the attempt to effectuate her life as if inside a bubble of dominant culture. To most of us, the bubble is transparent.[159] The culture we live in makes the specificity of our lives invisible to us. White interactions go on whether or not we intend to subordinate another person or to interact with consciousness of race. They are part of the meanings in the culture in which we live, and they are part of how we react to things emotionally, but since they are "normal" they are as invisible as air. Feeling unlike an agent in one's life, noticing *only* the ways in which one is not powerful, may be a vision of the self which depends on the transparency of the ways in which you are privileged.[160] The dominant mentality is protected by this invisibility which allows it to inflict pain deliberately or unawares.[161] For those defined outside this bubble of culture, it is not invisible at all. Defensiveness in the face of criticism can make this bubble as perceptible as armor.[162]

If the point of feminist endeavor is to undertake the transformation of society and achieve the liberation of women, then it matters a great deal how we undertake this transformative work. Transformative work, which is part of consciousness-raising and is the point of feminist struggle, involves listening respectfully to those who can see what we cannot. It involves consciousness-raising of our own, like Peggy McIntosh's lists, to try to undo the invisibility of whiteness. This work requires understanding and playing close attention to women as social actors.

---

158. Maria Lugones, *On the Logic of Pluralist Feminism*, in FEMINIST ETHICS 35 (Claudia Card ed., 1991).

159. Notable exceptions are white women whose lives are lived intimately connected with people of color—as lovers, spouses, mothers—and sometimes through friendship, *see supra* note 140. HOOKS, *supra* note 83, at 177 ("white people who shift locations . . . begin to see the world differently . . . . Understanding how racism works, [a white man who shifted position] can see the way in which whiteness acts to terrorize without seeing himself as bad, or all white people as bad, and all black people as good.").

160. BELL HOOKS, *Sisterhood: Political Solidarity Between Women*, in FEMINIST THEORY FROM MARGIN TO CENTER, *supra* note 100, at 43, 44-47 (criticizing bonding among women on the basis of shared victimization as reflecting class and race privilege). Examples of hidden privilege in claims of victimization can be found in the conversational asides in which middle-class professionals and academics discuss the disadvantage of white males in the current job market.

161. As Peggy McIntosh says, both the privileges everyone should have and the privileges no one should have are part of that package of privilege. McIntosh, *supra* note 90, at 10-14. Both are transparent to the person inside that bubble and quite visible to those outside it—those who have trouble cashing checks and know or suspect this is *not* true for everybody.

162. Franz Vital, a recent graduate of the University of Miami School of Law, has described the engagement of an almost visible shield when he uses the phrase "white people"—a reaction he compared to the force fields in science fiction films that are seen only by flashes and sparks as they repel attacks.

I am not suggesting that white privilege is an unchanging artifact. I am troubled by discourse on race and gender that treats identity as a set of fixed poles rather than as interactive, socially known, and contested. I believe that the societal tendency to see privilege as fixed and frozen is one reason MacKinnon hears discussion of privilege as antithetical to concepts of oppression. "Culture," "race," and "gender" should not be treated as fixed when they are lived constructions, fluid if extraordinarily powerful, and subject to change through struggle and resistance as well as to reinforcement and reproduction through interactive oppression(s). Identity is socially constructed, culturally known, and lived by women in the experience of oppression *and* in the lives we build despite being unable to escape the framework of oppression. Identity is also forged in the struggle against oppression, and therefore in the ways we conduct this struggle. For these reasons, I find it more useful to look at how white women live and what white women do than to try to say what a white woman "is." These are difficult but very important explorations.

In the second sentence of this essay, I used the term "defensive" to describe the essay to which I am replying. I used it deliberately, but the word is heavily charged. I vividly remember discussions of racism when I didn't agree with the criticisms made by people of color—thinking or saying, "but wait, that wasn't what I meant." Told I was being defensive about racism, I can still hear myself insisting (sometimes out loud, sometimes inwardly): "I'm not defensive—I just think you're wrong." Wasn't there any way to disagree with criticism, or to try to tell my version of what seemed to be true, without being labeled "defensive"?[163]

Marilyn Frye describes a feminist organization in which white women were criticized for their racism by women of color.[164] The white women decided (after consultation with women of color) to hold meetings of white women to work on this issue. Shortly thereafter, they were strongly criticized by a black woman for thinking they could understand it alone and for unilaterally deciding to exclude the women of color. Frye found this an intolerable double-bind—white women were racist if they didn't act, and racist if they did—and felt the criticism was "crazy." But this sense of "craziness" made her suspicious, because she knew how she herself had often seemed "crazy" to people who could not see the profound structure of sexism with which she was concerned. She responded by trying to listen differently and by trying to understand the ways in which her decisionmaking reflected a white privilege

---

163. I want to acknowledge here the inspiration I have found in two white women—Jeanne Adleman, my mother, and Stephanie Wildman, a friend—who have shown me examples that combine struggling against racism with the understanding that one will inevitably have absorbed some of the values society and culture have created. They consistently show a primary concern with fighting oppression and less concern with having been right about particular issues, something that many of us find very hard to relinquish. Stephanie sees this as part of being willing to move out of the "center" of discussion. Telephone Interview with Stephanie Wildman (Feb. 1993); *see also supra* note 59.

164. MARILYN FRYE, THE POLITICS OF REALITY: ESSAYS IN FEMINIST THEORY 111-12 (1983).

to define the terms and scope of white action against racism.[165]

I agree with the many feminists who assert the necessity of feminist struggle against all oppression. We can conclude that feminism must be concerned with struggle against racism, and that white feminists need an active agenda against racism (including white privilege), by recognizing that "women" will not be free until "women of color" experience freedom. We could reach the same conclusion by believing that racism is so deeply entwined and so profoundly implicated in all structures of gender oppression that it has harmed white women even as it has brought us privilege in many ways, so that we will never find freedom until we help transform all of these power relationships. Either way, white women need to work actively against white privilege.[166]

I also agree that feminism needs theory built out of the diverse experience and needs of women. How white women act will have a great deal to do with achieving the development of pluralist feminist theory. It matters how we talk with each other, and, especially, it matters how we listen. This does not mean that everything any person of color ever says must be taken by white women as objective truth, but that it be recognized as a truth, and as truth to the respected person from whom we hear it.[167] Close attention to positioned truths is respect fundamental to progress and change.[168]

Women can "coalesce across differences" to work on issues of concern to women. Martha Fineman has recently suggested that motherhood is such an area of shared concern and potentially of shared work to transform women's "gendered lives."[169] Recognizing the racially differentiated work of social reproduction and the differentiated images of single mothers should not preclude the development of shared work for mothers. Moving beyond shared sexual exploitation into other areas of life and struggle can help illuminate the potential for shared struggle. Recognizing shared interests in women that cross social and cultural boundaries is not the same as declaring women's shared sexual exploitation to be of primary significance in our struggles. Also, making difference visible and making white privilege non-neutral do not mean we need to declare against common ground for women.

As I reread MacKinnon's work while writing this essay, I found my respect for many of her insights reinforced and even increasing. My argument is not with the breadth or depth of her critique of oppression, nor with her relentless

---

165. *Id.* at 111-13.

166. This is not just about white women needing to "remember" that "other" women are "not the same as white women" and that we therefore should not make overbroad claims about "all of us"—concepts in which the tendency to treat whiteness as central recurs over and over again as we begin to try to work against it. *See supra* note 59.

167. *See* Lugones, *supra* note 158.

168. To understand what we do not see for ourselves, we need to be "listening with intent to hear." This sensitive phrase is from the anonymous client of a feminist therapist. Telephone Interview with Jeanne Adleman (Nov. 1992).

169. Fineman, *supra* note 68, at 20-23.

opposition to the pain, degradation, and suffering of women. However, her emphasis on the construction of gender through male power, and the centrality of sexual exploitation to her vision, tend to obscure the importance to white women of the social construction of race.

My first impulse was to articulate in this essay an alternative account of the construction of gender. But this quickly reminded me how many questions seemed truly important. These questions about what is happening and what to do about it are "theoretical" in ways that cannot be dismissed as academic and cannot be resolved without working to incorporate the diverse practice of women. These include questions about the construction of race, including whiteness as a racial construct and the interactive constructions of race and gender; understanding the relationship between theory and practice, and the ways in which culture and ideology mediate this relationship; recognizing both accommodation and resistance to oppression without falling into the dual traps of finding resistance in any act or of sentimentalizing accommodation; evaluating whether objective truths (which I might fear less than others, were I only certain of them) are necessary to liberatory vision; and exploring questions about valuing women's work without perpetuating enforced motherhood or other roles that have been forced upon us.

Solving these questions is a collective intellectual and political undertaking for our time. Transformative work depends on working toward understanding these questions. The quality of the understanding we achieve, and our ability to transform our lives and society depend on and are inevitably affected by the inclusive or exclusive nature of this work for change.

TRADITION, CHANGE, AND THE IDEA OF PROGRESS IN FEMINIST LEGAL THOUGHT

KATHARINE T. BARTLETT*

It often seems to me the progress of feminism is very much like that of psychoanalysis. Roughly speaking, there are two parts to analysis. First comes insight—collecting data on the damage within. Then comes extrication from the personality that has developed in response to the damage. The first part is easy, the second part hell. Insight comes in a rush: swift, exciting, dramatic. Extrication is interminable: repetitious, slogging, unesthetic. At least thirty-two times a year for six or seven years the patient repeats original insight as if for the first time. And then, when the analyst can hardly believe it is going to happen again, the patient announces, "Now I see clearly what I have not seen before." The analyst passes a tired hand across a weary brow and replies, "You saw that clearly last month, and last year, and the year before. When are you going to *act* on what you see?"[1]

Within feminist thought, there is great anxiety about progress: what it is, whether it is occurring, and how to make more of it happen. This anxiety is manifest in the range of reactions to the current "backlash"

---

* Professor of Law, Duke University. The initial version of this paper was given as the 1993 Rundell Lecture at the University of Wisconsin Law School on November 1, 1993. It benefitted from helpful comments I received at faculty workshops at University of North Carolina-Chapel Hill School of Law, Cornell Law School, and Harvard Law School; at lectures given at Vermont Law School, Dartmouth College, and New York University School of Law (Discourses Speaker Series); and at the 1993 Law and Society Annual Meeting. Much of the initial work for the paper was made possible by the support I received from the Rockefeller Foundation and the Cannon-Bost Faculty Research Fund of Duke Law School, which enabled me to spend the 1992-1993 academic year as a Fellow in the ideal research conditions provided at the National Humanities Center in Research Triangle Park, North Carolina. Special thanks go to Kathy Abrams, Linda Kerber, and Jeff Powell for their thoughtful comments, and to Jennifer Harrod for her research assistance.
1. Vivian Gornick, *Who Says We Haven't Made a Revolution?*, N.Y. TIMES, Apr. 15, 1990, § 6, at 24, 27 (emphasis added).

against feminism.[2] Some warn that women have asked for too much and weakened their legitimate claims to equality with special pleadings for women that cannot be justified.[3] Others charge that women have asked for too little and that incremental legal reforms within existing paradigms will only reinforce the status quo.[4] Some, among whom I count myself, are frustrated by claims made at both ends of the spectrum. Those worried about women's special pleadings seem to have missed the central feminist point about how the construction of principles as neutral and special serves systematically to rationalize women's subordination. Those insisting that incremental reform only reinforces women's subordination, in turn, undermine the slow and tedious work that might help to alter the social attitudes about gender that sustain it.

My aim in this Article is not to choose between extremes, or even to seek the happy middle between them. It is, rather, to improve the way feminists think about how to produce change—whatever its desired specifications. All too often today, feminists define progress in opposition to tradition and the past. The more "radical" the feminism, the more pervasive and enduring the oppressions of the past are seen to be, and thus the more urgent the need to fully repudiate its traditions.[5]

There is understandable reason for the feminist antipathy to tradition, which represents patriarchal gender role norms, the elimination of which is feminism's primary goal. Deepening the contemporary feminist hostility toward tradition has been its association with "family values," invoked in support of such conservative agenda items as state-encouraged prayer in the public schools, the reversal of *Roe v. Wade*, the privatization of responsibility for family support, the penalization of out-of-wedlock childbirth, and the rejection of purportedly "favored" treatment for women, gay men and lesbians, African-Americans, and third-world "aliens."

An oppositional stance toward tradition and the past, however, may do more to impede feminist progress than to accelerate it. What I

---

2. SUSAN FALUDI, BACKLASH: THE UNDECLARED WAR AGAINST AMERICAN WOMEN (1991).

3. *See, e.g.*, WENDY KAMINER, A FEARFUL FREEDOM: WOMEN'S FLIGHT FROM EQUALITY (1990); KATIE ROIPHE, THE MORNING AFTER: SEX, FEAR, AND FEMINISM ON CAMPUS (1993); CHRISTINA HOFF SOMMERS, WHO STOLE FEMINISM? HOW WOMEN HAVE BETRAYED WOMEN (1994); NAOMI WOLF, FIRE WITH FIRE: THE NEW FEMALE POWER AND HOW IT WILL CHANGE THE 21ST CENTURY (1993).

4. *See, e.g.*, MARTHA ALBERTSON FINEMAN, THE ILLUSION OF EQUALITY: THE RHETORIC AND REALITY OF DIVORCE REFORM (1991); CATHARINE A. MACKINNON, FEMINISM UNMODIFIED: DISCOURSES ON LIFE AND LAW (1987); Mary E. Becker, *Politics, Differences and Economic Rights*, 1989 U. CHI. LEGAL F. 169.

5. Radical feminists as varied in their approaches as Robin West and Catharine MacKinnon accept this oppositional view. *See infra* text accompanying notes 73-91.

contend in this Article is that a dichotomous view of change is both inaccurate and nonstrategic. It is inaccurate in the sense that the process of change occurs less in breaks from a fixed and stable past than in extensions of ever-mutating versions of it. The fact that change represents extensions of the past rather than its rejection is not due merely to the exigencies of compromise, cooptation, and the triumph of "special interests." The future brings along the past because, notwithstanding the allure of the brand new, what most individuals seek in their social relations is not something completely different, but rather a different familiar. I propose that the primary impulse for social change seeks reconciliation between the familiar and an evolving sense of what is just and good, rather than a radical break from the past.

The tradition/change dichotomy is nonstrategic because it fails to take into account this desire for the familiar. It sets the sights of reformers on efforts to engineer great leaps of freedom from an oppressive past to a sharply distinct, desirable future, rather than on building the connections essential to that future. In so doing, it increases the distance those who are being asked to change think they must move. This dichotomous view ignores the fact that the seemingly intractable views about gender which feminists seek to change are tied to individual and group identities, formed through the ongoing accretions and syntheses of old and new understandings of self and other. Feminist revelations can have little impact on identities they completely reject. They must make sense *in terms of* these identities. This requires not the triumph of new over old, but an integration between them that can generate transformed and transforming views about gender.

An approach to progress built on distance from, rather than identification with, the past creates dissonance and conflict. Dissonance and conflict can, of course, be useful in stimulating change. However, not just any dissonance and conflict will do. What feminists require is dissonance and conflict that enrich and extend a set of shared understandings, rather than further entrench old ones. Tradition is a key to identifying and reshaping the base of shared understandings on which desirable change, or progress, can build. It is a concept that feminists cannot afford to ignore.

This Article begins with an analysis of the oppositional view of tradition and change evident in recent Supreme Court decisions limiting the growth of constitutionally protected individual liberties in the family law area. I then demonstrate how feminist responses to these decisions incorporate and reinforce, rather than challenge, the dichotomous view of tradition and change that these decisions reveal, and show how this view is more damaging than helpful to feminist concepts of progress. I go on to lay out alternative views of tradition and change, including a view that sees tradition and change as mutually embodied rather than as opposites.

I contend that the embodiment view supplies the most promising framework for feminist progress. Within this view, tradition is seen as an important component of progress, which in turn is viewed less as a product of revolutionary insight implemented by the newly empowered, than as a product of mundane, necessarily repetitious narratives that reveal, teach about, and improve the ordinary, "traditional" meanings present in this society, including the ordinary meaning of gender. My argument is that although insight and power are necessary to feminist progress, changes in gender role attitudes depend upon the integration of insight and past understandings. These integrations cannot be achieved without, in Gornick's words, the "repetitious, slogging, unesthetic work[ing]" of these insights into the ordinary and familiar. In this view, strategies consistent with this more integrated approach to tradition and change are more likely to produce a deeper kind of progress—one that both endures and serves as a foundation for future progress—than are strategies based on the tradition/change dichotomy. I end with a review of feminist work from which this more integrated view of tradition and change might build.

I. THE TRADITION/CHANGE DICHOTOMY

A. Tradition and Precedent

Tradition has functioned in different ways in Supreme Court jurisprudence across a diverse set of constitutional contexts. In some cases, the Court has used tradition to refer to social norms and practices that have persisted for some period of time outside, or beyond the reach of, law. These norms and practices act as a limit on state acts that jeopardize these norms or practices[6] or as validation of state acts consistent with them.[7] In other cases, what is called tradition amounts

---

6. *See, e.g.*, Griswold v. Connecticut, 381 U.S. 479 (1965) (invalidating state prohibition against birth control based on deep-rooted tradition of marital privacy); Abington Sch. Dist. v. Schempp, 374 U.S. 203, 214, 226 (1962) (deep tradition of religious liberty as exercised in the private home, church, and the individual heart and mind supports First Amendment prohibition of state requirement that Bible passages be read and Lord's prayer be recited in public schools).

7. *See, e.g.*, Ingraham v. Wright, 430 U.S. 651, 657-64 (1977) (upholding corporal punishment in public schools based, in part, on use of such punishment "dat[ing] back to the colonial period"). Evidence of traditional norms and practices can also function as proof of the Bill of Rights drafters' "original intent" to allow certain challenged rules or practices. *See, e.g.*, Marsh v. Chambers, 463 U.S. 783, 786-88 (1983) (final agreement on language of the Bill of Rights three days after congressional authorization of appointment of paid congressional chaplains sheds light on what the drafters intended the First Amendment religion clauses to mean).

to rules or precedents internal to law, to which the Court refers in justifying continued adherence to these (or similar) rules and practices in the face of challenge by those urging an abandonment of tradition.[8] It is important to see that both usages function somewhat differently from legal precedent. Tradition and precedent each confer some sort of legitimating power on the past and impose constraints based on that power.[9] Whereas precedent consists of a holding in one legal case that is deemed to control directly the decision in another case,[10] however, tradition derives from outside of law, imposing limits not yet adjudicated by the courts. Once the legal relevance of a tradition has been adjudicated in a case, it becomes incorporated into a precedent and operates as such, subject of course to later reinterpretations of, or reliance upon, tradition (which might, in turn, alter precedent). A tradition that has become embodied in precedent may continue to operate not only as part of that precedent but as an independent, reinterpretable source of authority for future decisions. When authority functions as tradition, its strength increases with age; as precedent, it gains support from its recency.[11]

Typically, both precedent and tradition are viewed as constraints on authority, and rightly so. One commonly perceived difference between them is that precedent, especially as it operates in the common law, leaves

---

8.   *See, e.g.*, Burnham v. Superior Court, 495 U.S. 604 (1990) (upholding personal jurisdiction on the basis of physical presence, based on long tradition of American jurisdictional practice); Tison v. Arizona, 481 U.S. 137, 153 (1987) (finding that survey of state felony-murder rules indicates societal consensus that death penalty for murder under felony-murder rule is not "grossly excessive" and thus does not violate the Eighth Amendment); Bowers v. Hardwick, 478 U.S. 186, 191 (1986) (upholding anti-sodomy law on the basis of continued existence of such laws).

The distinction between tradition internal to the law and that which is external is prompted by Charles A. Miller's distinction between internal and external history. *See* CHARLES A. MILLER, THE SUPREME COURT AND THE USES OF HISTORY 20-21 (1969).

9.   Anthony T. Kronman views precedent as "merely one expression of [the general outlook of traditionalism,]" whereby the past has direct, inherent authority to which respect is owed, for its own sake. *See* Anthony T. Kronman, *Precedent and Tradition*, 99 YALE L.J. 1029, 1043-44 (1990).

10.   There are different theories, of course, by which it is determined whether a case is controlled by precedent. For an analysis of these theories, see Larry Alexander, *Constrained by Precedent*, 63 S. CAL. L. REV. 1 (1989); *see also* Earl Maltz, *The Nature of Precedent*, 66 N.C. L. REV. 367 (1988); Henry Monaghan, *Stare Decisis and Constitutional Adjudication*, 88 COLUM. L. REV. 723 (1988); Stephan R. Perry, *Judicial Obligation, Precedent and the Common Law*, 7 OXFORD J. LEGAL STUD. 215 (1987); Frederick Schauer, *Precedent*, 39 STAN. L. REV. 571 (1987).

11.   *See* David Luban, *Legal Traditionalism*, 43 STAN. L. REV. 1035, 1043 (1991).

room for evolution and change,[12] while tradition is fixed, stable, and unchanging. Indeed, scholars as noted as Oliver Wendell Holmes have applauded the common law's great responsiveness to changing conditions while deriding the inflexibility, purposelessness, and irrationality of the "merely historical."[13] This contrast, however, is based on a mistaken view of tradition, which in fact evolves and builds on what precedes it much like the common law. In the next section, I explore this common mistake about the rigidity and unchanging nature of tradition as it has appeared in Supreme Court decisions addressing constitutional rights and liberties relating to matters of family, procreation, and sexuality. It is with respect to matters of the family and sexuality that the Court has most often turned to tradition as a source of "previously unrecognized aspects of . . . liberty,"[14] and it is in the family law area that the Court, in recent years, has articulated a specific methodology for consulting tradition in adjudicating claims of individual rights and liberties not explicitly enumerated in the U.S. Constitution.[15] These decisions have provoked feminist critique which, as I will show, mirrors the dichotomous model of tradition and change pressed by Court conservatives. I go on to explain why this model, which is broadly present in feminist thought, provides a poor model for a concept of feminist progress.

B. Tradition as a "Living Thing"[16]

The use of tradition by the Supreme Court as a source of authority against state power began with two decisions challenging the state's power to regulate public education. *Meyer v. Nebraska*[17] addressed a Nebraska prohibition against teaching a modern language other than English in any school until after the eighth grade. *Pierce v. Society of Sisters*[18] examined an Oregon referendum initiative mandating that all children attend public, and not private, school. In each case, the Supreme Court

---

12. *See* MELVIN A. EISENBERG, THE NATURE OF THE COMMON LAW 1 (1988) (the common law evolves and adapts to the doctrinal and social propositions of the community).

13. *See* OLIVER WENDELL HOLMES, *The Path of the Law, in* COLLECTED LEGAL PAPERS 167, 192 (1920) (also found in 10 HARV. L. REV. 457, 472 (1897)) (explaining certain doctrines in contract law in which tradition "overrides rational policy"); *see also infra* note 78.

14. *See Developments in the Law—The Constitution and the Family*, 93 HARV. L. REV. 1156, 1177 (1980).

15. *See* Michael H. v. Gerald D., 491 U.S. 110 (1988). This case is discussed in detail *infra* text accompanying notes 54-61.

16. Poe v. Ullman, 367 U.S. 497, 542 (1961) (Harlan, J., dissenting).

17. 262 U.S. 390 (1923).

18. 268 U.S. 510 (1925).

held that the state regulation encroached too deeply upon matters which, by tradition over time and in various cultural contexts, had been left up to parents and teachers. In the case of *Meyer*, the relevant tradition was the "supreme importance" with which "[t]he American people have always regarded education and acquisition of knowledge"[19] and the institutional commitment to control over children by parents rather than by a homogeneous community within which the individual's identity might be submerged.[20] *Pierce* involved the specific tradition of private schools in this country, which have been "long regarded as useful and meritorious."[21] From these traditions the Court discerned an until then unidentified constitutional interest on the part of parents and guardians in "direct[ing] the upbringing and education of children under their control,"[22] which protected their right to resist state standardization of their children in public schools[23] and to engage a qualified teacher to instruct their children in subjects of their own choosing.[24]

Tradition functioned in both *Meyer* and *Pierce* as a source of liberty and privilege not otherwise explicitly found either in the Constitution or in other legal sources. The long-standing expectations held by parents with respect to the education and upbringing of their children became, by virtue of the depth and fundamental nature of these expectations, a limit on state power to intrude on them. Although this limit has been linked with the natural law of property and contract rights protected in *Lochner*[25] and later discredited in the New Deal era,[26] in *Meyer* and *Pierce* the traditions at issue were not those of a universal higher law of all mankind; they were identified, instead, as peculiarly American practices and expectations.[27] These traditions were at the same time general and specific in scope, drawing from parents' broad responsibility toward their children's upbringing to reaffirm specific expectations with respect to what those children should be taught, and by whom.

---

19.   *Meyer*, 262 U.S. at 400.

20.   *Id.* at 402.

21.   *Pierce*, 268 U.S. at 534.

22.   *Id.* at 534-35.

23.   *Id.* at 535.

24.   *Meyer*, 262 U.S. at 400.

25.   *See* Lochner v. New York, 198 U.S. 45 (1905).

26.   *See* West Coast Hotel Co. v. Parrish, 300 U.S. 379 (1937).

27.   *Pierce*, for example, spoke of "the fundamental theory of liberty upon which all governments *in this Union* repose," which "excludes any general power of the [s]tate to standardize its children by forcing them to accept instruction from public teachers only." 268 U.S. at 535 (emphasis added); *see also Meyer*, 262 U.S. at 400 ("The *American people* have always regarded education and acquisition of knowledge as matters of supreme importance which should be diligently promoted.") (emphasis added).

For forty years after *Meyer* and *Pierce*, the constitutional project of identifying fundamental liberties entitled to constitutional protection based on what came to be understood as "substantive due process" lay in dormant disrepute.[28] It reappeared in *Griswold v. Connecticut*,[29] in which the Court held that the deep-seated societal respect afforded to marriage and the spousal relationship supports a constitutional right for married persons to be free from state control in their decisions about whether to use birth control. At a superficial level, *Griswold* located the Court's authority to overturn intrusive state legislation in the "penumbra" of more explicit privacy rights found in the First, Third, Fourth, Fifth, and, in a residual sense, Ninth, Amendments to the Constitution, rather than in the Due Process Clause of the Fourteenth Amendment. Fundamentally, however, *Griswold* was based, no less than *Meyer* and *Pierce*, on a set of social practices and expectations in marital intimacy that were seen to predate, and at the same time transcend, existing legal sources.[30] The Court was protecting in *Griswold* a "way of life" that valued highly the privacy and sexual intimacy of a married couple. This way of life was worthy of protection not because it could be placed in a particular location or time, but rather because it could not. It was "older than the Bill of Rights . . . older than our political parties, . . . older than our school system."[31] Authority for this way of life came from its

---

28.   Perhaps it would be more accurate to say that substantive due process went underground, and was rearticulated through equal protection principles invoked less to protect certain "suspect" classes of individuals than to protect especially important individual rights and liberties. In Skinner v. Oklahoma, 316 U.S. 535 (1942), the Court held on equal protection grounds that the state could not arbitrarily classify crimes of moral turpitude that would be punished by sterilization. Since the classifications involved in *Skinner*—e.g., embezzlers and sex offenders—were not worthy of rigorous constitutional scrutiny, it is reasonable to conclude that it was the individual's special substantive (due process) interest in procreation that gave rise to the higher level of review. Similarly, in Loving v. Virginia, 388 U.S. 1 (1967), the Court invalidated anti-miscegenation laws that applied equally to whites and blacks on equal protection grounds, at least in part because of the special constitutional status afforded to marriage. *See also* Zablocki v. Redhail, 434 U.S. 374 (1978) (invalidating Wisconsin statute requiring parent with out-of-custody children to get court permission to marry); Stanley v. Illinois, 405 U.S. 645 (1972) (holding, on a procedural due process theory, that state may not irrebuttably presume the unfitness of an unwed father and deprive him of custody of his children); Eisenstadt v. Baird, 405 U.S. 438 (1971) (holding on equal protection grounds that unmarried, as well as married, persons have a constitutional right to access to contraceptives).

29.   381 U.S. 479 (1965).

30.   *Id*. at 486.

31.   *Id*.

acceptance and importance in society, which no other type of association could match.[32]

The reliance upon tradition as a source of constitutional liberty became even more explicit in *Moore v. City of East Cleveland*.[33] In *Moore*, the Court invalidated a zoning ordinance that defined "family" in such a way as to exclude a grandmother and her two grandchildren from a single-family-only residential district. The decision was based on what the Court's plurality identified as the "careful 'respect for the teachings of history [and] solid recognition of the basic values that underlie our society.'"[34]   As in *Griswold*, no constitutional language or precedent supported the particular right defined by the *Moore* plurality. The source of the right, rather, was the historical fact that millions of citizens have grown up in extended families of "uncles, aunts, cousins and especially grandparents," and that "the accumulated wisdom of civilization, gained over the centuries and honored throughout our history . . . [supports such a large] conception of the family."[35] As in *Griswold*, the Court's power derived from the fact that the extended family was a living practice generated "[o]ut of choice, necessity, or a sense of family responsibility"[36] and was "deeply rooted in this Nation's history and tradition."[37]

The organic dimensions of tradition, as well as its interrelationship with precedent, are apparent in each of these decisions. New precedent

---

32.   *Id.* (marriage is "an association for as noble a purpose as any involved in our prior decisions"); *see also id.* at 491 (Goldberg, J., concurring) (privacy in marriage is protected by the Ninth Amendment because it is "so basic and fundamental and so deep-rooted in our society"). According to Professor Bruce Ackerman, *Griswold* represents the reinterpretation of the Bill of Rights "in a post-New Deal world in which property and contract no longer serve the libertarian functions pre-supposed by the eighteenth century." *See* Bruce Ackerman, *Constitutional Politics/Constitutional Law*, 99 YALE L.J. 453, 527, 544 (1989). In emphasizing the right of parents to engage teachers and schools, *Meyer* and *Pierce* might well be seen as the analytical bridges in this new synthesis.

33.   431 U.S. 494 (1977). In one intervening case, Wisconsin v. Yoder, 406 U.S. 205 (1972), the Court relied heavily on the 300-year tradition of the Amish as a successful and self-sufficient segment of American society, as well as on the general American tradition of parents' concern for the nurture and upbringing of their children, in holding that the state unreasonably interfered with the liberty of Amish parents when it failed to accommodate their wish to withdraw their children from public schools after the eighth grade. However, the reasoning of the case relies even more heavily on the importance of the religious free exercise interests involved, and thus *Yoder* is more properly seen as a First Amendment case.

34.   *Moore*, 431 U.S. at 504 (citing *Griswold*, 381 U.S. at 501 (Harlan, J., concurring)).

35.   *Id.* at 505-06.

36.   *Id.* at 505.

37.   *Id.* at 504.

was created based on social practices and expectations extending back into a historical past. In each case, the state had acted within existing legal parameters but in so doing offended a set of moral values and social expectations deeply embedded within the culture. Insofar as the state legislation at issue in *Meyer* and *Pierce* was a response to some perceived emergency or crisis,[38] the Court's action in these cases can be viewed as an effort to protect long-standing, still-existing practices and expectations from inflamed popular prejudices of the moment. Even when the state rule was not a product of momentary legislative passions, however, the Court recognized that such a rule may violate deeply held cultural norms. The zoning ordinance struck down in *Moore* was at least ten years old,[39] while the statute challenged in *Griswold* was passed in 1879 and had been challenged unsuccessfully a few years previous to *Griswold* in *Poe v. Ullman*.[40] In *Loving v. Virginia*,[41] the Court struck down on due process grounds a state anti-miscegenation law, notwithstanding the illegality of interracial marriage in most states in the nineteenth century.[42]

This line of cases supports the proposition that a tradition upon which a due process claim could be based does not need to be identical to the claim at issue, fixed at one particular point in the past and continuing unbroken to the present. The tradition is, rather, a norm that has endured in different iterations in different times. It is a source of reasoned reversal—a mid-course correction, so to speak—of a state action which, upon reflection, in light of the sense that can be made of the past, represents excessive control over its citizens. Tradition thereby connects past and present and gives each meaning in terms of the other. It is old, yet in its timelessness acts as a source of new recognitions.

---

38.   The Nebraska statute at issue in *Meyer* was enacted in response to an "emergency" and fostered in the context of the post-war "aversion toward every characteristic of truculent adversaries." 262 U.S. 390, 402 (1923). The Oregon statute challenged in *Pierce* was a new statute enacted under the initiative provision of the state constitution. The voters were responding to "the great increase in juvenile crime in the United States," which was linked to "the great increase in the number of children . . . who were not attending public schools." 268 U.S. at 524-25. They believed that "religious suspicions" promoted "the separation of children along religious lines during the most susceptible years of their lives", and that "the mingling together . . . of the children of all races and sexes . . . might be the best safeguard against future internal dissensions and consequent weakening of the community against foreign dangers." *Id.* at 525.

39.   The East Cleveland Housing Code cited in the case is dated 1966. *Moore*, 431 U.S. at 496.

40.   367 U.S. 497 (1961).

41.   388 U.S. 1 (1967).

42.   *See* Planned Parenthood v. Casey, 112 S. Ct. 2791, 2805 (1992) (plurality opinion by O'Connor, Kennedy and Souter).

C. Tradition as a Fixed Source in a Particular Past

In recent years, the concept of tradition used by the Court in evaluating constitutional liberty claims has made a significant turn from the "living" tradition[43] of earlier cases. The shift was stimulated by concerns that the earlier approach permitted judges too much discretion to carve out new constitutional rights based on their individual, subjective preferences. Dissenting in *Moore*, for example, Justice White fiercely insisted that the Court's approach to extending constitutional protection of rights or liberties based on tradition gave a "far too expansive charter" to the Court.[44] A number of academics also objected to the Court's use of tradition to recognize new constitutional rights and liberties, largely on grounds that judges should not second-guess moral standards and norms set by legislatures.[45] Conservative justices added to the Court in the Reagan years were sympathetic to these objections, and by 1985, the Justice White view was in the majority.

Bowers v. Hardwick[46] involved a challenge to a Georgia criminal statute prohibiting sodomy—a challenge which the Court treated as an attack on the statute as applied only to homosexuals.[47] In addressing the challenge, Justice White did not abandon the concept of tradition, which was too embedded in Court precedent to ignore altogether, but rather began the steps that would transform its meaning. Only rights or liberties "deeply rooted in this Nation's history and tradition" are entitled to

---

43.   *See supra* note 16.

44.   Moore v. City of East Cleveland, 431 U.S. 494, 549 (1977) (White, J., dissenting). Justice White's opposition to the use of tradition in expanding, as opposed to checking, the evolution of constitutional rights and liberties in *Moore* was consistent with his views on the subject expressed earlier in Doe v. Bolton, 410 U.S. 179 (1973) (White, J., dissenting), Planned Parenthood v. Danforth, 428 U.S. 52 (1976) (White, J., dissenting), and Thornburgh v. American College of Obstetricians & Gynecologists, 476 U.S. 747, 790 (1986) (White, J., dissenting).

45.   *See, e.g.*, ROBERT BORK, THE TEMPTING OF AMERICA 231-35 (1990); JOHN HART ELY, DEMOCRACY AND DISTRUST 60-63 (1980); Robert Bork, *Neutral Principles and Some First Amendment Problems*, 47 IND. L.J. (1971); Bruce C. Hafen, *The Constitutional Status of Marriage, Kinship, and Sexual Privacy—Balancing the Individual and Social Interests*, 81 MICH. L. REV. 463, 553-55 (1983); *see also* Alfred H. Kelly, *Clio and the Court: An Illicit Love Affair*, 1965 SUP. CT. REV. 119, 150-55 (criticizing *Griswold* and many other decisions for relying on inaccurate "law-office history").

46.   478 U.S. 186 (1985).

47.   Michael Hardwick was arrested for an act of sodomy with another man. The prosecution was dropped, and Hardwick brought an action challenging the statute, stating that it placed him, and others, in fear of imminent arrest. *Id.* at 188. For a critical analysis of the Court's decision to treat the case as a challenge to the statute as applied to homosexuals, see Janet E. Halley, *Reasoning About Sodomy, Act and Identity in and After* Bowers v. Hardwick, 79 VA. L. REV. 1721, 1741-42 (1993).

constitutional protection, White declared. The "right to engage in homosexual sodomy"[48] has no such deep roots. To the contrary, anti-sodomy legislation itself has "ancient roots" and existed at a widespread level in the common law, in the laws of the original thirteen states at the time they ratified the Bill of Rights, and in 1868 when the Fourteenth Amendment was passed.[49] Twenty-four states and the District of Columbia still have anti-sodomy laws.[50] In the light of such "traditions," Justice White concluded, the statute implicated no fundamental liberty interest.

The differences between the old and the new traditionalism are fundamental in at least two respects. First, whereas in *Meyer*, *Pierce*, *Griswold*, and *Moore*, tradition was found in social practices, norms, and expectations external to the law, in *Hardwick* Justice White invoked a tradition constituted by the continued existence of legal rules and proscriptions that were consistent with those under attack. Although it was the state's authority to prohibit certain sexual practices between consenting adults that was at issue, the exercise of this authority by states provided the yardstick by which this authority was judged. Second, whereas the traditions in the earlier line of cases were important because of the fundamental part they played in a way of life pervasive and still persistent in a long and deep historical chain, the legal rules consulted in *Hardwick* were important because of their location in specific, discrete pasts—especially the years the Bill of Rights and the Fourteenth Amendment were ratified.[51] Tradition operated for the *Hardwick* majority not as an evolving continuity with the past but as evidence of the

---

48.   Dramatic differences in the articulations of the rights asserted mirror divisions on the Court in defining fundamental rights and liberties entitled to constitutional protection. Thus, for example, while Justice White speaks in *Bowers* of the "right to engage in homosexual sodomy," Justice Blackmun in his dissenting opinion discusses "the right to be let alone" and "the right to decide for [oneself] whether to engage in particular forms of private, consensual sexual activity." 478 U.S. at 129. A similar divergence marks the descriptions of the claims at issue in *Michael H.* and *Roe v. Wade. Compare* Michael H. v. Gerald D., 491 U.S. 110, 130 (Scalia, J.) (addressing the right of "an adulterous natural father" to obtain rights to his child) *and* Roe v. Wade, 410 U.S. 113, 179 (1973) (White, J., dissenting) (describing Court's holding as "investing women and doctors with the constitutionally protected right to exterminate [human life]" and describing women seeking abortion right as "those who seek to serve only their convenience") *with Michael H.*, 491 U.S. at 141 (Brennan, J., dissenting) (characterizing the right involved as "the freedom not to conform" and the right of "parenthood" by a father who has a "substantial" relationship with his child) and *Roe v. Wade*, 410 U.S. at 129, 153 (addressing the right of the pregnant woman "to choose to terminate her pregnancy" and the "right of privacy").

49.   *Bowers*, 478 U.S. at 192-93.

50.   *Id.* at 193-94.

51.   478 U.S. at 192-93.

drafters' "original understanding" of particular relevant constitutional provisions. As such, it was insignificant that, even by Justice White's own account, over half the states since 1961 had overcome the weight of legislative inertia and repealed their sodomy laws, and that the states which had such laws on the books did not enforce them.[52] No attention was given to what role those laws played in past societies; to what benefits they served then and serve now; to what harms they cause, including the growing violence against gays and lesbians associated with, and implicitly encouraged by, the state endorsement of intolerance toward them;[53] nor to the actual sexual practices of the people those laws affected, or their currently held expectations about privacy and sexual expression.

Justice White's approach to tradition was refined and expanded by Justice Scalia in *Michael H. v. Gerald D.*[54] In *Michael H.*, a biological father, who had lived on and off with his child and her mother, challenged a California statute that conclusively presumed that the husband of a child's mother is the child's father. His challenge was based on earlier Court decisions that protected the rights of fathers who had established functional parent-child relationships with their biological offspring.[55] Rejecting the application of these earlier precedents, Justice Scalia acknowledged that unmarried fathers may have rights, but only in the context of the "unitary" or marital family. The "adulterous natural father"[56] is outside the traditionally protected zone, Scalia insisted, and thus has no claim for a chance to demonstrate that continued involvement in his child's life is in her best interests.

The rigidity of Justice Scalia's conception is demonstrated in a number of different ways. First, Justice Scalia reinforced Justice White's supposition that the only appropriate use of tradition is one that limits the "individual predilections" of judges.[57] Only if the past is viewed as

---

52.   Indeed, the state dropped its prosecution in *Hardwick. Id.* at 188; *see supra* note 47.

53.   This violence and its connection to state criminal statutes are powerfully presented in Kendall Thomas, *Beyond the Privacy Principle*, 92 COLUM. L. REV. 1431 (1992).

54.   491 U.S. 110 (1988). Justice Scalia's approach to tradition was joined only by Chief Justice Rehnquist. Justices O'Connor and Kennedy, who otherwise concurred in Justice Scalia's plurality opinion, explicitly rejected his "historical analysis." *Id.* at 132 (O'Connor, J., dissenting).

55.   *See* Caban v. Mohammed, 441 U.S. 380 (1979); Stanley v. Illinois, 405 U.S. 645 (1972).

56.   491 U.S. at 120.

57.   *See Michael H.*, 491 U.S. at 122 n.2 (purpose of Due Process Clause is not "to enable this Court to invent new values"); *see also Hardwick*, 478 U.S. at 191 ("Announcing rights . . . involves much more than the imposition of the Justices' own

fixed, readily ascertainable, and unchanging can it be claimed to serve this function.[58]

Second, in *Michael H.* the Court assumed that *any* remnant of a past practice is sufficient to sustain a state law based on that practice. Just as in *Hardwick*, the Court in *Michael H.* relied on a diminishing body of state law that was rarely, if ever, enforced. For support, Justice Scalia leaned on a desiccated common law presumption and a single 1957 ALR annotation finding no statutes that recognized putative fathers in Michael H.'s position. Only a conception of tradition as fixed at some time, for all time, can support an approach that allows its continued recognition on such slim authority.

The rigidity of Justice Scalia's view of tradition was manifested also by his approach to potentially competing traditions. Unlike Justice White, Justice Scalia acknowledged the possibility of conflicting traditions. His view of tradition as fixed and stable, however, enabled easy resolution of such conflicts; priority must be given to the most specific applicable tradition—in *Michael H.*, the specific tradition of the nuclear family rather than the more general tradition supporting the rights of biological parents. Like Justice White in *Hardwick*, Justice Scalia deemed it unnecessary to justify the traditions relied upon in contemporary terms. Once identified, the relevant traditions took on independent significance—spoke for themselves, in effect. Tradition could be lifted from a specific time to show the intentions of a specific set of individuals and then frozen as a non-negotiable given for all time, without need for justification or explanation.[59] When this was done, other information, subsequent state

---

choice of values.").

58.   In fact, as others have noted, Justice Scalia has himself seemed to use tradition in a result-oriented fashion. *See infra* note 70.

59.   Justice Scalia in other contexts has been even more explicit about the independent and self-validating significance of past practices. In Rutan v. Republican Party of Illinois, 497 U.S. 62 (1990) (Scalia, J., dissenting), for example, he reasoned that political patronage practices were legitimated by their longstanding use:

> [W]hen a practice not expressly prohibited by the text of the Bill of Rights bears the endorsement of a long tradition of open, widespread, and unchallenged use that dates back to the beginning of the Republic, we have no proper basis for striking it down. Such a venerable and accepted tradition is not to be laid on the examining table and scrutinized. . . . To the contrary, such traditions are themselves the stuff out of which the Court's principles are to be formed. They are, in these uncertain areas, the very points of reference by which the legitimacy or illegitimacy of *other* practices are to be figured out.

Id. at 95-96; *see also* Burnham v. Superior Court, 495 U.S. 604, 621 (1990) (where a rule has traditionally been applied by states, there need be "no independent inquiry into the desirability or fairness of the [rule] leaving that judgment to the legislatures that are free to amend it; for our purposes its validation is its pedigree").

law developments,[60] the Court's own precedent on the rights of unmarried fathers,[61] and actual societal norms and expectations[62] became irrelevant.

There is much to criticize in Justice Scalia's concept of tradition, as many others have pointed out. To treat tradition as a coherent whole, subject to ready ascertainment, retrieval, and replication, and as distinguishable from what is modern is to engage in fictions that ignore some of tradition's most significant features. Traditions are not unitary, coherent, or integrated wholes. They are, as Jack Balkin has written,

> a motley collection of principles and counterprinciples, standing for one thing when viewed narrowly and standing for another when viewed more generally. Tradition never speaks with one voice, although, to be sure, persons of particular predilections may hear only one.[63]

At any one time in our society, traditions of close-knit family units have coexisted with traditions of family disintegration, violence, and abuse.[64] Traditions of equality have long shared ground with traditions of slavery and oppression. Traditions of conformity and community have cross-cut traditions of resistance and freedom of expression.[65] To say that only

---

60. Justice Scalia pays lip service to the fact that over time "bastardy laws" have become "less harsh" and "the rigid protection of the marital family has in other respects been relaxed." 491 U.S. at 125. These mitigations were treated as irrelevant, however, in the face of the continued existence in some jurisdictions of the type of statute at issue in the case.

61. *See* Lehr v. Robertson, 463 U.S. 248 (1983); Caban v. Mohammed, 441 U.S. 380 (1979); Quilloin v. Walcott, 434 U.S. 246 (1978); Stanley v. Illinois, 405 U.S. 645 (1972). Justice Brennan, in his dissenting opinion, insisted that these precedents were all highly relevant to the unwed father's claim in *Michael H.*

62. Frank Michelman presents as one of the central distinctions between Justice Brennan's and Justice Scalia's use of tradition in constitutional decisionmaking that Justice Brennan defines tradition in terms of practices approved by societal norms, whereas Justice Scalia tends to see the practices themselves as sufficient. *See* Frank I. Michelman, *Super Liberal: Romance, Community, and Tradition in William J. Brennan, Jr.'s Constitutional Thought*, 77 VA. L. REV. 1261, 1314 (1991); *see also* Peggy Cooper Davis, *Contested Images of Family Values: The Role of the State*, 107 HARV. L. REV. 1348, 1351-53 (1994) (arguing that the tradition upon which the Court should rely in constitutional decisionmaking encompasses the history and principles that produced it).

63. J.M. Balkin, *Tradition, Betrayal, and the Politics of Deconstruction*, 11 CARDOZO L. REV. 1613, 1618 (1990).

64. For a recent work addressing the mythology and idealization of the American nuclear family, see STEPHANIE COONTZ, THE WAY WE NEVER WERE: AMERICAN FAMILIES AND THE NOSTALGIA TRAP (1992).

65. *See* MICHAEL J. PERRY, THE CONSTITUTION, THE COURTS, AND HUMAN RIGHTS 93 (1982).

deeply rooted traditions should be protected presupposes a self-evidence about the content of this society's traditions that defies these diversities, as well as the range of criteria for deciding among them, such as a tradition's age, its degree of continuity, the strength of commitments to it, or how widely it is held. Justice Scalia's effort to solve the problem by looking to the most specific tradition fails, absent criteria for measuring specificity.[66]

Justice Scalia's view of tradition also presupposes an opposition between tradition and change that historians and sociologists have long rejected in describing how traditions are maintained and how change is accomplished. The better view is that tradition and change are frequently "mutually reinforcing, rather than systems in conflict" and that change often strengthens, rather than weakens, tradition.[67] Viewing one as contradictory to the other misdiagnoses both.[68]

Justice Scalia's concept of tradition makes little sense even in terms of traditional conservative principles. Edmund Burke tied the possibility of "conservation" to the ability to change and adapt to existing circumstances, crediting England's ability to maintain its core fabric during the Restoration and Revolution periods, for example, to its ability to regenerate the deficient part of its "constitution" while preserving those parts that were not impaired.[69] Scalia's aims, however, appear related not so much to stability as to the advancement of a particular substantive agenda.[70] For purposes of this agenda, the tradition/change dichotomy

---

66.   *See* Laurence H. Tribe & Michael C. Dorf, *Levels of Generality in the Definition of Rights*, 57 U. CHI. L. REV. 1057, 1090 (1990).

67.   *See* Joseph R. Gusfield, *Tradition and Modernity: Misplaced Polarities in the Study of Social Change, in* POLITICAL DEVELOPMENT AND SOCIAL CHANGE 15, 20-22 (Jason L. Finkle & Richard W. Gable eds., 2d ed. 1971).

68.   *See* LLOYD I. RUDOLPH & SUSANNE HOEBER RUDOLPH, THE MODERNITY OF TRADITION: POLITICAL DEVELOPMENT IN INDIA 3 (1967) (making the point in relation to tradition and modernity).

69.   *See* EDMUND BURKE, *Letter to Sir Hercules Langrishe on the Subject of the Roman Catholicks of Ireland and the Propriety of Admitting Them to the Elective Franchise, Consistently with the Principle of the Constitution, as Elaborated at the Revolution, in* 6 THE WORKS OF THE RIGHT HONOURABLE EDMUND BURKE 297, 340 (London, Rivington 1826); EDMUND BURKE, *Reflections on the Revolution in France, and the Proceedings of Certain Societies in London Relative to That Event, in* 5 THE WORKS OF THE RIGHT HONOURABLE EDMUND BURKE, *supra*, at 27, 59. The contemporary durability of Burke's views of tradition and their relevance to contemporary debates over constitutional rights and liberties is explored in Ernest Young, *Rediscovering Conservatism: Burkean Political Theory and Constitutional Interpretation*, 72 N.C. L. REV. 619 (1994), and in Anthony Kronman, *Precedent and Tradition*, 99 YALE L.J. 1029, 1047-64 (1990).

70.   Nor are they tied to the protection of legislative prerogative from unrestrained judicial activism. Evidence that Justice Scalia is at least as "result-oriented" in his use

may be successful, at least to the extent it is able to rationalize a particular set of norms and practices that have been successfully linked with tradition. It is not so clear, as I shall explain, that the dichotomy is as useful to those with a more progressive, feminist agenda.

D. Feminist Theory and the Tradition/Change Dichotomy

Feminists have reacted sharply against the Court's new traditionalism, as well as against the right's "family values" agenda more generally.[71] In doing so, however, they have tended to accept the same dichotomous way of viewing tradition and change as the supporters of the agenda they reject. I demonstrate this acceptance, first through an analysis of Robin West's specific critique of Justice Scalia's approach in *Michael H.*[72] I then examine how the dichotomy functions in aspects of feminist thought more generally, showing through the work of Catharine MacKinnon the difficulties the dichotomy causes for feminist theory and practice.

1. ROBIN WEST

The substance of Robin West's critique of Justice White's approach in *Michael H.* is that in requiring a claim of individual rights and liberties to be rooted in tradition, it prevents the reconceptualization of the ideal of liberty essential to progress. Constraining understandings of liberty by their historical associations cramps these understandings and hence human potential for freedom.[73] The alternative, to West, seems clear. Efforts to define liberty should be set free from tradition and undertaken "by reference to some understanding of the ideally free or autonomous individual life."[74]

---

of tradition as those whom he accuses of judicial activism is that when the legislation at issue infringes on interests that he deems fundamental, such as the right to the unrestrained private use of one's own property, he has sought to invoke tradition to invalidate the legislation. *See, e.g.*, Lucas v. South Carolina Coastal Council, 112 S. Ct. 2886 (1992). For examples of inconsistencies in Justice Scalia's application of tradition analysis which further demonstrate his willingness to manipulate the doctrine to his own ideological purposes, see L. Benjamin Young, Jr., *Justice Scalia's History and Tradition: The Chief Nightmare in Professor Tribe's Anxiety Closet*, 78 VA. L. REV. 581 (1992).

71.   *See, e.g.*, Katha Pollitt, *Why I Hate Family Values*, NATION, July 20, 1992, at 88; Anna Quindlen, *Public & Private*; *Digging a Divide*, N.Y. TIMES, June 14, 1992, at 19.

72.   Robin West, *The Ideal of Liberty: A Comment on* Michael H. v. Gerald D., 139 U. PA. L. REV. 1373 (1991).

73.   *Id.* at 1374.

74.   *Id.* at 1377.

While West urges a total rejection of tradition rather than its embrace, her reconceptualization casts tradition in the same dichotomous relationship to change as does Justice Scalia's formulation of tradition. For West, as for Scalia, tradition conserves the past and change undermines tradition. The only difference is the normative judgment that follows. For Justice Scalia, tradition is desirable because it means stability; change, represented by the creation of unenumerated constitutional liberties and rights, is undesirable because it lacks legitimacy. For West, conversely, tradition is corrupt, oppressive and conformist; change is liberating. Thus, while Scalia wants to anchor liberty to tradition, West seeks to cut free from tradition altogether, so that the "ideally free or autonomous individual[ist] life" can be imagined without encumbrance.

West's rejection of tradition and the past is so complete that she rejects as well Justice Brennan's synthesis of tradition and change expressed in dissent to *Michael H.*, which continues the dynamic evolution of substantive due process through the line of cases from *Meyer* to *Moore*.[75] According to Brennan, the Court's precedents protecting the rights of unmarried biological fathers should have been extended in favor of Michael H.[76] West argues that Brennan's method of analysis, like Justice Scalia's, is backward-looking—Scalia looks back at tradition, Brennan back at precedent—and as such is inconsistent with progress. Backward-looking approaches, West argues, can only force the individual to protect the oppressions and injustices of the past and prevent contemporaneous or future change.[77] Real change, by contrast, requires cutting ties with the past and developing new ideals based on forward-looking considerations.

If Scalia's error is to assume that tradition can supply answers which are not there, West's error is to assume that the past supplies nothing that might assist in building a progressive future. Her out-of-thin-air approach assumes the possibility of absolute truth uncorrupted by history and of liberation from an oppressive, conformist past.[78] Such assumptions are

---

75.   *See supra* text accompanying notes 16-42.

76.   *See supra* note 61.

77.   West, *supra* note 72, at 1378.

78.   For other examples of this view, see Helen Garfield, *Privacy, Abortion, and Judicial Review: Haunted by the Ghost of* Lochner, 61 WASH. L. REV. 293, 336 (1986) (advocating the pursuit of aspirations and principles rather than the prejudices of tradition); *see also* Anita L. Allen, *Autonomy's Magic Wand: Abortion and Constitutional Interpretation*, 72 B.U. L. REV. 683, 696 (1992) (praising Court in Planned Parenthood v. Casey, 112 S. Ct. 2791 (1992), for "refusing to limit constitutional interpretation to text and tradition"); John C. Wofford, *The Blinding Light: The Uses of History in Constitutional Interpretation*, 31 U. CHI. L. REV. 502, 528 (1964) (arguing on behalf of freedom "from the strictures of the past," although recognizing that knowledge of

as illusory as Scalia's assumption that the past can be retrieved for the present in its original form. To consider change is to draw upon "storehouses of possible relevant analogies to our present problems, ways of thinking about such problems, and successful and unsuccessful attempts to solve them."[79] Every resolution can be seen as an alternative arising from, and in relation to, that past, which is why revolutionary ideals often sound so familiar. Thus, Jaroslav Pelikan writes, Thomas Jefferson's "self-evident truths" about creation, equality, and inalienable rights "were so self-evident at least partly as a consequence of the traditional doctrine of the creation of the human race in the image of God, a doctrine whose roots lie in both Athens and Jerusalem."[80] While in an important sense tradition can be viewed as constructed or invented by those who interpret and make it their own in the present,[81] every culture has a history that shapes perceptions and analyses, and from which such inventions are drawn.[82] Ignoring this history may be perilous.

2. CATHARINE MACKINNON

I began with West's analysis of tradition because it directly engages Justice Scalia's own version of traditionalism. The dichotomous view of tradition and change that West adopts, however, is pervasive, if less explicit, in the work of other feminist writers. The most notable of these writers is Catharine MacKinnon. I have discussed elsewhere my

---

historical continuity is essential in judicial decisionmaking).

79.   Martin Krygier, *Law as Tradition*, 5 LAW & PHIL. 237, 257 (1968). Krygier also writes: "[A]ny particular 'present' is a slice through a continuously changing diachronic quarry of deposits made by generations of people with different, often inconsistent and competing values, beliefs, and views of the world." *Id.* at 242.

Steven Winter, in discussing the constituted and constituting "situated-subject," uses a similar concept of sedimentation: "The past is . . . the sedimented knowledge with which one interacts with the problems of the present. It is this sedimentation that is preservative of the past. At the same time, this sedimentation is always an interaction with a [sic] incessantly dynamic present." Steven Winter, *Indeterminacy and Incommensurability in Constitutional Law*, 78 CAL. L. REV. 1441, 1511 (1990).

80.   JAROSLAV PELIKAN, THE VINDICATION OF TRADITION 12 (1984).

81.   *See* ERIC HOBSBAWN & TERENCE RANGER, THE INVENTION OF TRADITION 1-14 (1983).

82.   *See* MICHAEL WALZER, EXODUS AND REVOLUTION 134-35 (1985). According to Walzer, these cultural patterns accommodate a broad range of alternatives; if they did not, they would not endure long. Still, different cultures "read [different] books, tell different stories, confront different choices" which provide the organizations of thought and action available to that culture. *Id.*; *see also* Michael Schudson, *The Present in the Past Versus the Past in the Present*, 11 COMMUNICATION 105 (1989) (arguing that although the past is constantly being retold, every culture presents structures which limit the available past from which this retelling can occur).

assessment of MacKinnon's extraordinary contributions to feminist theory, as well as the tensions and contradictions present in this theory.[83] Here I wish to focus on her theory of feminist change.

MacKinnon's theory of change begins with a system of male oppression of women that she deems "metaphysically nearly perfect."[84] Because it is a perfect system, anything short of its complete collapse tends only to reinforce it. According to MacKinnon, the very principles that appear to enhance freedom and autonomy most for all individuals are also the ones that are most effective in securing male dominance. Principles of free speech, for example, appear to give everyone the same opportunity to express their own interests and points of view; thus, the protection of free speech appears to be an important tool in furthering underrepresented points of view. However, insofar as men have the power to make their speech more effective than women and have used this power to define women as sexual, otherwise worthless objects for men's pleasure, protection of free speech rights does more to harm than to help women.[85] Equality doctrine likewise pretends to guarantee that women and men receive equal treatment under the law, but only as to those rules, practices, and accommodations already in place to serve men. Equality neither requires nor permits measures to take account of women's differences from men; to the contrary, it compels the invalidation of rules and practices designed with women in mind. Thus, as with free speech protections, the concept of equality creates the appearance of objectivity and neutrality, but in so doing only obscures, and thus helps to guarantee, that what passes for objectivity and neutrality represents male interests and male norms.[86]

MacKinnon's one method of escape from the male dominance trap is the feminist method of consciousness-raising, through which women gain insight, and thus power over their own lives, by filtering their personal experiences through the lens of women's collective oppression.[87] But within MacKinnon's method of consciousness-raising, the oppositional simplicity apparent in her analysis of male dominance reasserts itself. Insight, within this method, is an all-or-nothing proposition—either you get it or you don't. Moreover, insight consists

---

83. *See, e.g.*, Katharine T. Bartlett, *MacKinnon's Feminism: Power on Whose Terms?*, 75 CAL. L. REV. 1559 (1987); Katharine T. Bartlett, *Feminist Legal Methods*, 103 HARV. L. REV. 829, 873-77 (1990).

84. *See* Catharine MacKinnon, *Feminism, Marxism, Method, and the State: Toward Feminist Jurisprudence*, 8 SIGNS 635, 638 (1983).

85. *See* MACKINNON, *supra* note 4, at 146-62.

86. *Id.* at 32-45, 71-74.

87. *See* CATHARINE A. MACKINNON, TOWARD A FEMINIST THEORY OF THE STATE 83-105 (1989).

of an all-or-nothing break from the past—either you're part of the system of male oppression or you share her insights and opposition to that system. Progress either happens or it doesn't.[88]

MacKinnon's all-or-nothing approach to progress has helped to highlight the insidious dynamic by which gender oppression is reinforced, but it has also had other, less beneficial effects. It has led to the devaluation of successes made in eliminating sex-based discrimination and to the equation of remaining, still-being-discovered forms of discrimination with those that came before. In so doing, her approach has played into the hands of those engaged in the current backlash against feminism and its accompanying mischaracterizations about what feminists, and feminism, are about. As to those individuals already on the lookout for rationalizations for despising women, the loss is insignificant; no approach is likely to be successful in significantly revising their gender role attitudes. As to others, however, the approach sets a standard more likely to entrench existing attitudes than to change them. The rejection of familiar bedrock principles such as free speech and equality confirms suspicions, all too easily acquired, that feminism is a form of gender imperialism. On a more personal level, individuals who experience as progress their own growth in awareness about gender-based discrimination are offended when instead of being applauded for their changed behaviors and attitudes, they are criticized for other, more subtle behaviors which are equated with the more explicit forms of sex discrimination these individuals thought they had left behind. The process degenerates as gender sophisticates attain heightened awareness of residual, unconscious as well as conscious forms of discrimination and correspondingly raise their expectations.[89] The distance between those "in the know" and those who simply "don't get it" increases. The number of people

---

88.   Mary Becker reflects this same all-or-nothing approach to change and progress in her sweeping indictment of the Bill of Rights of the U.S. Constitution. Finding countless examples of the injustices to women that have been perpetuated under, or notwithstanding, this document, Becker goes so far as to wonder "whether other governmental structures and electoral systems would be more democratic." *See* Mary E. Becker, *The Politics of Women's Wrongs and the Bill of "Rights": A Bicentennial Perspective*, 59 U. CHI. L. REV. 453, 517 (1992).

89.   This same dynamic is apparent in debates over the resilience of racism. *See, e.g.*, DERRICK BELL, FACES FROM THE BOTTOM OF THE WELL (1992); Jerome M. Culp, Jr., *Water Buffalo and Diversity: Naming Names and Reclaiming the Racial Discourse*, 26 CONN. L. REV. 209, 220-30 (1993) (analyzing difficulty of getting through to racism of white liberals who hide behind the curtains of their well meaning "goodwill"); Richard Delgado, *Critical Legal Studies and the Realities of Race—Does the Fundamental Contradiction Have a Corollary?*, 23 HARV. C.R.-C.L. L. REV. 407, 407 (1988) (arguing that "white people rarely see acts of . . . racism, while minority people see them all the time").

potentially guilty of the more subtle forms of discrimination increases, while those able to spot new forms of discrimination become an increasingly narrow elite vanguard. To those who "get it," the enemy grows. Those forced off the bus[90] become alienated and even hostile.

This unfortunate phenomenon might be called the "no-progress" problem. The no-progress problem results when shifts and reforms are minimized and recast to fit an unchanging narrative of systemic gender oppression. This phenomenon is related to its mirror-image counterpart, identified by Deborah Rhode as the "no-problem" problem.[91] The no-problem problem occurs when it is assumed, falsely, that because the most obvious forms of discrimination have been eliminated, gender discrimination no longer exists. These problems are corollaries in that both treat the end of gender discrimination as an all-or-nothing phenomenon rather than a form of oppression which has, literally, no final end. Both are exaggerations, although one view exaggerates the extent of progress, while the other view exaggerates the lack of it.

By identifying the no-progress problem, I do not mean to suggest that feminists are to blame for being misunderstood—only that their interests in correcting the misunderstandings may require new concepts and strategies. Likewise, I do not mean to say that critical analyses of gender bias and the ongoing discovery of newer and more subtle forms of discrimination should stop. Pointing out, for example, the implicit, as well as explicit, coercion present in many sexual relationships, the relationship between dress and appearance expectations and sexual subordination and harassment, and the ways in which gender matters in evaluating employees with respect to their personal styles, their looks, and their sexual preferences are important steps in the feminist project, which is a long way from being completed. Pressing the gender critique into deeper and deeper territory, however, is not aided by exaggerated assessments about the failures to attain incremental feminist goals, however limited progress toward these goals may seem to be. Such assessments are less a product of noticing what needs to be changed than of an oversimplified view of change or progress.

The notion that progress occurs only as a result of those with insight taking power from those without insight is dangerously incomplete. This notion causes feminists to focus primarily on generating new insights and acquiring new power when, as Vivian Gornick recognizes in the opening passage of this essay, the biggest problem for contemporary feminists is

---

    90.   *See* TOM WOLFE, THE ELECTRIC KOOL-AID ACID TEST 74 (1968) ("You're either on the bus or off the bus.").

    91.   *See* Deborah L. Rhode, *The "No-Problem" Problem: Feminist Challenges and Cultural Change*, 100 YALE L.J. 1731 (1991).

the inability to bridge the gap between insight and practice. For Gornick, the dearth of progress in feminism is due not to lack of insight, but to the large gap between insight and extrication. The "radical" feminist view of change assumes that feminists have the necessary blueprint for a better future; all that is lacking is the muscle to enact it. What Gornick suggests is that insight is the easy part. The hard part is integrating that insight into real, lived lives, a messy and often ugly process.

The integration aspect of gender reform requires a different stance toward the past than the oversimplified, oppositional view that feminist theorists have often assumed. In Part II, I sketch out the alternatives to the dichotomous model of tradition and change and recommend a model that sees the two as embodiments of each other rather than as opposites. In Part III, I identify some feminist work that begins to imply a notion of progress compatible with this view, and suggest how closer attention to issues of tradition and change might help to make this work more useful to feminists.

II. PROGRESS, TRADITION, AND CHANGE

A. *Three Views of Progress*

Historians disagree about the origin of the idea of progress,[92] but acknowledge different conceptual models for understanding the relationships between progress and history. One view, generally attributed to the ancients, though by no means either exclusive to or universally held by them, is that history is circular and repetitious. Within this view progress is impossible and man is doomed to a "perpetual recurrence of the same joys, sorrows and trials."[93] What

---

92.   J.B. Bury, who wrote the first modern history of the idea of progress, finds its precursors in the work of Francis Bacon, its philosophical foundation in seventeenth-century Cartesianism, and its first explicit articulation in the work of the Abbé de Saint-Pierre in the eighteenth century. *See* J.B. BURY, THE IDEA OF PROGRESS 50-63, 64-65, 128 (1932). Some other historians trace the roots of the idea of progress back to ancient times. *See* LUDWIG EDELSTEIN, THE IDEA OF PROGRESS IN CLASSICAL ANTIQUITY (1967); ROBERT NISBET, HISTORY OF THE IDEA OF PROGRESS (1980).

93.   *See* VERNON J. BOURKE, WISDOM FROM SAINT AUGUSTINE 194 (1983). Bourke contends that St. Augustine "broke this wheel of fate" with his ideal of the City of God, in which equilibrium and harmony, made possible by Christ's death and resurrection, were achievable. *See id.* at 194-95. However, until this ideal, in itself a matter of grace rather than achievement, was attained, original sin doomed man's efforts to rise above his condition, making progress in the Western sense futile and meaningless. Cyclical views of history did not perish with the ancients. *See, e.g.,* FREDERICK NIETZSCHE, THE GAY SCIENCE (1974); OSWALD SPENGLER, THE DECLINE OF THE WEST (1928). For a study of cyclic theories of history, see MIRCEA ELIADE, THE MYTH OF

appears to be change is, in fact, the playing out of limited available scripts. All eventually return to where they started, only to begin anew.

A competing view is "the idea of progress," which is associated with the Enlightenment assumptions that progress is inevitable, knowledge is infinitely expandable, and civilization is on a steady, upward climb. Within this view, the expansion of knowledge leads inexorably to the more or less continuous movement from the inferior to the superior.[94] If the cyclical view of history is a closed circle, the idea-of-progress view is a linear arrow reaching out into the indefinite future. Within this ever-onward-and-upward framework, different explanations for progress are possible; some theories stress biological[95] or sociobiological[96] evolution, while others identify rational forces explained by factors that are largely economic,[97] political,[98] or scientific.[99] In each sense, the idea of progress incorporates an evolutionary, forward pressure in the direction of expanded knowledge and improved civilization.

A third view of progress tracks modernist challenges to objectivity, perfectibility, and grand narrative. This view rejects both the cyclical and the linear views of progress, insisting that no unified external measure exists by which it might be said whether change is, or is not, progress. Instead, diverse forces establish normative systems, exert pressure and influence on one another, and maintain their own various courses. The result is a historical organization relying on multiple narratives, local and regional histories, plural perspectives, thick descriptions, and irreducible particularities. Within this methodological framework, sometimes referred to as the "new historicism," progress is not a generalizable phenomenon, but rather a possibility whose accomplishment is judged locally, within communities sharing similar assumptions, stories, and aspirations.[100]

THE ETERNAL RETURN (W.R. Trask trans., 1954).

94.   See NISBET, supra note 92, at 5.

95.   See, e.g., CHARLES DARWIN, ON THE ORIGIN OF SPECIES (London, J. Murray 1859).

96.   See, e.g., DONALD SYMONS, THE EVOLUTION OF HUMAN SEXUALITY (1979); ROBERT WRIGHT, THE MORAL ANIMAL (1994).

97.   See, e.g., GARY BECKER, A TREATISE ON THE FAMILY (1981); KARL MARX, A CONTRIBUTION TO THE CRITIQUE OF POLITICAL ECONOMY (N.I. Stone trans., 1904); ADAM SMITH, THE WEALTH OF NATIONS (1904).

98.   See, e.g., GEORG W.F. HEGEL, PHILOSOPHY OF RIGHT (T.M. Knox trans., Oxford Univ. Press 1952) (1821); GEORG W.F. HEGEL, THE PHILOSOPHY OF HISTORY (J. Sibree trans., Dover Publications 1956) (1890).

99.   AUGUSTE COMTE, THE POSITIVE PHILOSOPHY OF AUGUSTE COMTE (Harriet Martineau trans., 1893).

100.   For a series of perspectives on the new historicism or "new history," see AHR Forum: The Old History and the New, 94 AM. HIST. REV. 581 (1989). The modern debate among historians on objectivity and the nature of the relationship between the

B. Cycles and Stairs

These views of progress each imply a different role for tradition. Within the ancient, cyclical model, tradition is that to which one inevitably returns—for better or worse. No moment gains in any lasting sense from what has come before nor leads to anything not yet discovered. Within the Enlightenment model of linear and inevitable improvement, tradition is that which one grows out of and discards, as civilization continually betters itself. The modernist view finds tradition neither circular nor linear, but complex and chaotic. There is no single narrative about which generalizations can be made and no transcendent criteria to form the basis of such generalizations. Traditions are plural, multi-layered and internally inconsistent.[101] The part they play in progress depends entirely on particular aspects of the narrative, not the least of which are who is telling the story and why it is being told.

On this oversimplified grid, Justice Scalia's new traditionalism may be seen as a contemporary version of the cyclical view of history. A return to the past is not inevitable, as it appeared to be in the dominant ancient view, but it is, in important respects, possible. A return to the past is also, for Justice Scalia, desirable. At least as to that past he

---

debate among historians on objectivity and the nature of the relationship between the historian and her subject was rehearsed decades earlier. *Compare* Theodore C. Smith, *The Writing of American History in America, from 1884 to 1934*, 40 AM. HIST. REV. 445 (1935) (expressing allegiance to the ideal of the effort to achieve objective truth) *with* Charles A. Beard, *That Noble Dream*, 41 AM. HIST. REV. 74 (1935) (scientific objectivity among historians an illusion); *see also* Joan C. Williams, *Culture and Certainty: Legal History and the Reconstructive Project*, 76 VA. L. REV. 713, 715 (1990) (drawing on the new historicism to explore how legal history might be useful in "rethinking justification in a world without absolutes").

101.   The implications this view of tradition has for history can be seen in James Kloppenberg, *The Virtues of Liberalism: Christianity, Republicanism and Ethics in Early American Political Discourse*, 74 J. AM. HIST. 9 (1987), *summarized in* Joan Williams, *Culture and Certainty: Legal History and the Reconstruction Project*, 76 VA. L. REV. 713, 718 (1990).

Within legal theory, David Luban has described two directions in which modernism has led, only one of which preserves a positive role for tradition. One strand, which he labels avant-gardism, negates premodernist tradition and wishes to bury the past and "end history." *See* David Luban, *Legal Modernism*, 84 MICH. L. REV. 1656, 1676, 1684 (1990). This strand is represented by certain scholars in the Critical Legal Studies movement, including Duncan Kennedy and Peter Gabel, and in Roberto Unger's words, is at "perpetual war against the fact of contextuality." *Id.* at 1676 (citing ROBERTO M. UNGER, PASSION: AN ESSAY ON PERSONALITY 36 (1984)). The other, neo-Kantian strand questions specific constraints according to specific criteria which are conceded to be contextual and contingent, and seeks "transformation followed by reconstitution," as opposed to "permanent revolution." *Id.* at 1694. It is this latter view which is most compatible with the modernist view I describe above.

chooses to acknowledge, the past has a kind of divine authority, to which the Court (and by extension, the states and the people) must be faithful in its "original" sense, rather than as it has been interpreted and revised over time.[102]   As such, Scalia's view of tradition is, as West implies, a jurisprudence of dominance and submission, in which decisionmakers of the present are required to respect a prior authority and denied active collaboration in reshaping it.[103]

Ironically enough, West's and MacKinnon's respective critiques of tradition-based politics also adhere to a cyclical model of progress. Within their quite different theories, efforts to improve women's oppressed position in society are doomed. The system responds to injustice with principles that would appear to address it. Since those principles emanate from the very system that produces the injustice, however, they are not capable of eliminating the injustice and, in this failure, simply legitimize it. Indeed, women themselves are fooled into thinking that their oppression is imaginary, since if it were real, the law would forbid it. There seems no way out of the cycle, except by a kind of grace not entirely unfamiliar to St. Augustine.[104] Even then, those who see the light find their insights appropriated and recycled by those who claim to get it, but don't.

If the dichotomous view of tradition and change leads to a cyclical view of progress, the approach to tradition represented in the line of cases from *Meyer* to *Moore* and in the dissenting opinions of Justices Harlan in *Poe v. Ullman*, Blackmun in *Hardwick*, and Brennan in *Michael H.* is roughly consistent with the Enlightenment idea of progress. These decisions consult the past not so the present can be returned to a purer state of being but so that the future can move forward on a stable foundation.[105] Thus, Justice Harlan writes that every effort to define fundamental rights and liberties must "take 'its place in relation to what went before and further [cut] a channel for what is to come.'"[106] Change is inevitable and the only question is what direction that change takes. Tradition is also inevitable; "a decision . . . which radically

---

102.   While implied in West, *supra* note 72, this point is explicitly made in Robert A. Burt, *Precedent and Authority in Antonin Scalia's Jurisprudence*, 12 CARDOZO L. REV. 1685, 1690-94 (1991).

103.   *Id.* at 1693.

104.   *See supra* note 93.

105.   Rebecca L. Brown develops a concept of tradition as insight, which captures this consultative dimension. *See* Rebecca L. Brown, *Tradition as Insight*, 103 YALE L.J. 177 (1993).

106.   Poe v. Ullman, 367 U.S. 497, 544 (1961) (Harlan, J., dissenting) (quoting Irvine v. California, 347 U.S. 128, 147 (1954) (dissenting opinion)).

departs from it could not long survive."[107]   Due process must be construed in light of the Constitution's "deliberately capacious language," as a "living charter," and in accordance with its broad principles.[108] Accordingly, tradition must not be followed doggedly in its specific detail, but rather must be understood in context, in light of its changing rationales and place in people's lives.[109]

Within the Harlan/Brennan evolutionary approach to due process, many factors ruled out of bounds by the White/Scalia fixed view become important. For Harlan in *Poe v. Ullman*, it is significant that Connecticut "has not chosen to press the enforcement of [its prohibition against use of birth control] against individual users, while it nevertheless persists in asserting its right to do so at any time."[110]   For Brennan in *Michael H.*, it is relevant that the tradition of laws denying putative fathers standing to assert paternity is crumbling[111] and that the rationale supporting traditional burdens of illegitimacy is no longer valid.[112]   In both cases, the rules in question, while perhaps once on a firm foundation in social mores and expectations, no longer sit on stable ground.   In this circumstance, the Court must step back and look at a particular state "intrusion" from the perspective of the broader, more basic interests at stake, such as marital intimacy (*Poe v. Ullman* and *Griswold*), and the sanctity of the parent-child relationship (*Michael H.*).   These broader principles are to be interpreted not in their original context (if such were even possible), but in light of the Court's more recent, evolving precedents which make it unnecessary to rethink continually the meaning of society's historical practice, and in light of the current social realities that form the context to such a challenge.   Accordingly, Justice Harlan finds his way along the "rational continuum" of these precedents to a liberty interest in marital intimacy,[113] and Justice Brennan demonstrates that the right claimed in *Michael H.* is "close enough to the interests we already have protected to be deemed an aspect of 'liberty.'"[114]   In both cases, precedent and tradition work in tandem, tracking and pulling each other along the steady incline.

---

107.   *Id.* at 542.

108.   Michael H. v. Gerald D., 491 U.S. 110, 140-41 (1988) (Brennan, J., dissenting); *see also Poe v. Ullman*, 367 U.S. at 542 (Harlan, J., dissenting) ("[T]radition is a living thing.").

109.   Michael H., 491 U.S. at 140-41.

110.   *Poe v. Ullman*, 367 U.S. at 554.

111.   *Michael H.*, 491 U.S. at 138.

112.   *Id.* at 140.

113.   *Poe v. Ullman*, 367 U.S. at 543.

114.   *Michael H.*, 491 U.S. at 142.

C. The Embodiment View of Tradition and Change

A third view of tradition and change, which I will call the embodiment view, follows from the more complicated view of progress associated with post-modernist historical analyses and social critique. This view begins with the interactive account of tradition and change inherent in the idea-of-progress, common law model, but it adds a more complex understanding of the contestability, multiplicity, and social constructedness of the norms by which any claim of progress would have to be evaluated. Within this view, the past, like the present, is always in flux and part of the process of negotiation about who we are, what matters, and what constitutes improvement. It is always "before us," not behind us,[115] and is something "one can never predict."[116]

The embodiment view of tradition and change recognizes that to constitute a tradition, a past belief or practice must be transmitted by some individuals, in one time and place, and received by others. Without transmission and reception, a tradition dies. Its transmitted quality means that a tradition is not a static thing in time, but rather something that necessarily changes as the particular individuals who receive the tradition interpret it, integrate it into their own experiences, and make it their own. As it is interpreted, tradition necessarily changes; in fact, tradition is altered by the very act of trying to understand it. Laying claim to a tradition requires work and imagination,[117] which again means change. Thus, far from anchoring law to a changeless past, tradition ensures that change is inevitable—all the more so if the tradition is well-worn.

The embodiment view of change and tradition treats the multiplicity of traditions not simply as inconvenient inconsistencies or problems to be solved through a fixed formula, but rather as the creative source of possibilities for the future. Tradition is not a single integrated thread, but a patchwork of multiple themes and commitments, often united only by agreement about what the terms of debate over these themes and commitments will be.[118] The question is not whether we choose or reject tradition, but which traditions among this patchwork we will come

---

115.   *See* SHEILA ROWBOTHAM, THE PAST IS BEFORE US: FEMINISM IN ACTION SINCE THE 1960s, at xi (1989). Similarly, according to Rowbotham, "the future is behind us." *Id.* at 294, 301.

116.   I owe this treasure to Kazimierz Grzybowski.

117.   T.S. Eliot puts the point as follows: "Tradition . . . cannot be inherited, and if you want it you must obtain it by great labour." T.S. ELIOT, *Tradition and the Individual Talent, in* SELECTED ESSAYS 3, 4 (1950). This essay was referred to me by Professor William D. Andrews.

118.   *See* ALASDAIR MACINTYRE, AFTER VIRTUE 222 (1984) (defining tradition as "argument").

to identify as our "own."[119]   Within this shifting and conflicting process, a tradition that stops making sense under existing circumstances will not last. For this reason, it can fairly be said that the strength of a tradition is not how closely it adheres to its original form but how well it is able to develop and remain relevant under changing circumstances.[120]

A critical aspect of the embodiment view of tradition is its recognition of the importance of the relationship between tradition and identity. Tradition might well be defined in terms of the social identities it produces; individuals draw from it what has meaning for them, which in turn is drawn from what others have found meaningful.[121]   The relationship is not simply a matter of choice, but of necessity. At the individual level, healthy identity formation requires the absorption of new challenges into the existing identity structure. Without a successful synthesis of new self-understandings with the old, the fragile identity is at risk of disintegration, self-doubt, and an inability to cope with still further challenges.[122]   So also at the level of larger social units, tradition functions as an identity structure—one that can not be shoved aside by the new any more than it can be held fixed.[123]   Ironically, forward progress—indeed, cultural identity itself—depends on recognizing

---

119.   Insofar as this view suggests that there are many equally sound views about which traditions are good ones, defenders of the Enlightenment view of progress are likely to complain about moral relativism.   Some have accompanied such charges with dire predictions about the fall of civilization, ironically foretelling the end of progress, even as they insist that faith in its inevitability is essential. *See, e.g.,* NISBET, *supra* note 92, at 317-57. Nisbet's view of progress depends upon certain "objective" entailments of progress, which he finds in decline in the late twentieth century West, including the desire for economic growth, the existence of political elites, and belief in God. *Id.* To most scholars attracted to a postmodern world view, the point is not that there are no truths, but that the criteria by which we might evaluate them (including Nisbet's) are local rather than universal.   *See* Katharine T. Bartlett, *Minow's Social-Relations Approach to Difference: Unanswering the Unmasked,* 17 LAW & SOC. INQUIRY 437, 463 & n.51 (1992).

120.   Jaroslav Pelikan writes on this subject: "It is . . . a mark of an authentic and living tradition that it points us beyond itself." PELIKAN, *supra* note 80, at 54. According to Pelikan, when tradition is conserved for its own sake rather than for ends beyond itself, it becomes a false tradition, or idol. *Id.* at 54-55.

121.   *See generally* CHARLES TAYLOR, SOURCES OF THE SELF: THE MAKING OF THE MODERN IDENTITY (1989).

122.   *See generally* ERIK H. ERIKSON, IDENTITY AND THE LIFE CYCLE (1980).

123.   The importance of matters of individual and group identity has also been noted in the context of changes in attitudes about race.   Gary Peller, for example, has analyzed how choices between two alternative traditions in race discourse—integrationalism and nationalism—have been affected by various anxieties about group and self-identity, especially among black moderates and among white liberals and progressives. *See* Gary Peller, *Race Consciousness,* 1990 DUKE L.J. 758.

and integrating, rather than ignoring, the past; only the "flies of a summer" can afford otherwise.[124]

My purpose in elaborating an alternative view of tradition is not to provide a more determinate method of constitutional decisionmaking relating to matters of family, procreation, and sexuality.[125] My aim, rather, is to improve how feminists understand tradition and change, in order to help develop better strategies for transforming how the culture views gender. With respect to this larger goal, it hardly matters that some feminists are capable of generating visions of progress that break free from the past if, in failing to take account of tradition, they are unable to root these visions in the larger society's imagination.

III. FEMINIST PROGRESS AND TRADITION

R.G. Collingwood states that progress "is not the replacement of the bad by the good, but of the good by the better."[126] This statement reflects a recognition that not all change is for the better, and that progress, when it occurs, is an organic and fluid process rather than a static, either/or choice. The cyclical view of reform and oppression implicated in West's and MacKinnon's analyses of legal change rejects the possibilities of existing good on which the better might build, instead relying on flashes of insight to break free from past and present. The idea-of-progress view recognizes that the process of change is dynamic, but fails to address the possibility that not all change is positive.

A more realistic and useful view of change locates its potential not solely or even primarily in flashes of insight or in some inevitable historical or scientific force, but rather in the tensions and contradictions of a society's values and practices[127]—past, present, and future. When

---

124.   The image is, of course, Edmund Burke's. *See* EDMUND BURKE, REFLECTIONS ON THE REVOLUTION IN FRANCE 193 (C. O'Brien rev. ed. 1969) (1790). For a contemporary analysis of this image that distinguishes a state of "circularity and repetition, the endless return of the same," represented by the flies of the summer, from the world of culture in which a liberating progress is possible, see Kronman, *supra* note 9, at 1048-55, 1064-68.

125.   Michael J. Perry concludes that no concept of tradition can provide a basis for determinate decisionmaking. *See* MICHAEL J. PERRY, THE CONSTITUTION, THE COURTS, AND HUMAN RIGHTS 93-96 (1982). Surely Justice Scalia's concept of tradition restrains judges no better than do the alternatives. *See supra* note 70. It is not clear, of course, that the goal of restraining judges is a worthy objective of constitutional theory. *See* H. JEFFERSON POWELL, THE MORAL TRADITION OF AMERICAN CONSTITUTIONALISM: A THEOLOGICAL INTERPRETATION 252 (1993). In any event, it is not the goal of this Article.

126.   R.G. COLLINGWOOD, THE IDEA OF HISTORY 326 (1946).

127.   Values may conflict with each other or with practices, and vice versa.

these tensions and contradictions are perceived, efforts are made to reconcile them. These efforts at reconciliation produce pressures of their own, stimulating new, possibly more satisfactory, values and practices.

Tradition plays a significant role in this process. Its significance arises, first, because the kinds of contradictions deep or important enough to create serious tensions are those that emerge from settled understandings and expectations. These settled understandings and expectations do not develop overnight; they represent layers of accretions and reconciliations of previous tensions and contradictions. Second, to participate in changes to these understandings and expectations is to engage in the same process—the same tradition, if you will—that produced them. This participation consists of identifying contradictions and offering relief from them, relief sufficiently connected to what has come before—tradition—as to appear to be plausible and acceptable. Third, the process is, at its core, social rather than individual; it occurs through the interactions of individuals, creating new meanings with others from some shared, if often contested, past, even as what is understood as shared is continually renegotiated.

An understanding of the interactive, organic processes of change and progress based on efforts to reconcile existing contradictions and tensions is hardly new. It is present in theories of social change as diverse as those of John Stuart Mill, Roberto Unger, Alasdair MacIntyre, William Connolly, and Martha Minow. Mill's case for women's liberation in 1869 was structured around the inconsistency between the liberal value of equality and the fact of women's legal subordination.[128] Unger's plea for creative destablizations requires exploitation of the conflicts between a society's ideal principles and its actual practices.[129] MacIntyre's commitment to tradition conceives it as an ongoing reinterpretation and reworking of the incoherences and inconsistencies of a society's basic principles.[130] Connolly's program for negotiations of identity in a heterogeneous society relies on the identification of gaps between prevailing perceptions and individual and group experiences. Identifying these gaps creates openings through which an understanding of other

---

128. *See* JOHN STUART MILL, *The Subjection of Women*, *in* THREE ESSAYS BY JOHN STUART MILL 427 (World's Classic ed. 1912) (1869).

129. *See* ROBERTO UNGER, LAW IN MODERN SOCIETY 153-54 (1976) ("The deepest root of historical change is manifest or latent conflict between the view of the ideal and the experience of actuality.").

130. *See* ALASDAIR MACINTYRE, WHOSE JUSTICE? WHICH RATIONALITY? 355 (1988) (incompatible interpretations and incoherences in tradition stimulate reworkings of the tradition); *cf.* MACINTYRE, *supra* note 118, at 222 (traditions embody continuities of conflict).

perspectives might be achieved.[131]   And Minow's resolution of the
problem of human agency in a socially constructed world turns on a
process of describing the "nonfit" between experience and the categories
a society provides to interpret that experience.[132]

Feminists are good at pointing out the contradictions between
society's stated norms and its practices and how existing patterns of
gender subordination are sustained by the very forces that purport to
oppose it.   This is feminist social critique or insight.   As to the
reconciliations needed to reduce or resolve the contradictions and to upset
existing patterns of subordination, however, the feminist project
flounders. This floundering is aggravated by the feminist commitment to
an anti-tradition, either/or view of progress.   Such a commitment
discourages reconciliations and obscures passages from past to present.
It ignores the reality that new insights cannot be simply substituted for
deeply rooted attitudes and understandings to the contrary.   Past and
present must be reconciled and new challenges integrated within structures
of identity, the stability of which is dependent upon the ability to adapt
and change.

Individuals attain new understandings of themselves and others by
struggling to resolve the incoherence between their deeply ingrained
habits and norms and their experiences and insights.[133]   These struggles
may be resolved either by adjusting one's practices or by adapting one's
norms—or, most likely, by altering both. Feminists can help by tapping
into this struggle against incoherence, offering ways of thinking that
integrate rather than totally reject the most promising of the commitments
individuals bring to the table. Reason is often helpful in achieving new
and better syntheses and, contrary again to the prevailing dichotomous
way of thinking about tradition, is not necessarily antithetical to tradition.
As one traditionalist puts it, reason often represents a narration of "how
the argument has gone so far."[134] Feminists often appear to have given
up the tools of reason as well as tradition. Robin West, for example,
argues that commitment and direction for legal reform are moral, and

---

131.   *See* WILLIAM E. CONNOLLY, IDENTITY/DIFFERENCE: DEMOCRATIC
NEGOTIATIONS OF POLITICAL PARADOX 80, 204 (1991).

132.   *See* MARTHA MINOW, MAKING ALL THE DIFFERENCE: INCLUSION,
EXCLUSION, AND AMERICAN LAW 371-72 (1990) (citing Mary Douglas). I analyzed
Minow's theory in Bartlett, *supra* note 119.

133.   On the psychological need to reduce dissonance between one's practices and
one's values, see C. Edwin Baker, *The Process of Change and the Liberty Theory of the
First Amendment*, 55 S. CAL. L. REV. 293, 318 (1981).

134.   MACINTYRE, *supra* note 130, at 8; *see also* MACINTYRE, *supra* note 118, at
222 (tradition as argument). For a discussion of the interdependence of reason and
tradition, including MacIntyre's views on the subject, see POWELL, *supra* note 125, at 22-
24.

must come from experience and narrative rather than from rational argument.[135] This rejection of reason demonstrates the same segmented view of truth and lie as does the rejection of tradition. Both rejections represent a disintegration in ways of thinking about wisdom in light of, rather than in opposition to, recognized identities. It may be true, as John Stuart Mill proposed, that some irrational attachments may be strengthened rather than weakened when the weight of logic is brought to bear against them.[136] This dynamic may say more, however, about the failure to integrate reason and identity rather than about any failure of reason itself.

What an interactive view of tradition and change helps to highlight is that without the right linkage between feminist insight and matters of collective and individual identity—of which tradition and reason are both important components—insights may be wasted. Insight will not "sink in" unless it is integrated into ongoing individual and collective identities. To disassociate oneself from the effort at integration is to fail to participate in the organization of society and time and, thereby, to take oneself out of the process through which a culture is created and maintained. This process is necessarily political, entailing characterizations of past, present, and future which shape how reality is viewed and what choices are seen to exist.[137] It is the kind of process to which Vivian Gornick may have been referring when she described the "interminable, repetitious, slogging, unesthetic" work of feminism.[138]

Historian John Lukacs points out that the best historian is not necessarily the one who makes the original discovery or uncovers an undiscovered truth. Historical thinking, according to Lukacs, is a *rethinking* of the past, and the great historian is one "who retells the same portion of the past for the twentieth or fiftieth time perhaps, . . . [drawing] attention to it, . . . shed[ding] light on it . . . [and] deepen[ing]

---

135. *See* Robin L. West, *The Constitution of Reasons*, 92 MICH. L. REV. 1409, 1432-37 (1994) (book review).

136. *See* MILL, *supra* note 128, at 427-28:

So long as an opinion is strongly rooted in the feelings, it gains rather than loses in stability by having a preponderating weight of argument against it. For if it were accepted as a result of argument, the refutation of the argument might shake the solidity of the conviction; but when it rests solely on feeling, the worse it fares in argumentative contest, the more persuaded its adherents are that their feeling must have some deeper ground, which the arguments do not reach; and while the feeling remains, it is always throwing up fresh entrenchment of argument to repair any breach made in the old.

137. *See* SHELDON S. WOLIN, THE PRESENCE OF THE PAST: ESSAYS ON THE STATE AND THE CONSTITUTION 1 (1989) ("The present is another name for the political organization of existence.").

138. *See supra* note 1 and accompanying text.

our understanding perhaps even more than [extending] our information."[139] Feminists could benefit from a model that appreciates the role of rethinking in relation to discovery of "fresh" insight. That rethinking should not proceed through condescension, as if everyone who doesn't "get it" is a fool. Instead, the process of repetition and rediscovery should be viewed as an opportunity to improve, expand, and regenerate the insights that inform the process, through bridges linking those insights to principles and aspirations that are already part of the cultural identity.

Many traditions are, of course, hopelessly oppressive—irredeemable, from a feminist point of view.[140] This point is terribly important, and it must be conceded that any reliance on tradition legitimates a source that is heavily weighted against the interests of outsider individuals and groups against whom a strong tradition of mistrust and hatred exists. These individuals and groups will have difficulty finding traditions that can be profitably reexpressed and reinterpreted. Gay men and lesbian women are among the most obvious contemporary examples.[141] This phenomenon, however, reflects on the difficulty of change, rather than on the dispensability of tradition in accomplishing change. The fact that many traditions are bad underlines the necessity of distinguishing between the bad and the good, rather than treating all tradition as oppressive.

Accepting the constructive power of the past need not entail embracing all of its aspects. Indeed, a tradition consists of those aspects of the past from which a society has broken, as well as those a society has endorsed and made its own.[142] In defining the aspects of the past from which the present seeks to establish distance, the tradition/change dichotomy may have a strategic value.[143] At the same time, it should

---

139. JOHN LUKACS, HISTORICAL CONSCIOUSNESS OR THE REMEMBERED PAST 34-35 (1968).

140. This is Robin West's principal point. See West, supra note 72, at 1385. Many others, not all feminists, have made it as well. See, e.g., GARRY WILLS, INVENTING AMERICA, at xii (1978) (paraphrasing Willmoore Kendall); David A. Strauss, Tradition, Precedent, and Justice Scalia, 12 CARDOZO L. REV. 1699, 1711-12 (1991).

141. Notwithstanding the growing evidence that the abhorrence of homosexuality is not as historically pervasive as is usually assumed. See, e.g., JOHN BOSWELL, SAME-SEX UNIONS IN PREMODERN EUROPE (1994) (describing medieval practice of gay marriage); JOHN BOSWELL, CHRISTIANITY, SOCIAL TOLERANCE, AND HOMOSEXUALITY (1980) (strong sanctions against sodomy were legal innovations of the twelfth and thirteenth centuries).

142. See Poe v. Ullman, 367 U.S. 497, 542 (1961) (Harlan, J., dissenting) (The "balance . . . between liberty and the demands of organized society. . . [is struck] having regard to what history teaches are the traditions from which it developed as well as the traditions from which it broke.").

143. The strategic or ideological value of the dichotomy between tradition and modernity, notwithstanding the profound reliance of modernization on tradition, is

be remembered that inventing concepts of justice and equality that are both free of the past and understandable and acceptable to society is virtually unthinkable.   These concepts are bred and nurtured within cultures of understanding and resistance that warrant continual repetition and reexpression. This repetition does not merely affirm but recirculates, displaces, subverts, and undermines existing meanings[144]—meanings which, no matter how universal they may seem, are never complete and can never be totally "correct" or final.[145]   It bears emphasizing that the change arising from this process will not necessarily meet one's particular criteria for progress, nor settle what those criteria ought to be.   Such criteria require their own articulation (and rearticulation) and defense (and redefense).   My claim in this Article is not that this process of rearticulation assures progress, but rather that progress does not occur without it.   If awareness of the inevitable role of tradition in change stimulates better use of tradition to accomplish change, so also should awareness that progress is not guaranteed, and may easily be co-opted, make those engaged in social reform cautious of the dangers and all the more aware of the need to articulate and defend the premises on which they base their claims.

Some feminists in the law have pursued theories of change that recognize the role of reexpressing and reinterpreting the past.   For Mary Joe Frug, for example, gender meanings are constantly being remade *in relationship to* those that preceded it.   This remaking is possible because meanings are created through interpretation, through efforts to eliminate dissonance between different meanings or between the received wisdom and one's experiences, and through spaces that exist within established texts and practices.   The relationship between new and old meanings is itself a matter of infinite variation; it could be, for example, a relationship "of opposition, nuanced difference, or an effort at repetition."[146]

---

discussed in Gusfield, *supra* note 67, at 22.

144.   The most sophisticated and well-developed feminist exploration of the possibilities of "subversive repetition" is JUDITH BUTLER, GENDER TROUBLE: FEMINISM AND THE SUBVERSION OF IDENTITY (1990). *See id.* at 29-33, 115-16, 139-50.

145.   *See* Bartlett, *Feminist Legal Methods*, *supra* note 83, at 880-88.

146.   Judith G. Greenberg, *Introduction* to MARY JOE FRUG, POSTMODERN LEGAL FEMINISM, at xxix (1992).   In the context of poetry, Harold Bloom provides a more refined set of creative, "rhetorical positions" that one can take in relation to one's predecessors. *See* HAROLD BLOOM, THE ANXIETY OF INFLUENCE: A THEORY OF POETRY 14-16 (1973). As summarized by Kenji Yoshino, these include

> *clinamen*, or swerving, where the poet seeks to correct an error in the preceding text; *tessera*, or completion, where the successor fills out lacunae in the predecessor's work; *kenosis*, or emptying out, where the iconoclast son demystifies the godlike father by showing him to be as fallible as the son; *daemonization*, where the successor adopts the antithesis of the precursor;

Frug's understanding of change is that it cannot come from out of the blue; it comes, rather, from playing around with and reshuffling old meanings and understandings.[147]

Frug's approach to change shares some similarity with a more psychoanalytic approach developed by Drucilla Cornell. For Cornell, meaning is established in a chain of signifiers, which can always slide, yielding new meanings.[148] This process in which "meaning continually glides to create new meaning" corresponds to Jacques Lacan's concept of metonymy, which "relies on the endless recreation of the context which results from the juxtaposition to one term with another through contiguity."[149] This process is interrupted, however, when old meanings that have been substituted by new meanings disappear into the unconscious, thus "congealing" a sign so that "the signifier is not free to generate new meanings"; to get beneath these congealed signs, and to reactivate the process of sliding, it is necessary to retrace the "repressed trajectory or passageway through which the congelation of meaning took place."[150]

For Cornell, as for Frug, the challenge with respect to gender meanings is to get beneath the culture's congealed understandings of gender difference, which determinedly see female as the "other" of the Male, and thus the lesser, the lack, or that which is absent or not real. Although it is not clear just exactly how the psychoanalytic process proceeds as to a whole culture whose understanding of gender difference may be stagnated through the suppression of unconscious symbols and fantasies,[151] Cornell is clear that the possibility of change frees the patient-culture from "determination by the congealed signifiers expressible only as symptoms." It is also clear that part of the process of repair is a reimagining of the future, which true to the psychoanalytic dynamic,

---

askesis, where the poet curtails his gift to truncate the precursor's achievement in a milder form of kenosis; and apophrades, where the successor so overwhelms the predecessor that he reverses the father-son relationship.

Kenji Yoshino, *What's Past Is Prologue: Precedent in Literature and Law*, 104 YALE L.J. 471, 474 (1994). Each of these methods is a useful way of thinking about the relationship between precedent and change in the legal context. Others who have explored the tension between creativity and influence (or precedent) and how this tension functions comparatively in law and literature include Paul Gewirtz, *Remedies and Resistance*, 92 YALE L.J. 585 (1983), and David Cole, *Agon at Agora: Creative Misreadings in the First Amendment Tradition*, 95 YALE L.J. 857 (1986).

147.   FRUG, *supra* note 146, at 137, 148-53.

148.   DRUCILLA CORNELL, TRANSFORMATIONS: RECOLLECTIVE IMAGINATION AND SEXUAL DIFFERENCE 184 (1993).

149.   *Id.*

150.   *Id.* at 186.

151.   Who, for example, will be the therapist?

requires a reimagining of the past "not as an accurate account, but as the fantasy figures that have come to have significance for us in the way they have congealed our definitions of difference."[152] The past is important, not as that to which we might return, or as that from which we are trying to distance ourselves, but as "the very process of envisioning 'what is' differently."[153] Recapitulation is not capitulation.

Frug's and Cornell's approaches to change seem, as I have described them thus far, highly abstract. It is useful, then, to think about what concrete differences they might make in practice. One example is methodological; understanding the role of repetition and reinterpretation in social change means even greater use of the narrative method. As Robin West herself has argued, narrative helps to reinterpret settled understandings of one's own conditions and, perhaps more importantly, of the conditions of others.[154] There are healthy questions to be asked about the criteria for evaluating these narratives.[155] Notwithstanding these questions, it can hardly be denied that the narrative method has tremendous potential to blend new meanings into the familiar.

Other possibilities are more substantive. For example, more integrated models of past and present might contribute to fashioning better strategies for addressing "hate speech." Hate speech regulation represents the exercise of power against oppression, based on the insight that some speech oppresses in ways that undermine the ability of the oppressed to counteract that speech.[156] A focus on the importance of creating new meanings by integrating insight into the familiar, rather than by overpowering those who lack the insight, suggests less regulatory approaches. Ending silencing speech of one kind by silencing another reinforces the process of silencing, when what is crucial to the ultimate end of non-oppressive conversation is trust, openness, and a greater willingness to take risks and expose one's own viewpoints. Any regulatory scheme that overpowers one form of dominance for another

---

152.   *Id.* at 187.

153.   *Id.* at 194.

154.   Robin L. West, *The Constitution of Reasons*, 92 MICH. L. REV. 1409, 1434–36 (1994) (book review). The literature on the benefits of narrative to dislodge settled understandings is now legion. Some examples include Kathryn Abrams, *Hearing the Call of Stories*, 79 CAL. L. REV. 971 (1991); Toni Massaro, *Empathy, Legal Storytelling, and the Rule of Law: New Words, Old Wounds?*, 87 MICH. L. REV. 2099 (1989); Carrie Menkel-Meadow, *The Power of Narrative in Empathetic Learning: Post-Modernism and the Stories of Law*, 2 UCLA WOMEN'S L.J. 87 (1992) (book review); Symposium, *Legal Storytelling*, 87 MICH. L. REV. 2073 (1989).

155.   *See, e.g.*, Abrams, *supra* note 154; Suzanna Sherry & Daniel A. Farber, *Telling Stories out of School: An Essay on Legal Narratives*, 45 STAN. L. REV. 807 (1993).

156.   *See supra* text accompanying note 85.

may rebalance the field, without helping to remake new meanings which substitute the dominance of one side or the other with "the dominance of egalitarian, communicative interaction."[157]

An appreciation of how important the processes of repetition and reimagination are to social change also highlights the importance of affirming human agency for women as an everyday phenomenon, rather than as a rare glimpse of feminist insight. Feminist analyses that emphasize women's victimization sometimes ignore this importance. Although the extent to which the women's movement has emphasized and reinforced women's victimization has been wildly exaggerated, the success of this exaggerated criticism should serve as a warning of the pitfalls of victimization themes. Martha Minow explains how "the rhetoric of victimization charts out a limited repertoire of responses . . . 'I didn't do it' and 'I'm the real victim here,'"[158] which makes it unlikely that anyone will either identify with the experiences of others or accept responsibility for their suffering.[159] The dangers are real. Some feminists, such as Elizabeth Schneider and Martha Mahoney, have addressed how victimization rhetoric reinforces women's own sense of powerlessness and how legal issues might be reframed to leave room for women's agency as well.[160] Others have analyzed how, in specific contexts, the processes which victimize women are less total and disempowering than sometimes represented. Susan Etta Keller, for example, questions the coherence some feminists assume among the definition, message, and effect of pornography, urging responses to pornography that take advantage of opportunities to interpret and reinterpret its meanings.[161] Attention must also be given to how victimization approaches up the ante of gender subordination and, accordingly, how they generate backlash and impede opportunities for the kind of boundary-crossing that might actually reduce that subordination.

Increasingly, feminist legal scholars are moving away from offering analyses that create distance between existing legal principles and

---

157.   Baker, *supra* note 133, at 319.

158.   Martha Minow, *Surviving Victim Talk*, 40 UCLA L. REV. 1411, 1413 (1993).

159.   *Id.* at 1430-31; *see also* Susan Wendell, *Oppression and Victimization: Choice and Responsibility*, in A READER IN FEMINIST ETHICS 279, 287 (Debra Shogan ed., 1992).

160.   *See, e.g.*, Martha R. Mahoney, *Legal Images of Battered Women: Redefining the Issue of Separation*, 90 MICH. L. REV. 1 (1991); Elizabeth M. Schneider, *Describing and Changing: Women's Self-Defense Work and the Problem of Expert Testimony on Battering*, 9 WOMEN'S RTS. L. REP. 195 (1986); Elizabeth M. Schneider, *Particularity and Generality: Challenges of Feminist Theory and Practice in Work on Woman-Abuse*, 67 N.Y.U. L. REV. 520 (1992).

161.   *See* Susan E. Keller, *Viewing and Doing: Complicating Pornography's Meaning*, 81 GEO. L.J. 2195, 2242 (1993).

women's interests toward approaches that attempt to articulate women's interests in light of these principles, as reformulated to accommodate those interests. Jennifer Nedelsky, for example, rejects the choice between abandoning existing legal principles and buying into them, defining the feminist project as that of "mov[ing] the accepted understandings of concepts and issues in the direction of feminist perspectives."[162] In this spirit, Nedelsky has attempted to "reconceiv[e] autonomy" in light of the feminist critique of liberal individualism and feminist concern for enlarged understandings of public responsibility for human flourishing.[163]   Along similar lines, Linda McClain has responded to the feminist trashing of liberalism by reclaiming some of its basic tenets in terms consistent with feminist insights about privacy, responsibility, and care.[164]   Ruth Gavison, following up on some piercing, brilliant feminist attacks over the past fifteen years on the public-private dichotomy, has begun to rework the dichotomy in ways that recognize feminist insights about the oppression that comes from privatizing certain realms of activity, while preserving the protections related to privacy that women, as well as men, need to secure their life, liberty, and happiness. These efforts, while hardly the final word on the recurring issues they address, illustrate how feminist approaches might usefully build from, or return to reinterpret, familiar principles in light of feminist insights. They are at the same time pragmatic and feminist, keeping intact the long-range ideals toward which feminists have wanted to work even as those ideals are adjusted in the present to respond temporarily and partially to the real, non-ideal circumstances in which women presently find themselves.[165]

---

162.   Jennifer Nedelsky, *The Practical Possibilities of Feminist Theory*, 87 Nw. U. L. Rev. 1286, 1300 (1993). Nedelsky advocates "both the theoretical work of developing alternative conceptions and the practical skill of finding analogies that aid judges to see links between what is familiar to them and what is essential to us." *Id.*

163.   Jennifer Nedelsky, *Reconceiving Autonomy: Sources, Thought and Possibilities*, 1 Yale J.L. & Feminism 7, 21, 32-33 (1989); Jennifer Nedelsky, *Law, Boundaries, and the Bounded Self*, Representations, Spring 1990, at 162, 168-69 (1990); *see also* Susan G. Kupfer, *Autonomy and Community in Feminist Legal Thought*, 22 Golden Gate U. L. Rev. 583 (1992) (reformulating autonomy in light of Robin West's notion of the "authentic self" and feminist commitment to community).

164.   *See* Linda McClain, *"Atomistic Man" Revisited: Liberalism, Connection, and Feminist Jurisprudence*, 65 S. Cal. L. Rev. 1171 (1992).

165.   *See* Margaret J. Radin, *The Pragmatist and the Feminist*, 63 S. Cal. L. Rev. 1699 (1990).

IV. CONCLUSION

I am worried about a movement whose identity seems too often connected with a relentless pushing away from a contaminated past. Feminism needs a view of change that combines its critical vantage point on gender subordination with a sensitivity to the need to translate feminist visions of the future into terms that can be transmitted and received as part of a complex, never-ending narrative of change.

But with this worry comes anxiety—anxiety about whether all this represents womanly compromise, about whether I have prescribed a solution ripe for co-optation, and about whether I have taken shots at forefront feminism only to abdicate to a watered-down sell-out.

My response to this anxiety about compromise is, in a sense, still more compromise. First, nothing I argue for undercuts the necessity for a continuing "deep" critique of gender subordination in as many of its various forms as we are able to identify. As the most blatant types of sex discrimination are being eliminated, the need for such critique to reach the more subtle and elusive types of discrimination becomes all the more necessary. I simply resist the either/or view of change that such critiques often unnecessarily incorporate.

Second, it is not necessary to my view of progress that all feminists view change in the way I have described. Nor is it important that *all* feminists focus on incrementalist, as opposed to revolutionary, strategies.[166] In fact, if the theory of change I wish to promote is accurate, there needs to be both flashes of insight that enable one to spot inconsistencies and contradictions in the existing system *and* the more slogging, unexciting work of pushing, gently at times, to reconcile the inconsistencies and contradictions in the right direction.

Finally, I believe that my own anxiety about being sufficiently radical reflects the same dichotomous way of thinking about change in opposition to the past—and by extension, the dichotomy between deep-seated radical change and superficial reform—which, in arguing against, I find so hard to shed.[167] If my thesis is correct, my approach is no less radical than the more radical-appearing alternatives. I turn here to an analogy to childrearing. Childbirth, like feminist insight, is a creative act. But once

---

166. *See* Martha Minow, *Breaking the Law: Lawyers and Clients in Struggles for Social Change*, 52 U. PITT. L. REV. 723 (1991) (urging multiple strategies in working toward social change); Martha Minow, *Beyond Universality*, 1989 U. CHI. LEGAL F. 115 (advocating multiple feminist perspectives).

167. This dichotomy between deep and superficial change is false in the same sense that the distinction between tradition and change is false. While at times rhetorically or strategically useful, it masks complex relations between alternative meanings, past and present, and creates hierarchies of action when multiple actions may be required.

beyond that first dramatic stage, the most difficult work lies ahead. Much of that work, alas, is repetitive and unesthetic. This work nurtures through affirmation, even as it makes clear those practices it deems unacceptable. It fails, repeatedly, and in failure looks to have another try, to start again, each time using the resources available and the lessons learned from previous efforts. Much is compromise. It never stops.

Acknowledgments

MacKinnon, Catharine A. "Difference and Dominance: On Sex Discrimination
(1984)." In *Feminism Unmodified: Discourses on Life and Law* (Cambridge:
Harvard University Press, 1987): 32–45, 240–45. Reprinted by permission of
the publisher. Copyright 1987 by the President and Fellows of Harvard College.

Crenshaw, Kimberle. "Demarginalizing the Intersection of Race and Sex: A Black
Feminist Critique of Antidiscrimination Doctrine, Feminist Theory and
Antiracist Politics." *University of Chicago Legal Forum* (1989): 139–67.
Reprinted with the permission of the University of Chicago Law School.

Fineman, Martha L. "Challenging Law, Establishing Differences: The Future of
Feminist Legal Scholarship." *Florida Law Review* 42 (1990): 25–43. Reprinted
with the permission of the *Florida Law Review*. Copyright 1990.

Harris, Angela P. "Race and Essentialism in Feminist Legal Theory." *Stanford Law
Review* 42 (1990): 581–616. Reprinted with the permission of the Board of
Trustees of the Leland Stanford Junior University. Copyright (1990).

Rhode, Deborah L. "Feminist Critical Theories." *Stanford Law Review* 42 (1990):
617–38. Reprinted with the permission of the Board of Trustees of the
Leland Stanford Junior University. Copyright (1990).

Banks, Taunya Lovell. "Toilets as a Feminist Issue: A True Story." *Berkeley Women's
Law Journal* 6 (1990–91): 263–89. Reprinted with the permission of the
University of California Press.

Baer, Judith A. "Nasty Law or Nice Ladies? Jurisprudence, Feminism, and Gender
Difference." *Women and Politics* 11 (1991): 1–31. Reprinted with the
permission of Haworth Press, Inc. Copyright 1991.

MacKinnon, Catharine A. "From Practice to Theory, or What is a White Woman
Anyway?" *Yale Journal of Law and Feminism* 4 (1991): 13–22. Reprinted with
the permission of the *Yale Journal of Law and Feminism*.

Romany, Celina. "Ain't I a Feminist?" *Yale Journal of Law and Feminism* 4 (1991): 23–33.
Reprinted with the permission of the *Yale Journal of Law and Feminism*.

Fineman, Martha Albertson. "Feminist Theory in Law: The Difference It Makes."
Columbia Journal of Gender and Law 2 (1992): 1–23. Reprinted with the
permission of the Columbia University, School of Law.

Mahoney, Martha R. "Whiteness and Women, In Practice and Theory: A Reply to
    Catharine MacKinnon." *Yale Journal of Law and Feminism* 5 (1993): 217–51.
    Reprinted with the permission of the *Yale Journal of Law and Feminism*.
Bartlett, Katharine T. "Tradition, Change, and the Idea of Progress in Feminist Legal
    Thought." *Wisconsin Law Review* (1995): 303–43. Reprinted with permission
    of the *Wisconsin Law Review*. Copyright 1995 by the Board of Regents of the
    University of Wisconsin System.